The CAM and Nursing Coding Manual

V2001R3

**This is a coding and procedural reference tool based on the ABCcodes
for Complementary & Alternative Medicine (CAM) and Conventional Nursing.**

The CAM & Nursing Coding Manual ABCodes® describes
and defines the services of practitioners who provide
the following healthcare services:

Acupuncture
Ayurvedic Medicine
Body Work
Botanical Medicine
Chiropractic
Clinical Nutrition
Conventional Nursing
Holistic Medicine
Holistic Nursing
Homeopathic Medicine
Indigenous Medicine
Massage Therapy
Mental Healthcare
Midwifery
Naturopathic Medicine
Oriental Medicine
Osteopathic Medicine
Physical Medicine
Somatic Re-education

DISCLAIMER

The CAM and Nursing Coding Manual has been prepared for use with a patented system and copyright protected information developed exclusively by Alternative Link, Inc. It is designed to provide accurate and authoritative information in regard to the subject covered, and every reasonable effort has been made to ensure the accuracy of the information contained herein.

Nevertheless, the ultimate responsibility for correct coding lies with the provider of services. The provider must have the necessary training mandated by state law to use these codes for billing purposes. State code reports for 13 practice licenses are available through Alternative Link to assure that each provider bills within their legal scope of practice.

Alternative Link makes no representation, warranty, or guarantee that this compilation of codes and narrative is error-free, or that the use of these codes will assure reimbursement; nor are they guaranteed to prevent differences of opinion or disputes with Medicare/Medicaid or other third-party payers as to the coverage of described services or payment amounts.

In addition, Alternative Link bears no responsibility or liability for the results or consequences of the use of this coding manual.

ABCodes® disclaimer

The Alternative Billing Concepts coding system (ABCodes®) is designed to promote uniform CAM and nursing service reporting and statistical data collection.

Inclusion of a service, procedure, treatment or supply does not constitute endorsement by Alternative Link.

Inclusion or exclusion of a service, procedure, treatment or supply does not imply any health insurance coverage or reimbursement policy.

The CAM and Nursing Coding Manual

V2001R3

Alternative Link Systems, Inc.

DELMAR

THOMSON LEARNING™   Australia   Canada   Mexico   Singapore   Spain   United Kingdom   United States

The CAM & Nursing Coding Manual
by Alternative Link Systems, Inc.

Business Unit Director:
William Brottmiller

Editorial Assistant:
Robin Irons

Project Editor:
Mary Ellen Cox

Product Development Manager:
Marion Waldman

Executive Marketing Manager:
Dawn F. Gerrain

Production Coordinator:
John Mickelbank

Product Development Editor:
Jill Rembetski

Channel Manager:
Gretta Oliver

Art/Design Coordinator:
Jay Purcell

For permission to use material from this text or product, contact us by
Tel (800) 730-2214
Fax (800) 730-2215
www.thomsonrights.com

Library of Congress Cataloging-in-Publication Data

The CAM and nursing coding manual, V2001R3 : a coding and procedural reference tool based on the ABCcodes for complementary & alternative medicine (CAM) and conventional nursing / Alternative Link Systems, Inc.
    p. cm.
  Includes bibliographical references and index.
  ISBN 0-7668-4276-2 (alk. paper)
  1. Nursing. 2. Health insurance claims—Code numbers.
  3. Medicine—Terminology—Code numbers. 4. Hospitals—Prospective payment. I. Alternative Link Systems.
RT42 .C26 2001
610.73'01'48—dc21

                      2001032448

NOTICE TO THE READER

Table of Contents

Foreword

Thank you for purchasing Alternative Link Systems, Inc.'s *The CAM and Nursing Coding Manual,* which is based on the ABCode® system. This coding system fulfills the need of CAM and nurse providers to accurately communicate procedures and services to health insurance companies or to monitor the practice charges of individual providers. The ABCode® were built to meet the business requirements of practitioners and insurance companies who use codes to price and monitor patient encounters.

The ABCode® are also the key component of an electronic claims support system. This claims system, licensed to health insurers, expands the capabilities of conventional medical claims processing to include identification of each provider's state scope of practice.

The company's product line, paired with the ABCode®, enhances a full range of reference tools:

Relative Values: a publication and electronic files that act as a pricing mechanism to define the dollar value of services (adjustable by region or payer). Available through Relative Value Studies, Inc. (www.rvsdata.com);

Scope of Practice: defines the range of services allowed by statutes and regulations for each provider type in every state;

Decision Support: full descriptions of service to decrease or eliminate written reports from providers to payers;

Training Standards: describe the education required for any service in any state;

Legal Guides: summaries of state scope of practice laws for each licensed provider type; also available in April 2001 as a hardcopy reference through Delmar, a Thomson Learning Company (www.delmar.com).

Alternative Link Systems, Inc. pledges to provide our clients with current information, adhere to stringent process controls for updates, and expand our electronic capabilities to keep pace with national and international mandates for standardization of healthcare e-commerce.

Sincerely,

Melinna Giannini
President and CEO
Alternative Link Systems, Inc.
Las Cruces, New Mexico
May 2001

Acknowledgments

Through contractual agreements with *The Center for Nursing Classification* at the University of Iowa and Mosby Publishers, portions of the *Nursing Intervention Classification* (NIC) system has been included in the ABCode® system for administrative claims processing.

The NIC codes are part of a published University of Iowa Intervention Project, developed by members of the Iowa Intervention Project Research Team and edited by Joanne C. McCloskey, PhD, RN, FAAN and Gloria M. Bulechek, PhD, RN, FAAN. NIC Codes are mapped to the ABCode® in the NIC Index of this manual.

Karen S. Martin, RN, MSN. FAAN and Nancy J. Scheet, RN, MSN were part of the research team that developed the *Omaha System Intervention Scheme*. Karen also reviewed selected *Omaha System Intervention Scheme* terms and the definitions that were developed by Alternative Link and are now included in the ABCode®.

The Home Health Care Classification (HHCC) was developed by Virginia K. Saba, EdD, RN, FAAN, Clinical Associate Professor of Georgetown University to code, index, and classify care, and also to document and track the nursing care process over time and across settings and geographic locations.

Linda Ledray, PhD, RN, FAAN submitted and reviewed codes for the Sexual Assault Nurse Examiner (SANE). SANE codes were developed to provide standardized nomenclature for evaluative nursing procedures in caring for victims of sexual assault.

Special thanks to the following institutions for supplying information to Dr. Ted Rozema which he kindly shared with Alternative Link:

· Traditional Acupuncture Institute, Inc;
· National College of Naturopathic Medicine;
· Emperor's College of Traditional Oriental Medicine;
· Bastyr University, Natural Health Clinic;
· Traditional Chinese Medicine Clinic;
· Logan College of Chiropractic;
· Minnesota Institute of Acupuncture and Herbal Studies;
· National College of Chiropractic;
· Western States Chiropractic College.

We also wish to thank the New Mexico Academy of Healing Arts and 125 New Mexico providers who believed in us as we developed the first codes through trial and error in 1997.

Special thanks to the National Library of Medicine Unified Medical Language System team for their edits to our system in 1997.

The following members of Alternative Link staff contributed to the development of the terminology and design of this publication:

· Melinna Giannini, CEO
· Connie Koshewa, CPM, MPH, Research Mgr.
· Kevon K. Arthurs, ND, Medical Manager
· Bernd G. Lucks, Layout Design

With staff support from Belen Nemec, Greg Cooper, Donna Fay, Bernadette Quinnell and Sue M. Sefscik.

Alternative Link would like to thank the following individuals for their contributions and efforts supplying terms, edits, reviews and/or business advice:

- Desh Ahuja, *Fox Systems*
- Virginia Anthony, LMT
- Donna Atwood, RN
- Sandra Barlows, *Medical Management*
- Dan Barrows, LMT, *AMTA*
- Susan Benting, LMT
- Ian Bier, ND
- David M. Blaiwas, Mac, LAc
- Gary Boog, DC, *NM Chiropractic Assn.*
- Michael Brown, DC, *NM Chiropractic Assn*
- Gloria Bulechek, PhD, RN, FAAN
- Carlo Calabrese, ND
- David Canzone, DOM, *NM Board of Acupuncture*
- R. B. Casselberry, MD
- John Chah, MD, *NIH - Office of Alternative Medicine*
- Bobby Clark, *Health Smart, Inc*
- Jonathan Crews, TM Instructor
- Martin Dayton, DO
- William Doggett, DC
- Subu Dubey, MD
- Jean R. Eckerly, MD
- Roger Edwards, ScD
- Dagmar Ehling, DOM, LAc
- Ralph G. Ellis, Jr., MD
- Mary Fedak, *PPO Director for American Western Life*
- Kathleen L. Fleury, MT, *VT AMTA*
- Pickens Gantt, MD
- John St. George, *St. George Consulting*
- Elizabeth Gilmore, LM, CPM, BS, *Taos School of Midwifery*
- Rich Gorsuch
- Susan Groh, MD
- Cammie Hauser, RN, CPM
- Ross A. Hauser, MD
- William Hoshimi-Wilkes, PhD, DOM, *NM AAOM*
- Russell Jaffe, PhD, MD, *Serimmune Labs*
- Grace K. Johnstone
- Kris Justesen, LAc
- Brian Klepper, PhD, *Healthcare Performance, Inc*
- Mark Lamden, ND
- Linda Ledray, PhD, RN, FAAN
- Judy Lee, CPM
- Betsy Lehrfeld, JD, *Swankin & Turner Law*
- Kathleen LeMone, CPM, MPH
- Myron B. Lezak, MD
- Rosemary Mann, RN, CNM, PhD
- Howard Margolskee, MD, *Alternative Healthcare Systems of Maine*
- Dan Martin, OMD

- Karen S. Martin, RN, MSN, FAAN
- Joanne McCloskey, PhD, RN, FAAN
- Jim McClure, DC, *NM Chiropractic Assn.*
- Kathleen McMahon, *CAAOM*
- Joseph McWherter, MD
- Barbara Mitchell, JD, LAc, *Standards Mgmt.*
- Leo Modzinski, DO, MD
- Gary L. Moore, MD
- Willow T. Moore, DC, ND
- Dee Ann Newbold, LAc
- Gayla Nickel, CMT, *'A Gift of Health' Clinic*
- Claire O'Connell, HPH, PAC
- Bruce Oran, DO
- Craig Ottenstein, DO, *Lovelace/CIGNA*
- Raymond Psonak, DO
- Guy Pugh, MD
- David Reiding, DC
- Robert Rowen, MD
- Daniel Fuller Royal, DO,HMD
- Theodore Rozema, MD, *ACAM*
- Virginia Saba, EdD, RN, FAAN
- Darrell E. Sample, *WV Board of Acupuncture*
- Michael Schachter, MD
- Nancy J. Scheet, RN, MSN
- Kenneth B. Sewell, PhD
- Mark Shishida, *Fox Systems*
- Marylou Singleton, LM
- James M. Sperry, Jr., RPAC
- Stephen L. Sporn, ND
- Lawrence G. Stern, DC
- Vlad I. Thomas, CNT
- Robert E. Thompson, MD
- Wanita Thompson, RN, LMT
- Jan Thorpe, LPN, *Alternative Healthcare Systems of Maine*
- Toni Tripp-Reimer, PhD, RN, FAAN, *University of Iowa*
- Theodore J. Tuinstra, DO
- James Turner, JD, *Swankin & Turner Law*
- Walter A. Ward, MD
- Bette Waters, CNM, RN, MT, *Sexual Assault Nurse Examiner (SANE)*
- Wynn Werner, *Ayurvedic Institute and Wellness Clinic*
- Robert White, PA, PhD, ND, *Am. Board of Specialties of Alternative Medicine*
- Sheila Williams, DC

If inadvertently, we have left off the names of any contributors, please call us and we will gladly publish your name in future updates.

Introduction

The ABCode® are built upon our firm belief that this system greatly improves the entrance of CAM and expanded nursing services into mainstream health care. The codes provide the infrastructure needed for insurance companies to measure the effectiveness of these services side by side with conventional medicine treatments, thus facilitating responsible patient access to integrated healthcare.

Structure of the codes

The codes are five-digit alpha codes. The first letter identifies the category or section where the code can be found. For example, all the codes contained in *Section A, Clinical Practice Charges,* begin with the letter "A" and all codes contained in *Section B, Multi Specialty Treatments,* begin with the letter "B".

The category sections are divided into sub-categories, such as *Diagnostician* and *Limited and non-diagnostician.* Finally, the sub-categories contain headings such as *New client* or *Existing client.* The organization of the CAM Coding Manual is reflected in the *Table of Contents.*

Example of the structural meaning of a code:

AEBAJ	Weight management, Group, each 15 minutes, Nutrition counseling, Education, Clinical practice charges
A	Section A: Clinical practice charges
E	Subsection E: Education
B	Heading B: Nutrition counseling
AJ	Procedure: Weight management, each 15 minutes

The first letter of each code always points to the category or section. The second letter points to a sub-category in that section and the third letter to the heading. Procedures and supply items are then defined by two alpha-characters at the end of the code.

What you must know to use this book

How to use code modifiers

Provider specific code modifiers in the ABCode® system convey the professional license of the provider filing the claim. They do not convey difficulty or indicate professional components. The provider modifiers are attached to the end of the procedure codes. All codes in sections A, B, C, D, E and N of the ABC coding manual must be followed by a code modifier. A list of code modifiers is found on page xxvi & xxvii.

Examples: if a nurse practitioner files a claim for a 10 minute initial office visit, then code AAAAA would be modified or followed by 1H (nurse practitioner modifier) in the modifier space on the HCFA 1500 form. If a naturopathic doctor filed for the same 10 minute office visit, then code AAAAA would have a code modifier of 1E (naturopathic doctor).

Reference codes and their use

All reference codes are found in *Section A* of the coding manual and consequently, all reference codes begin with the letter "A". Remember that the codes in *Section "A"* require use of a modifier.

To prescribe, compound or dispense

Codes ADZAA-ADZZZ always have modifiers and are used to link state scope of practice laws to each provider licensed to prescribe, compound or dispense remedies or prescriptive items as the claim is being processed.

Reference codes ADZAA-ADZZZ are followed by prescriptive item, preparation, compounded substance or dispensed item codes. Codes for these items are found in *Sections F, G and H.* Codes in *Sections F, G and H,* are not modified.

Herb, nutritional supplement, flower essence and homeopathic preparation codes

Codes from Sections F, G and H describe nutritional supplements, oriental and Western herbs and botanicals, flower essences and homeopathic preparations. These codes must be preceded by a reference code in Section A (ADZAA-ADZZZ). Do not use a modifier with codes in Sections F, G and H.

Reference codes to refer and track adjunct services

ABCODE® ADYAF-ADYZZ are used when referring a patient to an exercise class, yoga, hypnotherapy, meditation or other service that falls outside the jurisdiction of health care law. Reference codes are only used for these services when a licensed health care provider is not trained or certified to offer these services directly to the patient.

If the provider is trained or certified to offer these services, no reference code is needed. Remember that in order to bill directly for exercise, yoga or meditation, a provider must hold a state license as a healthcare provider and prove training or certification to bill for an adjunct service.

Using CPT™ and ABCODE® to bill for services

There are codes needed by CAM and Nurse providers to bill for diagnostic tests, x-rays and minor surgery that are found in CPT™. In order to verify that a CAM or Nurse provider is allowed to offer these services:

1.) Use ABC codes, ADYAA-ADYAE, before ordering diagnostic tests or services (i.e.: x-rays or cardiovascular tests in CPT™). Follow the directions and expanded definitions in this coding manual to determine the appropriate code.

2.) Use ABCcodes, ADWAA through ADWZZ, are used prior to billing for minor surgeries. Follow these codes with CPT™ Codes to code the actual minor surgery. The expanded definitions will help you determine which reference codes are appropriate for you to use.

CPT™ is a registered trademark of the American Medical Association.

The HCFA 1500 form and the UB-92

ABCode® can be filed on a HCFA 1500 form (for direct patient services) or on a UB-92 form (if the services originate from a hospital or clinic).

These forms are the accepted standard forms for filing healthcare claims. Each form contains a field indicating the state in which the claim is filed and each form has a field for listing coded procedures.

ABCode® fit into the procedure code fields of these forms, just like conventional procedure codes. Alternative Link's database system can connect the state field on these forms with the procedure code and modifier to determine if state law allows the provider to bill for the procedure. The system is usually licensed by health insurance payers to verify the legality of a claim.

The company's database tells the claims adjuster if the coded information on the form falls within the state scope of practice laws for the provider filing the claim. The code string also relays training information for that particular provider and clearly defines the meaning of the service. This gives the claims adjuster all of the necessary justification to approve or deny the claim for payment and reduces paperwork for the provider.

HCFA 1500 Example

A naturopathic doctor in Maine wants to bill an insurance carrier or capture office data for treating a patient. The patient hasn't been able to sleep and the naturopathic doctor's course of treatment is to prescribe a homeopathic remedy.

First, the naturopathic doctor would code the sleep disorder using an ICD-9CM diagnostic code in box 24 E on the HCFA 1500 form.

Box 24 E Diagnostic Code
760.51
Description: Sleep Disturbance, Other Insomnia

Next, he or she would use the appropriate ABCode® in the first and second procedure code slots of box 24 D on the HCFA 1500 form.

Box 24 D Procedures, Services or Supplies
ADZAD /1E
Description: Prescribe homeopathic preparation, no charge, Prescribing, preparation and dispensing, General, Clinical practice charges

HAIAD/no modifier needed
Description: Ignatia, St. Ignatius Bean, Scientific name I, Homeopathic Preparation

HCFA 1500 Fig. 1

PLEASE
DO NOT
STAPLE
IN THIS
AREA

HEALTH INSURANCE CLAIM FORM

| | PICA | | | | | | | | | | PICA | | |

1.	MEDICARE	MEDICAID	CHAMPUS	CHAMPVA	GROUP HEALTH PLAN	FECA BLK LUNG	OTHER	1a. INSURED'S I.D. NUMBER	(FOR PROGRAM IN ITEM 1)
	(Medicare #)	(Medicaid #)	(Sponsor's SSN)	(VA File #)	(SSN or ID)	(SSN)	(ID)		

2. PATIENT'S NAME (Last Name, First Name, Middle Initial)

3. PATIENT'S BIRTH DATE MM | DD | YY   SEX M   F

4. INSURED'S NAME (Last Name, First Name, Middle Initial)

5. PATIENT'S ADDRESS (No., Street)

6. PATIENT RELATIONSHIP TO INSURED   Self Spouse Child Other

7. INSURED'S ADDRESS (No., Street)

CITY   STATE

8. PATIENT STATUS   Single   Married   Other

CITY   STATE

ZIP CODE   TELEPHONE (Include Area Code) (   )

Employed   Full-Time Student   Part-Time Student

ZIP CODE   TELEPHONE (INCLUDE AREA CODE) (   )

9. OTHER INSURED'S NAME (Last Name, First Name, Middle Initial)

10. IS PATIENT'S CONDITION RELATED TO:

11. INSURED'S POLICY GROUP OR FECA NUMBER

a. OTHER INSURED'S POLICY OR GROUP NUMBER

a. EMPLOYMENT? (CURRENT OR PREVIOUS)   YES   NO

a. INSURED'S DATE OF BIRTH MM | DD | YY   SEX M   F

b. OTHER INSURED'S DATE OF BIRTH MM | DD | YY   SEX M   F

b. AUTO ACCIDENT?   PLACE (State)   YES   NO

b. EMPLOYER'S NAME OR SCHOOL NAME

c. EMPLOYER'S NAME OR SCHOOL NAME

c. OTHER ACCIDENT?   YES   NO

c. INSURANCE PLAN NAME OR PROGRAM NAME

d. INSURANCE PLAN NAME OR PROGRAM NAME

10d. RESERVED FOR LOCAL USE

d. IS THERE ANOTHER HEALTH BENEFIT PLAN?   YES   NO   *If yes*, return to and complete item 9 a-d.

READ BACK OF FORM BEFORE COMPLETING & SIGNING THIS FORM.

12. PATIENT'S OR AUTHORIZED PERSON'S SIGNATURE I authorize the release of any medical or other information necessary to process this claim. I also request payment of government benefits either to myself or to the party who accepts assignment below.

SIGNED _____   DATE _____

13. INSURED'S OR AUTHORIZED PERSON'S SIGNATURE I authorize payment of medical benefits to the undersigned physician or supplier for services described below.

SIGNED _____

14. DATE OF CURRENT: MM | DD | YY   ◄ ILLNESS (First symptom) OR INJURY (Accident) OR PREGNANCY(LMP)

15. IF PATIENT HAS HAD SAME OR SIMILAR ILLNESS. GIVE FIRST DATE MM | DD | YY

16. DATES PATIENT UNABLE TO WORK IN CURRENT OCCUPATION MM | DD | YY   FROM   TO   MM | DD | YY

17. NAME OF REFERRING PHYSICIAN OR OTHER SOURCE

17a. I.D. NUMBER OF REFERRING PHYSICIAN

18. HOSPITALIZATION DATES RELATED TO CURRENT SERVICES MM | DD | YY   FROM   TO   MM | DD | YY

19. RESERVED FOR LOCAL USE

20. OUTSIDE LAB?   YES   NO $ CHARGES

21. DIAGNOSIS OR NATURE OF ILLNESS OR INJURY. (RELATE ITEMS 1,2,3 OR 4 TO ITEM 24E BY LINE)

1. |___ . ___   3. |___ . ___

2. |___ . ___   4. |___ . ___

22. MEDICAID RESUBMISSION CODE   ORIGINAL REF. NO.

23. PRIOR AUTHORIZATION NUMBER

24. A		B	C	D		E	F	G	H	I	J	K
DATE(S) OF SERVICE From To		Place of Service	Type of Service	PROCEDURES, SERVICES, OR SUPPLIES (Explain Unusual Circumstances) CPT/HCPCS	MODIFIER	DIAGNOSIS CODE	$ CHARGES	DAYS OR UNITS	EPSDT Family Plan	EMG	COB	RESERVED FOR LOCAL USE
MM DD YY MM DD YY												

25. FEDERAL TAX I.D. NUMBER   SSN   EIN

26. PATIENT'S ACCOUNT NO.

27. ACCEPT ASSIGNMENT? (For govt. claims, see back)   YES   NO

28. TOTAL CHARGE $

29. AMOUNT PAID $

30. BALANCE DUE $

31. SIGNATURE OF PHYSICIAN OR SUPPLIER INCLUDING DEGREES OR CREDENTIALS (I certify that the statements on the reverse apply to this bill and are made a part thereof.)

SIGNED _____   DATE _____

32. NAME AND ADDRESS OF FACILITY WHERE SERVICES WERE RENDERED (If other than home or office)

33. PHYSICIAN'S, SUPPLIER'S BILLING NAME, ADDRESS, ZIP CODE & PHONE #

PIN#   GRP#

(APPROVED BY AMA COUNCIL ON MEDICAL SERVICE 8/88)   *PLEASE PRINT OR TYPE*   FORM HCFA-1500 (12-90), FORM RRB-1500,

Merely, by entering **760.51, ADZAD-1E** and **HAIAD** on the HCFA 1500 form, the provider and payer have communicated the above diagnosis and course of treatment, as well as capturing information about the provider's legal scope of practice in Maine.

Although the insurance carrier may not reimburse for this treatment, the data now becomes part of the treatment pattern for the patient. This data can be compared to conventional data for effectiveness, cost and patient outcomes for sleep disorders. Coded information is essential for computers to analyze this information.

Cross references

Using the index to locate procedures

The *Procedure Index* in the back of the book is a good place to begin looking for the service that you want to code. Refer to the *Supply and Product Index* for supply items you want to code. There is also an index to cross-reference nursing terms from the Nursing Intervention Classification system to the ABCode® in the back of the book.

Using the code tree to locate procedures

The code tree, located in the back of the book, groups services, procedures, treatments and supplies based on the hierarchy of the ABCode® system. The code tree helps users locate services based on the type of treatment being looked for. The code tree also helps users understand general placement of the terms by category, subcategory and heading.

Read the subsection and headings in the code tree. Turn to that section of the coding manual and read the descriptions and expanded definitions to select the code that best describes the service or supply that you are performing or prescribing.

General guidelines for providers

Provider modifiers

Provider-specific modifiers are two character codes that convey to a payer the license a provider holds. The modifiers are attached to the end of the procedure codes. Sections **A, B, C, D, E** and **N** of the ABCode® must be followed by a provider modifier. See page xiii, **'How to use Code modifiers'**.

Why use a provider modifier?

· Provider modifiers create data specific to each practitioner type;
· They allow each type of practitioner's services to be compared to conventional data;
· They link code, provider and state scope of practice laws;
· They link the provider to the education and training requirements for any coded service or supply item.

Provider specific guidelines

These codes have been designed by Alternative Link to provide a more thorough tracking and reporting system for billable procedures. Almost 4,000 codes describe what is said, done, ordered, supplied and distributed by CAM and Nurse providers. Expanded definitions for each code further describe procedures and reduce the paperwork burdens on practitioners.

There are about 4,000 procedures, services and nutriceuticals listed in this manual. Any practitioner may use any code in this manual as long as the practitioner is trained to offer the service to a patient and also allowed by the state to provide the treatment under scope of practice laws. Additional training requirements are indicated in the expanded definitions. Codes are listed by category in each section of the book. Follow the *Table of Contents* or the *Index* to find specific treatments, supplies or nutriceuticals.

Licensed Acupuncturists and Oriental Medicine Doctors

Acupuncturists or doctors of oriental medicine will find a cross-reference on page xxvi & xxvii to the different titles assigned by states for this license. All non-MD providers licensed to offer acupuncture services should use 1C to modify the codes.

Acupuncture and oriental medicine providers are required to strictly observe state scope of practice laws when using these codes. Any code, within the scope of practice laws for the license, may be used to bill for services. Use the *Table of contents* and the *Index* to find different types of services or supplies.

It is important that you carefully read the instructions on how to place codes and modifiers on billing forms on pages 3 - 6. Reference codes, previously explained in the directions, are necessary to use CPT™ codes within this coding system.

Referral codes are used when recommending yoga and other services you do not personally provide to the patient. Advanced study is required by state laws in order to use many of the ABCode®. Please check the specific requirement for the procedure in the expanded definition (e.g. surgical anesthesia using acupuncture).

Bodyworkers, Massage Therapists and Somatic Educators

There are many training levels of practitioners who practice bodywork, massage and somatic education. For the purposes of using the ABCode® to bill for services, national, state, city or county certification as a massage therapist (1B) is needed.

Many of the procedures listed under Bodywork/Massage/Somatic education require additional and specific training and/or certification, especially for specialized training such as Rolfing®, Structural Integration® and Feldenkrais®. Training/Certification for these and other course work require the practitioner to prove certification before assigning codes to claim forms.

Training standards have not been assigned by the states for these modalities but are usually based on certifications.

Limited massage codes have been assigned for use by various other provider types. However, use of any of the advanced training massage codes by MDs, DOs, NDs, Acupuncturists or others assumes massage training and/or certification as delineated, above.

Massage therapists are considered a type of non diagnostician for the purpose of insurance coverage because massage therapists may not originate a diagnosis or make decisions requiring medical diagnosis. Some states require a medical referral before providing massage or bodywork.

Massage therapists do take patient intake information. Codes ACAAD and ACBAD describe the time that a massage therapist spends with a patient in their office.

Codes ACAAD - ACBAD are also used for patient home visits, as well as in a nursing home or hospital setting. Codes ADAAB - ADCAE can be used for expanded services and travel time. Some plans allow massage visits as part of a wellness visit. If the patient is using this benefit, use codes ABAAA - ABAZZ to bill for these services.

Chiropractors

Chiropractors (1A) should use the ABCode® for evaluation and management when it is important to differentiate chiropractic from conventional services. The 1A provider modifier allows claims to be reviewed to show efficacy of chiropractic treatment patterns.

There are many procedures that are used by chiropractors throughout this manual, with definitions to describe the particular service. These procedures are listed by category in each section of the book (e.g. biofeedback in mental health).

Reference codes for x-rays and lab tests are used to tie the chiropractic license (1A) to the scope of practice in the state where the claim was filed. The ABC Code is followed by an x-ray or lab test code from CPT™. Chiropractic providers are required to strictly observe state scope of practice laws when using these codes. Scope of Practice Reports are available from Alternative Link.

It is important to carefully read the instructions on how to place codes and modifiers on billing forms. Referral codes, as explained previously, are necessary in order to map to CPT™ codes on the billing forms for x-rays and lab tests.

Advanced certification is required by state laws in order to use many of the ABCode®. Please check the specific requirement for the procedure in the expanded definition (e.g., Trigger Point Needling).

It is important to read instructions carefully on how to place codes and modifiers on billing forms. Referral codes, as explained previously, are necessary in order to map CPT™ codes to the entire chiropractic treatment pattern (e.g. radiological studies and lab tests). This mapping allows cost and outcome studies specific to chiropractors.

Licensed, Direct-Entry or Certified Professional Midwives and Nurse Midwives

There are two types of midwives included in Alternative Link's system: licensed, direct-entry or certified professional midwives (1D) and nurse or certified nurse midwives (1G). See the cross-reference of these two practitioner modifiers to abbreviations for the various titles used in different states on pages xxvi & xxvii.

The title, *Direct-entry Midwife* is commonly used to describe midwives who have entered directly into midwifery training without a nursing background. *Certified Professional Midwife* is the title for midwives who have been certified by the North American Registry of Midwives (NARM). Nineteen (19) states recognize licensure or certification of various types of registered midwives, while fifteen (15) states clearly prohibit the practice of non-nurse midwifery by statutes or case law.The remaining states have no statutes or regulations recognizing or prohibiting the practice of registered midwives and are considered unregulated. In legal states, registered midwives are independent practitioners with guidelines on working with non-complicated prenatal, delivery and postnatal care. Some of the legal states allow the administration of medications in emergency situations.

Certified Nurse Midwives (1G) are midwives with prior training as registered nurses. Many states consider nurse midwives a category of advanced practice nursing. Some of these states require a master's degree in addition to a registered nursing license in order to practice nurse midwifery. Some states also require national certification by the American College of Nurse Midwives (ACNM). Most states grant certified nurse midwives varying levels of prescriptive authority and many states allow nurse midwives to practice independently of physician oversight.

If allowed by state law, global midwifery codes are used to process maternity claims when the midwife is directing all patient care. These codes include the initial and subsequent history, physical examination, monitoring blood pressure and fetal heart tones and monthly visits up to 28 weeks gestational age, biweekly visits from 29 to 36 weeks, and weekly visits thereafter until birth, and postpartum care up to six weeks. Any other services or visits should be coded individually, including newborn care. For one to three prenatal visits only, use the appropriate office codes in Section A.

Many of the codes used by midwives are contained in the Midwifery subsection of Section C, Practice Specialties. Many other appropriate codes are in other sections of the manual, particularly in Section N, Nursing. For a complete list of codes allowed for RM or NM by state, license and scope of practice, please contact Alternative Link.

Naturopathic Doctors or Physicians

The ABCODE® have been designed by Alternative Link to provide a more thorough system for reporting and tracking the use of holistic procedures. Naturopathic doctors (1E) should use the ABCODE® for evaluation and management when it is important to differentiate services from conventional medical services. The 1E provider modifier allows claims to be reviewed to show efficacy of naturopathic treatment patterns when compared to conventional medicine.

Naturopathic medical providers are required to strictly observe state scope of practice laws when using these codes. Codes for naturopathic medicine are listed throughout the Coding Manual. Use any code that falls within the naturopathic doctor's scope of practice laws of the state. In states that do not license, but do not prohibit the practice of naturopathic medicine, no DEA license is available, therefore prescribing controlled substances is prohibited. Reports of the legally allowed codes for NDs in each state are available through Alternative Link.

It is important to read the instructions carefully on how to place codes and modifiers on billing forms. Referral codes, previously explained in the directions, are necessary in order to use CPT™ codes with in this coding system (e.g. radiological studies, minor surgical procedures and lab tests).

Advanced study is required by some state laws in order for naturopaths to use many of the ABCode®. Please check the specific requirement for the procedure in the expanded definition, (e.g., Labor induction using acupuncture).

Medical and Osteopathic Doctors

Medical and Osteopathic Doctors should use the ABCode® for evaluation and management when it is important to differentiate CAM services from conventional medical services. The 1M or 1L provider modifier allows claims to be reviewed to show efficacy of MD or DO holistic treatment patterns.

There are many procedures from which to choose, with definitions to describe the particular service. These procedures are listed by category in each section of the book. Follow the *Table of Contents* or the *Procedure Index* to find specific treatments.

It is important to read instructions carefully on how to place codes and modifiers on billing forms. Referral codes, as previously explained in the directions, are necessary in order to map to CPT™ codes on forms (e.g. radiological studies, heart or vascular studies, minor surgical procedures). Advanced study is required by different state laws in order for physicians to use many of the ABCode®. Please check the specific requirement for the procedure (e.g., surgical anesthesia using acupuncture).

Clinical Nurse Specialists, Nurse Midwives, Nurse Practitioners, Licensed Practical Nurses and Registered Nurses

There are five levels of nursing licensure included in Alternative Link's system. Each nurse type using the coding system would use a two character modifier after the codes in this book to indicate the license held.

The modifiers for each practitioner are: Registered Nurses (1K), Practical Nurses (1J), Clinical Nurse Specialists (1F), Nurse Practitioners (1H) and Certified Nurse Midwives (1G). Registered and Practical Nurses generally do not bill directly for services. However, hospitals, clinics and doctor's offices may want to track their services to assure legal compliance with state scope of practice laws.

The N Section contains nursing procedures from the Nursing Interventions Classification (NIC) system. NIC is a comprehensive standardized vocabulary to facilitate communicating nursing treatments between nurses, hospital staff and other providers. An index in the back of this manual maps NIC numeric identifiers and terms to the Alternative Link ABCode®.

The information contained in these nursing classification system was modified for reporting nursing services to insurance companies with attached relative values in 1998. Other contributors to nursing codes contained in this book are: Omaha System Intervention Scheme, Home Health Care Classification system and Sexual Assault Resource Service.

Many alternative medicine codes can also be used by nurses. For a complete list of codes for your state, license and scope of practice, please contact Alternative Link.

Nursing services are also found in different parts of this manual under the headings of midwifery, mental health and/or counseling.

Further instructions

The ABCode® contain instructional notes in the front of each section so the user can:

· Understand the intent of codes contained in specific sections and subsections;
· Locate the appropriate code;
· Assign additional codes to indicate expanded time or procedures, as necessary;

Please, be aware of services or procedures that are bundled into global services and cannot be filed with other codes. Expanded definitions identify which codes are global services.

The notes at the beginning of the sections will help you understand the codes contained in that section. Guidelines that are specific to individual codes are also included in the expanded definitions. Careful reading and adherence to section directions are recommended to assure appropriate code assignment.

Super tip for super efficiency

Create a super bill (see page 14, *Sample Superbill*) or a patient encounter form for your operation, office or clinic. A super bill is a listing of the coded services you use most often. Creating a superbill saves time looking up and writing down all the procedures that were performed during the office visit. The services can simply be checked off on the form. Most services will only have to be looked up once to create a superbill.

Background of the coding system

The development of the ABCode® began in 1996. The original goal was to provide CAM practitioners with codes to bill for services to insurance companies. Nursing procedures were included in 1998. The codes were designed to do five jobs:

· Accurately describe the services used to treat patients;
· Allow providers and payers to negotiate fees;
· Assure the insurance company that the coded treatments fall within the legal scope of practice rules in the state where the licensed practitioner performs the service;
· Aggregate data for each licensed practitioner to compare to conventional medicine;
· Fit inside existing claims processing and payment systems.

Establishing a common "language" for CAM and nursing allows services to be easily understood and helps promote health insurance covearge.

The creation of a coding system, compatible with mainstream medical billing and claims processing systems, was necessary to integrate CAM and Nursing services into the business structures of insurance reimbursement.

How the insurance industry uses codes

The insurance industry pairs diagnosis codes (ICD-9) with treatment codes (HCPCS including CPT™) in large data warehouses to determine the number of claims per diagnosis. The industry analyzes treatment patterns for each ICD-9 code and determines the average cost of treatments for each diagnosis. Claims data is also surveyed to track the average number of visits required before a patient ceases to see health care providers for the problem.

As a result of accurate coding on standard claim forms, cost-effectiveness and treatment-efficacy can be measured. This gives insurance underwriters, as well as the government, employers, actuaries and others, the ability to calculate risk and exposure and set insurance premiums for CAM and expanded nursing services.

Until the advent of Alternative Link's ABCODE®, no coded data for CAM or nursing services existed. Consequently, no data could be gathered to perform outcome analysis. With ABCODE®, the insurance industry can incorporate these expanded services into covered healthcare benefits using the same business structure used to cover conventional medicine.

Equally important, underwriters can now compare CAM and nursing services to conventional treatment patterns to assess the costs and benefits associated with adding these services to insurance coverage.

How the complete system works to support CAM and nursing

Our coding system database contains over 13 million units of information to support claims processing for CAM and nursing. The system passes claims for payment when codes fall within the scope of practice for the practitioner in the state(s) where the practitioner is licensed and fails claims that are not allowed by state law.

Having electronic access to this information reduces legal liability for insurance payers and providers. The electronic format lowers the cost of processing claims for CAM and nursing providers. It also reduces the cost of processing claims for the insurance companies. Reduction of cost and legal liability motivates payers to consider incorporating CAM and nursing services into fully insured benefits.

The State Legal Guide to Complementary and Alternative Medicine and Nursing, a book that outlines scope of practice for 13 practitioner types, was extracted from the coding system database. This book is also published by Delmar, a Thomson Learning Company, and is available by visiting our web site: www.delmar.com.

Relative Value Units

Relative value units (RVUs), provide a value indication for each procedure code. Relative values for CAM and nursing are available as a companion reference to our coding manuals.

Relative Values for Complementary and Alternative Medicine and Nursing describe the interrelationship of values between procedures. A conversion factor is used to determine rates or fees for services. The conversion factor can be adjusted up or down for different regions of the country or by insurance contract. This information was developed in cooperation with Relative Value Studies, Inc., creators of Relative Values for Physicians (*Relative Values for Physicians* are broadly used for non-government sponsored health services). The relative values in the publication and electronic files distributed by RVSI are attached to the ABCODE®.

Relation Based Relative Value Studies (RBRVS), developed by the Health Care Finance Administration, is the relative value system used when filing claims for Medicare or Medicaid.

The 2001 edition of "Relative Values for CAM & Nursing" contains RBRVS factors. To order, contact:

Relative Value Studies, Inc.
www.rvsdata.com/, 1675 Larimer Ste. 410, Denver,
CO 80202, Phone (303) 534-0506

Relative values for CAM and Nursing can also be ordered through Alternative Link by logging on to our website at www.alternativelink.com or by using the order form in the very back of this book.

Other Information

Providers can bill for more services if they provide documentation of certifications above their state license. Example: chiropractic training does not cover foot reflexology, but a chiropractor may use the codes for reflexology treatments if additional training has been obtained.

Over 11 million code combinations are possible within the ABCODE® structure to support emerging CAM and nursing services and modifiers can be added to support future licensed provider types. This coding system can grow and expand with time.

Conclusion

The need for a uniform CAM and Nursing coding system is apparent. Many health insurers and managed care organizations are moving to include CAM and private-practice Nursing in their policy offerings. States are beginning to mandate coverage of certain CAM and Nursing services.

In addition, the recent federal mandate for code standardization, HIPAA (Health Insurance Portability and Accountability Act of 1996) demands an accurate description of coded treatments. Until the ABCode® were created, there was simply no information to accurately describe the wealth of CAM and nursing treatments in the detail needed to support legal billing and to cause accurate data capture.

Frequently asked questions

Q: *Can a provider also use codes from CPT™ with this system?*

A: Yes. For example, if you order or administer x-rays, perform minor surgical procedures , order heart, vascular or vital capacity studies, you should code these services using CPT™.
Note, you must also use a reference code from the ABCode® system to generate scope of practice information.

Q: *Is there any certain way to use both code sets?*

A: Yes. If you need to use CPT™, you will find a reference code in the ABCode® under Section A.

Example: if you file code ADYAE and modify it with 1C, the provider tells the payer that they are a Doctor of Oriental Medicine and that they are going to order an x-ray. The code states that a CPT code for an x-ray will follow.

Alternative Link's electronic claims editing system will tell a payer the Doctor of Oriental Medicine is allowed to order x-rays in New Mexico. In Iowa, a licensed acupuncturist must work from a referral from a physician and may not order x-rays or any other diagnostic tests.

Q: *Why do I have to use a "no charge" reference code?*

A: Using the ABC reference code ties the service to the provider's legal scope of practice in the state where the service is provided. CPT™ does not convey this information. Modifiers for CPT™ have different rules than the codes in the ABC system.

Q: *What do I do if I don't find the code I need?*

A: We have provided a form before the indices of this book for you to request additional codes (see page 15). Simply fill it out and mail it to us. We will verify that other providers need this code. In the meantime, use an undefined (***ZZ) procedure code and attach a written report when billing for the service.

CPT™ is a registered trademark of the American Medical Association.

Provider Modifier	State Abbreviation	Provider Specialty
1A	DC	Doctor of Chiropractic
		Chiropractic Doctor
1B	MT	Massage Therapist
	CMT	Certified Massage Therapist
	LMP	Licensed Massage Practitioner
	LMT	Licensed Massage Therapist
	LMT	Licensed Massage Technician
	MP	Massage Practitioner
	no acronym	Master Massage Therapist
	no acronym	Massage and Bodywork Therapist
	no acronym	Massage and Bodywork Technician
	no acronym	Masseur/Masseuse
1C	DOM	Doctor of Oriental Medicine
	OMD	Oriental Medical Doctor
	AcT	Acupuncture Therapist
	AP	Acupuncture Physician
	CA	Certified Acupuncturist
	DAc	Doctor of Acupuncture
	LAc	Licensed Acupuncturist
1D	RM	Registered Midwife
	CM	Certified Midwife
	CPM	Certified Professional Midwife
	DEM	Direct Entry Midwife
	GM	Granny Midwife
	LLM	Licensed Lay Midwife
	LM	Lay Midwife
	LM	Licensed Midwife
	LTM	Licensed Traditional Midwife
	LDM	Licensed Direct-Entry Midwife
	LMP	Licensed Midwife Practitioner
1E	ND	Naturopathic Doctor
	ND	Naturopath Physician
	DN	Doctor of Naturopathy
1F	CNS	Clinical Nurse Specialist
	NS	Nurse Specialist
	CRNS	Clinical Registered Nurse Specialist
1G	CNM	Certified Nurse Midwife
	NM	Licensed Nurse Midwife
	CRNM	Certified Registered Nurse Midwife

Provider Modifier	State Abbreviation	Provider Specialty
1H	ANP	Advanced Nurse Practitioner
	APN	Advanced Practice Nurse
	APRN	Advanced Practice Registered Nurse
	ARNP	Advanced Registered Nurse Practitioner
	CNP	Certified Nurse Practitioner
	CRNP	Certified Registered Nurse Practitioner
	NP	Nurse Practitioner
	RN, NP, C	Registered Nurse, Nurse Practitioner, Certified
	RNP	Registered Nurse Practitioner
1J	LPN	Licensed Practical Nurse
	LVN	Licensed Vocational Nurse
1K	RN	Registered Nurse
	no acronym	Professional Nurse
	no acronym	Professional Registered Nurse
1L	DO	Doctor of Osteopathy
		Osteopathic Doctor
1M	MD	Medical Doctor
		Allopathic Physician
		Doctor of Allopathic Medicine
1N	PA	Physician's Assistant
2002	MH	Mental Health Professional *(not a Psychiatrist)*
	CPC	Certified Professional Counselor
	MFCC	Marriage and Family Counselor
	MSW	Master of Social Work
	PhD	Psychologist
	EdD	Psychologist
	PsyD	Psychologist
	LCP	Psychologist
	MFCC	Psychologist
	MA	Psychologist
2003	HD	Holistic Dentist
	DDS	Doctor of Dental Surgery
2003	OT	Occupational Therapist
2003	PT	Physical Therapist
n/a	HO	*Homeopath* is a secondary license for physicians

Sample Superbill—Modify all codes on this form by "1A" to indicate Chiropractic Doctor

Superbill for □		Date:□ _____		Provider Name:□ _____		
Chiropractors□		Patient:□ _____		Provider Type:□ _____		

Office Visit - New Patient□			General□			Ergonomics□		
ABC□	**DESCRIPTION**□	**# / $**□	**ABC**□	**DESCRIPTION**□	**# / $**□	**ABC**□	**DESCRIPTION**□	**# / $**□
AAAAA□	Simple, 10 minutes□		BAAAA□	Cold or ice pack□		CBDAA□	Digital wrist movements□	
AAAAB□	Usual, 20 minutes□		BABAB□	Electric.stimulation unattended□		CBDAB□	Gait training□	
AAAAC□	Complex, 30 minutes□		BABAG□	Galvanic, high voltage□		CBDAC□	Lifting□	
AAAAD□	Detailed, 45 minutes□		BABAJ□	Electrical stimulation attended□		CBDAD□	Lower body movements□	
AAAAE□	Comprehensive, 60 minutes□		BACAB□	Diathermy, short wave□		CBDAE□	Rotational activities□	
AAAZZ□	Undefined, narrative required□		BAGAD□	Ultrasound□		CBDAF□	Sitting□	
			BBCAA□	Manual traction□		CBDAG□	Standing□	
			BBCAB□	Mechanical traction□		CBDAH□	Supine functions□	
			BCAAA□	Orthotics fitting and movement□		CBDAI□	Upper body training□	
Office Visit - Existing Patient□			BDDAA□	Extremity or trunk w/o hands□		CBDAJ□	Functional activities□	
ABC□	**DESCRIPTION**□	**# / $**□				CBDAK□	Daily living activities training□	
AABAA□	Simple, 5 minutes□					CBDAL□	Isometric exercise□	
AABAB□	Usual, 10 minutes□					CBDAM□	Traction, gravity guidance□	
AABAC□	Complex, 15 minutes□		**X-Rays**□			CBDAN□	Body mechanics promotion□	
AABAD□	Detailed, 25 minutes□		Enter all CPT X-Ray codes that you use below□			CBDAO□	Balance, exercise therapy□	
AABAE□	Comprehensive, 40 minutes□		**ABC**□	**DESCRIPTION**□	**# / $**□	CBDAP□	Muscle control exercise□	
AABZZ□	Undefined, narrative required□		ADYAE□	Ordering X-Rays, no charge□	n/c□	CBDAQ□	Group psychomotor skills ed.□	
						CBDAR□	Individual psychomotor skills□	
						CBDZZ□	Undefined, narrative required□	
Chiropractic□								
ABC□	**DESCRIPTION**□	**# / $**□						
CCAAA□	Block Technique□							
CCAAB□	Educational Kinesiology□							
CCAAC□	Physical manipulation, 1 area□					**Other**□		
CCAAD□	Manipulation, each extra area□					**ABC**□	**DESCRIPTION**□	**# / $**□
CCAAE□	General spinal, 1 or 2 regions□							
CCAAF□	General spinal, 3 or 4 regions□							
CCAAG□	General spinal, 5 regions□							
CCAAH□	Manipulation other than spine□							
CCAZZ□	Undefined, narrative required□							

Unless noted differently, default time increment is 15 minutes□

Medicinal Items□			Return Visits□			Charges□	
			First return visit□				
			In:□	For:□	min□	**Services**	□
			Second return visit□				
			In:□	For:□	min□	**Medicinal Items**	□
			Third return visit□				
			In:□	For:□	min□	**Laboratory**	□
			Fourth return visit□				
			In:□	For:□	min□	**Adjustment**	□
			Supply Items□				
						TOTAL CHARGES	□
						AMOUNT PAID	□
						ICD-9□	**Diagnosis**□

Additional Code Request Form

Alternative Link is aware that the current code set is not all-inclusive and that you may not be able to find a particular procedure or supply item code. We highly encourage your participation to make this the best and most complete coding system possible. Please complete the following information and submit it to us. We will consider all recommendations for future publications.

Short description of the procedure, supply item, etc., you are recommending to include.

_____

_____

_____

Describe the procedure, supply item, etc., how and when it is used, and how you receive training for it.

_____

_____

_____

_____

_____

Does the state you practice in recognize this procedure?   ○ **Yes**   ○ **No**

Are you allowed to perform this procedure in your state? (please attach documentation if available)

_____

_____

About me (your name, specialty and contact address)

Send to:

Alternative Link
Research Department
1065 S. Main, Building C
Las Cruces, NM 88005

Section A: Clinical Practice Charges

Instructions

The following subsections are contained in Section A:

Diagnostician
New client in office
Existing client in office
New client house call
Existing client house call
New client nursing facility
Existing client nursing facility

Periodic
Wellness visit, new or existing client

Limited and non-diagnostician
New client in office
Existing client in office
New client house call
Existing client house call
New client nursing home
Existing client nursing home

General service and reference codes
Consultation between providers
Expanded services
Phone conversations
Interpretive services
Hospice care
Performing
Recommending
Ordering and referring
Prescription, preparation and dispensing

Education
General
Nutritional counseling

General

Alternative health practitioners and nurses use appropriate codes in Section A to describe office, outpatient, clinical practice, general services and non-billable references to services. Therapeutic services, performed during the encounter, should also be coded and are found in Sections B, C, D and N.

Codes AAAAA through AAFZZ are for client/patient visits (see explanation below) based on the amount of time, the complexity, and location of visits. Evaluation and Management Codes in CPT® are not defined in the same manner as these codes. Initial homeopathic intakes can take 60 minutes or longer. The ABC codes can be used to describe homeopathic services for new clients/patients. These codes can also be used by any provider with diagnostic authority. Codes ACAAA through ACZZZ are for limited diagnostic providers to report client/patient intake and assessment time.

Add modifiers (provider specific) to all codes in Section A. See pages xxvi-xxvii for a table of provider modifiers.

A **diagnostician** (see code range AAAAA through ABZZZ) is a practitioner whose scope of practice allows them to diagnose (using ICD–9 diagnostic codes to define health services) or make decisions regarding the patient's/client's condition.

A **limited and non-diagnostician** (see code range ABAAA through ACZZZ) is unable to originate a patient diagnose (using ICD–9 diagnostic codes). Some limited diagnosticians must receive orders from a diagnostician in order to provide a particular service or procedure to the patient/client.

A massage therapist must use codes ACAAD and ACBAD for client assessment.

All practitioners are encouraged to read their specific practitioner section in the introduction of the book:

Clinical practice charges

Diagnostician

New client in office

ABC Code	Procedure Description	Expanded Definition
AAAAA	Simple, 10 minutes, New client in office, Diagnostician, Clinical practice charges	Office visit for evaluation, management and ICD-9 diagnosis of a new client. Simple 10 minute personal meeting to provide counseling and coordination of healthcare recommendations for client and/or family. This code may be used by non-physician providers able to diagnose.
AAAAB	Usual, 20 minutes, New client in office, Diagnostician, Clinical practice charges	Office visit for evaluation, management and ICD-9 diagnosis of a new client. Usual 20 minute personal meeting to provide counseling and coordination of healthcare recommendations for client and/or family. This code may be used by non-physician providers able to diagnose.
AAAAC	Complex, 30 minutes, New client in office, Diagnostician, Clinical practice charges	Office visit for evaluation, management and ICD-9 diagnosis of a new client. Complex 30 minute personal meeting to provide counseling and coordination of healthcare recommendations for client and/or family and for examination of more complex health concerns. This code may be used by non-physician providers able to diagnose.
AAAAD	Detailed, 45 minutes, New client in office, Diagnostician, Clinical practice charges	Office visit for evaluation, management and ICD-9 diagnosis of a new client. Detailed 45 minute personal meeting to provide counseling and coordination of healthcare recommendations for client and/or family, to gather detailed medical history information and for examination of more complex health concerns. This code may be used by non-physician providers able to diagnose.
AAAAE	Comprehensive, 60 minutes, may include homeopathy, New client in office, Diagnostician, Clinical practice charges	Office visit for evaluation, management and ICD-9 diagnosis, and/or homeopathic followup of a new client. Comprehensive 60 minute personal meeting to provide counseling and coordination of healthcare recommendations to client and/or family, to gather medical history information and for examination of health concerns. This code may be used by non-physician providers able to diagnose.

New client in office

ABC Code	Procedure Description	Expanded Definition
AAAAF	Comprehensive, prolonged, 90 minutes, may include homeopathy, New client in office, Diagnostician, Clinical practice charges	Office visit for evaluation, management and ICD-9 diagnosis, and/or homeopathic followup of a new client. Comprehensive 90 minute personal meeting to provide counseling and coordination of healthcare recommendations to client and/or family, to gather medical history information and for examination of health concerns. This code may be used by non-physician providers able to diagnose.
AAAAG	Comprehensive, prolonged, 120 minutes, may include homeopathy, New client in office, Diagnostician, Clinical practice charges	Office visit for evaluation, management and ICD-9 diagnosis, and/or homeopathic followup of a new client. Comprehensive 120 minutes personal meeting to provide counseling and coordination of healthcare recommendations to client and/or family, to gather medical history information and for examination of health concerns. This code may be used by non-physician providers able to diagnose.
AAAAH	Comprehensive, prolonged, 150 minutes, also homeopathy, New client in office, Diagnostician, Clinical practice charges	Office visit for evaluation, management and ICD-9 diagnosis, and/or homeopathic followup of a new client. Comprehensive 150 minutes personal meeting to provide counseling and coordination of healthcare recommendations to client and/or family, to gather medical history information and for examination of health concerns. This code may be used by non-physician providers able to diagnose.
AAAZZ	Undefined, narrative required, New client in office, Diagnostician, Clinical practice charges	Anywhere else undefined new client in office visit. This code may be used by non-physician providers able to diagnose.

Existing client in office

ABC Code	Procedure Description	Expanded Definition
AABAA	Simple, 5 minutes, may include homeopathy, Existing client in office, Diagnostician, Clinical practice charges	Office visit for the purpose of evaluation, management and ICD-9 diagnosis and/or homeopathic followup of an existing client. Simple 5 minutes personal meeting to provide counseling and coordination of healthcare recommendations to client and/or family. This code may be used by non-physician providers able to diagnose.
AABAB	Usual, 10 minutes, may include homeopathy, Existing client in office, Diagnostician, Clinical practice charges	Office visit for the purpose of evaluation, management and ICD-9 diagnosis and/or homeopathic followup of an existing client. Usual 10 minutes personal meeting to provide counseling and coordination of healthcare recommendations to client and/or family. This code may be used by non-physician providers able to diagnose.

Existing client in office

ABC Code	Procedure Description	Expanded Definition
AABAC	Complex, 15 minutes, may include homeopathy, Existing client in office, Diagnostician, Clinical practice charges	Office visit for the purpose of evaluation, management and ICD-9 diagnosis and/or homeopathic followup of an existing client. Complex 15 minutes personal meeting to provide counseling and coordination of healthcare recommendations to client and/or family, and for examination of more complex health concerns. This code may be used by non-physician providers able to diagnose.
AABAD	Detailed, 25 minutes, may include homeopathy, Existing client in office, Diagnostician, Clinical practice charges	Office visit for the purpose of evaluation, management and ICD-9 diagnosis and/or homeopathic followup of an existing client. Detailed 25 minutes personal meeting to provide counseling and coordination of healthcare recommendations to client and/or family, to gather detailed medical history information and for examination of more complex health concerns. This code may be used by non-physician providers able to diagnose.
AABAE	Comprehensive, 40 minutes, may include homeopathy, Existing client in office, Diagnostician, Clinical practice charges	Office visit for the purpose of evaluation, management and ICD-9 diagnosis and/or homeopathic followup of an existing client. Comprehensive 40 minutes personal meeting to provide counseling and coordination of healthcare recommendations to client and/or family, to gather detailed medical history information and for examination of more complex health concerns. This code may be used by non-physician providers able to diagnose.
AABAF	Comprehensive, 60 minutes, may include homeopathy, Existing client in office, Diagnostician, Clinical practice charges	Office visit for the purpose of evaluation, management and ICD-9 diagnosis and/or homeopathic followup of an existing client. Comprehensive 60 minutes personal meeting to provide counseling and coordination of healthcare recommendations to client and/or family, to gather detailed medical history information and for examination of more complex health concerns. This code may be used by non-physician providers able to diagnose.
AABAG	Comprehensive, prolonged, 90 minutes, may include homeopathy, Existing client in office, Diagnostician, Clinical practice charges	Office visit for the purpose of evaluation, management and ICD-9 diagnosis and/or homeopathic followup of an existing client. Comprehensive 90 minute personal meeting to provide counseling and coordination of healthcare recommendations to client and/or family, to gather detailed medical history information and for examination of more complex health concerns. This code may be used by non-physician providers able to diagnose.

Existing client in office

ABC Code	Procedure Description	Expanded Definition
AABAH	Comprehensive, prolonged, 120 minutes, may include homeopathy, Existing client in office, Diagnostician, Clinical practice charges	Office visit for the purpose of evaluation, management and ICD-9 diagnosis and/or homeopathic followup of an existing client. Comprehensive 120 minutes personal meeting to provide counseling and coordination of healthcare recommendations to client and/or family, to gather detailed medical history information and for examination of more complex health concerns. This code may be used by non-physician providers able to diagnose.
AABAI	Comprehensive, prolonged, 150 minutes, may include homeopathy, Existing client in office, Diagnostician, Clinical practice charges	Office visit for the purpose of evaluation, management and ICD-9 diagnosis and/or homeopathic followup of an existing client. Comprehensive 150 minutes personal meeting to provide counseling and coordination of healthcare recommendations to client and/or family, to gather detailed medical history information and for examination of more complex health concerns. This code may be used by non-physician providers able to diagnose.
AABZZ	Undefined, narrative required, Existing client in office, Diagnostician, Clinical practice charges	Anywhere else undefined existing client in office visit. This code may be used by non-physician providers able to diagnose.

New client house call

ABC Code	Procedure Description	Expanded Definition
AACAA	Simple, 10 minutes, New client house call, Diagnostician, Clinical practice charges	Home visit for the purpose of evaluation, management and ICD-9 diagnosis and/or homeopathic followup of a new client. Simple 10 minutes personal meeting to provide counseling and coordination of healthcare recommendations to client and/or family. This code may be used by non-physician providers able to diagnose.
AACAB	Usual, 20 minutes, New client house call, Diagnostician, Clinical practice charges	Home visit for the purpose of evaluation, management and ICD-9 diagnosis and/or homeopathic followup of a new client. Usual 20 minutes personal meeting to provide counseling and coordination of healthcare recommendations to client and/or family. This code may be used by non-physician providers able to diagnose.

New client house call

ABC Code	Procedure Description	Expanded Definition
AACAC	Complex, 30 minutes, New client house call, Diagnostician, Clinical practice charges	Home visit for the purpose of evaluation, management and ICD-9 diagnosis and/or homeopathic followup of a new client. Complex 30 minutes personal meeting to provide counseling and coordination of healthcare recommendations to client and/or family and for examination of more complex health concerns. This code may be used by non-physician providers able to diagnose.
AACAD	Detailed, 45 minutes, New client house call, Diagnostician, Clinical practice charges	Home visit for the purpose of evaluation, management and ICD-9 diagnosis and/or homeopathic followup of a new client. Detailed 45 minutes personal meeting to provide counseling and coordination of healthcare recommendations to client and/or family, to gather detailed medical history information and for examination of more complex health concerns. This code may be used by non-physician providers able to diagnose.
AACAE	Comprehensive, 60 minutes, may include homeopathy, New client house call, Diagnostician, Clinical practice charges	Home visit for the purpose of evaluation, management and ICD-9 diagnosis and/or homeopathic followup of a new client. Comprehensive 60 minutes personal meeting to provide counseling and coordination of healthcare recommendations to client and/or family, to gather detailed medical history information and for examination of more complex health concerns. This code may be used by non-physician providers able to diagnose.
AACAF	Comprehensive, prolonged, 90 minutes, may include homeopathy, New client house call, Diagnostician, Clinical practice charges	Home visit for the purpose of evaluation, management and ICD-9 diagnosis and/or homeopathic followup of a new client. Comprehensive 90 minutes personal meeting to provide counseling and coordination of healthcare recommendations to client and/or family, to gather detailed medical history information and for examination of more complex health concerns. This code may be used by non-physician providers able to diagnose.
AACAG	Comprehensive, prolonged, 120 minutes, may include homeopathy, New client house call, Diagnostician, Clinical practice charges	Home visit for the purpose of evaluation, management and ICD-9 diagnosis, and/or homeopathic followup of a new client. Comprehensive 120 minutes personal meeting to provide counseling and coordination of healthcare recommendations to client and/or family, to gather medical history information and for examination of more complex health concerns. This code may be used by non-physician providers able to diagnose.

Diagnostician

New client house call

ABC Code	Procedure Description	Expanded Definition
AACAH	Comprehensive, prolonged, 150 minutes, may include homeopathy, New client house call, Diagnostician, Clinical practice charges	Home visit for the purpose of evaluation, management and ICD-9 diagnosis, and/or homeopathic followup of a new client. Comprehensive 150 minutes personal meeting to provide counseling and coordination of healthcare recommendations to client and/or family, to gather medical history information and for examination of more complex health concerns. This code may be used by non-physician providers able to diagnose.
AACZZ	Undefined, narrative required, New client house call, Diagnostician, Clinical practice charges	Anywhere else undefined new client house call. This code may be used by non-physician providers able to diagnose.

Existing client house call

ABC Code	Procedure Description	Expanded Definition
AADAA	Simple, 5 minutes, may include homeopathy, Existing client house call, Diagnostician, Clinical practice charges	Home visit for the purpose of evaluation, management and ICD-9 diagnosis and/or homeopathic followup of an existing client. Simple 5 minutes personal meeting to provide counseling and coordination of healthcare recommendations to client and/or family. This code may be used by non-physician providers able to diagnose.
AADAB	Usual, 10 minutes, may include homeopathy, Existing client house call, Diagnostician, Clinical practice charges	Home visit for the purpose of evaluation, management and ICD-9 diagnosis and/or homeopathic followup of an existing client. Usual 10 minutes personal meeting to provide counseling and coordination of healthcare recommendations to client and/or family. This code may be used by non-physician providers able to diagnose.
AADAC	Complex, 15 minutes, may include homeopathy, Existing client house call, Diagnostician, Clinical practice charges	Home visit for the purpose of evaluation, management and ICD-9 diagnosis and/or homeopathic followup of an existing client. Complex 15 minutes personal meeting to provide counseling and coordination of healthcare recommendations to client and/or family and for examination of more complex health concerns. This code may be used by non-physician providers able to diagnose.

Diagnostician

Existing client house call

ABC Code	Procedure Description	Expanded Definition
AADAD	Detailed, 25 minutes, may include homeopathy, Existing client house call, Diagnostician, Clinical practice charges	Home visit for the purpose of evaluation, management and ICD-9 diagnosis and/or homeopathic followup of a new client. Detailed 45 minutes personal meeting to provide counseling and/or coordination of healthcare recommendations to client and/or family, to gather detailed medical history information and for examination of more complex health concerns. This code may be used by non-physician providers able to diagnose.
AADAE	Comprehensive, 40 minutes, may include homeopathy, Existing client house call, Diagnostician, Clinical practice charges	Home visit for the purpose of evaluation, management and ICD-9 diagnosis and/or homeopathic followup of an existing client. Comprehensive 40 minutes personal meeting to provide counseling and coordination of healthcare recommendations to client and/or family, to gather detailed medical history information and for examination of more complex health concerns. This code may be used by non-physician providers able to diagnose.
AADAF	Comprehensive, 60 minutes, may include homeopathy, Existing client house call, Diagnostician, Clinical practice charges	Home visit for the purpose of evaluation, management and ICD-9 diagnosis and/or homeopathic followup of an existing client. Comprehensive 60 minutes personal meeting to provide counseling and coordination of healthcare recommendations to client and/or family, to gather detailed medical history information and for examination of more complex health concerns. This code may be used by non-physician providers able to diagnose.
AADAG	Comprehensive, prolonged, 90 minutes, may include homeopathy, Existing client house call, Diagnostician, Clinical practice charges	Home visit for the purpose of evaluation, management and ICD-9 diagnosis and/or homeopathic followup of an existing client. Comprehensive 90 minutes personal meeting to provide counseling and coordination of healthcare recommendations to client and/or family, to gather detailed medical history information and for examination of more complex health concerns. This code may be used by non-physician providers able to diagnose.

Existing client house call

ABC Code	Procedure Description	Expanded Definition
AADAH	Comprehensive, prolonged, 120 minutes, may include homeopathy, Existing client house call, Diagnostician, Clinical practice charges	Home visit for the purpose of evaluation, management and ICD-9 diagnosis and/or homeopathic followup of an existing client. Comprehensive 120 minutes personal meeting to provide counseling and coordination of healthcare recommendations to client and/or family, to gather detailed medical history information and for examination of more complex health concerns. This code may be used by non-physician providers able to diagnose.
AADAI	Comprehensive, prolonged, 150 minutes, may include homeopathy, Existing client house call, Diagnostician, Clinical practice charges	Home visit for the purpose of evaluation, management and ICD-9 diagnosis and/or homeopathic followup of an existing client. Comprehensive 150 minutes personal meeting to provide counseling and coordination of healthcare recommendations to client and/or family, to gather detailed medical history information and for examination of more complex health concerns. This code may be used by non-physician providers able to diagnose.
AADZZ	Undefined, narrative required, Existing client house call, Diagnostician, Clinical practice charges	Anywhere else undefined existing client house call. This code may be used by non-physician providers able to diagnose.

New client nursing facility

ABC Code	Procedure Description	Expanded Definition
AAEAA	Simple, 10 minutes, New client nursing facility, Diagnostician, Clinical practice charges	Nursing facility visit for the purpose of evaluation, management and ICD-9 diagnosis and/or homeopathic followup of a new client. Simple 10 minutes personal meeting to provide counseling and coordination of healthcare recommendations to client and/or family. This code may be used by non-physician providers able to diagnose.
AAEAB	Usual, 20 minutes, New client nursing facility, Diagnostician, Clinical practice charges	Nursing facility visit for the purpose of evaluation, management and ICD-9 diagnosis and/or homeopathic followup of a new client. Usual 20 minutes personal meeting to provide counseling and coordination of healthcare recommendations to client and/or family. This code may be used by non-physician providers able to diagnose.

New client nursing facility

ABC Code	Procedure Description	Expanded Definition
AAEAC	Complex, 30 minutes, New client nursing facility, Diagnostician, Clinical practice charges	Nursing facility visit for the purpose of evaluation, management and ICD-9 diagnosis and/or homeopathic followup of a new client. Complex 30 minutes personal meeting to provide counseling and coordination of healthcare recommendations to client and/or family and for examination of more complex health concerns. This code may be used by non-physician providers able to diagnose.
AAEAD	Detailed, 45 minutes, New client nursing facility, Diagnostician, Clinical practice charges	Nursing facility visit for the purpose of evaluation, management and ICD-9 diagnosis of a new client. Detailed 45 minutes personal meeting to provide counseling and/or coordination of healthcare recommendations to client and/or family, to gather detailed medical history information and for examination of more complex health concerns. This code may be used by non-physician providers able to diagnose.
AAEAE	Comprehensive, 60 minutes, New client nursing facility, Diagnostician, Clinical practice charges	Nursing facility visit for the purpose of evaluation, management and ICD-9 diagnosis and/or homeopathic followup of a new client. Comprehensive 60 minutes personal meeting to provide counseling and coordination of healthcare recommendations to client and/or family, to gather detailed medical history information and for examination of more complex health concerns. This code may be used by non-physician providers able to diagnose.
AAEAF	Comprehensive, prolonged, 90 minutes, New client nursing facility, Diagnostician, Clinical practice charges	Nursing facility visit for the purpose of evaluation, management and ICD-9 diagnosis and/or homeopathic followup of a new client. Comprehensive 90 minutes personal meeting to provide counseling and coordination of healthcare recommendations to client and/or family, to gather detailed medical history information and for examination of more complex health concerns. This code may be used by non-physician providers able to diagnose.
AAEAG	Comprehensive, prolonged, 120 minutes, New client nursing facility, Diagnostician, Clinical practice charges	Nursing facility visit for the purpose of evaluation, management and ICD-9 diagnosis and/or homeopathic followup of a new client. Comprehensive 120 minutes personal meeting to provide counseling and coordination of healthcare recommendations to client and/or family, to gather detailed medical history information and for examination of more complex health concerns. This code may be used by non-physician providers able to diagnose.

Diagnostician

New client nursing facility

ABC Code	Procedure Description	Expanded Definition
AAEAH	Comprehensive, prolonged, 150 minutes, New client nursing facility, Diagnostician, Clinical practice charges	Nursing facility visit for the purpose of evaluation, management and ICD-9 diagnosis and/or homeopathic followup of a new client. Comprehensive 150 minutes personal meeting to provide counseling and coordination of healthcare recommendations to client and/or family, to gather detailed medical history information and for examination of more complex health concerns. This code may be used by non-physician providers able to diagnose.
AAEZZ	Undefined, narrative required, New client nursing facility, Diagnostician, Clinical practice charges	Anywhere else undefined new client nursing facility visit. This code may be used by non-physician providers able to diagnose.

Existing client nursing facility

ABC Code	Procedure Description	Expanded Definition
AAFAA	Simple, 5 minutes, Existing client nursing facility, Diagnostician, Clinical practice charges	Nursing facility visit for the purpose of evaluation, management and ICD-9 diagnosis and/or homeopathic followup of an existing client. Simple 5 minutes personal meeting to provide counseling and coordination of healthcare recommendations to client and/or family. This code may be used by non-physician providers able to diagnose.
AAFAB	Usual, 10 minutes, Existing client nursing facility, Diagnostician, Clinical practice charges	Nursing facility visit for the purpose of evaluation, management and ICD-9 diagnosis and/or homeopathic followup of an existing client. Usual 10 minutes personal meeting to provide counseling and coordination of healthcare recommendations to client and/or family. This code may be used by non-physician providers able to diagnose.
AAFAC	Complex, 15 minutes, Existing client nursing facility, Diagnostician, Clinical practice charges	Nursing facility visit for the purpose of evaluation, management and ICD-9 diagnosis and/or homeopathic followup of an existing client. Complex 15 minutes personal meeting to provide counseling and coordination of healthcare recommendations to client and/or family, and for examination of more complex health concerns. This code may be used by non-physician providers able to diagnose.

Diagnostician

Existing client nursing facility

ABC Code	Procedure Description	Expanded Definition
AAFAD	Detailed, 25 minutes, Existing client nursing facility, Diagnostician, Clinical practice charges	Nursing facility visit for the purpose of evaluation, management and ICD-9 diagnosis and/or homeopathic followup of an existing client. Detailed 25 minutes personal meeting to provide counseling and/or coordination of healthcare recommendations to client and/or family, to gather detailed medical history information and for examination of more complex health concerns. This code may be used by non-physician providers able to diagnose.
AAFAE	Comprehensive, 40 minutes, Existing client nursing facility, Diagnostician, Clinical practice charges	Nursing facility visit for the purpose of evaluation, management and ICD-9 diagnosis and/or homeopathic followup of an existing client. Comprehensive 40 minutes personal meeting to provide counseling and coordination of healthcare recommendations to client and/or family, to gather detailed medical history information and for examination of more complex health concerns. This code may be used by non-physician providers able to diagnose.
AAFAF	Comprehensive, 60 minutes, Existing client nursing facility, Diagnostician, Clinical practice charges	Nursing facility visit for the purpose of evaluation, management and ICD-9 diagnosis and/or homeopathic followup of an existing client. Comprehensive 60 minutes personal meeting to provide counseling and coordination of healthcare recommendations to client and/or family, to gather detailed medical history information and for examination of more complex health concerns. This code may be used by non-physician providers able to diagnose.
AAFAG	Comprehensive, prolonged, 90 minutes, Existing client nursing facility, Diagnostician, Clinical practice charges	Nursing facility visit for the purpose of evaluation, management and ICD-9 diagnosis and/or homeopathic followup of an existing client. Comprehensive 90 minutes personal meeting to provide counseling and coordination of healthcare recommendations to client and/or family, to gather detailed medical history information and for examination of more complex health concerns. This code may be used by non-physician providers able to diagnose.

Diagnostician

Existing client nursing facility

ABC Code	Procedure Description	Expanded Definition
AAFAH	Comprehensive, prolonged, 120 minutes, Existing client nursing facility, Diagnostician, Clinical practice charges	Nursing facility visit for the purpose of evaluation, management and ICD-9 diagnosis and/or homeopathic followup of an existing client. Comprehensive 120 minutes personal meeting to provide counseling and coordination of healthcare recommendations to client and/or family, to gather detailed medical history information and for examination of more complex health concerns. This code may be used by non-physician providers able to diagnose.
AAFAI	Comprehensive, prolonged, 150 minutes, Existing client nursing facility, Diagnostician, Clinical practice charges	Nursing facility visit for the purpose of evaluation, management and ICD-9 diagnosis and/or homeopathic followup of an existing client. Comprehensive 150 minutes personal meeting to provide counseling and coordination of healthcare recommendations to client and/or family, to gather detailed medical history information and for examination of more complex health concerns. This code may be used by non-physician providers able to diagnose.
AAFZZ	Undefined, narrative required, Existing client nursing facility, Diagnostician, Clinical practice charges	Anywhere else undefined existing client nursing facility visit. This code may be used by non-physician providers able to diagnose.

Periodic

Wellness visit, new or existing client

ABC Code	Procedure Description	Expanded Definition
ABAAA	15 minute wellness visit by diagnostician or non diagnostician, Wellness visit, new or existing client, Periodic, Clinical practice charges	Fifteen minute periodic consultation with a new or existing client without medical or physical complaints, by either a diagnostician or non-diagnostician.
ABAAB	30 minute wellness visit by diagnostician or non diagnostician, Wellness visit, new or existing client, Periodic, Clinical practice charges	Thirty minute periodic consultation with a new or existing client without medical or physical complaints, by either a diagnostician or non-diagnostician.
ABAAC	45 minute wellness visit by diagnostician or non diagnostician, Wellness visit, new or existing client, Periodic, Clinical practice charges	Fourtyfive minute periodic consultation with a new or existing client without medical or physical complaints, by either a diagnostician or non-diagnostician.
ABAAD	60 minute wellness visit by diagnostician or non diagnostician, Wellness visit, new or existing client, Periodic, Clinical practice charges	One hour periodic consultation with a new or existing client without medical or physical complaints, by either a diagnostician or non-diagnostician.

Wellness visit, new or existing client

ABC Code	Procedure Description	Expanded Definition
ABAAE	90 minute wellness visit by diagnostician or non diagnostician, Wellness visit, new or existing client, Periodic, Clinical practice charges	Ninety minute periodic consultation with a new or existing client without medical or physical complaints, by either a diagnostician or non-diagnostician.
ABAAF	120 minute wellness visit by diagnostician or non diagnostician, Wellness visit, new or existing client, Periodic, Clinical practice charges	Two hour periodic consultation with a new or existing client without medical or physical complaints, by either a diagnostician or non-diagnostician.
ABAZZ	Undefined, narrative required, Wellness visit, new or existing client, Periodic, Clinical practice charges	Anywhere else undefined wellness visit for new or existing client, by either a diagnostician or non-diagnostician.

Limited and non-diagnostician

New client in office

ABC Code	Procedure Description	Expanded Definition
ACAAA	10 minutes, New client in office, Limited diagnostician, Clinical practice charges	Office visit for the purpose of assessment of a new client. 10 minutes personal meeting to assess health status and for development of a treatment plan. This code is for use by providers trained to do complex patient assessments, but who are not allowed to use ICD-9 codes for diagnostic purposes or are required to have a prior medical diagnosis or referral.
ACAAB	25 minutes, New client in office, Limited diagnostician, Clinical practice charges	Office visit for the purpose of assessment of a new client. 25 minutes personal meeting to assess health status and for development of a treatment plan. This code is for use by providers trained to do complex patient assessments, but who are not allowed to use ICD-9 codes for diagnostic purposes or are required to have a prior medical diagnosis or referral.
ACAAC	45 minutes, New client in office, Limited diagnostician, Clinical practice charges	Office visit for the purpose of assessment of a new client. 45 minutes personal meeting to assess health status and for development of a treatment plan. This code is for use by providers trained to do complex patient assessments, but who are not allowed to use ICD-9 codes for diagnostic purposes or are required to have a prior medical diagnosis or referral.
ACAAD	Initial assessment massage therapist, New client in office, Limited diagnostician, Clinical practice charges	Client intake for the purpose of subjective, objective assessment and treatment plan for somatic education, massage or bodywork.

Limited and non-diagnostician

New client in office

ABC Code	Procedure Description	Expanded Definition
ACAZZ	Undefined, narrative required, New client in office, Limited diagnostician, Clinical practice charges	Anywhere else undefined new client in office visit for personal meeting to assess health status and for development of a treatment plan. This code is for use by providers trained to do complex patient assessments, but who are not allowed to use ICD-9 codes for diagnostic purposes or are required to have a prior medical diagnosis or referral.

Existing client in office

ABC Code	Procedure Description	Expanded Definition
ACBAA	5 minutes, Existing client in office, Limited diagnostician, Clinical practice charges	Office visit for the purpose of assessment of an existing client. 5 minutes personal meeting to assess health status and for development of a treatment plan. This code is for use by providers trained to do complex patient assessments, but who are not allowed to use ICD-9 codes for diagnostic purposes or are required to have a prior medical diagnosis or referral.
ACBAB	15 minutes, Existing client in office, Limited diagnostician, Clinical practice charges	Office visit for the purpose of assessment of an existing client. 15 minutes personal meeting to assess health status and for development of a treatment plan. This code is for use by providers trained to do complex patient assessments, but who are not allowed to use ICD-9 codes for diagnostic purposes or are required to have a prior medical diagnosis or referral.
ACBAC	30 minutes, Existing client in office, Limited diagnostician, Clinical practice charges	Office visit for the purpose of assessment of an existing client. 30 minutes personal meeting to assess health status and for development of a treatment plan. This code is for use by providers trained to do complex patient assessments, but who are not allowed to use ICD-9 codes for diagnostic purposes or are required to have a prior medical diagnosis or referral.
ACBAD	Subsequent assessment massage therapist, Existing client in office, Limited diagnostician, Clinical practice charges	Subsequent client intake for the evaluation of prior somatic education, massage or bodywork treatment.
ACBZZ	Undefined, narrative required, Existing client in office, Limited diagnostician, Clinical practice charges	Anywhere else undefined existing client in office for personal meeting to assess health status and for development of a treatment plan. This code is for use by providers trained to do complex patient assessments, but who are not allowed to use ICD-9 codes for diagnostic purposes or are required to have a prior medical diagnosis or referral.

New client house call

ABC Code	Procedure Description	Expanded Definition
ACCAA	25 minutes, New client house call, Limited diagnostician, Clinical practice charges	Home visit for the purpose of assessment of a new client. 25 minutes personal meeting to assess health status and for development of a treatment plan. This code is for use by providers trained to do complex patient assessments, but who are not allowed to use ICD-9 codes for diagnostic purposes or are required to have a prior medical diagnosis or referral.
ACCAB	45 minutes, New client house call, Limited diagnostician, Clinical practice charges	Home visit for the purpose of assessment of a new client. 45 minutes personal meeting to assess health status and for development of a treatment plan. This code is for use by providers trained to do complex patient assessments, but who are not allowed to use ICD-9 codes for diagnostic purposes or are required to have a prior medical diagnosis or referral.
ACCAC	60 minutes, New client house call, Limited diagnostician, Clinical practice charges	Home visit for the purpose of assessment of a new client. 60 minutes personal meeting to assess health status and for development of a treatment plan. This code is for use by providers trained to do complex patient assessments, but who are not allowed to use ICD-9 codes for diagnostic purposes or are required to have a prior medical diagnosis or referral.
ACCZZ	Undefined, narrative required, New client house call, Limited diagnostician, Clinical practice charges	Anywhere else undefined new client house call for personal meeting to assess health status and for development of a treatment plan. This code is for use by providers trained to do complex patient assessments, but who are not allowed to use ICD-9 codes for diagnostic purposes or are required to have a prior medical diagnosis or referral.

Existing client house call

ABC Code	Procedure Description	Expanded Definition
ACDAA	15 minutes, Existing client house call, Limited diagnostician, Clinical practice charges	Home visit for the purpose of assessment of an existing client. 15 minutes personal meeting to assess health status and for development of a treatment plan. This code is for use by providers trained to do complex patient assessments, but who are not allowed to use ICD-9 codes for diagnostic purposes or are required to have a prior medical diagnosis or referral.

Limited and non-diagnostician

Existing client house call

ABC Code	Procedure Description	Expanded Definition
ACDAB	30 minutes, Existing client house call, Limited diagnostician, Clinical practice charges	Home visit for the purpose of assessment of an existing client. 30 minutes personal meeting to assess health status and for development of a treatment plan. This code is for use by providers trained to do complex patient assessments, but who are not allowed to use ICD-9 codes for diagnostic purposes or are required to have a prior medical diagnosis or referral.
ACDAC	60 minutes, Existing client house call, Limited diagnostician, Clinical practice charges	Home visit for the purpose of assessment of an existing client. 60 minutes personal meeting to assess health status and for development of a treatment plan. This code is for use by providers trained to do complex patient assessments, but who are not allowed to use ICD-9 codes for diagnostic purposes or are required to have a prior medical diagnosis or referral.
ACDZZ	Undefined, narrative required, Existing client house call, Limited diagnostician, Clinical practice charges	Anywhere else undefined existing client house call for personal meeting to assess health status and for development of a treatment plan. This code is for use by providers trained to do complex patient assessments, but who are not allowed to use ICD-9 codes for diagnostic purposes or are required to have a prior medical diagnosis or referral.

New client nursing facility

ABC Code	Procedure Description	Expanded Definition
ACEAA	25 minutes, New client nursing facility, Limited diagnostician, Clinical practice charges	Nursing facility visit for the purpose of assessment of a new client. 25 minutes personal meeting to assess health status and for development of a treatment plan. This code is for use by providers trained to do complex patient assessments, but who are not allowed to use ICD-9 codes for diagnostic purposes or are required to have a prior medical diagnosis or referral.
ACEAB	45 minutes, New client nursing facility, Limited diagnostician, Clinical practice charges	Nursing facility visit for the purpose of assessment of a new client. 45 minutes personal meeting to assess health status and for development of a treatment plan. This code is for use by providers trained to do complex patient assessments, but who are not allowed to use ICD-9 codes for diagnostic purposes or are required to have a prior medical diagnosis or referral.

New client nursing facility

ABC Code	Procedure Description	Expanded Definition
ACEAC	60 minutes, New client nursing facility, Limited diagnostician, Clinical practice charges	Nursing facility visit for the purpose of assessment of a new client. 60 minutes personal meeting to assess health status and for development of a treatment plan. This code is for use by providers trained to do complex patient assessments, but who are not allowed to use ICD-9 codes for diagnostic purposes or are required to have a prior medical diagnosis or referral.
ACEZZ	Undefined, narrative required, New client nursing facility, Limited diagnostician, Clinical practice charges	Anywhere else undefined new client nursing facility visit for personal meeting to assess health status and for development of a treatment plan. This code is for use by providers trained to do complex patient assessments, but who are not allowed to use ICD-9 codes for diagnostic purposes or are required to have a prior medical diagnosis or referral.

Existing client nursing facility

ABC Code	Procedure Description	Expanded Definition
ACFAA	15 minutes, Existing client nursing facility, Limited diagnostician, Clinical practice charges	Nursing facility visit for the purpose of assessment of an existing client. 15 minutes personal meeting to assess health status and for development of a treatment plan. This code is for use by providers trained to do complex patient assessments, but who are not allowed to use ICD-9 codes for diagnostic purposes or are required to have a prior medical diagnosis or referral.
ACFAB	30 minutes, Existing client nursing facility, Limited diagnostician, Clinical practice charges	Nursing facility visit for the purpose of assessment of an existing client. 30 minutes personal meeting to assess health status and for development of a treatment plan. This code is for use by providers trained to do complex patient assessments, but who are not allowed to use ICD-9 codes for diagnostic purposes or are required to have a prior medical diagnosis or referral.
ACFAC	60 minutes, Existing client nursing facility, Limited diagnostician, Clinical practice charges	Nursing facility visit for the purpose of assessment of an existing client. 60 minutes personal meeting to assess health status and for development of a treatment plan. This code is for use by providers trained to do complex patient assessments, but who are not allowed to use ICD-9 codes for diagnostic purposes or are required to have a prior medical diagnosis or referral.

Limited and non-diagnostician

Existing client nursing facility

ABC Code	Procedure Description	Expanded Definition
ACFZZ	Undefined, narrative required, Existing client nursing facility, Limited diagnostician, Clinical practice charges	Anywhere else undefined existing client nursing facility visit for personal meeting to assess health status and for development of a treatment plan. This code is for use by providers trained to do complex patient assessments, but who are not allowed to use ICD-9 codes for diagnostic purposes or are required to have a prior medical diagnosis or referral.

General

ABC Code	Procedure Description	Expanded Definition
ACZZZ	Undefined, narrative required, General, Limited diagnostician, Clinical practice charges	Any above undefined general, non-diagnostic clinical practice charge. Narrative required.

General service and reference codes

Consultation between providers

ABC Code	Procedure Description	Expanded Definition
ADAAA	15 minutes, Consultation between providers, General service and reference codes, Clinical practice charges	Fifteen minutes of providing client care information to other health professionals.
ADAAB	30 minutes, Consultation between providers, General service and reference codes, Clinical practice charges	Thirty minutes of providing client care information to other health professionals.
ADAAC	40 minutes, Consultation between providers, General service and reference codes, Clinical practice charges	Forty minutes of providing client care information to other health professionals.
ADAAD	60 minutes, Consultation between providers, General service and reference codes, Clinical practice charges	Sixty minutes of providing client care information to other health professionals.
ADAAE	80 minutes, Consultation between providers, General service and reference codes, Clinical practice charges	Eighty minutes of providing client care information to other health professionals.
ADAZZ	Undefined, narrative required, Consultation between providers, General service and reference codes, Clinical practice charges	Anywhere else undefined consultation with provider. Narrative required.

Expanded services

ABC Code	Procedure Description	Expanded Definition
ADBAA	Care provided after hours until 10 p.m., Expanded services, General service and reference codes, Clinical practice charges	Client care provided after hours until 10 p.m. in addition to basic service.

Expanded services

ABC Code	Procedure Description	Expanded Definition
ADBAB	Care provided from 10 p.m. until 8 a.m., Expanded services, General service and reference codes, Clinical practice charges	Client care provided from 10 p.m. until 8 a.m. in addition to basic service.
ADBAC	Care provided, Sundays or on holidays, Expanded services, General service and reference codes, Clinical practice charges	Client care provided on Sundays or holidays in addition to basic service.
ADBAD	Client related travel, extraordinary, narrative required, Expanded services, General service and reference codes, Clinical practice charges	Client related travel, transportation or escorting beyond basic service. Narrative required.
ADBZZ	Undefined, narrative required, Expanded services, General service and reference codes, Clinical practice charges	Anywhere else undefined expanded general service.

Phone conversations

ABC Code	Procedure Description	Expanded Definition
ADCAA	Brief, 15 minutes, Phone conversations, General service and reference codes, Clinical practice charges	Phone conversations between patient or family member and provider for consultation, clarification of instructions, reporting or evaluating test results or new information, brief, 15 minutes.
ADCAB	Intermediate, 30 minutes, Phone conversations, General service and reference codes, Clinical practice charges	Phone conversations between patient or family member and provider for consultation, clarification of instructions, reporting or evaluating in detail test results or new information, intermediate, 30 minutes.
ADCAC	Extended, 45 minutes, Phone conversations, General service and reference codes, Clinical practice charges	Phone conversations between patient or family member and provider for consultation, clarification of instructions, reporting or evaluating in detail test results or new information, extended, 45 minutes.
ADCAD	Prolonged, 60 minutes, Phone conversations, General service and reference codes, Clinical practice charges	Phone conversations between patient or family member and provider for consultation, clarification of instructions, reporting or evaluating in detail test results or new information, prolonged, 60 minutes.
ADCAE	Telephone followup, each 15 minutes, Phone conversations, General service and reference codes, Clinical practice charges	Fifteen minutes of phone conversations where the health care provider relays results of testing or evaluates response and assesses potential for problems of previous treatment, examination, or testing to the patient.
ADCZZ	Undefined, narrative required, Phone conversations, General service and reference codes, Clinical practice charges	Anywhere else undefined phone conversations.

Interpretive services

ABC Code	Procedure Description	Expanded Definition
ADDAA	Analysis and interpretation of computer data, report required, Interpretive services, General service and reference codes, Clinical practice charges	Critical analysis of computer data to assist with clinical decision-making.
ADDAB	Analysis and interpretation of laboratory findings, Interpretive services, General service and reference codes, Clinical practice charges	Critical analysis of laboratory findings to assist with clinical decision-making.
ADDAC	Analysis and interpretation of radiological films, report required, Interpretive services, General service and reference codes, Clinical practice charges	Critical analysis of radiological films to assist with clinical decision-making.
ADDAD	Documentation, Interpretive services, General service and reference codes, Clinical practice charges	Recording and documentation of pertinent client data in a clinical record. Not a billable charge.
ADDZZ	Undefined, narrative required, Interpretive services, General service and reference codes, Clinical practice charges	Anywhere else undefined interpretive services.

Hospice care

ABC Code	Procedure Description	Expanded Definition
ADEAP	Dying care, initial hour, Hospice care, General service and reference codes, Clinical practice charges	Initial hour of promotion of physical comfort and psychological peace in the final phase of life; use with code ADEAQ.
ADEAQ	Dying care, each additional hour, Hospice care, General service and reference codes, Clinical practice charges	Each additional hour of promotion of physical comfort and psychological peace in the final phase of life; use with code ADEAP.
ADEZY	Undefined, narrative required, Hospice care, General service and reference codes, Clinical practice charges	Anywhere else undefined hospice care.

Performing

ABC Code	Procedure Description	Expanded Definition
ADWAA	General minor surgery procedures, refer to CPT (TM) codes for minor surgery, no charge, Performing, General service and reference codes, Clinical practice charges	This code is used for mapping provider types planning to perform minor surgical procedures. CPT (TM) Codes should be used to bill for the actual procedures.
ADWAB	General minor surgery procedures of the skin, refer to CPT (TM) codes for minor surgery, no charge, Performing, General service and reference codes, Clinical practice charges	This code is used for mapping provider types planning to perform minor surgical procedures of the skin. CPT (TM) Codes should be used to bill for the actual procedures.

Performing

ABC Code	Procedure Description	Expanded Definition
ADWAC	Nail procedures, minor surgery, refer to CPT (TM) codes for minor surgery, no charge, Performing, General service and reference codes, Clinical practice charges	This code is used for mapping provider types planning to perform minor surgery on a nail. CPT (TM) Codes should be used to bill for the actual procedures.
ADWAD	Shaving skin lesions, refer to CPT (TM) codes for minor surgery, no charge, Performing, General service and reference codes, Clinical practice charges	This code is used for mapping provider types planning to shave skin lesions. CPT (TM) Codes should be used to bill for the actual procedures.
ADWAE	Skin excisions, refer to CPT (TM) codes for minor surgery, no charge, Performing, General service and reference codes, Clinical practice charges	This code is used for mapping provider types planning to perform skin excisions. CPT (TM) Codes should be used to bill for the actual procedures.
ADWAF	Suturing of skin, refer to CPT (TM) codes for minor surgery, no charge, Performing, General service and reference codes, Clinical practice charges	This code is used for mapping provider types planning to perform suturing of skin. CPT (TM) Codes should be used to bill for the actual procedures.
ADWZZ	Undefined, narrative required, no charge, Performing, General service and reference codes, Clinical practice charges	Anywhere else undefined performing. CPT (TM) Codes should be used to bill for the actual procedures.

Recommending

ABC Code	Procedure Description	Expanded Definition
ADXAA	Recommend nutritional supplements, no charge, Recommending, General service and reference codes, Clinical practice charges	Recommendation for preparation and use of a nutritional supplement. The practitioner needs to verify recommendations using a peer-reviewed reference tool such as a Materia Medica. Notices of contraindications need to be given to clients and/or patients. Any provider using this code is required to show training and/or certification.
ADXAB	Recommend homeopathic remedy, no charge, Recommending, General service and reference codes, Clinical practice charges	Recommendation for preparation and use of a homeopathic remedy. The practitioner needs to verify recommendations using a peer-reviewed reference tool such as a Materia Medica. Notices of contraindications need to be given to clients and/or patients. Any provider using this code is required to show training and/or certification.
ADXAC	Recommend oral chelation agent, no charge, Recommending, General service and reference codes, Clinical practice charges	Recommendation for preparation and use of an oral chelation agent. The practitioner needs to verify recommendations using a peer-reviewed reference tool such as a Materia Medica. Notices of contraindications need to be given to clients and/or patients. Any provider using this code is required to show training and/or certification.

General service and reference codes

Recommending

ABC Code	Procedure Description	Expanded Definition
ADXAD	Recommend oriental herb or botanical, no charge, Recommending, General service and reference codes, Clinical practice charges	Recommendation for preparation and use of an oriental herb or botanical. The practitioner needs to verify recommendations using a peer-reviewed reference tool such as a Materia Medica. Notices of contraindications need to be given to clients and/or patients. Any provider using this code is required to show training and/or certification.
ADXAE	Recommend western herb or botanical, no charge, Recommending, General service and reference codes, Clinical practice charges	Recommendation for preparation and use of a western herb or botanical. The practitioner needs to verify recommendations using a peer-reviewed reference tool such as a Materia Medica. Notices of contraindications need to be given to clients and/or patients. Any provider using this code is required to show training and/or certification.
ADXZZ	Undefined, narrative required, Recommending, General service and reference codes, Clinical practice charges	Anywhere else undefined recommendation. Any provider using this code is required to show training and/or certification.

Ordering and referring

ABC Code	Procedure Description	Expanded Definition
ADYAA	Ordering heart or vascular study, no charge, Ordering and referring, General service and reference codes, Clinical practice charges	This code is for mapping which provider type is ordering an electrocardiogram for a heart or vascular study. CPT (TM) Codes should be used to bill for the actual study.
ADYAB	Ordering laboratory procedures, no charge, Ordering and referring, General service and reference codes, Clinical practice charges	This code is for mapping which provider type is ordering a laboratory procedure. CPT (TM) Codes should be used to bill for the actual study.
ADYAC	Ordering neurological studies, no charge, Ordering and referring, General service and reference codes, Clinical practice charges	This code is for mapping which provider type is ordering a neurological study. CPT (TM) Codes should be used to bill for the actual study.
ADYAD	Ordering pulmonary or vital capacity breathing study, no charge, Ordering and referring, General service and reference codes, Clinical practice charges	This code is for mapping which provider type is ordering a pulmonary or vital capacity breathing study. CPT (TM) Codes should be used to bill for the actual study.
ADYAE	Ordering x-rays, no charge, Ordering and referring, General service and reference codes, Clinical practice charges	This code is to map which provider type is ordering x-rays. CPT (TM) codes should be used to bill for the actual x-ray services.
ADYAF	Referral to hypnotherapy, no charge, Ordering and referring, General service and reference codes, Clinical practice charges	Although the billing provider may not be providing the hypnotherapy service, they may be attaching a bill for hypnotherapy as part of the client treatment. The ABC Code to follow will be CDAAG.

Ordering and referring

ABC Code	Procedure Description	Expanded Definition
ADYAG	Referral to rebirthing services, no charge, Ordering and referring, General service and reference codes, Clinical practice charges	Although the billing provider may not be providing the rebirthing service, they may be attaching a bill for the rebirthing service as part of the client treatment. The ABC Code to follow for rebirthing will be CDAAI.
ADYAI	Referral to Tai Chi class, no charge, Ordering and referring, General service and reference codes, Clinical practice charges	Although the billing provider may not be providing the Tai Chi class/service, they may be attaching a bill for the Tai Chi service as part of the client treatment. The ABC Codes to follow will be BBADB and/or BBABI.
ADYAJ	Referral to Yoga class, no charge, Ordering and referring, General service and reference codes, Clinical practice charges	Although the billing provider may not be providing the Yoga class/service, they may be attaching a bill for the Yoga class/service as part of the client treatment. The ABC Codes to follow will be BBABF and/or BBABJ.
ADYAK	Referral to meditation service or class, no charge, Ordering and referring, General service and reference codes, Clinical practice charges	Although the billing provider may not be providing the meditation class/service, they may be attaching a bill for the meditation class/service as part of the client treatment. The codes to follow will be CDAFF, CDAFG, CDAFH, CDAFI, CDAFJ and/or CDAFK.
ADYAL	Referral to specialist, no charge, Ordering and referring, General service and reference codes, Clinical practice charges	This code is for tracking when it is necessary to refer a patient to a higher level of care.
ADYAM	Transfer of care for Cesarean section, no charge, Ordering and referring, General service and reference codes, Clinical practice charges	This code is for tracking when it is necessary to transfer care of a delivery to an OB-GYN for complications requiring a C-Section.
ADYZZ	Undefined, narrative required, Ordering and referring, General service and reference codes, Clinical practice charges	Anywhere else undefined ordering and referring.

Prescription, preparation and dispensing

ABC Code	Procedure Description	Expanded Definition
ADZAA	Prescribe nutritional supplements, no charge, Prescription, preparation and dispensing, General service and reference codes, Clinical practice charges	Written instructions for preparation and use of a nutritional supplement. This code must appear before any claim is attached for a dietary supplement.
ADZAB	Prescribe oriental herb or botanical, no charge, Prescription, preparation and dispensing, General service and reference codes, Clinical practice charges	Written instructions for preparation and use of an oriental herb or botanical. This code must appear before any claim is attached for an oriental supplement.

Prescription, preparation and dispensing

ABC Code	Procedure Description	Expanded Definition
ADZAC	Prescribe western herb or botanical, no charge, Prescription, preparation and dispensing, General service and reference codes, Clinical practice charges	Written instructions for preparation and use of a western herb or botanical. This code must appear before any claim is attached for a western supplement.
ADZAD	Prescribe homeopathic remedy, no charge, Prescription, preparation and dispensing, General service and reference codes, Clinical practice charges	Written instructions for preparation and use of a flower essence or homeopathic remedy. This code must appear before any claim is attached for a Bach or homeopathic supplement.
ADZAF	Prescribe oral chelation agents, no charge, Prescription, preparation and dispensing, General service and reference codes, Clinical practice charges	Written instructions for preparation and use of an oral chelation. This code must appear before any claim is attached for an oral chelation agent.
ADZAG	Prescribe pharmaceutical, no charge, Prescription, preparation and dispensing, General service and reference codes, Clinical practice charges	Written instructions for preparation and use of a pharmaceutical. This code must appear before any claim is attached for a pharmaceutical item.
ADZAI	Dispense oral medication, Prescription, preparation and dispensing, General service and reference codes, Clinical practice charges	Preparing and giving medications by mouth and monitoring patient responsiveness.
ADZAJ	Dispense reservoir medication, Prescription, preparation and dispensing, General service and reference codes, Clinical practice charges	Administration and monitoring of medication through an artificial receptacle placed in a vein.
ADZAK	Dispense topical medication, Prescription, preparation and dispensing, General service and reference codes, Clinical practice charges	Preparing and applying medications to the skin and mucous membranes.
ADZAL	Compounding western herb, each 5 minutes, Prescription, preparation and dispensing, General service and reference codes, Clinical practice charges	Making a substance by combining two or more ingredients found in the western herb section of this code set. This code must be preceded by code ADZAC and may only be used with codes GAAAA through GAZZZ.
ADZAM	Compounding oriental herb, each 5 minutes, Prescription, preparation and dispensing, General service and reference codes, Clinical practice charges	Making a substance by combining two or more ingredients found in the oriental herb section of this code set. This code must be preceded by code ADZAB and may only be used with codes GBAAA through GBZZZ.
ADZAN	Compounding homeopathic preparation, each 5 minutes, Prescription, preparation and dispensing, General service and reference codes, Clinical practice charges	Making a substance by combining two or more ingredients found in the homeopathic or flower remedy section of this code set. Narrative is required. This code must be preceded by code ADZAD and may only be used with codes HAAAA through HZZZZ.

Prescription, preparation and dispensing

ABC Code	Procedure Description	Expanded Definition
ADZAO	Compounding pharmaceuticals, each 5 minutes, Prescription, preparation and dispensing, General service and reference codes, Clinical practice charges	Making a substance by combining two or more pharmaceutical ingredients to create a drug; must be preceded by code ADZAG.
ADZAP	Dispense western herb, Prescription, preparation and dispensing, General service and reference codes, Clinical practice charges	Distribute any substance found in the western herb set of this code set; must be preceded by code ADZAC.
ADZAQ	Dispense oriental herb, Prescription, preparation and dispensing, General service and reference codes, Clinical practice charges	Distribute any substance found in the oriental herb portion of this code set; must be preceded by code ADZAB.
ADZAR	Dispense nutritional supplement, Prescription, preparation and dispensing, General service and reference codes, Clinical practice charges	Distribute any substance found in the nutritional supplement set of this code set; must be preceded by code ADZAA.
ADZAS	Dispense homeopathic preparation, Prescription, preparation and dispensing, General service and reference codes, Clinical practice charges	Distribute any substance found in the homeopathic or flower remedy section of this code set; must be preceded by code ADZAD.
ADZAT	Dispense pharmaceutical, Prescription, preparation and dispensing, General service and reference codes, Clinical practice charges	Distribute any pharmaceutical; must be preceded by code ADZAG.
ADZZZ	Undefined, narrative required, Prescription, preparation and dispensing, General service and reference codes, Clinical practice charges	Prescribe, compound, dispense anywhere else undefined material; narrative required.

Education

General

ABC Code	Procedure Description	Expanded Definition
AEAAL	Oriental botanical training, individual, each 15 minutes, General, Education, Clinical practice charges	Fifteen minutes of individual instruction on the preparation and use of oriental herbs or formulas for medicinal use.
AEAAM	Western botanical training, individual, each 15 minutes, General, Education, Clinical practice charges	Fifteen minutes of individual instruction on the preparation and use of western herbs or formulas for medicinal use.
AEAAN	Home care training, each 15 minutes, General, Education, Clinical practice charges	Fifteen minutes of counseling another to perform activities of daily living in the home setting.
AEAAO	Homeopathic training, individual, each 15 minutes, General, Education, Clinical practice charges	Fifteen minutes of individual training on the use of homeopathic agents for medicinal use.

General

ABC Code	Procedure Description	Expanded Definition
AEAAS	Homeopathic training, group, each 15 minutes, General, Education, Clinical practice charges	Fifteen minutes of group training on the use of homeopathic agents for medicinal use.
AEABB	Oriental botanical training, group, each 15 minutes, General, Education, Clinical practice charges	Fifteen minutes of group training on the preparation and use of oriental herbs or formulas for medicinal use.
AEABC	Western botanical training, group, each 15 minutes, General, Education, Clinical practice charges	Fifteen minutes of group training on the preparation and use of western herbs or formulas for medicinal use.
AEAZZ	Undefined, narrative required, General, Education, Clinical practice charges	Any above undefined general education charges. Narrative required.

Nutritional counseling

ABC Code	Procedure Description	Expanded Definition
AEBAA	Nutritional counseling, individual, each 15 minutes, Nutritional counseling, Education, Clinical practice charges	Fifteen minutes of use of an interactive helping process focusing on the needs of an individual for diet modification.
AEBAB	Nutritional counseling, group, each 15 minutes, Nutritional counseling, Education, Clinical practice charges	Fifteen minutes of an interactive helping process focusing on the need in a group setting for diet modification.
AEBAC	Holistic nutrition education, individual, each 15 minutes, Nutritional counseling, Education, Clinical practice charges	Fifteen minutes of an interactive helping process focusing on the needs of an individual for holistic and nutritional diet modification.
AEBAD	Holistic nutrition education, group, each 15 minutes, Nutritional counseling, Education, Clinical practice charges	Fifteen minutes of an interactive helping process focusing on the need in a group setting for holistic and nutritional diet modification.
AEBAE	Nutrition management, each 15 minutes, Nutritional counseling, Education, Clinical practice charges	Fifteen minutes of assisting with or providing a balanced dietary intake of foods and fluids.
AEBAF	Nutrition therapy, each 15 minutes, Nutritional counseling, Education, Clinical practice charges	Fifteen minutes of administration of food to support metabolic processes of a patient who is malnourished or at high risk for becoming malnourished.
AEBAG	Weight gain assistance, individual, each 15 minutes, Nutritional counseling, Education, Clinical practice charges	Fifteen minutes of facilitating gain of body weight in an individual.

Nutritional counseling

ABC Code	Procedure Description	Expanded Definition
AEBAH	Weight gain assistance, group, each 15 minutes, Nutritional counseling, Education, Clinical practice charges	Fifteen minutes of facilitating gain of body weight in a group setting.
AEBAI	Weight management, individual, each 15 minutes, Nutritional counseling, Education, Clinical practice charges	Fifteen minutes of facilitating maintenance of optimal body weight and percent body fat in an individual.
AEBAJ	Weight management, group, each 15 minutes, Nutritional counseling, Education, Clinical practice charges	Fifteen minutes of facilitating maintenance of optimal body weight and percent body fat in a group setting.
AEBAK	Weight reduction assistance, individual, each 15 minutes, Nutritional counseling, Education, Clinical practice charges	Fifteen minutes of facilitating loss of weight and/or body fat in an individual.
AEBAL	Weight reduction assistance, group, each 15 minutes, Nutritional counseling, Education, Clinical practice charges	Fifteen minutes of facilitating loss of weight and/or body fat in a group setting.
AEBAM	Prescribed diet teaching, individual, each 15 minutes, Nutritional counseling, Education, Clinical practice charges	Fifteen minutes of preparing a patient to correctly follow a prescribed diet.
AEBAN	Prescribed diet teaching, group, each 15 minutes, Nutritional counseling, Education, Clinical practice charges	Fifteen minutes of preparing a patient to correctly follow a prescribed diet in a group setting.
AEBAO	Nutrition monitoring, each 15 minutes, Nutritional counseling, Education, Clinical practice charges	Fifteen minutes of collection and analysis of patient data to prevent or minimize risk of malnourishment.
AEBZZ	Undefined, narrative required, Nutritional counseling, Education, Clinical practice charges	Anywhere else undefined nutritional counseling procedures.

Section B: Multi Specialty Treatments

Instructions

The following subsections are contained in Section B:

Physical modalities
  Cold
  Electrical or magnetic
  Heat
  Water
  Light therapy
  Mechanical
  Sound
  General

Rehabilitative
  General
  Work conditioning

Tests and measurements
  General
  Body composition
  Electronic muscle testing
  Manual muscle testing
  Physical performance
  Range of motion

Movement modalities
  Activity or exercise
  Joint mobilization
  Traction
  General
  Aquatic

General
  Allergy

Any practitioner, if appropriately trained or certified, may use this section if the scope of practice laws for their state or region allow them to perform these services.

Add modifiers (provider specific) to codes in Section B. For example, a massage therapist doing cold pack applications would use BAAAA-1B to report this service.

Unless otherwise indicated, the codes in this section represent fifteen (15) minute increments. If more than fifteen (15) minutes of the service or treatment is provided, report each increment according to payer requirements. Some payers may require that the code is listed once on the claim and the number of increments provided is indicated in item 24G of the HCFA 1500 claims form. Other payers may direct the provider to list the same code again to report each increment. Use incremental reporting to indicate the amount of time spent performing the same modality only.

Unless otherwise indicated by the term "supervised", these codes require direct provider contact with the patient. If the term "supervised" is included in the description, that service or treatment requires that the provider be present but not in direct contact with the patient

For Body Work procedures, see codes CBBAA through CBBZZ. For Ergonomic services, see codes CBDAA through CBDZZ. For naturopathic manipulation procedures, see codes CFAAA through CFCZZ; and for osteopathic manipulations, see codes CGAAA through CGBZZ.

All practitioners are encouraged to read their specific practitioner section in the introduction of the book:

Multi specialty treatments

Physical modalities

Cold

ABC Code	Procedure Description	Expanded Definition
BAAAA	Cold or ice pack, Cold, Physical modalities, Multi specialty treatments	Application of cold locally to one or more areas by cold or ice pack, cap, collar, or compress of cool water or alcohol.
BAAAB	Cryotherapy chamber, Cold, Physical modalities, Multi specialty treatments	Therapeutic use of cold by deliberate reduction of temperature of all or part of the body using a chamber device.
BAAAC	Hypothermia treatment, one area, Cold, Physical modalities, Multi specialty treatments	Therapeutic use of cold by deliberate reduction of temperature of one part or one region of the body.
BAAAD	Hypothermia treatment, entire body, Cold, Physical modalities, Multi specialty treatments	Therapeutic use of cold by deliberate reduction of temperature of the whole body.
BAAAE	Ice massage, Cold, Physical modalities, Multi specialty treatments	Application of ice by rubbing it over an area for the purpose of decreasing the blood, lymph and inflammatory medicators to collect in a area of injury.
BAAAF	Cold friction, Cold, Physical modalities, Multi specialty treatments	Vigorous rubbing using any type of cold or cooling agent.
BAAZZ	Undefined, narrative required, Cold, Physical modalities, Multi specialty treatments	Any above undefined use of cold. Narrative required.

Electrical or magnetic

ABC Code	Procedure Description	Expanded Definition
BABAC	Microelectric current, Electrical or magnetic, Physical modalities, Multi specialty treatments	Use of low level electrical current on an area or regions of the body for the deep warming and circulatory effects.
BABAD	Transcutaneous electrical neuro stimulation, Electrical or magnetic, Physical modalities, Multi specialty treatments	Application of transcutaneous electrical neuro stimulator (TENS) equipment to the skin in close proximity to and in blocking positions of nerve pain receptors.
BABAE	Magnet therapy, Electrical or magnetic, Physical modalities, Multi specialty treatments	Use of polarized objects placed in strategic points on the body for relief of pain and inflammation.

Physical modalities

Electrical or magnetic

ABC Code	Procedure Description	Expanded Definition
BABAF	Interferential current, Electrical or magnetic, Physical modalities, Multi specialty treatments	Use of a machine to provide bi-polar medium frequency currents, conduction pads are placed in positions so that currents intersect within the muscle tissue.
BABAG	Galvanic, high voltage, Electrical or magnetic, Physical modalities, Multi specialty treatments	Use of steady high electromotive force applied to a body part or region.
BABAH	Galvanic, low voltage, Electrical or magnetic, Physical modalities, Multi specialty treatments	Use of steady low electromotive force applied to a body part or region.
BABAI	Sine wave current, Electrical or magnetic, Physical modalities, Multi specialty treatments	Use of an alternating current that cycles, contracting the organs or tissue beneath the conduction pads.
BABAL	Iontophoresis, Electrical or magnetic, Physical modalities, Multi specialty treatments	Use of a direct or galvanic current to introduce soluble salt and/or drug ions into an area of the body.
BABAN	Diathermy, high frequency, Electrical or magnetic, Physical modalities, Multi specialty treatments	Use of high frequency electric current for therapeutic or surgical purposes.
BABAO	Diathermy, short wave, Electrical or magnetic, Physical modalities, Multi specialty treatments	Use of small incremental waves of electrical current for therapeutic or surgical purposes.
BABAP	Microwave, Electrical or magnetic, Physical modalities, Multi specialty treatments	Use of typical electromagnetic radiation between far infrared and radiowaves to a body part or region.
BABZZ	Undefined, narrative required, Electrical or magnetic, Physical modalities, Multi specialty treatments	Any above undefined use of electrical current. Narrative required.

Heat

ABC Code	Procedure Description	Expanded Definition
BACAC	Hot pack therapy, Heat, Physical modalities, Multi specialty treatments	Application of heat locally to one or more areas by heat pad, pack, cap, collar, or compress of hot water.
BACAE	Paraffin bath, Heat, Physical modalities, Multi specialty treatments	Application of heated purified mixture of solid hydrocarbons obtained from petroleum to a body part or region.
BACAF	Steam cabinet, Heat, Physical modalities, Multi specialty treatments	Use of a single person sized unit containing steam to encourage perspiration and excretion of toxins from the skin, elevating basal body temperature activating the immune system and increasing the metabolic rate.

Heat

ABC Code	Procedure Description	Expanded Definition
BACAG	Steam room, Heat, Physical modalities, Multi specialty treatments	Use of a multi-person sized unit containing steam to encourage perspiration and excretion of toxins from the skin, elevating basal body temperature activating the immune system and increasing the metabolic rate.
BACAH	Sauna, Heat, Physical modalities, Multi specialty treatments	Use of a single person or multiperson sized bath unit in which the bather is subjected to steam caused by water released directly over heated stones.
BACAI	Heat lamp, Heat, Physical modalities, Multi specialty treatments	Use of a heat lamp for therapeutic purposes.
BACAJ	Hot fomentation, Heat, Physical modalities, Multi specialty treatments	Warm moist application to a body part or region.
BACAK	Steam inhalation, Heat, Physical modalities, Multi specialty treatments	Use of a vaporizer or other device which allows the drawing of steam with or without medication into the sinuses and lungs. Assists the liquifaction, draining and expectoration of mucus, therefore decreasing congestion.
BACZZ	Undefined, narrative required, Heat, Physical modalities, Multi specialty treatments	Any above undefined use of heat. Narrative required.

Water

ABC Code	Procedure Description	Expanded Definition
BADAA	Contrast bath, Water, Physical modalities, Multi specialty treatments	Immersion in sudden and alternating extremes of first hot and then cold water, an intense vascular reaction occurs greatly stimulating peripheral circulation through dilation, then constriction and rebound dilation of the blood vessels and lymphatics. Has an added derivative effect.
BADAD	Hubbard Tank, Water, Physical modalities, Multi specialty treatments	Full immersion in a tub with turbine for facilitating underwater exercises increasing strength, flexability and range of motion. The bouyancy of the water aids the exercise and mild heating of the water facilitates stretching the turbine increases circulation and mobilization.
BADAG	Whirlpool, Water, Physical modalities, Multi specialty treatments	Immersion in a whirlpool bath or rapidly spinning or swirling water having a relaxing and massaging effect on the body or body part which will lessen muscle spasm, improve coordination and mobility.

Physical modalities

Water

ABC Code	Procedure Description	Expanded Definition
BADAI	Constitutional hydrotherapy with sine, Water, Physical modalities, Multi specialty treatments	Use of hot and cold compresses (thin cotton towels) to the chest, abdomen and back during which the patient is wrapped snugly in wool blankets. Gentle electrical stimulation is applied to the abdomen and back.
BADAJ	Constitutional hydrotherapy, Water, Physical modalities, Multi specialty treatments	Use of water in any form for the purpose to balance or assist the make up or functional habit of the body and the mind.
BADAL	Epsom salt bath, Water, Physical modalities, Multi specialty treatments	Use of a bath given in magnesium sulphate for the effect on the cutaneous eliminative systems and peripheral circulation.
BADAO	Sitz bath, Water, Physical modalities, Multi specialty treatments	Immersion of the buttocks and/or hips in hot or cold water or alternating temperatures, to focus the flow of fresh blood and nutrients to the lower pelvic, parianal and pereneal areas of the body area. The water may contain medicinal agents.
BADAQ	Percussion hydrotherapy, Water, Physical modalities, Multi specialty treatments	Spraying with percussion hose in a particular pattern, beginning and ending at the feet.
BADZZ	Undefined, narrative required, Water, Physical modalities, Multi specialty treatments	Any above undefined use of water. Narrative required.

Light therapy

ABC Code	Procedure Description	Expanded Definition
BAEAA	Infrared light therapy, Light therapy, Physical modalities, Multi specialty treatments	Therapeutic application infrared spectrum radiation from the red end of the invisible spectrum capable of penetrating body tissues to a depth of 10 mm for a deep heating effect.
BAEAB	Ultraviolet light therapy, Light therapy, Physical modalities, Multi specialty treatments	Use of ultraviolet light as an anti-fungal treatment for conditions such as eczema, psoriasis and candida albicans. Also known as actinotherapy when used in diagnosing and treating dermatological conditions. The Woods ultraviolet lamp is used to detect fungal infections on the skin.
BAEAC	Cold laser treatment, Light therapy, Physical modalities, Multi specialty treatments	Use of a low-level laser beam developed to focus light in a narrow intense beam. It is used to help reduce pain and enhance the natural healing process. This treatment can be applied to skin disorders, nerve trauma and infections.

Light therapy

ABC Code	Procedure Description	Expanded Definition
BAEAD	Mixed wavelength light, Light therapy, Physical modalities, Multi specialty treatments	Application of light containing a purposeful varying of the distances between the top of one wave and the identical phase of the succeeding one in the advance of waves of radiant energy.
BAEAE	Color therapy, Light therapy, Physical modalities, Multi specialty treatments	Use of a form of phototherapy using color to influence health to treat various physical or mental disorders. Any provider must show certification to use this code.
BAEAF	Infrared hemorrhoid cauterization, Light therapy, Physical modalities, Multi specialty treatments	The process of sealing the end of a hemorrhoid by using infrared light or a laser beam. The tiny burn causes the hemorrhoid to close off and shrink.
BAEZZ	Undefined, narrative required, Light therapy, Physical modalities, Multi specialty treatments	Any above undefined use of light. Narrative required.

Mechanical

ABC Code	Procedure Description	Expanded Definition
BAFAA	Percussion with a device, Mechanical, Physical modalities, Multi specialty treatments	Tapping a body part, region or full body with a device so that the vibration is sent deep into the tissue.
BAFAB	Vibration, Mechanical, Physical modalities, Multi specialty treatments	Use of a device on the body to create rapid movement.
BAFZZ	Undefined, narrative required, Mechanical, Physical modalities, Multi specialty treatments	Any above undefined use of mechanical device. Narrative required.

Sound

ABC Code	Procedure Description	Expanded Definition
BAGAA	Infratonic QGM, Sound, Physical modalities, Multi specialty treatments	Therapeutic use of a device on the body that produces coherent, chaotic sound waves in the range of 8 to 14 Hz. Used to increase vitality, accelerate healing and strengthen immune function.
BAGAC	Tuning fork, Sound, Physical modalities, Multi specialty treatments	Therapeutic use of a two pronged fork-like vibrating instrument made of steel that produces a particular musical note when struck. Can be used for diagnosis or treatment including hearing acuity testing, acupuncture point or chakra stimulation. Training and/or certification is needed to perform this service. See referral codes ADYAF through ADYAK if referring to a person or entity who is trained to provide this service to the public.

Physical modalities

Sound

ABC Code	Procedure Description	Expanded Definition
BAGAD	Ultrasound therapy, Sound, Physical modalities, Multi specialty treatments	Use of sound waves or vibrations that are of a frequency beyond the audibility of the human ear. They penetrate to a depth of 5 cm or more and generate heat an area of injury, inflammation, spasm or damaged tissue. See DDADT for phonophoresis code. Provider must be in attendance.
BAGZZ	Undefined, narrative required, Sound, Physical modalities, Multi specialty treatments	Any above undefined use of sound. Narrative required.

General

ABC Code	Procedure Description	Expanded Definition
BAHZZ	Undefined, narrative required, General, Physical modalities, Multi specialty treatments	Any above undefined physical modality. Narrative required.

Movement modalities

Activity or exercise

ABC Code	Procedure Description	Expanded Definition
BBAAA	Abdominal exercise, Activity or exercise, Movement modalities, Multi specialty treatments	Abdominal exercise to accomplish a therapeutic effect.
BBAAB	Breathing exercise, Activity or exercise, Movement modalities, Multi specialty treatments	Use of regulated breathing to develop the lung capacity and diaphramatic tone thereby increasing the ability of the body to obtain an increased level of oxygen.
BBAAD	Eye therapy, Activity or exercise, Movement modalities, Multi specialty treatments	Developing the muscular accomodation and binocularity (vergence and convergence) of the eye.
BBAAE	Flexibility exercise, Activity or exercise, Movement modalities, Multi specialty treatments	Increasing the body to elongate/bend. The ability of the muscle to relax and yield to force that stretches and elongates the muscle group. It also refers to the ability of the joints to extend.
BBAAF	Hiatal hernia toning exercise, Activity or exercise, Movement modalities, Multi specialty treatments	Exercising the diaphragm musculature to strengthen and reduce the incidence of the protrusion of any structure through the esophageal hiatus of the diaphragm.
BBAAH	Postural exercise, Activity or exercise, Movement modalities, Multi specialty treatments	Developing conscious awareness of and ability to maintain postural alignment, proper movement, balance and control.

Activity or exercise

ABC Code	Procedure Description	Expanded Definition
BBAAS	Free weights, Activity or exercise, Movement modalities, Multi specialty treatments	Use of graduated forms of weight to create resistance to muscles and increase strength, endurance and power.
BBAAT	Machine weights, Activity or exercise, Movement modalities, Multi specialty treatments	Active exertion of energy while using a force of additional moving weight of an apparatus to oppose the direction of the exertion in order to enhance the effectiveness and potency of an area, region or full body.
BBAAU	Weights training, Activity or exercise, Movement modalities, Multi specialty treatments	Active exertion of energy while using a force of additional free moving weight to oppose the direction of the exertion in order to enhance the effectiveness and potency of an area, region or full body.
BBAAW	Low impact aerobics, Activity or exercise, Movement modalities, Multi specialty treatments	Instruction, demonstration and oversight of physical exercises that do not include bouncing and jumping, but requires one foot remain on the ground at all times. The exercises are designed to deplete the normal store of oxygen in the body through strenuous exertion and to replace it through deep breathing.
BBAAX	Step aerobics, Activity or exercise, Movement modalities, Multi specialty treatments	Instruction, demonstration and oversight of the techniques of an individual in performance of a form of physical exercise that requires one leg at a time to move from a floor level platform onto a box in an up-up-down-down combination of steps. This is performed with or without weights, varies in both intensity and propulsion and may be either low or high impact in nature.
BBAAY	Exercise promotion, stretching, group, Activity or exercise, Movement modalities, Multi specialty treatments	Exercises in a group setting of two or more persons of facilitating systematic slow-stretch-hold muscle exercises to induce relaxation, to prepare muscles and/or joints for more vigorous exercise, or to increase or maintain body flexibility.
BBAAZ	Strength training, individual, Activity or exercise, Movement modalities, Multi specialty treatments	Facilitating regular resistive muscle training to maintain or increase muscle strength in an individual.
BBABA	Exercise promotion, stretching, individual, Activity or exercise, Movement modalities, Multi specialty treatments	Facilitating systematic slow-stretch-hold muscle exercises to induce relaxation, to prepare muscles and/or joints for more vigorous exercise, or to increase or maintain body flexibility.

Activity or exercise

ABC Code	Procedure Description	Expanded Definition
BBABD	Tai Chi, group, Activity or exercise, Movement modalities, Multi specialty treatments	Exercise in a group setting of two or more individuals of instruction, demonstration and oversight that combines movement, meditation, and breath regulation to enhance the flow of vital energy in the body, improve blood circulation and enhance immune function to create a therapeutic effect. See referral codes ADYAF through ADYAK if referring to a person or entity who is trained to provide this service to the public.
BBABF	Yoga, group, Activity or exercise, Movement modalities, Multi specialty treatments	Performance in a group setting of two or more individuals of instruction, demonstration and oversight of a discipline that focuses on the muscles and posture of the body, breathing mechanisms and consciousness and mental well-being by exercising, holding positions of the body combined with proper breathing and meditation. See referral codes ADYAF through ADYAK if referring to a person or entity who is trained to provide this service to the public.
BBABG	Self massage training, group, Activity or exercise, Movement modalities, Multi specialty treatments	Performance in a group setting of two or more individuals of instruction, demonstration and oversight manipulation of the soft tissues of their own bodies.
BBABH	Self massage training, individual, Activity or exercise, Movement modalities, Multi specialty treatments	Instruction, demonstration and oversight of the techniques of an individual in manipulation of the soft tissues of their own body.
BBABI	Tai Chi, individual, Activity or exercise, Movement modalities, Multi specialty treatments	Instruction, demonstration and oversight of exercise that combines movement, meditation, and breath regulation to enhance the flow of vital energy in the body, improve blood circulation and enhance immune function to create a therapeutic effect. See referral codes ADYAF through ADYAK if referring to a person or entity who is trained to provide this service to the public.
BBABK	Yoga, individual, Activity or exercise, Movement modalities, Multi specialty treatments	Instruction, demonstration and oversight of a discipline that focuses on the muscles and posture of the body, breathing mechanisms and consciousness and mental well-being by exercising, holding positions of the body combined with proper breathing and meditation. See referral codes ADYAF through ADYAK if referring to a person or entity who is trained to provide this service to the public.
BBABL	Strength training, group, Activity or exercise, Movement modalities, Multi specialty treatments	Two or more individuals of facilitating regular resistive muscle training to maintain or increase muscle strength in a group setting.

Activity or exercise

ABC Code	Procedure Description	Expanded Definition
BBABM	Qigong, individual, Activity or exercise, Movement modalities, Multi specialty treatments	Oriental exercise with an individual, incorporating movement, breath coordination, meditative focus and deep relaxation.
BBABN	Qigong, group, Activity or exercise, Movement modalities, Multi specialty treatments	Oriental exercise in a group setting, incorporating movement, breath coordination, meditative focus and deep relaxation.
BBABO	Balance therapy, Activity or exercise, Movement modalities, Multi specialty treatments	Use of specific activities, postures, and movements to maintain, enhance, or restore balance.
BBABP	Muscle control therapy, Activity or exercise, Movement modalities, Multi specialty treatments	Specific activity or exercise protocols to enhance or restore controlled body movement.
BBABQ	Sotai, Activity or exercise, Movement modalities, Multi specialty treatments	Japanese techniques of gentle manipulation of joints which stretches, supports and balances the physical body. It also takes into consideration breath, food, movement and thoughts as a total system.
BBABR	Pelvic floor exercise training, Activity or exercise, Movement modalities, Multi specialty treatments	Instruction on strengthening and training the pubococcygeal muscles through voluntary, repetitive contraction of the pelvic muscles to improve urine retention and strengthen these muscles for childbirth.
BBAZZ	Undefined, narrative required, Activity or exercise, Movement modalities, Multi specialty treatments	Any above undefined use of exercise activities. Narrative required.

Joint mobilization

ABC Code	Procedure Description	Expanded Definition
BBBAA	Articular decompression, Joint mobilization, Movement modalities, Multi specialty treatments	Purposeful slow lessening of pressure at the place of union or joint between two or more bones of the skeleton.
BBBAB	Distraction, approximation, Joint mobilization, Movement modalities, Multi specialty treatments	Purposeful separation of joint surfaces without rupture of their binding ligaments and without displacement.
BBBAC	Oscillations, Joint mobilization, Movement modalities, Multi specialty treatments	Active or passive process of purposeful exertion of energy in a swinging motion to release tension residual in the muscle.
BBBAD	Static tissue confinement and support, Joint mobilization, Movement modalities, Multi specialty treatments	Use of materials to accomplish the purposeful holding of an area of the body at rest, in balance and without motion.

Movement modalities

Joint mobilization

ABC Code	Procedure Description	Expanded Definition
BBBAE	Exercise therapy, joint mobility, group, Joint mobilization, Movement modalities, Multi specialty treatments	Active or passive body movement in a group setting to maintain or restore joint flexibility.
BBBAF	Exercise therapy, joint mobility, individual, Joint mobilization, Movement modalities, Multi specialty treatments	Active or passive body movement to maintain or restore joint flexibility.
BBBZZ	Undefined, narrative required, Joint mobilization, Movement modalities, Multi specialty treatments	Any above undefined joint mobilization activities. Narrative required.

Traction

ABC Code	Procedure Description	Expanded Definition
BBCAA	Manual traction, Traction, Movement modalities, Multi specialty treatments	Exerting a steady or intermittent pulling force, applied by hand, in which part of the body is placed under tension to correct the alignment of two adjoining structures or to hold them in position.
BBCAB	Mechanical traction, Traction, Movement modalities, Multi specialty treatments	Exerting steady or intermittent pulling force, applied by device, in which part of the body is placed under tension to correct the alignment of two adjoining structures or to hold them in position.
BBCZZ	Undefined, narrative required, Traction, Movement modalities, Multi specialty treatments	Any above undefined use of traction. Narrative required.

General

ABC Code	Procedure Description	Expanded Definition
BBDZZ	Undefined, narrative required, General, Movement modalities, Multi specialty treatments	Any above undefined general movement modalities. Narrative required.

Aquatic

ABC Code	Procedure Description	Expanded Definition
BBEAA	Water exercises, individual, Aquatic, Movement modalities, Multi specialty treatments	Exertion of energy, done in water, to enhance the effectiveness of an area, region or full body to create a therapeutic effect. Any provider using this code is required to show training and/or certification.

Movement modalities

Aquatic

ABC Code	Procedure Description	Expanded Definition
BBEAB	Water exercises, group, Aquatic, Movement modalities, Multi specialty treatments	Active exertion of energy in a group setting, with a portion of the body submersed in water. Performed while using the force of water as additional weight to oppose the direction of the exertion in order to enhance the effectiveness of an area, region or full body to create a therapeutic effect. Any provider using this code is required to show training and/or certification.
BBEZZ	Undefined, narrative required, Aquatic, Movement modalities, Multi specialty treatments	Any above undefined aquatic activity. Narrative required.

Rehabilitative

General

ABC Code	Procedure Description	Expanded Definition
BCAAA	Orthotics fitting and movement education, General, Rehabilitative, Multi specialty treatments	Fitting and educating a patient on the use of supportive braces to correct a congenital or developmental weakness. Can include orthoses like collars, spinal supports, belts, corsets, leg callipers splints and special footwear.
BCAAB	Prosthetic movement education, General, Rehabilitative, Multi specialty treatments	Instruction and practice in the proper application, care and use of an artificial body part.
BCAAC	Self care training, family, General, Rehabilitative, Multi specialty treatments	Training family members to assist an individual to perform activities of daily living.
BCAAE	RECOVERING, psychophysiological reordering of the nervous system, Page Bailey 10 day program, General, Rehabilitative, Multi specialty treatments	A ten day/forty hour science-based and curriculum-driven text-supported group study process using cognitive restructuring to reorder the nervous system and concurrently accelerate recovery experience following onset of any chronic illness, injury or pain. Training/certification is required to perform this service.
BCAAF	RECOVERING, psychophysiological reordering of the nervous system, Page Bailey program, each two hours, General, Rehabilitative, Multi specialty treatments	Two hour period of a science-based and curriculum-driven text-supported group study process using cognitive restructuring to reorder the nervous system and concurrently accelerate recovery experience following onset of any chronic illness, injury or pain. Training/certification is required to perform this service.
BCAAG	Self care training, individual, General, Rehabilitative, Multi specialty treatments	Training an individual to perform activities of daily living. Includes sitting, standing, transferring from one position to another, feeding, grooming and managing bodily functions.

Rehabilitative

General

ABC Code	Procedure Description	Expanded Definition
BCAAH	Self care training, group, General, Rehabilitative, Multi specialty treatments	Group training to perform activities of daily living. Includes sitting, standing, transferring from one position to another, feeding, grooming and managing bodily functions.
BCAAI	Therapeutic exercise, active, General, Rehabilitative, Multi specialty treatments	Use of exertion to obtain or restore normal function as well as improve and maintain appropriate mobility and flexibility, strength, coordination and relaxarion of the body.
BCAAJ	Therapeutic exercise, assistive, General, Rehabilitative, Multi specialty treatments	Use of exertion, with assistance, to obtain or restore normal function as well as improve and maintain appropriate mobility and flexibility, strength, coordination and relaxation of the body.
BCAAK	Therapeutic exercise, passive, General, Rehabilitative, Multi specialty treatments	A practitioner aiding movement while client is passive, to obtain or restore normal function as well as improve and maintain appropriate mobility and flexibility, strength, coordination and relaxarion of the body.
BCAAL	Therapeutic exercise, resistive, General, Rehabilitative, Multi specialty treatments	Exertion, with a practitioner resisting the direction of exertion, to measure the degree of normal function of a region of the body.
BCAAM	Therapeutic exercise, endurance, General, Rehabilitative, Multi specialty treatments	Exertion to obtain or restore normal function as well as improve and maintain appropriate mobility and flexibility, strength, coordination and relaxarion of the body.
BCAAN	Therapeutic exercise, balance and coordination, General, Rehabilitative, Multi specialty treatments	Active exertion of energy to enhance an area, region or full body to create an harmonious working together of parts in the normal sequence of functions.
BCAAQ	Therapeutic exercise, strengthening, General, Rehabilitative, Multi specialty treatments	Development of a muscle or group of muscles to exert maximum effort, tension, and sustain force in response to resistance.
BCAAR	Therapeutic exercise, stretching, General, Rehabilitative, Multi specialty treatments	Assisting a client in overcoming the limitation from soft tissue tightness or from muscle shortening due to immobilization or trauma and returning the body to normal range of motion.
BCAAS	Therapeutic exercise, range of motion, General, Rehabilitative, Multi specialty treatments	Active or passive acts of bending to decrease the angle at the joint between any two bones combined with rotational activities and exertion of energy to accomplish the therapeutic effect of increasing the measurable degrees of a circle through which a joint can be extended and flexed.

Rehabilitative

General

ABC Code	Procedure Description	Expanded Definition
BCAAT	Therapeutic exercise, individual, General, Rehabilitative, Multi specialty treatments	Instruction, demonstration and oversight of an individual in specific actions or skills that exert the muscles and are performed repeatedly in order to condition the body, improve health or maintain fitness level.
BCAAU	Therapeutic exercise, group, General, Rehabilitative, Multi specialty treatments	Exercise of two or more individuals in a group setting of instruction, demonstration and oversight specific actions or skills that exert muscles and are performed repeatedly in order to condition the body, improve health or maintain fitness level.
BCAZZ	Undefined, narrative required, General, Rehabilitative, Multi specialty treatments	Any above undefined use of training activity. Narrative required.

Work conditioning

ABC Code	Procedure Description	Expanded Definition
BCBAA	Work conditioning, initial two hours, Work conditioning, Rehabilitative, Multi specialty treatments	Initial two hour period of supervised, active and regular association of physical functions that includes exertion of energy to enhance the effectiveness and potency of an area, region or full body to strengthen the ability of the body to sustain similar activity that is necessary to perform a job role without yielding. Use with code BCBAB for additional time.
BCBAB	Work conditioning, each additional hour, Work conditioning, Rehabilitative, Multi specialty treatments	Each additional hour after the first two of supervised, active and regular association of physical functions that includes exertion of energy to enhance the effectiveness and potency of an area, region or full body and to strengthen the ability of the body to sustain similar activity that is necessary to perform a job role without yielding. Use with code BCBAA for initial time.
BCBAC	Worker safety management, individual, Work conditioning, Rehabilitative, Multi specialty treatments	Monitoring and manipulation of the worksite environment to promote safety and health of workers.
BCBAD	Worker safety management, group, Work conditioning, Rehabilitative, Multi specialty treatments	Monitoring and manipulation of the worksite environment in a group setting to promote safety and health of workers.
BCBZZ	Undefined, narrative required, Work conditioning, Rehabilitative, Multi specialty treatments	Anywhere else undefined work conditioning procedures. Narrative required.

General

ABC Code	Procedure Description	Expanded Definition
BDAAA	Biological terrain testing, General, Tests and measurements, Multi specialty treatments	Analysis of the metabolic status by taking the major points of physiologic measurement, including pH balance in urine, saliva, blood and sweat, and oxidation potential.
BDAAB	Electrodermal testing, General, Tests and measurements, Multi specialty treatments	Use of a galvanometric device to detect resistance on acupuncture meridian points. Also used to diagnose sensitivities and energetic responses to food and environmental elements and weakness in organs and internal metabolic systems as well as excesses or deficiencies in the meridians.
BDAAC	Ryodoraku, General, Tests and measurements, Multi specialty treatments	Diagnosis and treatment during which the client is placed on a very low electrical circuit device with a computerized testing instrument to measure a series of acupuncture points that evaluate electrical imbalances. Any practitioner other than an acupuncturist must show training and/or certification.
BDAAD	Acuscope, General, Tests and measurements, Multi specialty treatments	A form of computerized neural stimulation microcurent that facilitates healing by using a feedback loop-current control technology. This device is set up to detect tissue dysfunction with Voll capability and to treat with the microcurrent stimulation to the affected tissue.
BDAAE	Vasopneumatic device, General, Tests and measurements, Multi specialty treatments	Vasopneumatic devices operate according to the injector principle, in which a low-pressure suction is produced in the electrodes by a constant flow of compressed air.
BDAAF	Kirlian photography, General, Tests and measurements, Multi specialty treatments	The use of Kirlian technology to capture or photograph the essential energy and life force (aura) inherent in living organisms and natural substances. Training/certification is required to perform this service. See referral codes ADYAF through ADYAK if referring to a person or entity who is trained to provide this service to the public.
BDAZZ	Undefined, narrative required, General, Tests and measurements, Multi specialty treatments	Any above undefined general test and measurement procedure. Narrative required.

Body composition

ABC Code	Procedure Description	Expanded Definition
BDBAA	Caliper testing, Body composition, Tests and measurements, Multi specialty treatments	Using an instrument with a two-hinged jaw to measure the thickness of specific areas of the body to determine composition.

Body composition

ABC Code	Procedure Description	Expanded Definition
BDBAB	Impedance measuring devices, Body composition, Tests and measurements, Multi specialty treatments	Use of a device to determine the amount of incumberment or obstruction in body function.
BDBZZ	Undefined, narrative required, Body composition, Tests and measurements, Multi specialty treatments	Any above undefined test or measurement. Narrative required.

Electronic muscle testing

ABC Code	Procedure Description	Expanded Definition
BDCAA	Isokinetic testing, one area, Electronic muscle testing, Tests and measurements, Multi specialty treatments	A test to resist a movement in one body area measured electronically with a printed record generated, indicating the greatest amount of force used at each point in the range of motion. Use with code BDCAB for additional body areas.
BDCAB	Isokinetic testing, total body, Electronic muscle testing, Tests and measurements, Multi specialty treatments	Patients effort to resist a movement in full body is measured electronically with a printed record generated indicating the greatest amount of force used at each point in the range of motion. Use with code BDCAA for initial body area.
BDCAC	Isokinetic testing reevaluation, Electronic muscle testing, Tests and measurements, Multi specialty treatments	A test of the ability of a client to resist a movement in one or more body areas is measured electronically for comparison with original measurement. A printed record generated indicates the greatest amount of force used at each point in the range of motion. Used to determine efficacy of current treatment or exercise regime.
BDCAD	Electronic muscle testing, one area, Electronic muscle testing, Tests and measurements, Multi specialty treatments	Use of an electronic device to determine the ability and power during contraction of a bundle of long slender fibers for locomotion in one body area. Use with code BDCAE for additional body areas.
BDCAE	Electronic muscle testing, total body, Electronic muscle testing, Tests and measurements, Multi specialty treatments	Use of an electronic device to determine the ability and power during contraction of a bundle of long slender fibers responsible for locomotion over the entire body. Use with code BDCAD for initial body area.
BDCZZ	Undefined, narrative required, Electronic muscle testing, Tests and measurements, Multi specialty treatments	Any above undefined electronic test. Narrative required.

Manual muscle testing

ABC Code	Procedure Description	Expanded Definition

Manual muscle testing

ABC Code	Procedure Description	Expanded Definition
BDDAA	Extremity or trunk, without hands, Manual muscle testing, Tests and measurements, Multi specialty treatments	Use of resistance provided manually to determine the power and force able to be exerted in an extremity or the trunk of body without use of the hands.
BDDAB	Extremity or trunk, with hands, Manual muscle testing, Tests and measurements, Multi specialty treatments	Use of resistance provided manually to determine the power and force able to be exerted in an extremity or the trunk of body including use of the hands.
BDDAC	Total body, with hands, Manual muscle testing, Tests and measurements, Multi specialty treatments	Use of resistance provided manually to determine the power and force able to be exerted in all areas of the body including the use of the hands.
BDDAD	Total body, without hands, Manual muscle testing, Tests and measurements, Multi specialty treatments	Use of resistance provided manually to determine the power and force able to be exerted in all areas of the body without use of the hands.
BDDZZ	Undefined, narrative required, Manual muscle testing, Tests and measurements, Multi specialty treatments	Any above undefined manual test. Narrative required.

Physical performance

ABC Code	Procedure Description	Expanded Definition
BDEAA	Functional capacity, Physical performance, Tests and measurements, Multi specialty treatments	Determining the actual percent of normal or proper action of the body as compared to a statistical norm.
BDEAB	Musculoskeletal, Physical performance, Tests and measurements, Multi specialty treatments	Determining the actual percent of normal or proper action of the muscles and bones of the body as compared to a statistical norm.
BDEAC	Physical performance, Physical performance, Tests and measurements, Multi specialty treatments	Determining the actual percent of normal or proper physical action of the body as compared to a statistical norm.
BDEAD	Postural analysis, Physical performance, Tests and measurements, Multi specialty treatments	Analyzing the position of the body with respect to surrounding space, to determine and enhance coordination of the various muscles that move the limbs and maintain balance.
BDEZZ	Undefined, narrative required, Physical performance, Tests and measurements, Multi specialty treatments	Any above undefined physical performance testing. Narrative required.

Range of motion

ABC Code	Procedure Description	Expanded Definition

Range of motion

ABC Code	Procedure Description	Expanded Definition
BDFAA	Electronic testing, initial area, Range of motion, Tests and measurements, Multi specialty treatments	Electronic testing of the range of motion of an initial area, see BDFAB for additional areas.
BDFAB	Electronic testing, each additional area, Range of motion, Tests and measurements, Multi specialty treatments	Electronic testing of the range of motion of each additional area, see BDFAA for the initial area.
BDFAC	Electronic testing, each extremity other than hand, Range of motion, Tests and measurements, Multi specialty treatments	Electronic testing of the range of motion of each extremity other than hand.
BDFAD	Electronic testing, each spinal section, Range of motion, Tests and measurements, Multi specialty treatments	Electronic testing of the range of motion of each spinal section.
BDFAE	Electronic testing, each hand, Range of motion, Tests and measurements, Multi specialty treatments	Electronic testing of the range of motion of a hand with or without bilateral comparison.
BDFZZ	Undefined, narrative required, Range of motion, Tests and measurements, Multi specialty treatments	Any above undefined range of motion testing. Narrative required.

General

Allergy

ABC Code	Procedure Description	Expanded Definition
BEAAO	NAET, allergy testing and initial treatment, Allergy, General, Multi specialty treatments	Nambudripad Allergy Elimination Technique [NAET] (TM). Personal information is gathered and assessed during an allergy elimination initial examination and work-up. Includes vital signs and history. History includes a minimum of chief complaints, associated complaints, present and past medical history, family history, social history, other treatments for specific conditions, any unusual history, commonly eaten foods and drinks in everyday life, work, hobby, accidents, special procedures or surgery, accidents, etc. NAET (TM) muscle response testing is performed and verified by electrodermal testing to detect allergies. Heart rate variability information gathering and education is done. Supporting in-office tests to back up muscle response test findings are performed. Blood serum tests may or may not also be performed/ordered and billed separately, including ELISA or ALCAT tests. Any provider using these codes must show training.

Allergy

ABC Code	Procedure Description	Expanded Definition
BEAAP	NAET allergy treatment, Allergy, General, Multi specialty treatments	Nambudripad Allergy Elimination Technique [NAET] (TM) is utilized in the presence of a specific allergen that has been pre-determined by initial examination and testing. Acupressure massage is performed along and around the specific spinal segments identified. Those chiropractors and doctors of osteopathy who are fully licensed where practicing may also perform an adjustment in the specific area, using either thumbs or activator method. Those acupuncturists who are fully licensed where practicing may also place needles on selected acupoints. Any provider using these codes must show training.
BEAAQ	NAET, allergy recheck, no charge, Allergy, General, Multi specialty treatments	Nambudripad Allergy Elimination Technique [NAET] (TM) recheck is utilized after completion of the full recommended course of treatment to determine effectiveness. No charge. Includes re-evaluation by NAET (TM) muscle response testing and verification by electrodermal testing to detect any allergies that may still exist. Heart rate variability information gathering and education is also done. Supporting in-office tests to back up muscle response test findings may or may not also be performed. Any provider using these codes must show training.
BEAZY	Undefined, narrative required, Allergy, General, Multi specialty treatments	Anywhere else undefined allergy procedure. Narrative required.

Section C: Practice Specialties

Instructions

The following subsections are contained in Section C:

Oriental medicine
Anesthesia
General
Modalities
Therapies

Somatic education and massage
Body Mind
Bodywork
Energy work
Ergonomics
Massage
Oriental massage

Chiropractic services
General
Closed joint adjustment
Strapping

Mental health services
Counseling
Psychotherapy

Midwifery
General
Antepartum
Delivery
Postpartum
Newborn care
Family planning

Naturopathic manipulation
Osseous
Visceral
General

Osteopathic manipulation
Manipulation
General

Indigenous Medicine
Ayurvedic medicine
Native American
Curandera

Any practitioner, if appropriately trained or certified, may use codes in this section if the scope of practice laws for their state or region allows them to perform these services.

Add modifiers to the codes in Section C. For example, complete prenatal care performed by a naturopathic physician would be coded as CEBAC-1E. If a Cesarean Section is required, the provider should use transfer code ADYAM and/or labor support code CECAX when appropriate. ADYAM is a reference code. Read "*Reference codes and their use*" on page xiv.

Midwifery service codes are used for uncomplicated maternity cases. Global midwifery care includes the initial and subsequent history, physical examination, monitoring blood pressure and fetal heart tones and monthly visits up to 28 weeks gestational age, biweekly from 29-36 weeks, and weekly visits thereafter until birth. Any other services or visits, due to a complaint or complication, should be coded individually. The postpartum period is considered that time from delivery to six (6) weeks after delivery. Normal postpartum care is considered two (2) visits immediately following delivery and a final visit six weeks post-delivery. For one (1) to three (3) prenatal visits only, use appropriate office codes in Section A, Clinical practice charges, diagnostician (AAAAA-AAAZZ).

Mental health and midwifery service codes are not always in logical order, because they are added to the data system of Alternative Link as codes develop. Use the Index to look up procedures that are related.

All licensed practitioners are encouraged to read their specific practitioner section in the introduction of the book:

Acupuncture and Oriental Medicine guidelines	page xviii
Body work, Massage and Somatic Education guidelines	page xviii
Chiropractic guidelines	page xix
Indigenous Medicine (guidelines available in 2002)	
Medical and Osteopathic physician guidelines	page xxi
Mental Health Services (guidelines available in 2002)	
Midwifery guidelines	page xx
Naturopathic doctor guidelines	page xx
Nursing guidelines	page xxi

Practice specialties

Oriental medicine

Anesthesia

ABC Code	Procedure Description	Expanded Definition
CAAAA	Acupuncture anesthesia for dental, initial two hours, Anesthesia, Oriental medicine, Practice specialties	Initial two hours of administration of any acupuncture or oriental medicine modality or modalities, or of any herbal medicines for purposes of providing anesthesia and/or analgesia for one or more dental procedures performed on a single occasion. When performed by the attending dentist or surgeon, no other oriental medical procedures or modalities are billable for any services provided in relation to such dental procedures if such services could reasonably have been provided within one hour of conclusion of such dental procedures. For up to two hours of attendance by provider, regardless of complexity. These are high level codes. Any provider must show certification to use these codes. For additional time requirements see code CAAAE.
CAAAB	Acupuncture anesthesia for surgical, initial two hours, Anesthesia, Oriental medicine, Practice specialties	Initial two hours of administration of any acupuncture or oriental medicine modality or modalities or of any herbal medicines for purposes of providing anesthesia and/or analgesia for one or more surgical procedures performed on a single occasion. When performed by the same provider who is qualified and is performing the surgery, no other oriental medical procedures or modalities are billable for any services provided in relation to such surgical procedures if such services could reasonably have been provided within one hour of conclusion of such surgical procedures. For up to two hours in attendance by provider, regardless of complexity. These are high level codes. Any provider must show certification to use these codes. For additional time requirements see code CAAAE.

Anesthesia

ABC Code	Procedure Description	Expanded Definition
CAAAC	Acupuncture anesthesia for labor, includes post delivery, initial two hours, Anesthesia, Oriental medicine, Practice specialties	Initial two hours of administration of any acupuncture or oriental medicine modality or modalities or of any herbal medicines for purposes of inducing labor and is provided either by someone other than the primary attendant of the birth, or by the primary attendant. Requires anesthesia provider attendance for up to two hours. No other oriental medical procedures or modalities are billable for any services provided in relation to such induction procedures if such services, e.g., placental expulsion or hemostasis, could reasonably have been provided during the first two hours of attendance. These are high level codes. Any provider must show certification to use these codes. For additional time requirements see code CAAAE.
CAAAD	Cesarean section delivery using acupuncture anesthesia, initial two hours, Anesthesia, Oriental medicine, Practice specialties	Initial two hours of administration of any acupuncture or oriental medicine modality or modalities or of any herbal medicines by a provider other than the surgeon for the purposes of providing anesthesia or analgesia for Cesarean Section delivery. Requires provider attendance for up to two hours. No other oriental medical procedures or modalities are billable for any services provided in relation to such Cesarean procedure if such services could reasonably have been provided during first two hours of attendance. These are high level codes. Any provider must show certification to use these codes. For additional time requirements see code CAAAE.
CAAAE	Acupuncture anesthesia, each additional hour, Anesthesia, Oriental medicine, Practice specialties	For any anesthesia or analgesia procedure under codes CAAAA through CAAAD, additional time over that specified if at least 30 minutes in excess of specified time.
CAAZZ	Undefined acupuncture anesthesia, narrative required, Anesthesia, Oriental medicine, Practice specialties	Any elsewhere undefined anesthesia or analgesia procedure or modality involving stimulation of acupoints, provided for purposes of assisting in a surgical procedure or for determining appropriateness of acupuncture anesthesia or analgesia in a given patient for a specific proposed or imminent surgery. Narrative required.

General

ABC Code	Procedure Description	Expanded Definition
CABAB	Auricular acupuncture, General, Oriental medicine, Practice specialties	Piercing of one or more known acupoints in the pinna of the ear with filiform needles for treating or preventing disease or disorder or for relieving pain.

Oriental medicine

General

ABC Code	Procedure Description	Expanded Definition
CABAC	Plum Blossom Therapy, General, Oriental medicine, Practice specialties	Application of a Plum Blossom Seven-Star hammer-needle by tapping it along the meridians until the whole route is reddened, to alleviate paralysis or atrophy of muscles or Xu conditions.
CABAD	Points bleeding and dressing, General, Oriental medicine, Practice specialties	Application of surgical instrument to produce extravasation of blood to include application and/or administration of any related wound dressings and/or antiseptics or antibiotics.
CABAE	Acupuncture, initial 15 minutes, General, Oriental medicine, Practice specialties	Initial fifteen minutes of piercing of one or more known acupoints with needles, other than auricular acupoints, with filiform needles for purposes of treating or preventing disease or disorder, or for relieving pain. See code CABAF for additional time.
CABAF	Acupuncture, each additional 15 minutes, General, Oriental medicine, Practice specialties	Each additional fifteen minutes of piercing of one or more known acupoints with needles, other than auricular acupoints, with filiform needles for purposes of treating or preventing disease or disorder, or for relieving pain. See code CABAE for initial time.
CABAG	Trigger point needling, each region, General, Oriental medicine, Practice specialties	Each region of myofascial release by applying acupuncture needles to trigger points.
CABZZ	Undefined acupuncture, narrative required, General, Oriental medicine, Practice specialties	Any elsewhere undefined method of stimulating one or more acupoints. Narrative required.

Modalities

ABC Code	Procedure Description	Expanded Definition
CACAA	Cauterizing laser acupuncture, Modalities, Oriental medicine, Practice specialties	Use of laser output to cauterize one or more specific acupoints.
CACAB	Cupping, Modalities, Oriental medicine, Practice specialties	Cutaneous application of a vacuum to induce rubefaction or ecchymosal condition.
CACAC	Ear seeds or pellets, Modalities, Oriental medicine, Practice specialties	Affixing, with tape, of one or more beadlike objects or pellets to the pinna of the ear to apply extended pressure to auricular acupoint or acupoints.
CACAD	Electrical acupuncture, Modalities, Oriental medicine, Practice specialties	Applying an electrical current to acupuncture needles in situ, or any method of transdermal current application between two or more acupoints.
CACAE	Moxibustion, each region, Modalities, Oriental medicine, Practice specialties	Application of heat to acupoints using moxa or other incandescent material without causing pain or burning.

Oriental medicine

Modalities

ABC Code	Procedure Description	Expanded Definition
CACAF	O-Ring testing, Modalities, Oriental medicine, Practice specialties	Assessment of muscle resistance using thumb and finger. One form of applied Kinesiology.
CACAG	Non-cauterizing laser acupuncture, Modalities, Oriental medicine, Practice specialties	Non-cauterizing application of laser or maser output to acupoint or acupoints.
CACAH	Auricular tacks or microneedles, Modalities, Oriental medicine, Practice specialties	Placement of tacks or microneedles in the pinna of the ear.
CACZZ	Undefined, narrative required, Modalities, Oriental medicine, Practice specialties	Any elsewhere undefined modality of oriental medicine. Narrative required.

Therapies

ABC Code	Procedure Description	Expanded Definition
CADAA	Aquapuncture, point injection, Therapies, Oriental medicine, Practice specialties	Injection of saline solution into acupoint or acupoints with or without adjuvant fluids.
CADAB	Stress reduction techniques, Therapies, Oriental medicine, Practice specialties	Working with an individual for the purpose of reducing stress, using Oriental medicine techniques.
CADAD	Scar therapy, moxa, Therapies, Oriental medicine, Practice specialties	Techniques using moxibustion to reduce or effect adhesion or fibrosis of any body part.
CADZZ	Undefined, narrative required, Therapies, Oriental medicine, Practice specialties	Any elsewhere undefined injection of material into acupoint or acupoints. Narrative required.

Somatic education and massage

Body Mind

ABC Code	Procedure Description	Expanded Definition
CBAAA	Core Energetics, Body Mind, Somatic education and massage, Practice specialties	Release of body armoring with transformation effects on psyche. Any provider using this code is required to show training and/or certification.
CBAAB	Emotional Release, Body Mind, Somatic education and massage, Practice specialties	Point pressure holding technique together with the use of guided imagery to facilitate release of stored emotions. Any provider using this code must show training and/or certification.
CBAAD	Orgone therapy, Body Mind, Somatic education and massage, Practice specialties	Holistic body-mind psychotherapy which addresses the bioenergetic underpinnings of psychoemotional distress. Any provider using this code must show training and/or certification.

Somatic education and massage

Body Mind

ABC Code	Procedure Description	Expanded Definition
CBAAE	BodyMind Clearing, Body Mind, Somatic education and massage, Practice specialties	A combination of verbal communication, altered breathing patterns, positional changes, applied pressure and facilitated movement to assist in the release of the held thoughts, memory, and emotions which are resulting in body armoring, limitation of movement and appearance of pain. Any provider using this code must show training and/or certification.
CBAAF	Mind Body Communication, Body Mind, Somatic education and massage, Practice specialties	Use of the neural pathways, pain and position receptors, touch and movement to facilitate new moving patterns and awareness. Any provider using this code must show training and/or certification.
CBAAH	Jin Shin Do (R), Body Mind, Somatic education and massage, Practice specialties	Body mind therapy, treating the energetic system through point holding. Any provider using this code must show training and/or certification.
CBAAI	Jin Shin Jyutsu (R), Body Mind, Somatic education and massage, Practice specialties	Japanese art of treating body, mind and emotions through point pressure gently applied to the body. Attained by placing the fingertips on designated safety energy locks, to harmonize and restore the energy flow. Any provider using this code must show training and/or certification.
CBAZZ	Undefined, narrative required, Body Mind, Somatic education and massage, Practice specialties	Anywhere else undefined general BodyMind somatic education procedure. Narrative required. Any provider using this code must show training and/or certification.

Bodywork

ABC Code	Procedure Description	Expanded Definition
CBBAA	Alexander Technique (R), Bodywork, Somatic education and massage, Practice specialties	Psychophysical method of re-education to identify faulty habit patterns, consciously inhibit them and then initiate action to correct head, neck, back relationship to regain well being through postural and gait therapy. Any provider using this code must show training and/or certification.
CBBAB	Aston-Patterning (R), Bodywork, Somatic education and massage, Practice specialties	A specialized form of structural integration and movement education used to release muscle tension which helps to release functional and structural holding patterns from skin surface to bone. The body surface is used to make new movement options available. Establishes ease of movement in three dimensional asymmetrical patterns by unwinding. Any provider using this code must show training and/or certification.

Bodywork

ABC Code	Procedure Description	Expanded Definition
CBBAC	Bioenergetics, Bodywork, Somatic education and massage, Practice specialties	Point pressure and guided imagery to facilitate release of emotional holdings. Any provider using this code must show training and/or certification.
CBBAD	Biokinetics, Bodywork, Somatic education and massage, Practice specialties	Stimulation of the brain stem with gentle repetitive force, clears blockages to the metabolic and structural bodies while also clearing the energetic pathways. Any provider using this code must show training and/or certification.
CBBAE	Bio magnetics, Bodywork, Somatic education and massage, Practice specialties	Therapeutic application of magnetic fields to the body. Any provider using this code must show training and/or certification.
CBBAH	Core Work, Bodywork, Somatic education and massage, Practice specialties	Improving structure and function of myofascial system. Any provider using this code must show training and/or certification.
CBBAL	Hellerwork, Bodywork, Somatic education and massage, Practice specialties	Deep tissue body work affecting the nervous and muscular systems. Includes movement re-education training that uses a video feedback system to view how simple acts of daily life are accomplished. This technique is designed to realign the body and release chronic tension and stress. Consists of body work and movement therapy. Any provider using this code must show training and/or certification.
CBBAM	Bowen Technique, Bodywork, Somatic education and massage, Practice specialties	Physical manipulation of muscle and connective tissue designed to balance the body and stimulate energy flow. Any provider using this code must show training and/or certification.
CBBAN	LooyenWork (TM), Bodywork, Somatic education and massage, Practice specialties	A painless, deep-tissue therapy, introduced by Ted Looyen in 1985, that does not cause repetition of the initial trauma. A combination of rolfing, postural integration, Feldenkrais and Aston-Patterning. Any provider using this code must show training and/or certification.
CBBAO	Mechanical Link, Bodywork, Somatic education and massage, Practice specialties	Use of a system of evaluation to locate and release primary restriction with the fascial system and utilize gentle techniques to reduce structural tensions allowing the body to adjust and regulate its systems, including the auto immune system. Any provider using this code must show additional training and/or certification.

Bodywork

ABC Code	Procedure Description	Expanded Definition
CBBAP	Ortho-Bionomy (TM), Bodywork, Somatic education and massage, Practice specialties	Use of comfortable positions and gentle movements to ease the body into releasing tension and pain and to re-establish structural realignment. The body is re-educated using pressure point techniques to facilitate proprioceptor nerve ending activity within the muscles, and stretch-relax action to educate the body to identify its own patterns that support its ability to find balance. Facilitates the release of mental and emotional holding patterns within the body. Any provider using this code must show training and/or certification.
CBBAQ	Postural Integration, Bodywork, Somatic education and massage, Practice specialties	Bodywork using a method of working directly with the muscles, the position, the postures and/or movements of the body integrated with the mind and emotions. Any provider using this code must show training and/or certification.
CBBAR	Rolfing (R), Bodywork, Somatic education and massage, Practice specialties	Structural integration therapy, softens and re-organizes connective tissue in entire body by working specific body segments. Direct manipulation of body fascia over the entire body to alter structural dysfunction. Any provider using this code must show training and/or certification.
CBBAS	Rosen Method, Bodywork, Somatic education and massage, Practice specialties	Intuitive soft work allowing transformation based on psychological changes. Any provider using this code must show training and/or certification.
CBBAT	Sensory Integration, Bodywork, Somatic education and massage, Practice specialties	Facilitating neural sensory input reorganization. Any provider using this code must show training and/or certification.
CBBAU	SomatoEmotional Release, Bodywork, Somatic education and massage, Practice specialties	Releasing pain and dysfunction following psycho-emotional trauma. Any provider using this code must show training and/or certification.
CBBAV	Structural Integration, Bodywork, Somatic education and massage, Practice specialties	Direct manipulation of body fascia over the entire body to alter structural dysfunction. Any provider using this code must show training and/or certification.
CBBAX	Tooth therapy, Bodywork, Somatic education and massage, Practice specialties	Point pressure and oscillation of teeth with reflexes to other parts of the body. Any provider using this code must show training and/or certification.

Bodywork

ABC Code	Procedure Description	Expanded Definition
CBBAY	Touch for Health (R), Bodywork, Somatic education and massage, Practice specialties	Combining methods and techniques of acupuncture principles, using acupressure, muscle testing, massage and dietary guidelines. A variety of techniques are used such as finger pressure on neurovascular holding points on the head and pressure on identified holding points to relieve pain and improve function. Any provider using this code must show training and/or certification.
CBBAZ	Trager, Mentastics (R), Bodywork, Somatic education and massage, Practice specialties	Providing client with gentle, self-directed movements that enhance the value of a Trager session. Used in conjunction with code CBBBA. Any provider using this code must show training and/or certification.
CBBBA	Trager Psychophysical Integration (R), Bodywork, Somatic education and massage, Practice specialties	Hands-on work of fluid, gentle rhythmic rocking movements. This motion in the joints and muscles produces a positive sensory feedback into the central nervous system to enhance flexibility. Any provider using this code must show training and/or certification.
CBBBB	Trauma release, Bodywork, Somatic education and massage, Practice specialties	Therapeutic movement and breath work for the release of pain and emotion from psycho-emotional trauma. Any provider using this code must show training and/or certification.
CBBBC	Zero Balancing, Bodywork, Somatic education and massage, Practice specialties	Aligning body energy with body structure impacting body, mind and emotions. Any provider using this code must show additional training and/or certification.
CBBBD	Feldenkrais (R) Awareness Through Movement (R), individual, Bodywork, Somatic education and massage, Practice specialties	Verbally guiding gentle, exploratory movement sequences organized to promote a specific human function with the intention of increasing awareness of multiple possibilities of action. Thinking, sensory perception and imagery are involved in examining each function. Any provider using this code must show additional training and/or certification.
CBBBE	Feldenkrais (R) Awareness Through Movement (R), group, Bodywork, Somatic education and massage, Practice specialties	Verbally guiding gentle, exploratory movement sequences organized to promote a specific human function, with the intention of increasing awareness of multiple possibilities of action in a group setting. Thinking, sensory perception and imagery are involved in examining each function. Any provider using this code must show additional training and/or certification.

Bodywork

ABC Code	Procedure Description	Expanded Definition
CBBBF	Feldenkrais (R) Functional Integration (R), individual, Bodywork, Somatic education and massage, Practice specialties	Use of words and gentle, non-invasive touch to guide a patient to an awareness of existing and alternative movement patterns. The practitioner communicates to the patient how to organize him/herself and suggests additional choices for functional movement patterns. The intent of the touch is to communicate and not to correct. Any provider using this code must show additional training and/or certification.
CBBBG	Network Spinal Analysis (C), Level One Entrainment, Bodywork, Somatic education and massage, Practice specialties	NSA (C), Level One, Basic Care clinical application of a low force contact (of one second or less) to tissues overlying the spine in the area of the vertebral-spinal cord attachments for the purpose of developing: frequency entrained spinal oscillators; and/or self-generated somatopsychic responses to advance spinal and neural integrity; and/or automatic self-regulatory processes for adverse mechanical spinal cord tension and/or advance in the wellness index. Any provider using this code is required to show training and/or certification.
CBBBH	Network Spinal Analysis (C) Level Two Entrainment, Bodywork, Somatic education and massage, Practice specialties	Level Two, intermediate care including clinical application of low force contacts or impulses (that may last several seconds) to tissues overlying the spine in the area of the vertebral-spinal cord attachments on the articulation of greatest motion and ease for the purpose of developing an intermediate level of NSA (C). Any provider using this code must show training and/or certification.
CBBBI	Somato respiratory integration, Bodywork, Somatic education and massage, Practice specialties	Coordinating breath, movement and touch through patient directed movements by connecting client to their natural body rhythms to accomplish wellness. Any provider using this code must show training and/or certification.
CBBZZ	Undefined, narrative required, Bodywork, Somatic education and massage, Practice specialties	Anywhere else undefined general massage therapy procedure. Narrative required. Any provider using this code must show training and/or certification.

Energy work

ABC Code	Procedure Description	Expanded Definition
CBCAA	Energy integration, Energy work, Somatic education and massage, Practice specialties	Non-invasive work with energy fields, meridian and chakra systems. Any provider using this code must show training and/or certification.

Somatic education and massage

Energy work

ABC Code	Procedure Description	Expanded Definition
CBCAB	Therapeutic Touch, Energy work, Somatic education and massage, Practice specialties	Non-physical contact work with subtle body energies, facilitating the flow of healing energy through centering, intentionally, and the use of hands to help or promote healing. Any provider using this code must show training and/or certification.
CBCAC	Polarity Therapy, Energy work, Somatic education and massage, Practice specialties	gentle manipulation to balance subtle positive and negative energies. In addition to physical manipulation, a cleansing and nutritional diet and simple exercises of polarity and yoga are a part of the therapy. Any provider using this code must show training and/or certification.
CBCAD	Breath work, Energy work, Somatic education and massage, Practice specialties	Emotional release therapy using breathing techniques, often with point pressure.
CBCAE	Healing touch, Energy work, Somatic education and massage, Practice specialties	Use of standardized techniques that clear, energize and balance the human and environmental energy fields. These techniques include both contact and non-contact work. Any provider using this code must show training and/or certification.
CBCZZ	Undefined, narrative required, Energy work, Somatic education and massage, Practice specialties	Anywhere else undefined general energy work procedure. Narrative required.

Ergonomics

ABC Code	Procedure Description	Expanded Definition
CBDAA	Digital wrist movements, Ergonomics, Somatic education and massage, Practice specialties	Educating or reeducating proper wrist movement, including full range of motion when possible.
CBDAB	Gait training, Ergonomics, Somatic education and massage, Practice specialties	Education or reeducation in establishing a normal gait pattern when walking, including initial contact, midstance, swing through, single leg support to terminal stance and pre-swing.
CBDAC	Lifting, Ergonomics, Somatic education and massage, Practice specialties	Educating or reeducating to correct lifting techniques, including proper use of legs and back positioning.
CBDAD	Lower body movements, Ergonomics, Somatic education and massage, Practice specialties	Educating or reeducating lower body movement, including full range of motion when possible.
CBDAE	Rotational activities, Ergonomics, Somatic education and massage, Practice specialties	Educating or reeducating to correct rotational techniques, including full range of motion when possible.

Somatic education and massage

Ergonomics

ABC Code	Procedure Description	Expanded Definition
CBDAF	Sitting, Ergonomics, Somatic education and massage, Practice specialties	Educating or reeducating to correct sitting techniques, including proper use of legs, back, neck, head and arms positioning.
CBDAG	Standing, Ergonomics, Somatic education and massage, Practice specialties	Educating or reeducating to correct standing techniques, including proper weight distribution, use of legs, back, neck, head and arms positioning.
CBDAH	Supine functions, Ergonomics, Somatic education and massage, Practice specialties	Educating or reeducating to correct supine functions.
CBDAI	Upper body training, Ergonomics, Somatic education and massage, Practice specialties	Educating and reeducating upper body movement, including full range of motion when possible.
CBDAJ	Functional activities, Ergonomics, Somatic education and massage, Practice specialties	Analysis and instruction to correctly bend, stoop, kneel, rotate, lift, squat, use arms, etc.
CBDAK	Daily living activities training, Ergonomics, Somatic education and massage, Practice specialties	Analysis and instruction to correctly clean, drive, wash dishes, including coordination and use of muscles and fine motor dexterity.
CBDAL	Isometric exercise, Ergonomics, Somatic education and massage, Practice specialties	Use of force production by a muscle without joint movement through a range of motion, with some applied resistance.
CBDAM	Manual traction, gravity guidance, Ergonomics, Somatic education and massage, Practice specialties	Exerting a pulling force by hand to maintain proper position and facilitate healing, or to overcome muscle spasms in musculoskeletal disorders.
CBDAN	Body mechanics promotion, Ergonomics, Somatic education and massage, Practice specialties	Facilitating the use of posture and movement in daily activities to prevent fatigue and musculoskeletal strain or injury.
CBDAQ	Psychomotor skills teaching, group, Ergonomics, Somatic education and massage, Practice specialties	Preparing a client to perform a psychomotor skill in a group setting.
CBDAR	Psychomotor skills teaching, individual, Ergonomics, Somatic education and massage, Practice specialties	Preparing a client to perform a psychomotor skill.
CBDZZ	Undefined, narrative required, Ergonomics, Somatic education and massage, Practice specialties	Anywhere else undefined general massage therapy procedure. Narrative required.

Massage

ABC Code	Procedure Description	Expanded Definition

Massage

ABC Code	Procedure Description	Expanded Definition
CBEAB	Craniosacral Therapy, Massage, Somatic education and massage, Practice specialties	Evaluating and enhancing the function of craniosacral system. Use of light touch to assist the natural movement of the natural healing processes to balance restrictions in the craniosacral system.
CBEAC	Deep connective tissue therapy, Massage, Somatic education and massage, Practice specialties	Deep tissue frictioning and static pressure to access the deep muscle.
CBEAD	Dermal frictioning, Massage, Somatic education and massage, Practice specialties	Point pressure with friction movement over specific body points.
CBEAE	Facilitated stretching, Massage, Somatic education and massage, Practice specialties	Active and active-assisted stretching to increase flexibility and mobility.
CBEAF	Fascial mobilization, Massage, Somatic education and massage, Practice specialties	Deep frictioning and static pressure to fascial covering of muscles for therapeutic purposes.
CBEAG	Infant massage, Massage, Somatic education and massage, Practice specialties	Massage that includes infant caregiver instruction, performed on premature and full term infants. Promotes weight gain, neurological development, increases quiet alert periods as well as increasing bonding of baby with parent or caregiver.
CBEAH	Integrative manual therapy, Massage, Somatic education and massage, Practice specialties	Manual procedure based on systems approach to structural and functional rehabilitation.
CBEAI	Integrated neuromuscular technique, Massage, Somatic education and massage, Practice specialties	Capacitating neural responses, point pressure friction, position and movement.
CBEAJ	Lymphatic massage, Massage, Somatic education and massage, Practice specialties	Gently massaging key body points to unclog glands and passage ways that circulate lymphatic fluid to bodily organs.
CBEAL	Myofascial release, Massage, Somatic education and massage, Practice specialties	Deep frictioning and static pressure to fascial covering of muscles.
CBEAM	Myotherapy, Massage, Somatic education and massage, Practice specialties	Non-invasive hands on technique of pressure at the origin and continuing to the insertion of the muscle. Soft tissue mobilization to relieve pain and dysfunction.
CBEAN	Neuro-muscular re-education, Massage, Somatic education and massage, Practice specialties	Increasing appropriate neural response capacity using point pressure friction, position and movement.

Massage

ABC Code	Procedure Description	Expanded Definition
CBEAO	Neuro-muscular therapy, Massage, Somatic education and massage, Practice specialties	Soft tissue manipulation to balance the nervous system with the musculoskeletal system. Decreases distortion and biomechanical dysfunction. Also used to locate and release spasm and hypercontraction in the tissues, eliminate trigger points that cause referred pain, restore postural alignment and flexibility, restore strength of injured tissues and assist venous and lymphatic flow.
CBEAP	Origin insertion technique, Massage, Somatic education and massage, Practice specialties	Point pressure applied to Golgi tendon organs and approximation of muscle fibers.
CBEAQ	Proprioceptive Neuromuscular Facilitation, PNF, Massage, Somatic education and massage, Practice specialties	Diagonal cross body facilitated contraction movement and stretching of specific body parts or entire body.
CBEAR	Parasympathetic massage, Massage, Somatic education and massage, Practice specialties	Soft tissue mobilization of neural receptors and energy channels.
CBEAS	Postpartum massage, Massage, Somatic education and massage, Practice specialties	Stress reduction and relaxation with massage for the post partum woman beginning at the birth of a child and ending six weeks later.
CBEAT	Prenatal massage, Massage, Somatic education and massage, Practice specialties	Stress reduction, relaxation, skin and muscle tone improvement massage during pregnancy to assist in general discomforts and prevent premature labor. Includes massage during labor.
CBEAU	Reflexology, Massage, Somatic education and massage, Practice specialties	Application of firm pressure to specific nerve endings in the foot to create a reflex response to stimulate body organs such as pituitary glands, lungs, bladder, kidneys, stomach and spleen to return the body to optimal functioning.
CBEAV	Relaxation massage, Massage, Somatic education and massage, Practice specialties	Psychophysical relaxation through soft tissue mobilization.
CBEAW	Russian conditioning, Massage, Somatic education and massage, Practice specialties	Massage strokes similar to Swedish massage.
CBEAX	Spinal release, Massage, Somatic education and massage, Practice specialties	Massaging the eight muscle groups of the lower back.
CBEAY	Sports massage, pre-event, Massage, Somatic education and massage, Practice specialties	Massage to reduce injuries, alleviate inflammation and provide warm up for athletes.
CBEAZ	Lomi-lomi, Massage, Somatic education and massage, Practice specialties	Hawaiian massage techniques (often to music) using hot oils and long pressured strokes to relax the body.

Massage

ABC Code	Procedure Description	Expanded Definition
CBEBA	Sports massage, post-event, Massage, Somatic education and massage, Practice specialties	Massage performed after event to reduce injuries, alleviate inflammation, and provide warm up for athletes.
CBEBB	Sports massage, conditioning, Massage, Somatic education and massage, Practice specialties	Massage designed to reduce injuries, alleviate inflammation, and provide warm up for athletes. Part of training in preparation for a sporting event.
CBEBC	Sports massage, rehabilitation, Massage, Somatic education and massage, Practice specialties	Massage designed to reduce injuries, alleviate inflammation, and provide warm up for athletes.
CBEBD	Stress relief massage, Massage, Somatic education and massage, Practice specialties	Relaxation and psychophysical stress relief through soft tissue mobilization to increase blood circulation.
CBEBE	Stress, strain, counterstrain, Massage, Somatic education and massage, Practice specialties	Post-injury treatment of muscle and joint dysfunction.
CBEBF	Swedish massage, Massage, Somatic education and massage, Practice specialties	Soft tissue mobilization effleurage, pertrissage, tapping, friction and/or kneading to stimulate the flow of blood. All strokes go toward the heart.
CBEBG	Temporomandibular muscle therapy, Massage, Somatic education and massage, Practice specialties	Point pressure and connective tissue therapy to improve jaw tracking function and relieve pain.
CBEBH	Trigger point therapy, Massage, Somatic education and massage, Practice specialties	Application of pressure or manipulation to meridians and acupoints.
CBEBI	Visceral manipulation, Massage, Somatic education and massage, Practice specialties	Manipulation abdominal tissues to improve function, relieve contractures, scarring and adhesions.
CBEBJ	Zone therapy, Massage, Somatic education and massage, Practice specialties	Dividing the body into bilateral zones of reflexes of therapeutic impact.
CBEBK	Thai Massage, Massage, Somatic education and massage, Practice specialties	Use of a procedure that involves peripheral stimulation, facilitated stretching, joint distraction and is carried out on a firm mat on the floor rather than on a table, which allows effective use of the weight of the practitioner.
CBEBL	Watsu, Massage, Somatic education and massage, Practice specialties	Use of a combination of Zen Shiatsu and water therapy, practiced immersed in warm water. Promotes the relaxation and weightlessness, with the practitioner supporting, rocking and moving the whole body. Massage and stretching of the extremities can be incorporated.

Somatic education and massage

Massage

ABC Code	Procedure Description	Expanded Definition
CBEBM	Basic massage, Massage, Somatic education and massage, Practice specialties	Application of a combination of standard massage techniques.
CBEBN	Percussion and or tappotement, Massage, Somatic education and massage, Practice specialties	Tapping body parts, region or full body so that vibration is sent deep into the tissue.
CBEBO	Cross patterning, Massage, Somatic education and massage, Practice specialties	Cross crawl, creeping and other movement techniques facilitating neurological development and organization in patients who have experienced injuries or dysfunction due to birth, trauma, anoxia, accidents, or stroke.
CBEBP	Chair massage, Massage, Somatic education and massage, Practice specialties	Application of standard massage techniques to a client in a sitting position.
CBEZZ	Undefined, narrative required, Massage, Somatic education and massage, Practice specialties	Anywhere else undefined general massage therapy procedure. Narrative required.

Oriental massage

ABC Code	Procedure Description	Expanded Definition
CBGAA	Acupressure, Oriental massage, Somatic education and massage, Practice specialties	Application of firm, sustained pressure to acupuncture meridianpoints for stimulating or sedating the energy flow. Any practitioner, other than an acupuncturist, must show training and/or certification.
CBGAB	Amma therapy, Oriental massage, Somatic education and massage, Practice specialties	Application of deep tissue manipulation with pressure friction and touch to specific points that works on primary and tenden muscle energy pathways and affects the mind and body complex. Any practitioner, other than an acupuncturist, must show training and/or certification.
CBGAC	Anma therapy, Oriental massage, Somatic education and massage, Practice specialties	Massage by palpation, used to treat a wide range of illnesses and can clear the meridian vessels, stimulate circulation of energy and blood, loosen stiff joints and increase body resistance to disease. Any practitioner, other than an acupuncturist, must show training and/or certification.
CBGAD	Chinese massage, Oriental massage, Somatic education and massage, Practice specialties	Providing massage with modern and traditional oriental massage techniques. Any practitioner, other than an acupuncturist, must show training and/or certification.

Somatic education and massage

Oriental massage

ABC Code	Procedure Description	Expanded Definition
CBGAI	Shiatsu, Oriental massage, Somatic education and massage, Practice specialties	Chinese point pressure working with meridians and movement of body. Any practitioner, other than an acupuncturist, must show training and/or certification.
CBGAK	Tui Na, Oriental massage, Somatic education and massage, Practice specialties	Chinese massage and manipulation using hand techniques on soft tissue, acupressure to directly affect the flow of Qi, and manipulation to realign the musculoskeletal and ligamentous relationships. Any practitioner, other than an acupuncturist, must show training and/or certification.
CBGAL	Guasha, Oriental massage, Somatic education and massage, Practice specialties	Skin scraping with a moistened copper disc using a back and forth motion. May be accompanied by a pinch and pull movement called chih sha. Sites include occipital depression of the neck, both sides of the thoracic vertebrae, both sides of laryngeal prominence, the bridge of the nose, the tai yang depression, the inter-eyebrow space, the anterior chest, and the elbow and knee spaces. Any practitioner, other than an acupuncturist, must show training and/or certification.
CBGAP	Auricular therapy, Oriental massage, Somatic education and massage, Practice specialties	Application of needles to acupoints in the pinna of the ear that relate to areas of the body. The ear is used to diagnose and treat conditions such as arthritis, asthma, indigestion, migraine, urinary problems and nervous disorders. It has also been shown to be highly effective in the treatment of addictions, whether to drugs, alcohol, food or tobacco. Any provider using this code must show training and/or certification.
CBGZZ	Undefined, narrative required, Oriental massage, Somatic education and massage, Practice specialties	Anywhere else undefined oriental massage therapy procedure. Narrative required. Any provider using this code must show training and/or certification.

Chiropractic services

Chiropractic manipulation

ABC Code	Procedure Description	Expanded Definition
CCAAA	Block technique, Chiropractic manipulation, Chiropractic services, Practice specialties	Use of very specific blocks or wedges to correct the position of the sacrum and ileum, stabilizing the spinal column. Blocks are placed under the pelvis according to the malposition detected.
CCAAB	Educational Kinesiology, Chiropractic manipulation, Chiropractic services, Practice specialties	Muscle testing to determine whether the relationship between a muscle and its joints is compromised.

Chiropractic services

Chiropractic manipulation

ABC Code	Procedure Description	Expanded Definition
CCAAC	Extraspinal manipulation, initial area, Chiropractic manipulation, Chiropractic services, Practice specialties	The application of force by hand or device to osseous and/or connective tissue structures other than the spine to restore normal anatomical and/or physiological structure and function. For additional areas see code CCAAD.
CCAAD	Extraspinal manipulation, each additional area, Chiropractic manipulation, Chiropractic services, Practice specialties	The application of force by hand or device to osseous and/or connective tissue structures other than of the spine to restore normal anatomical and/or physiological structure and function. For initial area see code CCAAC.
CCAAE	Spinal manipulation, initial area, Chiropractic manipulation, Chiropractic services, Practice specialties	The application of force by hand or device to osseous and/or connective tissue structures of the spine to restore normal anatomical and/or physiological structure and function. See code CCAAF for additional areas.
CCAAF	Spinal manipulation, each additional area, Chiropractic manipulation, Chiropractic services, Practice specialties	The application of force by hand or device to osseous and/or connective tissue structures of the spine to restore normal anatomical and/or physiological structure and function. See code CCAAE for initial area.
CCAAJ	Soft tissue manipulation, Chiropractic manipulation, Chiropractic services, Practice specialties	The application of force by hand or device to soft tissue structures to restore normal anatomical and/or physiological structure and function.
CCAAK	Organ tissue manipulation, Chiropractic manipulation, Chiropractic services, Practice specialties	The application of force by hand or device to organ tissue structures to restore normal anatomical and/or physiological structure and function.
CCAZZ	Undefined, narrative required, Chiropractic manipulation, Chiropractic services, Practice specialties	Anywhere else undefined general chiropractic procedure. Narrative required.

Closed joint adjustment

ABC Code	Procedure Description	Expanded Definition
CCBAA	Acromioclavicular, Closed joint adjustment, Chiropractic services, Practice specialties	The application of force by hand or device to osseous and/or adjacent soft tissue structures of the acromioclavicular to restore normal anatomical and/or physiological structure and function.
CCBAB	Ankle, Closed joint adjustment, Chiropractic services, Practice specialties	The application of force by hand or device to osseous and/or adjacent soft tissue structures of the ankle to restore normal anatomical and/or physiological structure and function.

Closed joint adjustment

ABC Code	Procedure Description	Expanded Definition
CCBAC	Radius carpal, Closed joint adjustment, Chiropractic services, Practice specialties	The application of force by hand or device to osseous and/or adjacent soft tissue structures of the radius carpal to restore normal anatomical and/or physiological structure and function.
CCBAD	Elbow, Closed joint adjustment, Chiropractic services, Practice specialties	The application of force by hand or device to osseous and/or adjacent soft tissue structures of the elbow to restore normal anatomical and/or physiological structure and function.
CCBAE	Hip joint, Closed joint adjustment, Chiropractic services, Practice specialties	The application of force by hand or device to osseous and/or adjacent soft tissue structures of the hip joint to restore normal anatomical and/or physiological structure and function.
CCBAF	Knee joint, Closed joint adjustment, Chiropractic services, Practice specialties	The application of force by hand or device to osseous and/or adjacent soft tissue structures of the knee joint to restore normal anatomical and/or physiological structure and function.
CCBAG	Toe joint, Closed joint adjustment, Chiropractic services, Practice specialties	The application of force by hand or device to osseous and/or adjacent soft tissue structures of the toe joint to restore normal anatomical and/or physiological structure and function.
CCBAH	Patella, Closed joint adjustment, Chiropractic services, Practice specialties	The application of force by hand or device to osseous and/or adjacent soft tissue structures of the patella to restore normal anatomical and/or physiological structure and function.
CCBAI	Rib fracture, Closed joint adjustment, Chiropractic services, Practice specialties	The application of force by hand or device to osseous and/or adjacent soft tissue structures of each rib facet to restore normal anatomical and/or physiological structure and function.
CCBAJ	Shoulder, Closed joint adjustment, Chiropractic services, Practice specialties	The application of force by hand or device to osseous and/or adjacent soft tissue structures of the shoulder to restore normal anatomical and/or physiological structure and function.
CCBAK	Temporomandibular Joint Therapy, TMJ, Closed joint adjustment, Chiropractic services, Practice specialties	The application of force by hand or device to osseous and/or adjacent soft tissue structures of the temporomandibular joint to restore normal anatomical and/or physiological structure and function.
CCBAL	Wrist, Closed joint adjustment, Chiropractic services, Practice specialties	The application of force by hand or device to osseous and/or adjacent soft tissue structures of the wrist to restore normal anatomical and/or physiological structure and function.

Chiropractic services

Closed joint adjustment

ABC Code	Procedure Description	Expanded Definition
CCBAM	Scaphoid through lunate, Closed joint adjustment, Chiropractic services, Practice specialties	The application of force by hand or device to osseous and/or adjacent soft tissue structures of the scaphoid through lunate to restore normal anatomical and/or physiological structure and function.
CCBAN	Lunate, Closed joint adjustment, Chiropractic services, Practice specialties	The application of force by hand or device to osseous and/or adjacent soft tissue structures of the lunate to restore normal anatomical and/or physiological structure and function.
CCBAO	Sternum and clavicle, Closed joint adjustment, Chiropractic services, Practice specialties	The application of force by hand or device to osseous and/or adjacent soft tissue structures of the sternum and clavicle to restore normal anatomical and/or physiological structure and function.
CCBZZ	Undefined, narrative required, Closed joint adjustment, Chiropractic services, Practice specialties	Anywhere else undefined closed joint dislocation. Narrative required.

Strapping

ABC Code	Procedure Description	Expanded Definition
CCCAA	Elbow or wrist, Strapping, Chiropractic services, Practice specialties	Casting, splinting, taping and/or strapping to stabilize, reduce, or support a fracture, injury or dislocation in the elbow or wrist.
CCCAB	Knee, Strapping, Chiropractic services, Practice specialties	Casting, splinting, taping and/or strapping to stabilize, reduce, or support a fracture, injury or dislocation in the knee.
CCCZZ	Undefined, narrative required, Strapping, Chiropractic services, Practice specialties	Anywhere else undefined casting, splinting, taping and/or strapping to stabilize, reduce, or support a fracture, injury or dislocation. Narrative required.

Mental health services

Counseling

ABC Code	Procedure Description	Expanded Definition
CDAAA	Initial mental health interview with complete history, Counseling, Mental health services, Practice specialties	Commencement of mental health services for evaluation, management and ICD-9 diagnosis.
CDAAD	Clinical hypnotherapy, Counseling, Mental health services, Practice specialties	Application of techniques designed to induce relaxation so the client may be more receptive to suggestions designed to further the goals of therapy.

Mental health services

Counseling

ABC Code	Procedure Description	Expanded Definition
CDAAF	Guided imagery, Counseling, Mental health services, Practice specialties	Use of imagination processes under the guidance of the therapist to achieve relaxation, anxiety reduction, or pain control.
CDAAG	Hypnotherapy, Counseling, Mental health services, Practice specialties	Inducing an altered state of consciousness to create acute awareness and directed focus during a therapy session. Credentialed training and/or certification is needed. See referral codes ADYAF through ADYAK if referring to a trained person.
CDAAI	Rebirthing, Counseling, Mental health services, Practice specialties	Breathing process that increases the ability to feel and resolve past experience resulting in an increase of physical and spiritual energy. Credentialed training and/or certification is needed. See referral codes ADYAF through ADYAK if referring to a trained person.
CDAAJ	Activity therapy, individual, Counseling, Mental health services, Practice specialties	Prescription and assistance with specific physical, cognitive, social, and spiritual activities to increase the range, frequency, or duration of the activities.
CDAAK	Abuse protection, adult, individual, Counseling, Mental health services, Practice specialties	Identifying high risk, dependent relationships and actions to prevent further infliction of physical or emotional harm.
CDAAL	Abuse protection, adult, group, Counseling, Mental health services, Practice specialties	Identifying high risk, dependent relationships in a group setting and actions to prevent further infliction of physical or emotional harm.
CDAAM	Anticipatory guidance training, Counseling, Mental health services, Practice specialties	Preparing client for an anticipated developmental and/or situational crisis.
CDAAN	Behavior management, hyperactivity, Counseling, Mental health services, Practice specialties	Teaching cognitive and behavioral skills to help the client cope with dysfunctional overactivity.
CDAAO	Bibliotherapy, individual, Counseling, Mental health services, Practice specialties	Use of literature to enhance the expression of feelings and the gaining of insight of an individual.
CDAAP	Biofeedback, Counseling, Mental health services, Practice specialties	Assisting the client to modify a body function using feedback from instrumentation.
CDAAR	Abuse protection, child, individual, Counseling, Mental health services, Practice specialties	Identifying high risk, dependent child relationships and actions to prevent possible or further infliction of physical, sexual, or emotional harm or neglect of basic necessities of life.

Counseling

ABC Code	Procedure Description	Expanded Definition
CDAAS	Abuse protection, child, group, Counseling, Mental health services, Practice specialties	Identifying high-risk, dependent child relationships in a group setting and actions to prevent possible or further infliction of physical, sexual, or emotional harm or neglect of basic necessities of life.
CDAAT	Child development education, Counseling, Mental health services, Practice specialties	Assisting parents to understand and promote the physical, psychological, and social growth and development of their child/children.
CDAAU	Environmental management, comfort, Counseling, Mental health services, Practice specialties	Manipulation of the surroundings of the client for promotion of optimal comfort.
CDAAW	Environmental management, community, Counseling, Mental health services, Practice specialties	Monitoring and influencing of the physical, social, cultural, economic, and political conditions that affect the health of groups and communities.
CDAAX	Complex relationship building training, individual, Counseling, Mental health services, Practice specialties	Establishing a therapeutic relationship with an individual client who has difficulty interacting with others.
CDAAY	Crisis intervention counseling, individual, Counseling, Mental health services, Practice specialties	Assisting an individual to cope with an immediate crisis that threatens his or her well-being. Crisis intervention counseling involves the use of support and stabilization, problem solving, hope instillation, and resource mobilization to move the client through the acute crisis event or period.
CDAAZ	Abuse protection, domestic partner, individual, Counseling, Mental health services, Practice specialties	Identification of high risk, dependent, domestic relationships and actions to prevent possible or further infliction of physical, sexual or emotional harm or exploitation of a domestic partner.
CDABA	Delusion management training, Counseling, Mental health services, Practice specialties	Promoting the comfort, safety, and reality orientation of a client experiencing false, fixed beliefs that have little or no basis in reality.
CDABB	Dementia management training, Counseling, Mental health services, Practice specialties	Providing a modified environment for the client who is experiencing a chronic confusional state.
CDABC	Abuse protection, elder, individual, Counseling, Mental health services, Practice specialties	Identifying high-risk, dependent elder relationships and actions to prevent possible or further infliction of physical, sexual, or emotional harm, neglect of basic necessities of life or exploitation.

Counseling

ABC Code	Procedure Description	Expanded Definition
CDABD	Abuse protection, elder, group, Counseling, Mental health services, Practice specialties	Identifying high-risk, dependent elder relationships in a group setting and actions to prevent possible or further infliction of physical, sexual, or emotional harm, neglect of basic necessities of life or exploitation.
CDABE	Family integrity promotion, Counseling, Mental health services, Practice specialties	Promoting family cohesion and unity in a family setting.
CDABF	Family involvement training, Counseling, Mental health services, Practice specialties	Facilitating family participation in the emotional and physical care of the client in a family setting.
CDABG	Family mobilization training, Counseling, Mental health services, Practice specialties	Utilizing family strengths in a family setting to influence the health of the client in a positive direction.
CDABH	Family process maintenance, Counseling, Mental health services, Practice specialties	Minimizing family process disruption effects.
CDABI	Family support training, Counseling, Mental health services, Practice specialties	Promoting family values, interests and goals.
CDABK	Guilt reduction facilitation, individual, Counseling, Mental health services, Practice specialties	Helping another to cope with painful feelings of responsibility, actual or perceived.
CDABL	Active listening training, individual, Counseling, Mental health services, Practice specialties	Training an individual to attend closely to and attach significance to verbal and nonverbal messages.
CDABM	Active listening training, group, Counseling, Mental health services, Practice specialties	Training a group to attend closely to and attach significance to verbal and nonverbal messages.
CDABN	Active listening training, family, Counseling, Mental health services, Practice specialties	Training family members to attend closely to and attach significance to verbal and nonverbal messages.
CDABO	Teen parent education, individual, Counseling, Mental health services, Practice specialties	Assisting a teen parent to understand and promote the physical, psychological, and social growth and development of their children.
CDABP	Anger control training, individual, Counseling, Mental health services, Practice specialties	Facilitating the expression of anger in an adaptive nonviolent manner in an individual client.
CDABQ	Anger control training, group, Counseling, Mental health services, Practice specialties	Facilitating the expression of anger in an adaptive nonviolent manner in a group setting.
CDABR	Anger control training, family, Counseling, Mental health services, Practice specialties	Facilitating the expression of anger in an adaptive nonviolent manner in a family setting.

Counseling

ABC Code	Procedure Description	Expanded Definition
CDABS	Animal assisted therapy, individual, Counseling, Mental health services, Practice specialties	Purposeful use of animals to provide affection, attention, diversion, and relaxation.
CDABT	Animal assisted therapy, group, Counseling, Mental health services, Practice specialties	Purposeful use of animals in a group setting to provide affection, attention, diversion, and relaxation.
CDABU	Anxiety reduction training, individual, Counseling, Mental health services, Practice specialties	Minimizing apprehension, dread foreboding, or uneasiness in an individual related to an unidentified source of anticipated danger.
CDABV	Anxiety reduction training, group, Counseling, Mental health services, Practice specialties	Minimizing apprehension, dread foreboding, or uneasiness in an individual within a group setting related to an unidentified source of anticipated danger.
CDABW	Art therapy, individual, Counseling, Mental health services, Practice specialties	Employing a variety of artistic media and techniques to encourage the expression and processing of emotional material. Training and/or certification is required to perform this service.
CDABX	Art therapy, group, Counseling, Mental health services, Practice specialties	Employing a variety of artistic media and techniques in a group setting to encourage the expression and processing of emotional material. Training and/or certification is required to perform this service.
CDABY	Assertiveness training, individual, Counseling, Mental health services, Practice specialties	Assisting client with the effective expression of feelings, needs, and ideas while respecting the rights of others.
CDABZ	Eye Movement Desensitization and Reprocessing Therapy, Counseling, Mental health services, Practice specialties	Specific Eye Movement Desensitization and Reprocessing (EMDR) therapy techniques that are incorporated into a comprehensive approach that processes and releases information trapped in the body-mind (by activating the information processing system of the brain). Utilizing eye movements or other forms of rhythmical stimulation to stimulate the information processing system of the brain.
CDACA	Assertiveness training, group, Counseling, Mental health services, Practice specialties	Assisting a client in a group setting with the effective expression of feelings, needs, and ideas while respecting the rights of others.
CDACB	Autogenic training, individual, Counseling, Mental health services, Practice specialties	Assistance with self-suggestions about feelings of heaviness and warmth for the purpose of inducing relaxation.

Counseling

ABC Code	Procedure Description	Expanded Definition
CDACC	Autogenic training, group, Counseling, Mental health services, Practice specialties	Assistance in a group setting with self-suggestions about feelings of heaviness and warmth for the purpose of inducing relaxation.
CDACD	Behavior management training, individual, Counseling, Mental health services, Practice specialties	Helping a client to manage negative behavior.
CDACE	Behavior management training, group, Counseling, Mental health services, Practice specialties	Helping a client in a group setting to manage negative behavior.
CDACF	Behavior management training, family, Counseling, Mental health services, Practice specialties	Helping a client in a family setting to manage negative behavior.
CDACG	Behavior management training, self harm, individual, Counseling, Mental health services, Practice specialties	Assisting the client to decrease or eliminate self-mutilating or self-abusive behavior.
CDACH	Behavior management training, self harm, group, Counseling, Mental health services, Practice specialties	Assisting the client in a group setting to decrease or eliminate self-mutilating or self-abusive behavior.
CDACI	Behavior modification training, individual, Counseling, Mental health services, Practice specialties	Promoting a behavior change.
CDACJ	Behavior modification training, group, Counseling, Mental health services, Practice specialties	Promoting a behavior change in a group setting.
CDACK	Body image enhancement, individual, Counseling, Mental health services, Practice specialties	Improving the conscious or subconscious perceptions and attitudes of a client towards his/her body.
CDACL	Body image enhancement, group, Counseling, Mental health services, Practice specialties	Improving the conscious or subconscious perceptions and attitudes of a client in a group setting towards his/her body.
CDACM	Coping enhancement training, individual, Counseling, Mental health services, Practice specialties	Assisting the client to adapt to perceived stressors, changes, or threats which interfere with meeting life demands and roles.
CDACN	Coping enhancement training, group, Counseling, Mental health services, Practice specialties	Assisting the client in a group setting to adapt to perceived stressors, changes, or threats which interfere with meeting life demands and roles.

Counseling

ABC Code	Procedure Description	Expanded Definition
CDACO	Coping enhancement training, family, Counseling, Mental health services, Practice specialties	Assisting the client in a family setting to adapt to perceived stressors, changes, or threats which interfere with meeting life demands and roles.
CDACP	Decision making support, individual, Counseling, Mental health services, Practice specialties	Providing information and support for a client who is making a decision regarding health care.
CDACQ	Decision making support, group, Counseling, Mental health services, Practice specialties	Providing information and support in a group setting for a client who is making a decision regarding health care.
CDACR	Decision making support, family, Counseling, Mental health services, Practice specialties	Providing information and support in a family setting for a client who is making a decision regarding health care.
CDACZ	Forgiveness facilitation, individual, Counseling, Mental health services, Practice specialties	Assisting an individual to forgive and/or experience forgiveness in relationship with self, others, and higher power.
CDADA	Impulse control training, individual, Counseling, Mental health services, Practice specialties	Assisting the client to mediate impulsive behavior through applications of problem solving strategies to social and interpersonal situations.
CDADB	Impulse control training, group, Counseling, Mental health services, Practice specialties	Assisting the client in a group setting to mediate impulsive behavior through applications of problem solving strategies to social and interpersonal situations.
CDADC	Impulse control training, family, Counseling, Mental health services, Practice specialties	Assisting the client in a family setting to mediate impulsive behavior through applications of problem solving strategies to social and interpersonal situations.
CDADD	Meditation training, individual, Counseling, Mental health services, Practice specialties	Training an individual to alter their level of awareness by focusing specifically on an image or thought.
CDADE	Meditation training, group, Counseling, Mental health services, Practice specialties	Training individuals in a group setting to alter their level of awareness by focusing specifically on an image or thought.
CDADF	Memory training, individual, Counseling, Mental health services, Practice specialties	Facilitating memory in an individual.
CDADG	Memory training, group, Counseling, Mental health services, Practice specialties	Facilitating memory in individuals in a group setting.

Counseling

ABC Code	Procedure Description	Expanded Definition
CDADH	Mood management, individual, Counseling, Mental health services, Practice specialties	Providing for safety and stabilization of a client who is experiencing dysfunctional mood.
CDADI	Mood management training, group, Counseling, Mental health services, Practice specialties	Providing for safety and stabilization in a group setting for a client who is experiencing dysfunctional mood.
CDADJ	Mood management training, family, Counseling, Mental health services, Practice specialties	Providing for safety and stabilization in a family setting for a client who is experiencing dysfunctional mood.
CDADK	Substance abuse treatment, individual, Counseling, Mental health services, Practice specialties	Supportive care of individual client with physical and psychological problems associated with the use of alcohol or drugs.
CDADL	Substance abuse treatment, group, Counseling, Mental health services, Practice specialties	Supportive care of group members with physical and psychological problems associated with alcohol or drugs.
CDADM	Goal setting training, individual, Counseling, Mental health services, Practice specialties	Individual collaboration to identify and prioritize care goals, then developing a plan for achieving those goals through use of goal attainment scaling.
CDADN	Goal setting training, group, Counseling, Mental health services, Practice specialties	Collaboration in a group setting to identify and prioritize care goals, then develop a plan for achieving those goals through the use of goal attainment scaling.
CDADO	Parent education, individual, Counseling, Mental health services, Practice specialties	Assisting individual parents to understand and promote the physical, psychological and social growth and development their adolescent child/children.
CDADP	Parent education, group, Counseling, Mental health services, Practice specialties	Assisting parents in a group setting to understand and promote the physical, psychological and social growth and development their adolescent child/children.
CDADQ	Role enhancement training, individual, Counseling, Mental health services, Practice specialties	Assisting an individual to improve relationships by clarifying and supplementing specific role behaviors.
CDADR	Role enhancement training, group, Counseling, Mental health services, Practice specialties	Assisting an individual and/or significant other in a group setting to improve relationships by clarifying and supplementing specific role behaviors.
CDADS	Role enhancement training, family, Counseling, Mental health services, Practice specialties	Assisting an individual, significant other, and/or family in a family setting to improve relationships by clarifying and supplementing specific role behaviors.

Counseling

ABC Code	Procedure Description	Expanded Definition
CDADT	Safe sex education, individual, Counseling, Mental health services, Practice specialties	Providing instruction concerning sexual protection during sexual activity.
CDADU	Safe sex education, group, Counseling, Mental health services, Practice specialties	Providing instruction in a group setting concerning sexual protection during sexual activity.
CDADV	Self awareness enhancement, individual, Counseling, Mental health services, Practice specialties	Assisting an individual to explore and understand their thoughts, feelings, motivations, and behaviors.
CDADW	Self awareness enhancement, group, Counseling, Mental health services, Practice specialties	Assisting an individual in a group setting to explore and understand their thoughts, feelings, motivations, and behaviors.
CDADX	Self esteem enhancement, individual, Counseling, Mental health services, Practice specialties	Assisting an individual to increase personal judgement of self-worth.
CDADY	Self esteem enhancement, group, Counseling, Mental health services, Practice specialties	Assisting an individual in a group setting to increase personal judgement of self-worth.
CDADZ	Parenting promotion, Counseling, Mental health services, Practice specialties	Providing parenting information, support and coordination of comprehensive services to high risk families.
CDAEA	Self modification assistance training, individual, Counseling, Mental health services, Practice specialties	Reinforcing self-directed change to achieve personally important goals.
CDAEB	Self modification assistance training, group, Counseling, Mental health services, Practice specialties	Reinforcing self-directed change in a group setting to achieve personally important goals.
CDAEC	Self responsibility facilitation, individual, Counseling, Mental health services, Practice specialties	Encouraging an individual to assume responsibility for own behavior.
CDAED	Self responsibility facilitation, group, Counseling, Mental health services, Practice specialties	Encouraging an individual in a group setting to assume responsibility for own behavior.
CDAEE	Self responsibility facilitation, family, Counseling, Mental health services, Practice specialties	Encouraging an individual in a family setting to assume responsibility for own behavior.
CDAEF	Compulsive behavior treatment, sexual, individual, Counseling, Mental health services, Practice specialties	Identifying and changing the cognitive, behavioral, and emotional components of compulsive sexual behavior.

Mental health services

Counseling

ABC Code	Procedure Description	Expanded Definition
CDAEG	Sexual behavior management training, group, Counseling, Mental health services, Practice specialties	Delineation and prevention in a group setting of socially unacceptable sexual behavior.
CDAEH	Sexual counseling, individual, Counseling, Mental health services, Practice specialties	Use of an interactive helping process in focusing to adjust sexual practice or to enhance coping with a sexual event and/or disorder.
CDAEI	Sexual counseling, group, Counseling, Mental health services, Practice specialties	Use of an interactive helping process in a group setting to adjust sexual practice or to enhance coping with a sexual event and/or disorder.
CDAEL	Simple relaxation therapy, individual, Counseling, Mental health services, Practice specialties	Encouraging relaxation in an individual to decrease undesirable signs and symptoms such as pain, muscle tension, or anxiety.
CDAEM	Simple relaxation therapy, group, Counseling, Mental health services, Practice specialties	Encouraging relaxation in an individual in a group setting to decrease undesirable signs and symptoms such as pain, muscle tension, or anxiety.
CDAEN	Smoking cessation, individual, Counseling, Mental health services, Practice specialties	Helping an individual to stop smoking.
CDAEO	Smoking cessation, group, Counseling, Mental health services, Practice specialties	Helping an individual in a group setting to stop smoking.
CDAEP	Behavior modification training, social skills, individual, Counseling, Mental health services, Practice specialties	Developing or improving interpersonal social skills.
CDAEQ	Behavior modification training, social skills, group, Counseling, Mental health services, Practice specialties	Assisting a client in a group setting to develop or improve interpersonal social skills.
CDAER	Spiritual support, individual, Counseling, Mental health services, Practice specialties	Counseling and assisting the individual feel balance and connection with a greater power.
CDAES	Spiritual support, group, Counseling, Mental health services, Practice specialties	Counseling and assisting the individual in a group setting to feel balance and connection with a greater power.
CDAET	Stress reduction management, individual, Counseling, Mental health services, Practice specialties	Counseling and working with an individual for reducing stress.
CDAEU	Stress reduction management, group, Counseling, Mental health services, Practice specialties	Working with an individual in a group setting for reducing stress.

Counseling

ABC Code	Procedure Description	Expanded Definition
CDAEV	Substance use prevention, individual, Counseling, Mental health services, Practice specialties	Counseling to prevent an alcoholic or drug use lifestyle.
CDAEW	Substance use prevention, group, Counseling, Mental health services, Practice specialties	Counseling in a group setting to prevent an alcoholic or drug use lifestyle.
CDAEX	Substance use prevention, family, Counseling, Mental health services, Practice specialties	Counseling family members to prevent an alcoholic or drug use lifestyle.
CDAEZ	Abuse protection, institution and organizational, individual, Counseling, Mental health services, Practice specialties	Identifying dysfunctional and harmful thoughts, feelings and behaviors associated with the relationship of an individual to an institution or organization and changing these activities to promote adaptive functioning and personal autonomy. The institution/organization may be a religious entity, cult, fraternal organization, employment setting, or other similar entity that may exert influence and control over the individual.
CDAFC	Support system enhancement, individual, Counseling, Mental health services, Practice specialties	Facilitating support by family, friends, and community.
CDAFD	Support system enhancement, group, Counseling, Mental health services, Practice specialties	Facilitating support by family, friends, and community in a group setting.
CDAFE	Support system enhancement, family, Counseling, Mental health services, Practice specialties	Facilitating support by family, friends, and community in a family setting.
CDAFF	Individual transcendental meditation, advanced course, 6 hours, Counseling, Mental health services, Practice specialties	Advanced six hour course training an individual to alter awareness level by using techniques as taught by Maharishi Vedic Universities and Schools.
CDAFG	Transcendental meditation, advanced course, group, six hours, Counseling, Mental health services, Practice specialties	Advanced six hour course in a group setting training an individual to alter awareness level by using techniques as taught by Maharishi Vedic Universities and Schools.
CDAFH	Transcendental meditation, residence course, individual, three days and nights, Counseling, Mental health services, Practice specialties	Residence three days and nights course training an individual to alter awareness level by using techniques as taught by Maharishi Vedic Universities and Schools.

Counseling

ABC Code	Procedure Description	Expanded Definition
CDAFI	Transcendental meditation, residence course, group, three days and nights, Counseling, Mental health services, Practice specialties	Residence three days and nights course in a group setting training an individual to alter awareness level by using techniques as taught by Maharishi Vedic Universities and Schools.
CDAFJ	Transcendental meditation, short course, individual, sixteen hours, Counseling, Mental health services, Practice specialties	Short 16 hour course training an individual to alter awareness level by using techniques as taught by Maharishi Vedic Universities and Schools.
CDAFK	Transcendental meditation, short course, group, sixteen hours, Counseling, Mental health services, Practice specialties	Short 16 hour course in a group setting training an individual to alter awareness level by using techniques as taught by Maharishi Vedic Universities and Schools.
CDAFL	Values clarification training, individual, Counseling, Mental health services, Practice specialties	Assisting another individual to clarify values.
CDAFM	Values clarification training, group, Counseling, Mental health services, Practice specialties	Assisting individuals in a group to clarify values.
CDAFN	Learning facilitation, individual, Counseling, Mental health services, Practice specialties	Promoting an individual to process and comprehend information.
CDAFP	Limit setting training, Counseling, Mental health services, Practice specialties	Establishing the parameters of desirable and acceptable behavior.
CDAFQ	Milieu therapy, Counseling, Mental health services, Practice specialties	Use of people, resources, and events in the immediate environment for optimal psychosocial functioning.
CDAFR	Goal setting training, family, Counseling, Mental health services, Practice specialties	Collaborating with clients in a family setting to identify and prioritize care goals, then developing a plan for achievement through the construction and use of goal attainment scaling.
CDAFS	Pain management training, individual, Counseling, Mental health services, Practice specialties	Client education regarding cognitive restructuring techniques and coping skills to reduce chronic pain. Typically includes client education regarding emotions and lifestyle choices in increasing or decreasing pain.
CDAFU	Play therapy, individual, Counseling, Mental health services, Practice specialties	Use in an individual context of playthings and play activities to encourage the expression and processing of emotional material.
CDAFV	Reality orientation, individual, Counseling, Mental health services, Practice specialties	Promoting the awareness of personal identity, time, and environment.

Counseling

ABC Code	Procedure Description	Expanded Definition
CDAFW	Reality orientation, group, Counseling, Mental health services, Practice specialties	Promoting the awareness of personal identity, time, and environment in a group setting.
CDAFX	Reminiscence therapy, Counseling, Mental health services, Practice specialties	Recalling past events, feelings, and thoughts to facilitate adaptation to present circumstances.
CDAFZ	Compulsive behavior treatment, religious, individual, Counseling, Mental health services, Practice specialties	Identifying and changing the cognitive, behavioral, and emotional components of compulsive religious behavior.
CDAGA	Sibling support, Counseling, Mental health services, Practice specialties	Assisting a sibling to cope with the illness of a brother or sister.
CDAGC	Socialization enhancement, individual, Counseling, Mental health services, Practice specialties	Facilitating the ability of an individual to interact with others.
CDAGE	Suicide prevention counseling, Counseling, Mental health services, Practice specialties	Reducing risk of self-inflicted harm for a client in crisis or severe depression.
CDAGF	Support group, Counseling, Mental health services, Practice specialties	Activity within a group context designed to encourage the identification and expression of feelings regarding mental health issues and provide for the mutual support of group members.
CDAGJ	Human sexuality education, individual, Counseling, Mental health services, Practice specialties	Educating an individual to become comfortable with their developmental state while focusing on attitudes, feelings and behaviors related to male/female roles.
CDAGK	Human sexuality education, group, Counseling, Mental health services, Practice specialties	Educating individuals in a group setting to become comfortable with their developmental state while focusing on attitudes, feelings and behaviors related to male/female roles.
CDAGO	Spiritual growth facilitation, individual, Counseling, Mental health services, Practice specialties	Growth for the client to identify, connect with, and call upon the source of meaning, purpose, comfort, strength, and hope in their lives.
CDAGP	Spiritual growth facilitation, group, Counseling, Mental health services, Practice specialties	Growth for the client in a group setting to identify, connect with, and call upon the source of meaning, purpose, comfort, strength, and hope in their lives.
CDAGQ	Spiritual growth facilitation, family, Counseling, Mental health services, Practice specialties	Growth for the client in a family setting to identify, connect with, and call upon the source of meaning, purpose, comfort, strength, and hope in their lives.

Counseling

ABC Code	Procedure Description	Expanded Definition
CDAGR	Hakomi, Counseling, Mental health services, Practice specialties	Guidance based on of non-separation, complexity, mindfulness, non-violence and the Mind-Body connection. Practitioners create healing relationships through personhood and compassion (loving presence). Any provider using this code must show training and/or certification.
CDAGT	Bibliotherapy, group, Counseling, Mental health services, Practice specialties	Use of literature to enhance feelings and insight in a group setting.
CDAGU	Learning facilitation, group, Counseling, Mental health services, Practice specialties	Promoting the ability to process and comprehend information in a group setting.
CDAGV	Counseling, individual, Counseling, Mental health services, Practice specialties	Psychological intervention that employs counseling techniques designed to alleviate or resolve mental health disorders through insight, increasing adaptive functioning skills, identifying and processing emotions and changing dysfunctional thoughts, feelings and behaviors.
CDAGW	Counseling, couples, Counseling, Mental health services, Practice specialties	Psychological intervention of a couple that employs counseling techniques designed to alleviate or resolve mental health disorders through insight, increasing adaptive functioning skills, identifying and processing emotions and changing dysfunctional thoughts, feelings and behaviors.
CDAGX	Counseling, group, Counseling, Mental health services, Practice specialties	Psychological intervention in a group setting that employs counseling techniques designed to alleviate or resolve mental health disorders through insight, increasing adaptive functioning skills, identifying and processing emotions and changing dysfunctional thoughts, feelings and behaviors.
CDAGY	Counseling, family, Counseling, Mental health services, Practice specialties	Psychological intervention of family members that employs counseling techniques designed to alleviate or resolve mental health disorders through insight, increasing adaptive functioning skills, identifying and processing emotions and changing dysfunctional thoughts, feelings and behaviors.
CDAGZ	Inpatient psychotherapy, individual, initial 30 minutes, Counseling, Mental health services, Practice specialties	Initial thirty minute period of psychotherapy for an inpatient. For additional time requirements see code CDAHA.
CDAHA	Inpatient psychotherapy, individual, each additional 15 minutes, Counseling, Mental health services, Practice specialties	Additional fifteen minute period of psychotherapy for an inpatient. For initial time see code CDAGZ.

Mental health services

Counseling

ABC Code	Procedure Description	Expanded Definition
CDAHB	Outpatient psychotherapy, individual, initial 30 minutes, Counseling, Mental health services, Practice specialties	Initial thirty minute period of psychotherapy for an outpatient. For additional time requirements see code CDAHC.
CDAHC	Outpatient psychotherapy, individual, each additional 15 minutes, Counseling, Mental health services, Practice specialties	Additional fifteen minute period of psychotherapy for an outpatient. For initial time see code CDAHB.
CDAHD	Psychotherapy, couples, Counseling, Mental health services, Practice specialties	In-depth psychological intervention within a committed relationship between two people. Various psychotherapeutic techniques are employed to develop insight into core issues that underlie different mental health problems, and to work through said issues towards a healthier and fulfilling relationship.
CDAHE	Psychotherapy, family, Counseling, Mental health services, Practice specialties	In-depth psychological intervention within a nuclear or extended family unit. Various psychotherapeutic techniques are employed to develop insight into core issues that underlie different mental health problems, and to work through said issues towards healthier and fulfilling relationships.
CDAHF	Psychotherapy, multi family, Counseling, Mental health services, Practice specialties	In-depth psychological intervention in a multi-family setting. Various counseling techniques designed to alleviate or resolve conflict and discord within a nuclear or extended family unit. Psychotherapeutic change is achieved through insight, increasing healthy relationships, identifying and processing emotions, and changing dysfunctional thoughts, feelings and behaviors.
CDAHG	Psychotherapy, group, Counseling, Mental health services, Practice specialties	In-depth psychological intervention of a formal therapy group. Various psychotherapeutic techniques are employed to develop insight into core issues that underlie different mental health problems, and to work through said issues to alleviate or resolve psychological distress and increase adaptive functioning.
CDAHH	Eating disorder therapy, individual, Counseling, Mental health services, Practice specialties	Counseling on prevention and treatment of severe diet restriction and overexercising or bingeing and purging of food and fluids.
CDAHI	Eating disorder therapy, group, Counseling, Mental health services, Practice specialties	Counseling in a group setting on prevention and treatment of severe diet restriction and overexercising or bingeing and purging of food and fluids.
CDAHJ	Eating disorder therapy, family, Counseling, Mental health services, Practice specialties	Counseling in a family setting on prevention and treatment of severe diet restriction and overexercising or bingeing and purging of food and fluids.

Counseling

ABC Code	Procedure Description	Expanded Definition
CDAHK	Music therapy, individual, Counseling, Mental health services, Practice specialties	Use of music to achieve a change in behavior or feeling in an individual. Credentialed training and/or certification is needed to perform this service. See referral codes ADYAF through ADYAK if referring to a trained person or entity to provide this service.
CDAHL	Music therapy, group, Counseling, Mental health services, Practice specialties	Use of music in a group setting to achieve a specific change in behavior or feeling. Training and/or certification is needed to perform this service. See referral codes ADYAF through ADYAK if referring to a trained person or entity to provide this service.
CDAHM	Grief coping skills teaching, individual, Counseling, Mental health services, Practice specialties	Teaching how to deal effectively with mental suffering or distress over affliction or loss.
CDAHN	Grief coping skills teaching, group, Counseling, Mental health services, Practice specialties	Teaching in a group how to deal effectively with mental suffering or distress over affliction or loss.
CDAHO	Grief coping skills teaching, family, Counseling, Mental health services, Practice specialties	Teaching family members how to deal effectively with mental suffering or distress over affliction or loss.
CDAHP	Grief coping, individual, Counseling, Mental health services, Practice specialties	Helping an individual deal with acute mental suffering or distress over affliction or loss.
CDAHQ	Grief coping, family, Counseling, Mental health services, Practice specialties	Helping a family deal with mental suffering or distress over a recent affliction or loss.
CDAHR	Grief coping, group, Counseling, Mental health services, Practice specialties	Helping a group deal with mental suffering or distress over a recent affliction or loss.
CDAHS	Guilt reduction facilitation, group, Counseling, Mental health services, Practice specialties	Helping a group to cope with painful feelings of responsibility, actual or perceived.
CDAHT	Dance therapy, individual, Counseling, Mental health services, Practice specialties	Use of the body in fluid dance movements to achieve a change in behavior or feeling in an individual. Credentialed training and/or certification is required.
CDAHU	Activity therapy, group, Counseling, Mental health services, Practice specialties	Assistance with specific physical, cognitive, social, and spiritual activities to increase the range, frequency, or duration of a group of two or more persons.
CDAHV	Complex relationship building training, group, Counseling, Mental health services, Practice specialties	Establishing a therapeutic relationship in a group setting with individuals, who have difficulty interacting with others.

Counseling

ABC Code	Procedure Description	Expanded Definition
CDAHW	Abuse protection, domestic partner, group, Counseling, Mental health services, Practice specialties	High risk, dependent, domestic relationships and actions in a group setting to prevent further infliction of physical, sexual or emotional harm or exploitation of a domestic partner.
CDAHX	Socialization enhancement, group, Counseling, Mental health services, Practice specialties	Facilitating individuals in a group setting to interact with others.
CDAHY	Forgiveness facilitation, group, Counseling, Mental health services, Practice specialties	Assisting individuals in a group setting to forgive in relationship with self, others, and higher power.
CDAHZ	Play therapy, group, Counseling, Mental health services, Practice specialties	Use of playthings and play activities in a group setting to encourage the expression and processing of emotional material.
CDAIA	Behavior management, inattention, Counseling, Mental health services, Practice specialties	Teaching cognitive and behavioral skills to help the client cope with a diminished ability to concentrate and maintain attention that adversely impacts their interactions with their environment.
CDAIB	Compulsive behavior treatment, sexual, group, Counseling, Mental health services, Practice specialties	Identifying and changing within a group setting the cognitive, behavioral, and emotional components of compulsive sexual behavior.
CDAIC	Compulsive behavior treatment, gambling, individual, Counseling, Mental health services, Practice specialties	Identifying and changing the cognitive, behavioral, and emotional components of compulsive gambling behavior of the client.
CDAID	Compulsive behavior treatment, gambling, group, Counseling, Mental health services, Practice specialties	Identifying and changing within a group setting the cognitive, behavioral, and emotional components of compulsive gambling behavior.
CDAIE	Compulsive behavior treatment, religious, group, Counseling, Mental health services, Practice specialties	Identifying and changing within a group setting the cognitive, behavioral, and emotional components of compulsive religious behavior.
CDAIF	Crisis intervention counseling, family, Counseling, Mental health services, Practice specialties	Counseling and training family members to deal with mental health crisis. Crisis intervention counseling typically involves early identification of impending crises, support and stabilization techniques, and resource mobilization.
CDAIG	Crisis intervention peer training, group, Counseling, Mental health services, Practice specialties	Counseling and training of the social network of a client to deal with mental health crisis. Crisis intervention counseling involves early identification of impending crises, support and stabilization techniques and resource mobilization.

Counseling

ABC Code	Procedure Description	Expanded Definition
CDAIH	Pain management training, group, Counseling, Mental health services, Practice specialties	Education in a group regarding cognitive restructuring and coping skills to reduce chronic pain. Pain management training includes client education regarding emotions and lifestyle choices in increasing or decreasing pain.
CDAII	Depression management training, individual, Counseling, Mental health services, Practice specialties	Use of psychological techniques to manage the cognitive, behavioral and emotional symptoms of depression. Depression management training includes client education about the symptoms of depression, coping skills to reduce the impact of depression, and when to seek professional help.
CDAIJ	Depression management training, group, Counseling, Mental health services, Practice specialties	Use of psychological techniques in a group setting to manage the cognitive, behavioral and emotional symptoms of depression. Depression management training includes client education about the symptoms of depression, coping skills to reduce the impact of depression, and when to seek professional help.
CDAIK	Phobia management training, individual, Counseling, Mental health services, Practice specialties	Use of psychological techniques to manage the cognitive, behavioral and emotional symptoms of phobia. Phobia management training includes client education about the symptoms of phobia, coping skills to reduce the impact of phobia, and when to seek professional help.
CDAIL	Phobia management training, group, Counseling, Mental health services, Practice specialties	Use of psychological techniques in a group setting to manage the cognitive, behavioral and emotional symptoms of phobia. Phobia management training includes client education about the symptoms of phobia, coping skills to reduce the impact of phobia, and when to seek professional help.
CDAIM	Substance abuse treatment, family, Counseling, Mental health services, Practice specialties	Supportive care of family members with physical and psychological problems associated with use of alcohol or drugs.
CDAIN	Mediation, Counseling, Mental health services, Practice specialties	Helping two or more individuals reach a compromise that benefits both parties. Mediation involves helping each party understand the needs and wants of the other(s), realize the importance of reaching a mutually beneficial compromise, and join in reducing conflict and increasing productive problem solving.

Mental health services

Counseling

ABC Code	Procedure Description	Expanded Definition
CDAIO	Teen parent education, group, Counseling, Mental health services, Practice specialties	Assisting teen parents in a group setting to understand and promote the physical, psychological and social growth and development of their toddler, preschool, or elementary school-aged child or children.
CDAIP	Abuse protection, institutional or organizational, group, Counseling, Mental health services, Practice specialties	Identifying within a group setting dysfunctional and harmful thoughts, feelings and behaviors associated with an individual to an institution or organization and changing these activities to promote adaptive functioning and personal autonomy. The institution/organization may be a religious entity, cult, fraternal organization, employment setting, or other entity that seemingly exerts influence and control.
CDAIQ	Dance therapy, group, Counseling, Mental health services, Practice specialties	Use of the body in fluid dance movements to achieve a change in behavior or feeling in a group setting. Credentialed training and/or certification is required.
CDAZZ	Undefined, narrative required, Counseling, Mental health services, Practice specialties	Anywhere else undefined mental health counseling procedure. Narrative required.

Testing, evaluation and interpretation

ABC Code	Procedure Description	Expanded Definition
CDBAP	Psychological testing, brief assessment, Testing, evaluation and interpretation, Mental health services, Practice specialties	Brief interviews and measures for an initial assessment of psychological, cognitive, and emotional functioning.
CDBAQ	Psychological testing, comprehensive, Testing, evaluation and interpretation, Mental health services, Practice specialties	Objective and subjective tests for a comprehensive evaluation of the psychological functioning, intellectual capacity, achievement potential, or personality structure.
CDBAR	Psychological test interpretation, Testing, evaluation and interpretation, Mental health services, Practice specialties	Systematic interpretation by a psychologist of objective and subjective tests to obtain a comprehensive, integrated evaluation of the personality structure, psychological functioning, cognitive functioning, and/or achievement potential.
CDBAS	Neuropsychological testing, Testing, evaluation and interpretation, Mental health services, Practice specialties	Objective and subjective tests for a comprehensive evaluation of the neuropsychological functioning. Neuropsychological testing may involve the assessment of intellectual capacity, cognitive functioning and limitations, achievement potential and learning disability, and neuropsychological deficits from brain injury and disease morbidity.

Mental health services

Testing, evaluation and interpretation

ABC Code	Procedure Description	Expanded Definition
CDBAT	Neuropsychological test interpretation, Testing, evaluation and interpretation, Mental health services, Practice specialties	Systematic interpretation by a psychologist of objective and subjective tests to obtain a comprehensive, integrated evaluation of the neuropsychological functioning. This may include intellectual capacity, cognitive functioning and limitations, achievement potential, learning disabilities and neuropsychological deficits.
CDBAU	Records and test psychiatric evaluation services, Testing, evaluation and interpretation, Mental health services, Practice specialties	Evaluating hospital or other psychiatric records and test results.
CDBZY	Undefined, narrative required, Testing, evaluation and interpretation, Mental health services, Practice specialties	Anywhere else undefined mental health test, evaluation or interpretation. Narrative required.

Midwifery services

General

ABC Code	Procedure Description	Expanded Definition
CEAAD	Pelvic exam with pap smear, General, Midwifery services, Practice specialties	Pelvic exam to include visualization of vulva, perineum, then vagina and cervix with speculum and bimanual evaluation. Pap smear carried out at time of pelvic exam.
CEAAE	Pelvic exam without pap smear, General, Midwifery services, Practice specialties	Pelvic exam to include visualization of vulva, perineum, then vagina and cervix with speculum and bimanual evaluation.
CEAAG	Annual gynecological exam with pap smear, General, Midwifery services, Practice specialties	Medical history review, pelvic exam with labs, breast exam and general health education including self breast exam.
CEAAH	Cervical escharotic treatments, General, Midwifery services, Practice specialties	Tissue destruction utilizing corrosive and/or caustic agent or extreme cold.
CEAAL	Pap smear, repeat, General, Midwifery services, Practice specialties	Repeat pap smear in management of general health or past abnormal pap smear evaluation.
CEAAM	Breast examination, comprehensive, General, Midwifery services, Practice specialties	Comprehensive physical breast examination for abnormal shape, identification of lumps, masses or lesions, nipple appearance and/or nipple discharge.
CEAAQ	Family integrity promotion, group, General, Midwifery services, Practice specialties	Growth of individuals in a group setting who are adding an infant to the family unit.

General

ABC Code	Procedure Description	Expanded Definition
CEAAR	Family integrity promotion, individual, General, Midwifery services, Practice specialties	Growth of an individual who is adding an infant to the family unit.
CEAAW	Pregnancy termination care, initial hour, General, Midwifery services, Practice specialties	First hour of management and stabilization of the physical and psychological needs of the woman undergoing a spontaneous or elective abortion. For additional time requirements, see code CEAAX.
CEAAX	Pregnancy termination care, each additional 15 minutes, General, Midwifery services, Practice specialties	Additional fifteen minute period of management of the physical and psychological needs of the woman undergoing a spontaneous or elective abortion. For initial time see code CEAAW.
CEAAY	Grief work facilitation, perinatal death, General, Midwifery services, Practice specialties	Assistance with the resolution of a perinatal loss.
CEAAZ	Developmental care, General, Midwifery services, Practice specialties	Structuring the environment and providing care in response to the behavioral cues and states of the pre-term infant.
CEABG	Equipment transport for off site delivery, General, Midwifery services, Practice specialties	Transfer of emergency and non-emergency equipment to an off-site location for obstetrical delivery.
CEABH	Home preparation prior to labor and delivery, General, Midwifery services, Practice specialties	Preparing the home for safe and effective delivery of care.
CEABJ	Pessary management, General, Midwifery services, Practice specialties	Placement and monitoring of a vaginal device for treating stress urinary incontinence, uterine retroversion, genital prolapse, or incompetent cervix.
CEABL	Pregnancy termination counseling, General, Midwifery services, Practice specialties	Management and counseling for the psychological needs of the woman undergoing a spontaneous or elective abortion.
CEABM	Counseling for Cesarean birth, General, Midwifery services, Practice specialties	Educating and/or counseling on Cesarean birth, including when it is indicated, what can be done to reduce chances of having a C-Section, and what is involved with the surgical procedure. If the procedure is necessary, recommendations are made towards simplifying delivery for the mother, baby and family.
CEABO	Breast care training, General, Midwifery services, Practice specialties	Breast self-care training, including self examination and its significance.

General

ABC Code	Procedure Description	Expanded Definition
CEAZZ	Undefined, narrative required, General, Midwifery services, Practice specialties	Anywhere else undefined midwifery procedure. Narrative required.

Antepartum

ABC Code	Procedure Description	Expanded Definition
CEBAA	Prenatal care, 4 to 6 visits, Antepartum, Midwifery services, Practice specialties	Antepartum care for four through six visits. Initial visit with complete history and physical exam and subsequent antepartum follow-up for evaluation of mother and fetus well-being. This code should not be used with other office visit codes. For one to three prenatal visits, use codes AAAAE through AAAAH.
CEBAB	Prenatal care, 7 or more visits, Antepartum, Midwifery services, Practice specialties	Antepartum care for seven or more visits. Initial visit with complete history and physical exam and subsequent antepartum follow-up for evaluation of mother and fetus well-being. This code should not be used with other office visit codes. For one to three prenatal visits, use codes AAAAE through AAAAH.
CEBAC	Prenatal care, complete, Antepartum, Midwifery services, Practice specialties	Complete antepartum care. Initial visit with complete history and physical exam and subsequent antepartum follow-up for evaluation of mother and fetus well-being. Included in global fee for delivery.
CEBAD	Prenatal electronic fetal monitoring, Antepartum, Midwifery services, Practice specialties	Electronic evaluation of fetal heart rate response to movement, external stimuli, or uterine contractions during antepartal testing.
CEBAE	Prenatal monitoring of uterus, Antepartum, Midwifery services, Practice specialties	Monitoring the uterus of a pregnant woman to asses uterine integrity.
CEBAG	Bleeding reduction, antepartum uterus, initial stabilization, Antepartum, Midwifery services, Practice specialties	Initial fifteen minute period of monitoring the uterus of a pregnant woman to assess uterine integrity and to reduce abnormal bleeding. For additional time requirements, see code CEBAH.
CEBAH	Bleeding reduction, antepartum uterus, each additional 15 minutes, Antepartum, Midwifery services, Practice specialties	Additional fifteen minute period of monitoring the uterus of a pregnant woman to assess uterine integrity and to reduce abnormal bleeding. For initial time requirements, see code CEBAG.
CEBAI	Childbirth preparation, group, Antepartum, Midwifery services, Practice specialties	Providing information and support in a group setting to facilitate childbirth and to enhance the ability of an individual to develop and perform the role of parent.
CEBAJ	Childbirth preparation, individual, Antepartum, Midwifery services, Practice specialties	Providing information and support to facilitate childbirth and to enhance the ability of an individual to develop and perform the role of parent.

Antepartum

ABC Code	Procedure Description	Expanded Definition
CEBAK	False labor monitoring, initial hour, Antepartum, Midwifery services, Practice specialties	First hour of monitoring and management of a woman when labor fails to establish. For additional time requirements, see code CEBAL.
CEBAL	False labor monitoring, each additional 15 minutes, Antepartum, Midwifery services, Practice specialties	Additional fifteen minute period of continued monitoring and management of a woman when labor fails to establish. For initial time requirements, see code CEBAK.
CEBAM	High risk pregnancy identification, Antepartum, Midwifery services, Practice specialties	Identification of a high risk pregnancy to promote healthy outcomes for mother and baby.
CEBAN	Labor suppression, initial hour, Antepartum, Midwifery services, Practice specialties	Initial hour of controlling uterine contractions prior to 37 weeks of gestation to prevent pre-term birth. For additional time requirements, see code CEBAO.
CEBAO	Labor suppression, each additional 15 minutes, Antepartum, Midwifery services, Practice specialties	Additional fifteen minute period of controlling uterine contractions prior to 37 weeks of gestation to prevent pre-term birth. For initial time requirements, see code CEBAN.
CEBAP	Late pregnancy surveillance, Antepartum, Midwifery services, Practice specialties	Purposeful and ongoing acquisition, interpretation, and synthesis of maternal-fetal data for treatment, observation or admission.
CEBAQ	Ultrasonography, Antepartum, Midwifery services, Practice specialties	Performance of ultrasound exams to determine ovarian, uterine, or fetal status.
CEBAT	Doula, prenatal services, each hour, Antepartum, Midwifery services, Practice specialties	One hour period of professional, non-medical support of a pregnant woman to provide stress reduction and education regarding birthing plan options. Usually provided during the second or third trimester and facilitates and significantly improves labor and delivery in childbirth.
CEBZZ	Undefined, narrative required, Antepartum, Midwifery services, Practice specialties	Anywhere else undefined antepartum midwifery procedure. Narrative required.

Delivery

ABC Code	Procedure Description	Expanded Definition
CECAA	Vaginal delivery only, Delivery, Midwifery services, Practice specialties	Spontaneous vaginal delivery without prenatal care. May include vacuum extraction. Includes immediate postpartum care during the first 72 hours and immediate postdelivery care. Does not include six weeks postpartum visits.

Delivery

ABC Code	Procedure Description	Expanded Definition
CECAB	Vaginal delivery and postpartum care only, Delivery, Midwifery services, Practice specialties	Vaginal delivery, including postpartum care through the six weeks postpartum period. Does not include prenatal care. Delivery may include vacuum extraction.
CECAC	Delivery of placenta only, Delivery, Midwifery services, Practice specialties	Manual delivery of placenta only. Not billable if delivery was performed by the same provider.
CECAH	Global OB care after prior Cesarean section, Delivery, Midwifery services, Practice specialties	Vaginal delivery, with or without vacuum extraction, with complete antepartum and postpartum care, with or without episiotomy, with previous Cesarean section delivery.
CECAI	Vaginal delivery only after prior Cesarean delivery, Delivery, Midwifery services, Practice specialties	Vaginal delivery, with or without vacuum extraction with previous Cesarean section delivery. Includes immediate postdelivery care. Does not include immediate or final six weeks postpartum care.
CECAK	Vaginal delivery and postpartum care after prior Cesarean delivery, Delivery, Midwifery services, Practice specialties	Vaginal delivery on woman with previous Cesarean section delivery, with or without vacuum extraction or episiotomy, and postpartum care through the six weeks postpartum period.
CECAN	Amnioinfusion, Delivery, Midwifery services, Practice specialties	Infusion of fluid into the uterus during labor to relieve umbilical cord compression or to dilute meconium-stained fluid.
CECAQ	High risk delivery assistance, Delivery, Midwifery services, Practice specialties	Assisting high risk vaginal births.
CECAR	Intrapartal care, Delivery, Midwifery services, Practice specialties	Monitoring and management of stages one and two of the birth process, when care transferred to a new provider.
CECAS	Intrapartum electronic fetal monitoring, Delivery, Midwifery services, Practice specialties	Electronic evaluation of fetal heart rate response to uterine contractions during intrapartal care.
CECAT	Labor induction, initial hour, Delivery, Midwifery services, Practice specialties	Initial hour of initiation or augmenting labor by mechanical or pharmacological methods. For additional time requirements, see code CECAU.
CECAU	Labor induction, each additional 15 minutes, Delivery, Midwifery services, Practice specialties	Additional fifteen minute period of augmenting labor by mechanical or pharmacological methods. For initial time requirements, see code CECAT.
CECAV	Labor monitoring off site, Delivery, Midwifery services, Practice specialties	Monitoring and management of stages one and two of the birth process, at location other than delivery site.

Delivery

ABC Code	Procedure Description	Expanded Definition
CECAW	Labor monitoring, Delivery, Midwifery services, Practice specialties	Monitoring and management of stages one and two of the birth process, at delivery site.
CECAX	Labor support, Delivery, Midwifery services, Practice specialties	Continued support of patient by provider who has transferred medical responsibility.
CECAY	Global OB care, Delivery, Midwifery services, Practice specialties	Normal vaginal delivery with or without episiotomy, including the monitoring and management of the pregnant patient (prenatal care) as well as comprehensive postpartum care.
CECAZ	Home birth facility preparation, Delivery, Midwifery services, Practice specialties	Includes all equipment set up, break down, clean up, re-sterilization of instruments. For false labor , etc., use house call codes AADAC through AADAI, CEBAK and CEBAL, as appropriate.
CECBA	Free standing birth facility, charge A, Delivery, Midwifery services, Practice specialties	Use of a free-standing birthing facility for first 12 hours. Facility complies with and maintains current city business license as a place for midwifery care. For portion used for false labor monitoring, etc., use code CECBB.
CECBB	Free standing birth facility, charge A2, each hour, Delivery, Midwifery services, Practice specialties	Use of a free-standing birthing facility for each additional one hour period. Facility complies with and maintains current city business license status as a place for midwifery care. For initial time, see code CECBA.
CECBC	Free standing birth facility, charge B, Delivery, Midwifery services, Practice specialties	Use of a free-standing birthing facility for first twelve hours. For portion used for false labor monitoring, etc., use code CECBD. Facility complies with and maintains current city business license status as a place for delivery of midwifery care.
CECBD	Free standing birth facility, charge B2, each hour, Delivery, Midwifery services, Practice specialties	Use of a free-standing birthing facility for each additional hour. Facility complies with and maintains current city business license status as a place for midwifery care. For initial time, see code CECBC.
CECBE	Free standing birth facility, charge C, Delivery, Midwifery services, Practice specialties	Use of a free-standing birthing facility for first eight hours. Facility has accreditation as a licensed birth center. For portion used for false labor monitoring, etc., use code CECBF.
CECBF	Free standing birth facility, charge C2, each hour, Delivery, Midwifery services, Practice specialties	Use of a free-standing birthing facility for additional one hour period. Facility has accreditation as a licensed birth center.

Delivery

ABC Code	Procedure Description	Expanded Definition
CECBG	Hospital based birth center facility, charge D, Delivery, Midwifery services, Practice specialties	Use of hospital-based birth center for first 24 hours. Facility has national accreditation as a hospital-based birth center. For portion used for false labor monitoring, etc., use code CECBH.
CECBH	Hospital based birth center facility, charge D2, each hour, Delivery, Midwifery services, Practice specialties	Use of hospital-based birth center facility for each additional one hour period. Facility has national accreditation as a hospital-based birth center.
CECBI	Vaginal delivery and prenatal care only, Delivery, Midwifery services, Practice specialties	Vaginal delivery, includes prenatal care. May include vacuum extraction. Includes immediate postdelivery care and may include episiotomy.
CECBJ	Use of a waterbirth tub, tub supplied by provider, must be used with a delivery code, Delivery, Midwifery services, Practice specialties	Use and/or preparation of a waterbirth tub for labor and/or birth. Tub is supplied by provider.
CECBK	Use of a waterbirth tub, tub supplied by client, must be used with a delivery code, Delivery, Midwifery services, Practice specialties	Use and/or preparation of a waterbirth tub for labor and/or birth. Tub is supplied by client.
CECBL	Ordering cryopreservation services for umbilical cord blood stem cells, no charge, Delivery, Midwifery services, Practice specialties	Ordering the cryopreservation of stem cells collected from umbilicus venous blood.
CECBM	Stem cell collection from umbilical cord blood, Delivery, Midwifery services, Practice specialties	Withdrawing blood from umbilical cord vein as a source of stem cell platelets.
CECBN	Second midwife assist with delivery, includes postdelivery care, initial hour, Delivery, Midwifery services, Practice specialties	Initial hour of a second midwife assisting primary midwife with delivery and postpartum care. See code CECBO for additional time.
CECBO	Second midwife assist with delivery, includes postdelivery care, each additional hour, Delivery, Midwifery services, Practice specialties	Additional hour of a second midwife assisting primary midwife with delivery and postpartum care. See code CECBN for initial time.
CECBP	Vaginal delivery after prior Cesarean delivery, including prenatal care, Delivery, Midwifery services, Practice specialties	Vaginal delivery, with or without vacuum extraction, after a Cesarean section delivery. Includes prenatal care and immediate postpartum care.
CECBQ	Doula, intrapartum services, each hour, Delivery, Midwifery services, Practice specialties	One hour period of professional, non-medical support of a laboring woman provided to reduce stress, improve comfort and environment, and provide continuity of care to facilitate and improve natural delivery and birthing outcomes.

Midwifery services

Delivery

ABC Code	Procedure Description	Expanded Definition
CECZZ	Undefined, narrative required, Delivery, Midwifery services, Practice specialties	Anywhere else undefined midwifery delivery procedure. Narrative required.

Postpartum

ABC Code	Procedure Description	Expanded Definition
CEDAA	Postpartum care only, up to six weeks, Postpartum, Midwifery services, Practice specialties	Up to six weeks of monitoring and management of the patient who has recently given birth.
CEDAB	Home visit, Postpartum, Midwifery services, Practice specialties	Postpartum home visit for physical assessment and management.
CEDAD	Bleeding reduction, postpartum uterus, initial stabilization, Postpartum, Midwifery services, Practice specialties	Initial measures to reduce blood loss from the postpartum uterus. For additional time requirements, see code CEDAE.
CEDAE	Bleeding reduction, postpartum uterus, each additional 15 minutes, Postpartum, Midwifery services, Practice specialties	Additional fifteen minute period of limiting the blood loss from the postpartum uterus. For initial measures, see code CEDAD.
CEDAF	Perineal care, Postpartum, Midwifery services, Practice specialties	Maintenance of perineal skin integrity and relief of perineal discomfort.
CEDAG	Episiotomy, Postpartum, Midwifery services, Practice specialties	Episiotomy and/or repair of vaginal region. Includes administration of local anesthesia and surgical incision of midline or mediolateral fourchette with suturing after delivery.
CEDAH	Lactation suppression, Postpartum, Midwifery services, Practice specialties	Assisting a woman in the suppression of milk flow when breastfeeding is not desired.
CEDAI	Lactation counseling, Postpartum, Midwifery services, Practice specialties	An interactive process to assist with successful breastfeeding.
CEDAJ	Vaginal suturing, Postpartum, Midwifery services, Practice specialties	Suturing of vaginal tear following vaginal delivery. May include administration of local anesthesia.
CEDAK	Doula, postpartum services, each hour, Postpartum, Midwifery services, Practice specialties	One hour period of professional, non-medical support to reduce stress, educate regarding self care, newborn care, and feeding and eating decisions. Provided to facilitate and improve family-infant bonding, growth and development, and reduce postpartum complications.
CEDZZ	Undefined, narrative required, Postpartum, Midwifery services, Practice specialties	Anywhere else undefined postpartum procedure. Narrative required.

Newborn care

ABC Code	Procedure Description	Expanded Definition
CEEAA	Newborn resuscitation with positive pressure ventilation and or chest compression, Newborn care, Midwifery services, Practice specialties	Resuscitation of the immediate newborn with positive pressure ventilation and/or chest compression. May include visualization of vocal chords and suction of the trachea.
CEEAB	Newborn care following delivery with physical examination and conference with parent, Newborn care, Midwifery services, Practice specialties	Immediate wewborn care with physical examination and assessment and conference with parent/parents. Includes state required blood screenings.
CEEAC	Newborn care at office with physical exam and conference with parent, Newborn care, Midwifery services, Practice specialties	Newborn care at office with physical examination and assessment and conference with parent/parents. Includes state required blood screenings.
CEEAE	Attachment promotion, Newborn care, Midwifery services, Practice specialties	Development of the parent-infant relationship.
CEEAF	Bottle feeding counseling, Newborn care, Midwifery services, Practice specialties	Teaching the preparation and administration of fluids to an infant via a bottle.
CEEAH	Breastfeeding assistance, Newborn care, Midwifery services, Practice specialties	Preparing a new mother to breastfeed her infant.
CEEAI	Breastfeeding education, Newborn care, Midwifery services, Practice specialties	Teaching a new mother to breastfeed her infant.
CEEAK	Infant care teaching, individual, Newborn care, Midwifery services, Practice specialties	Teaching about nurturing and physical care of infant.
CEEAL	Kangaroo care, Newborn care, Midwifery services, Practice specialties	Promoting closeness between parent and physiologically stable preterm infant by preparing the parent and providing the environment for skin-to-skin contact.
CEEAN	Neonate phototherapy, each hour, Newborn care, Midwifery services, Practice specialties	One hour period of using light therapy to reduce bilirubin levels in newborn infants.
CEEAP	Newborn monitoring, each hour during the first 48 hours, Newborn care, Midwifery services, Practice specialties	Measurement and interpretation of physiologic status of the neonate in the first 48 hours after delivery.
CEEAQ	Nonnutritive sucking, Newborn care, Midwifery services, Practice specialties	Provision of sucking opportunities for infant who is gavage fed or who can receive nothing by mouth.
CEEAS	Infant care teaching, group, Newborn care, Midwifery services, Practice specialties	Teaching a group about nurturing and physical care of infant.

Newborn care

ABC Code	Procedure Description	Expanded Definition
CEEAT	Infant nutrition teaching, individual, Newborn care, Midwifery services, Practice specialties	Individual instruction on nutrition and feeding practices during the first year of life.
CEEAU	Infant nutrition teaching, group, Newborn care, Midwifery services, Practice specialties	Instruction in a group setting on nutrition and feeding practices during the first year of life.
CEEAV	Infant safety teaching, individual, Newborn care, Midwifery services, Practice specialties	Instruction on safety during first year of life.
CEEAW	Infant safety teaching, group, Newborn care, Midwifery services, Practice specialties	Instruction in a group setting on safety during first year of life.
CEEAZ	Newborn resuscitation, initial measures, Newborn care, Midwifery services, Practice specialties	Initial administration of emergency measures to sustain life in a newborn. For additional time requirements, see code CEEBA.
CEEBA	Newborn resuscitation, each additional 15 minutes, Newborn care, Midwifery services, Practice specialties	Additional fifteen minute period of administering emergency measures to sustain life in a newborn. For initial measures, see code CEEAZ.
CEEZZ	Undefined, narrative required, Newborn care, Midwifery services, Practice specialties	Anywhere else undefined newborn midwifery procedure. Narrative required.

Family planning

ABC Code	Procedure Description	Expanded Definition
CEFAA	Contraception instruction, group, Family planning, Midwifery services, Practice specialties	Facilitating pregnancy prevention in a group setting by providing information about the physiology of reproduction and methods to control contraception.
CEFAB	Contraception instruction, individual, Family planning, Midwifery services, Practice specialties	Facilitating pregnancy prevention by providing information about the physiology of reproduction and methods to control contraception.
CEFAC	Unplanned pregnancy, Family planning, Midwifery services, Practice specialties	Facilitating decision making regarding pregnancy outcome.
CEFAD	Diaphragm, cervical cap fitting, Family planning, Midwifery services, Practice specialties	Fitting a diaphragm or cervical cap method of birth control for appropriate size and comfort.
CEFAE	Contraceptive capsule implantation, Family planning, Midwifery services, Practice specialties	Implanting contraceptive capsules containing progestogen subcutaneously (beneath the skin) in the upper arm.
CEFAF	Contraceptive capsule implant removal, Family planning, Midwifery services, Practice specialties	Removing contraceptive capsules containing progesteron subcutaenously (beneath the skin) from the upper arm.

Midwifery services

Family planning

ABC Code	Procedure Description	Expanded Definition
CEFAG	Contraceptive capsule, removal and reimplantation, Family planning, Midwifery services, Practice specialties	Removing and reimplanting contraceptive capsules containing progestogen subcutaneously (beneath the skin) from the upper arm.
CEFAH	Fertility preservation, Family planning, Midwifery services, Practice specialties	Providing information, counseling, and treatment that facilitates reproductive health and the ability to conceive.
CEFAI	Genetic counseling, Family planning, Midwifery services, Practice specialties	Use of an interactive helping process focusing on the prevention of a genetic disorder or on the ability to cope with a family member who has a genetic disorder.
CEFAJ	Infertility, Family planning, Midwifery services, Practice specialties	Management, education, and support of the patient and partner undergoing evaluation and treatment for infertility.
CEFAK	Preconception counseling, Family planning, Midwifery services, Practice specialties	Screening and counseling done before pregnancy to avoid or decrease the risk for birth defects.
CEFAL	Reproductive technology management, Family planning, Midwifery services, Practice specialties	Assisting a patient through complex infertility treatment.
CEFZZ	Undefined, narrative required, Family planning, Midwifery services, Practice specialties	Anywhere else undefined family planning procedure. Narrative required.

Naturopathic manipulation

Osseous

ABC Code	Procedure Description	Expanded Definition
CFAAA	Cervical, Osseous, Naturopathic manipulation, Practice specialties	Manipulation of the cervical vertebrae.
CFAAB	Thoracic, Osseous, Naturopathic manipulation, Practice specialties	Manipulation of the thoracic vertebrae.
CFAAC	Lumbar, Osseous, Naturopathic manipulation, Practice specialties	Manipulation of the lumbar vertebrae.
CFAAD	Sacrum, Osseous, Naturopathic manipulation, Practice specialties	Manipulation of the sacrum.
CFAAE	Coccyx, Osseous, Naturopathic manipulation, Practice specialties	Manipulation of the coccyx.

Naturopathic manipulation

Osseous

ABC Code	Procedure Description	Expanded Definition
CFAAF	One extremity, Osseous, Naturopathic manipulation, Practice specialties	Manipulation or manual therapy of a peripheral joint of the body. For additional extremities, see code CFAAG.
CFAAG	Each additional extremity, Osseous, Naturopathic manipulation, Practice specialties	Manipulation or manual therapy of an additional peripheral joint of the body. For initial extremity, see code CFAAF.
CFAAH	Multiple areas, Osseous, Naturopathic manipulation, Practice specialties	Manipulation of multiple areas of the spine or peripheral joints. For initial area, see code CFAAF.
CFAAI	Craniosacral, Osseous, Naturopathic manipulation, Practice specialties	Includes techniques which enhance the vitality of the cranial rhythmic impulse, reduce neural entrapment from exit foramen at the base of the skull, improve motion and circulation in articular and membranous restrictions.
CFAZZ	Undefined, narrative required, Osseous, Naturopathic manipulation, Practice specialties	Anywhere esle undefined manipulation or mobilization of any articulating surface. Narrative required.

Visceral

ABC Code	Procedure Description	Expanded Definition
CFBAA	Diaphragm, Visceral, Naturopathic manipulation, Practice specialties	Manipulation or manual therapy to effect mobility and motility of the diaphragm.
CFBAB	Gynecological, Visceral, Naturopathic manipulation, Practice specialties	Manipulation or manual therapy to effect mobility, motility, metabolism, secretion, excretion of the uterus or adnexal structures.
CFBAC	Liver pump, Visceral, Naturopathic manipulation, Practice specialties	Manipulation or manual therapy to effect metabolism, secretion, or excretion of the liver.
CFBAD	Prostatic massage, Visceral, Naturopathic manipulation, Practice specialties	Manipulation or manual therapy to effect metabolism, secretion, or excretion of the prostate.
CFBAE	Thoracic pump, Visceral, Naturopathic manipulation, Practice specialties	Manipulation or manual therapy to effect mobility, motility, metabolism, secretion, excretion of any thoracic organ.
CFBZZ	Undefined, narrative required, Visceral, Naturopathic manipulation, Practice specialties	Anywhere else undefined manipulation or manual therapy to any visceral organ. Narrative required.

General

ABC Code	Procedure Description	Expanded Definition

Naturopathic manipulation

General

ABC Code	Procedure Description	Expanded Definition
CFCAA	Binasal specifics, General, Naturopathic manipulation, Practice specialties	Finger cots attached to a sphygmomanometer bulb inserted into the nasal passage which quickly inflates and releases to open and mobilize the bony structures surrounding the frontal and maxillary sinuses.
CFCAB	Nasosimpatico, General, Naturopathic manipulation, Practice specialties	Aromatic oils inserted into the nasal passages to open and drain the sinuses.
CFCAC	Scar therapy, manual, General, Naturopathic manipulation, Practice specialties	Manual reduction or release of adhesions, contractures of scar tissue, or fibrosis in the body.
CFCZZ	Undefined, narrative required, General, Naturopathic manipulation, Practice specialties	Anywhere else undefined techniques using naturopathic manipulation. Narrative required.

Osteopathic manipulation

Manipulation

ABC Code	Procedure Description	Expanded Definition
CGAAA	1 or 2 body regions, Manipulation, Osteopathic manipulation, Practice specialties	Therapeutic application of manually guided forces to one or two body regions to improve physiological function and/or support homeostasis.
CGAAB	3 or 4 body regions, Manipulation, Osteopathic manipulation, Practice specialties	Therapeutic application of manually guided forces to three or four body regions to improve physiological function and/or support homeostasis.
CGAAC	5 or 6 body regions, Manipulation, Osteopathic manipulation, Practice specialties	Therapeutic application of manually guided forces to five or six body regions to improve physiological function and/or support homeostasis.
CGAAD	7 or 8 body regions, Manipulation, Osteopathic manipulation, Practice specialties	Therapeutic application of manually guided forces to seven or eight body regions to improve physiological function and/or support homeostasis.
CGAAE	9 or 10 body regions, Manipulation, Osteopathic manipulation, Practice specialties	Therapeutic application of manually guided forces to nine or ten body regions to improve physiological function and/or support homeostasis.
CGAAF	Cranial osteopathy, Manipulation, Osteopathic manipulation, Practice specialties	Evaluation of cyclic expansion and contraction of the membranous tissues through the cranial sacral mechanism and manipulation to correct membranous, articular, ligamentous strains.
CGAAG	Muscle energy technique, Manipulation, Osteopathic manipulation, Practice specialties	A manual, direct, diagnostic, and treatment technique to reduce or remove restriction in range of motion.
CGAZZ	Undefined, narrative required, Manipulation, Osteopathic manipulation, Practice specialties	Anywhere else undefined osteopathic manipulation. Narrative required.

Osteopathic manipulation

General

ABC Code	Procedure Description	Expanded Definition
CGBZZ	Undefined, narrative required, General, Osteopathic manipulation, Practice specialties	Anywhere else undefined general osteopathic procedure. Narrative required.

Indigenous medicine

Ayurvedic medicine

ABC Code	Procedure Description	Expanded Definition
CHAAA	Ahara counseling, individual, Ayurvedic medicine, Indigenous medicine, Practice specialties	Preventative or remedial counseling, including advice on how to maintain good nutrition or recommendations on the changes needed to counteract the imbalances creating an underlying cause of the presenting medical problem.
CHAAB	Netra Basti, each application, Ayurvedic medicine, Indigenous medicine, Practice specialties	Each therapeutic application of oil for eyes by provider.
CHAAC	Panchakarma therapy, each treatment day, Ayurvedic medicine, Indigenous medicine, Practice specialties	Three stage process of five major purification procedures and adjunct therapies for purifying and rejuvenating the body by reversing the disease mechanisms which carry toxic waste products from the digestive tract into the tissues. Cleansing actions may or may not include Purvakarma, Vaman, Virechan, Basti, Nasya Raktamoksha. Each treatment.
CHAAD	Raktamoksha, each treatment, Ayurvedic medicine, Indigenous medicine, Practice specialties	Purification and cleansing of the blood by releasing or liberating an excess of specific energies carried in the blood. Typically accomplished with herbs or leeches. Each treatment.
CHAAE	Shaman, Ego, each hour, Ayurvedic medicine, Indigenous medicine, Practice specialties	One hour period of supervised release of ego demands when client is too weak for other detoxification measures.
CHAAF	Shaman, moonlight, each hour, Ayurvedic medicine, Indigenous medicine, Practice specialties	One hour period of supervised night detoxification when client is too weak for other detoxification measures.
CHAAG	Shaman, water, each hour, Ayurvedic medicine, Indigenous medicine, Practice specialties	One hour period of supervised limitation of water intake when client is too weak for other detoxification measures.
CHAAH	Shaman, detoxification, each treatment, Ayurvedic medicine, Indigenous medicine, Practice specialties	Therapeutic measure by provider to release toxins when client is too weak for other detoxification measures. Each treatment.

Ayurvedic medicine

ABC Code	Procedure Description	Expanded Definition
CHAAI	Shaman, exercise, each hour, Ayurvedic medicine, Indigenous medicine, Practice specialties	One hour period of supervised exercise when client is too weak for other detoxification measures.
CHAAJ	Shaman, fast, each hour, Ayurvedic medicine, Indigenous medicine, Practice specialties	One hour period of supervised fast when client is too weak for other detoxification measures.
CHAAK	Shaman, kindling, each treatment, Ayurvedic medicine, Indigenous medicine, Practice specialties	Rekindling of digestive fire by provider to burn toxins when client is too weak for other purification measures. Each treatment.
CHAAL	Shirodhara, each application, Ayurvedic medicine, Indigenous medicine, Practice specialties	Each therapeutic application of a stream of warm oil poured on forehead.
CHAAM	Snehan, per provider, Ayurvedic medicine, Indigenous medicine, Practice specialties	External application of herbs and/or medicated oils to the entire body by two providers to induce the body to eliminate accumulated toxins; enhance secretions for elimination; lubricate and protect tissues, organs and systems from damage; and to soothe, pacify and nourish tissues and remove obstructions. Treatment per provider.
CHAAN	Swedan, Ayurvedic medicine, Indigenous medicine, Practice specialties	Supervised sudation or sweating.
CHAAO	Uttara Basti, each treatment, Ayurvedic medicine, Indigenous medicine, Practice specialties	Urethral for men or vaginal for women, application of liquids. Each treatment.
CHAAP	Vaman, each treatment, Ayurvedic medicine, Indigenous medicine, Practice specialties	Supervised emesis/vomiting therapy. Each treatment.
CHAAQ	Vihara counseling, Ayurvedic medicine, Indigenous medicine, Practice specialties	Lifestyle analysis, education and counseling, preventative or intervention oriented. Includes guidelines for daily activities to maintain optimum health and balance.
CHAAR	Virechan, each treatment, Ayurvedic medicine, Indigenous medicine, Practice specialties	Supervised purging therapy. Each treatment.
CHAAS	Anuvasana, each enema, Ayurvedic medicine, Indigenous medicine, Practice specialties	Oil enema.
CHAAT	Bruhana Basti, each treatment, Ayurvedic medicine, Indigenous medicine, Practice specialties	Introduction of nutritional liquids into the colon through the rectum to the ileocecal valve for therapeutic purification and rejuvenation of the colon. Beneficial effect on other organs, tissues and systems. Each treatment.

Ayurvedic medicine

ABC Code	Procedure Description	Expanded Definition
CHAAU	Kala Basti, each series, Ayurvedic medicine, Indigenous medicine, Practice specialties	Introduction of medicated oily liquids into the colon through the rectum to the ileocecal valve for therapeutic purification and rejuvenation of the colon. Beneficial effect on other organs, tissues and systems. Schedule of 15 enemas, 10 oils and 5 decoctions. Per series.
CHAAV	Karma Basti, each series, Ayurvedic medicine, Indigenous medicine, Practice specialties	Introduction of medicated oily liquids into the colon through the rectum to the ileocecal valve for therapeutic purification and rejuvenation of the colon. Beneficial effect on other organs, tissues and systems. Schedule of 30 enemas. Per series.
CHAAW	Matra Basti, each treatment, Ayurvedic medicine, Indigenous medicine, Practice specialties	Introduction of medicated oily liquids into the colon through the rectum to the ileocecal valve for therapeutic purification and rejuvenation of the colon. Beneficial effect on other organs, tissues and systems. Each treatment.
CHAAX	Niruha Asthapana, each treatment, Ayurvedic medicine, Indigenous medicine, Practice specialties	Decoction enema. Each treatment.
CHAAY	Yoga Basti, each series, Ayurvedic medicine, Indigenous medicine, Practice specialties	Introducing medicated oily liquids into the colon through the rectum to the ileocecal valve for therapeutic purification and rejuvenation of the colon. Beneficial effect on other organs, tissues and systems. Schedule of 8 enemas, 5 oils and 3 decoctions.
CHAAZ	Bruhana Nasya, each application, Ayurvedic medicine, Indigenous medicine, Practice specialties	Each nasal application of a nutritive solution for a positive effect. Massage of face and scalp and herbalized steam inhalation or fomentation.
CHABA	Marshya Nasya, each application, Ayurvedic medicine, Indigenous medicine, Practice specialties	Each nasal application of ghee or oil for therapeutic effect. Massage of face and scalp and herbalized steam inhalation or fomentation.
CHABB	Navaran Nasya, each application, Ayurvedic medicine, Indigenous medicine, Practice specialties	Each nasal application of a solution for a decoction effect. Massage of face and scalp and herbalized steam inhalation or fomentation.
CHABC	Pradhamana Nasya, each application, Ayurvedic medicine, Indigenous medicine, Practice specialties	Each nasal application of a dry powder or powders for a purging and cleansing effect. Massage of face and scalp and herbalized steam inhalation or fomentation.
CHABD	Prati Marshya, each application, Ayurvedic medicine, Indigenous medicine, Practice specialties	Each application of daily oil nasya.

Ayurvedic medicine

ABC Code	Procedure Description	Expanded Definition
CHABE	Shaman Nasya, each application, Ayurvedic medicine, Indigenous medicine, Practice specialties	Each nasal application of a solution for a sedative effect. Massage of face and scalp and herbalized steam inhalation or fomentation.
CHAZZ	Undefined, narrative required, Ayurvedic medicine, Indigenous medicine, Practice specialties	Anywhere else undefined Ayurvedic Medicine. Narrative required.

Native American

ABC Code	Procedure Description	Expanded Definition
CHBZZ	Undefined, narrative required, Native American, Indigenous medicine, Practice specialties	Anywhere else undefined Native American Healing. Narrative required.

Curandera

ABC Code	Procedure Description	Expanded Definition
CHCZZ	Undefined, narrative required, Curandera, Indigenous medicine, Practice specialties	Anywhere else undefined Curandera Procedures. Narrative required.

Section D: Laboratory and In-Office Procedures

Instructions

The following subsections are contained in section D:

Heart or vascular services*

Neurological*

Substance administration*
General
Injections
Insertion and removal management

Laboratory
General blood analysis
Mineral analysis
Nutritional analysis
Metabolic analysis
Blood vitamin analysis
Saliva analysis
Stool analysis
Tissue and bone
Urinalysis
General laboratory services
Organ and disease panels
Male testing
Female testing
Allergy
Sample collection

Radiology**
General (undefined code)

General procedures and services
Spectroscopy
Irradiation (undefined code)
Thermography

Any practitioner, if appropriately trained or certified, may use codes in this section, provided that the scope of practice for their state or region allows them to perform these laboratory procedures. These codes do not include the physical examination and/or treatment of the patient.

Add modifiers (provider specific) to the codes in Section D. For example, a nurse practitioner ordering a thyroid test would use the ordering code in Section A, ADYAB-1H and DEAAZ-1H for a Free T3 thyroid measurement.

*Most "Heart and vascular services" and "Neurological services" have extensive coding in CPT™. Only use ABC Codes under these headings when no appropriate service is found in CPT™. Codes DAAAI and DBBAD are not found in CPT™.

**For "Radiology" and "Minor surgery", use CPT™ codes.

Laboratory and office procedures

Heart or vascular services

Electrocardiogram

ABC Code	Procedure Description	Expanded Definition
DAAAI	CUPID (TM), cardiac ultra phase information diagnosis, each test, Electrocardiogram, Heart or vascular services, Laboratory and office procedures	Non-invasive, portable device that transforms the recordings of a conventional 12-lead ECG from time domain to frequency domain is used to diagnose major heart diseases. CUPID also gives confirmation of re-vascularization and re-perfusion suggesting endocrinologic or nervous dysfunction and helps differentiate between atrial and ventricular arrhythmias. See code ADYAA for other services.

General heart or vascular procedures

ABC Code	Procedure Description	Expanded Definition
DAFZZ	Undefined, narrative required, General heart or vascular procedures, Heart or vascular services, Laboratory and office procedures	Anywhere else undefined general heart or vascular procedures. Narrative required. Coding found in CPT (TM). Only use this code if the heart or vascular service is not found in CPT (TM).

Neurological

Nerve conduction procedures

ABC Code	Procedure Description	Expanded Definition
DBBAD	Trigger point injection, Nerve conduction procedures, Neurological, Laboratory and office procedures	The injection of a substance into the hyperirritable point in a muscle bundle. Substances may range from normal saline, B12, anesthetics to steroids.

General neurological procedures

ABC Code	Procedure Description	Expanded Definition
DBDZZ	Undefined, narrative required, General neurological procedures, Neurological, Laboratory and office procedures	Anywhere else undefined general neurological procedures. Narrative required. Coding found in CPT (TM). Only use this code if the neurological service is not found in CPT (TM).

Substance administration

General

ABC Code	Procedure Description	Expanded Definition

General

ABC Code	Procedure Description	Expanded Definition
DDAAZ	Chelation suppository, General, Substance administration, Laboratory and office procedures	The placement of an easily fusible chelating agent mass into the vagina, rectum or urethra. Oxidation therapy selectively destroys pathogenic bacteria, viruses and deactivates toxic substances without injury to healthy cells.
DDABZ	Ear medication administration, General, Substance administration, Laboratory and office procedures	Preparing and instilling otic (ear) medications.
DDACP	Chelation therapy, oral, General, Substance administration, Laboratory and office procedures	Use of an oral chelating substance for the therapeutic purpose of binding with specific detrimental materials in the blood so that they may be eliminated.
DDACS	Chelation therapy, intramuscular, General, Substance administration, Laboratory and office procedures	Use of a chelating substance, administered into the muscle, for the therapeutic purpose of binding with specific detrimental materials in the blood to eliminate them.
DDACT	Chelation therapy, intravenous, General, Substance administration, Laboratory and office procedures	Use of an intravenous solution for the purpose of binding with specific detrimental materials in the blood to eliminate them.
DDACU	Chelation therapy, subcutaneous, General, Substance administration, Laboratory and office procedures	Use of a chelating substance, administered under the skin, for the therapeutic purpose of binding with specific detrimental materials in the blood to eliminate them.
DDACZ	Eye medication administration, General, Substance administration, Laboratory and office procedures	Preparing and instilling ophthalmic (eye) medication.
DDADB	Oxidative medicine, intramuscular, General, Substance administration, Laboratory and office procedures	Use of oxidative agents, administered into the muscle, to restore oxidative balance by increasing the amount of oxygen necessary for optimal function of the body. Oxidation therapy selectively destroys pathogenic bacteria, viruses and deactivates toxic substances without injury to healthy cells.
DDADC	Oxidative medicine, intravenous, General, Substance administration, Laboratory and office procedures	Use of intravenous solution to increase the amount of oxygen in the blood to achieve a therapeutic effect. Oxidation therapy selectively destroys pathogenic bacteria, viruses and deactivates toxic substances without injury to healthy cells.

General

ABC Code	Procedure Description	Expanded Definition
DDADD	Oxidative medicine, subcutaneous, General, Substance administration, Laboratory and office procedures	Use of oxidating agents, administered under the skin, to restore balance by increasing the amount of oxygen necessary for optimal function of the body. Oxidation therapy selectively destroys pathogenic bacteria, viruses and deactivates toxic substances without injury to healthy cells.
DDADE	Transdermal, General, Substance administration, Laboratory and office procedures	Administration of medication or other therapeutic substance through the skin, as applied in ointment or patch form.
DDADF	Inhalant, General, Substance administration, Laboratory and office procedures	Administration of medication or other therapeutic substance by way of nose and trachea, or through the respiratory system.
DDADG	Sublingual, General, Substance administration, Laboratory and office procedures	Administration of medication or other therapeutic substance beneath the tongue.
DDADH	Intravenous autotransfusion, General, Substance administration, Laboratory and office procedures	Collection and reinfusion of blood which has been lost intraoperatively or postoperatively from clean wounds.
DDADK	Rectal medication administration, General, Substance administration, Laboratory and office procedures	Preparing and inserting rectal suppositories.
DDADL	Skin medication administration, General, Substance administration, Laboratory and office procedures	Preparing and applying medications to the skin.
DDADM	Suppository, General, Substance administration, Laboratory and office procedures	The placement of an easily fusible therapeutic mass into the vagina, rectum or urethra.
DDADN	Vaginal medication administration, General, Substance administration, Laboratory and office procedures	Preparing and inserting vaginal medications.
DDADQ	Total parenteral nutrition (TPN) administration, General, Substance administration, Laboratory and office procedures	Administration of full nutrition via a catheter placed in a vein that drains into the superior vena cava.
DDADR	Medication administration, ventricular reservoir, General, Substance administration, Laboratory and office procedures	Administration and monitoring of medication through an indwelling catheter into the lateral ventricle.

Substance administration

General

ABC Code	Procedure Description	Expanded Definition
DDADS	Oral medication administration, General, Substance administration, Laboratory and office procedures	Administration of medication by mouth.
DDADT	Phonophoresis, General, Substance administration, Laboratory and office procedures	The use of ultrasound to enhance the transcutaneous delivery of topically applied drugs through the transfer of ions into the tissue.
DDADU	Oral immunization, General, Substance administration, Laboratory and office procedures	Provision of immunization for prevention of communicable disease. Single dose oral immunization.
DDAZZ	Undefined, narrative required, General, Substance administration, Laboratory and office procedures	Anywhere else undefined substance administration. Narrative required.

Injections

ABC Code	Procedure Description	Expanded Definition
DDBAZ	Epidural medication administration, Injections, Substance administration, Laboratory and office procedures	Preparing and administering medications via the space surrounding the dural membrane.
DDBBJ	Intramuscular administration of autogenous solution, Injections, Substance administration, Laboratory and office procedures	Administration of a solution with components which originated from the patient (i.e. the patients own blood products) by injection into the muscle for therapeutic purposes.
DDBBK	Diagnostic intravenous, initial substance, Injections, Substance administration, Laboratory and office procedures	Use of intravenous route and solution to introduce a single substance for diagnostic purposes. For additional substance requirements see code DDBBL.
DDBBL	Diagnostic intravenous, each additional substance, Injections, Substance administration, Laboratory and office procedures	Use of intravenous route and solution to introduce additional substances for diagnostic purposes. Each additional substance. For initial substance see code DDBBK.
DDBBM	Enteral tube infusion, Injections, Substance administration, Laboratory and office procedures	Delivery of substance or substances introduced through a gastrointestinal tube using the force of gravity.
DDBBN	Enteral tube injection, Injections, Substance administration, Laboratory and office procedures	Forcing a substance or substances for delivery through a gastrointestinal tube.
DDBBO	Intrapleural infusion, Injections, Substance administration, Laboratory and office procedures	Administration of substance or substances through an intrapleural infusion for therapeutic purposes.

Injections

ABC Code	Procedure Description	Expanded Definition
DDBBP	Intrapleural injection, Injections, Substance administration, Laboratory and office procedures	Administration of substance or substances through an intrapleural injection for therapeutic purposes.
DDBBQ	Intra arterial, one substance, Injections, Substance administration, Laboratory and office procedures	Administration of a single substance into an artery for therapeutic purposes.
DDBBR	Intra arterial, two or more substances, Injections, Substance administration, Laboratory and office procedures	Administration of two or more substances into an artery for therapeutic purposes.
DDBBS	Intracutaneous, one substance, Injections, Substance administration, Laboratory and office procedures	Administration of a single substance within the layers of skin for therapeutic purposes.
DDBBT	Intracutaneous, two or more substances, Injections, Substance administration, Laboratory and office procedures	Administration of two or more substances within the layers of skin for therapeutic purposes.
DDBBV	Intramuscular, one substance, Injections, Substance administration, Laboratory and office procedures	Administration of a single substance by injection into the muscle for therapeutic purposes.
DDBBW	Intramuscular, two or more substances, Injections, Substance administration, Laboratory and office procedures	Administration of two or more substances by injection into the muscle for therapeutic purposes.
DDBBZ	Intradermal medication administration, Injections, Substance administration, Laboratory and office procedures	Preparing and giving medications via the intradermal route.
DDBCA	Intraspinal infusion, Injections, Substance administration, Laboratory and office procedures	Administration of substances within the spine by infusion, using the force of gravity, for therapeutic purposes.
DDBCB	Intraspinal injection, Injections, Substance administration, Laboratory and office procedures	Administration of substances within the spine by injection for therapeutic purposes.
DDBCF	Percutaneous, sequential and incremental, Injections, Substance administration, Laboratory and office procedures	Administration of substance or substances by injection through the skin.
DDBCH	Percutaneous, 1 substance, Injections, Substance administration, Laboratory and office procedures	Administration of a single substance by injection through the skin.

Injections

ABC Code	Procedure Description	Expanded Definition
DDBCI	Percutaneous, 2 or more substances, Injections, Substance administration, Laboratory and office procedures	Administration of two or more substances by injection through the skin.
DDBCJ	Peripherally inserted central catheter infusion, Injections, Substance administration, Laboratory and office procedures	Administration of substance or substances by infusion, using the force of gravity, into a peripherally inserted central catheter.
DDBCK	Peripherally inserted central catheter injection, Injections, Substance administration, Laboratory and office procedures	Administration of substance or substances by injection into a peripherally inserted central catheter.
DDBCL	Shunt infusion, Injections, Substance administration, Laboratory and office procedures	Administration of substance or substances by infusion, using the force of gravity, into a shunt.
DDBCM	Shunt, 1 substance, Injections, Substance administration, Laboratory and office procedures	Administration of substance or substances by injection into a shunt.
DDBCN	Shunt, 2 or more substances, Injections, Substance administration, Laboratory and office procedures	Administration of two or more substances by injection into a shunt.
DDBCO	Single injection vaccination, one substance, Injections, Substance administration, Laboratory and office procedures	Immunization for prevention of communicable disease. Single injection of one substance. For two or more substances, see code DDBCP.
DDBCP	Single injection vaccination, two or more substances, Injections, Substance administration, Laboratory and office procedures	Immunization for prevention of communicable disease. Single injection of two or more substances. For one substance, see code DDBCO.
DDBCQ	Allergy injection with provision of extracts, initial injection, Injections, Substance administration, Laboratory and office procedures	Initial injection of specific allergen extract that can be used for diagnostic or therapeutic purposes. See code DDBDB for additional injections
DDBCR	Allergy injection without provision of extracts, initial injection, Injections, Substance administration, Laboratory and office procedures	Initial injection of allergen solution for therapeutic purposes. See code DDBDC for additional injections.
DDBCS	Skin end point titration, 1 injection, Injections, Substance administration, Laboratory and office procedures	Intradermal test using a single allergen extract to determine sensitivity to various drugs, materials, foods and/or pollens.

Injections

ABC Code	Procedure Description	Expanded Definition
DDBCT	Skin end point titration, 2 or more injections, Injections, Substance administration, Laboratory and office procedures	Intradermal test using two or more allergen extracts to determine sensitivity to various drugs, materials, foods and/or pollens.
DDBCV	Subcutaneous, 1 substance, Injections, Substance administration, Laboratory and office procedures	Administration of a single substance by injection just beneath the skin.
DDBCW	Subcutaneous, 2 or more substances, Injections, Substance administration, Laboratory and office procedures	Administration of two or more substances by injection just beneath the skin.
DDBDB	Allergy injection with provision of extracts, each additional injection, Injections, Substance administration, Laboratory and office procedures	Each additional injection of specific allergen extracts that can be used for diagnostic or therapeutic purposes. See code DDBCQ for initial injection.
DDBDC	Allergy injection without provision of extracts, each additional injection, Injections, Substance administration, Laboratory and office procedures	Each additional injection of allergen solutions for therapeutic purposes. See code DDBCR for initial injection.
DDBDD	Rapid intravenous fluid resuscitation, Injections, Substance administration, Laboratory and office procedures	Administering prescribed intravenous fluids at full gravity flow capacity. May or may not also include manual pressure on bag to speed up delivery during emergencies.
DDBDG	Analgesic intravenous administration, Injections, Substance administration, Laboratory and office procedures	Use of medication by intravenous route to reduce or eliminate pain.
DDBDH	Analgesic intramuscular administration, Injections, Substance administration, Laboratory and office procedures	Use of medication by intramuscular route to reduce or eliminate pain.
DDBDI	Local anesthesia administration, Injections, Substance administration, Laboratory and office procedures	Administration of anesthesia by injection to a defined area of the body.
DDBDJ	Intravenous insertion, Injections, Substance administration, Laboratory and office procedures	Insertion of a needle into a peripheral vein for the purpose of administering fluids, blood or medications.
DDBDK	Intravenous blood products administration, Injections, Substance administration, Laboratory and office procedures	Use of intravenous route for purpose of administering blood products for therapeutic purposes.

Injections

ABC Code	Procedure Description	Expanded Definition
DDBDL	Therapeutic intravenous infusion, initial substance, Injections, Substance administration, Laboratory and office procedures	Use of a solution delivered through the intravenous route for therapeutic purposes. For additional substance requirements see code DDBCY.
DDBDM	Therapeutic intravenous infusion, each additional substance, Injections, Substance administration, Laboratory and office procedures	Use of a solution delivered through the intravenous route for therapeutic purposes. Each additional substance. For initial substances see code DDBCX.
DDBZZ	Undefined, narrative required, Injections, Substance administration, Laboratory and office procedures	Anywhere else undefined use of injections. Narrative required.

Insertion and removal management

ABC Code	Procedure Description	Expanded Definition
DDCAC	Airway insertion and stabilization, non tracheotomy, Insertion and removal management, Substance administration, Laboratory and office procedures	Insertion, or assistance with insertion, and stabilization of an artificial airway.
DDCAG	Chest tube placement for drainage, Insertion and removal management, Substance administration, Laboratory and office procedures	Placement of external water-seal drainage device exiting the chest cavity.
DDCAL	Enteral tube placement, Insertion and removal management, Substance administration, Laboratory and office procedures	Placement of a tube directly into the digestive tract for the purpose of delivering substances.
DDCAP	Gastrointestinal tube placement, intubation, Insertion and removal management, Substance administration, Laboratory and office procedures	Insertion of a tube into the stomach or intestinal tract.
DDCAQ	Gastrointestinal tube removal, extubation, Insertion and removal management, Substance administration, Laboratory and office procedures	Removal of a tube from the stomach or intestinal tract.
DDCAU	Insertion of invasive hemodynamic line, Insertion and removal management, Substance administration, Laboratory and office procedures	Insertion of a venous or arterial line for multiple purposes.
DDCAW	Intrapleural tube placement for substance administration, Insertion and removal management, Substance administration, Laboratory and office procedures	Interpleural catheter for substance administration.

Substance administration

Insertion and removal management

ABC Code	Procedure Description	Expanded Definition
DDCAX	Pediatric intraosseous medication administration, Insertion and removal management, Substance administration, Laboratory and office procedures	Insertion of a needle through the bone cortex of an infant into the medullary cavity for the purpose of short term emergency administration of fluid, blood, or medication.
DDCAZ	Intrapleural tube placement for drainage, Insertion and removal management, Substance administration, Laboratory and office procedures	Insertion of a chest tube for drainage.
DDCBA	Intraspinal tube placement for substance administration, Insertion and removal management, Substance administration, Laboratory and office procedures	Insertion of a tube into the spine for substance administration.
DDCBH	Peripherally inserted central catheter placement, Insertion and removal management, Substance administration, Laboratory and office procedures	Insertion of a peripheral intravenous line.
DDCBJ	Invasive hemodynamic line removal, Insertion and removal management, Substance administration, Laboratory and office procedures	Removal of an invasive hemodynamic line as appropriate.
DDCBM	Umbilical line, tube placement, Insertion and removal management, Substance administration, Laboratory and office procedures	Placement of a tube into the umbilicus for venous or arterial access.
DDCBN	Urinary catheter placement, Insertion and removal management, Substance administration, Laboratory and office procedures	Insertion and/or removal of a hollow, flexible tube into the bladder for drainage of urine.
DDCBZ	Endotracheal extubation, Insertion and removal management, Substance administration, Laboratory and office procedures	Removal of an endotracheal tube from the nasopharyngeal or oropharyngeal airway.
DDCZY	Undefined, narrative required, Insertion and removal management, Substance administration, Laboratory and office procedures	Anywhere else undefined insertion and removal management. Narrative required.

Laboratory

General blood analysis

ABC Code	Procedure Description	Expanded Definition

General blood analysis

ABC Code	Procedure Description	Expanded Definition
DEAAZ	Free T3, General blood analysis, Laboratory, Laboratory and office procedures	Measurement of an active thyroid hormone.
DEABF	Enzyme isolation, General blood analysis, Laboratory, Laboratory and office procedures	Isolating enzymes in general blood analysis.
DEABW	Comprehensive melatonin profile, General blood analysis, Laboratory, Laboratory and office procedures	Salivary assessment that analyzes the secretion pattern of the hormone crucial for healthy sleep patterns, antioxidant defense, proper immune response, and balanced endocrine function.
DEABZ	Glucose tolerance test, initial hour, General blood analysis, Laboratory, Laboratory and office procedures	Initial hour of blood glucose level analysis after glucose injection or ingestion.
DEACB	Glucose assay, testing, each report, General blood analysis, Laboratory, Laboratory and office procedures	Analysis of glucose levels in blood.
DEACE	Liver function panel, liver profile, General blood analysis, Laboratory, Laboratory and office procedures	Series of blood chemistry tests that detects changes in the way the liver is making new substances, breaking down and/or excreting old ones and whether liver cells are healthy or being damaged.
DEACF	GGT Panel, General blood analysis, Laboratory, Laboratory and office procedures	Gamma Glutamyl Transferase (GGT) analysis, provides information about liver function or damage.
DEACG	Caffeine clearance, General blood analysis, Laboratory, Laboratory and office procedures	This test is a sensitive indicator of biological detoxification status.
DEACH	Glyco hemoglobin, General blood analysis, Laboratory, Laboratory and office procedures	Analysis of glycosylated hemoglobin levels in blood.
DEACI	TT3, total RIA, General blood analysis, Laboratory, Laboratory and office procedures	Resin tri-iodothyronine uptake; T3 uptake ratio; T3UR; used in confirming diagnosis of hyperthyroidism or hypothyroidism.
DEACJ	Thyroid hormone binding ratio, General blood analysis, Laboratory, Laboratory and office procedures	Analysis of thyroid hormone binding ratio (THBR), useful in determining whether thyroid hormone changes are due to thyroid disease or to abnormalities in thyroxine-binding globulin (TBG).
DEACK	Proinsulin assay, General blood analysis, Laboratory, Laboratory and office procedures	Analysis of proinsulin levels in blood, a precursor of insulin, normally less than or equal to 20% of total insulin.
DEACN	Thyroid stimulating hormone, General blood analysis, Laboratory, Laboratory and office procedures	Analysis of thyroid stimulating hormone (TSH) levels in blood, helpful in differentiating primary hypothyroidism from other causes.

General blood analysis

ABC Code	Procedure Description	Expanded Definition
DEACO	Pure thyroxine assay, total free T4, General blood analysis, Laboratory, Laboratory and office procedures	Measurement of biologically active thyroxin.
DEACP	Thyroid uptake T3 or T4, General blood analysis, Laboratory, Laboratory and office procedures	Measurement of resin-binding capacity of serum thyroid hormone.
DEACQ	24 hour thyroid profile, each report, General blood analysis, Laboratory, Laboratory and office procedures	Analysis over a 24-hour period of any of the thyroid tests, see DEACO, DEACP.
DEACR	Low density lipoprotein testing, General blood analysis, Laboratory, Laboratory and office procedures	Analysis of low density lipoprotein (LDL) level in blood.
DEACS	Glucose tolerance test, 2 hours, General blood analysis, Laboratory, Laboratory and office procedures	Analysis of blood glucose level, 2 hours after glucose injection or ingestion.
DEACT	Glucose tolerance test, 3 hours, General blood analysis, Laboratory, Laboratory and office procedures	Analysis of blood glucose level, 3 hours after glucose injection or ingestion.
DEACU	Glucose tolerance test, each additional hour beyond four hours, General blood analysis, Laboratory, Laboratory and office procedures	Additional hour of analysis of blood glucose levels after fasting; then, after an injection or ingestion of glucose. For initial time, see code DEACV.
DEACV	Glucose tolerance test, initial four hours, General blood analysis, Laboratory, Laboratory and office procedures	Analysis of blood glucose levels after fasting; then, after an injection or ingestion of glucose, again at 30 minutes, 1 hour, 90 minutes, 2 hours, and 3 hours. For additional time, see code DEACU.
DEAZZ	Undefined, narrative required, General blood analysis, Laboratory, Laboratory and office procedures	Anywhere else undefined general blood analysis. Narrative required.

Mineral analysis

ABC Code	Procedure Description	Expanded Definition
DEBAA	Beta carotene, Mineral analysis, Laboratory, Laboratory and office procedures	Measurement of Beta carotene level. Mineral analyses can be performed on a variety of physical substances such as hair, blood, urine etc.
DEBAB	Calcium, total, Mineral analysis, Laboratory, Laboratory and office procedures	Measurement of Calcium level. Mineral analyses can be performed on a variety of physical substances such as hair, blood, urine etc.

Mineral analysis

ABC Code	Procedure Description	Expanded Definition
DEBAC	Chloride, Mineral analysis, Laboratory, Laboratory and office procedures	Measurement of Chloride level. Mineral analyses can be performed on a variety of physical substances such as hair, blood, urine etc.
DEBAD	Iron, Mineral analysis, Laboratory, Laboratory and office procedures	Measurement of Iron level. Mineral analyses can be performed on a variety of physical substances such as hair, blood, urine etc.
DEBAE	Magnesium, Mineral analysis, Laboratory, Laboratory and office procedures	Measurement of Magnesium level. Mineral analyses can be performed on a variety of physical substances such as hair, blood, urine etc.
DEBAF	Phosphorus, Mineral analysis, Laboratory, Laboratory and office procedures	Measurement of Phosphorus level. Mineral analyses can be performed on a variety of physical substances such as hair, blood, urine etc.
DEBAG	Potassium, Mineral analysis, Laboratory, Laboratory and office procedures	Measurement of Potassium level. Mineral analyses can be performed on a variety of physical substances such as hair, blood, urine etc.
DEBAH	Selenium, Mineral analysis, Laboratory, Laboratory and office procedures	Measurement of Selenium level. Mineral analyses can be performed on a variety of physical substances such as hair, blood, urine etc.
DEBAI	Serum ferritin, Mineral analysis, Laboratory, Laboratory and office procedures	Measurement of Serum Ferritin level. Mineral analyses can be performed on a variety of physical substances such as hair, blood, urine etc.
DEBAJ	Serum sodium, Mineral analysis, Laboratory, Laboratory and office procedures	Measurement of Serum Sodium level. Mineral analyses can be performed on a variety of physical substances such as hair, blood, urine etc.
DEBAK	Total iron binding capacity, Mineral analysis, Laboratory, Laboratory and office procedures	Measurement of total iron binding capacity. Mineral analyses can be performed on a variety of physical substances such as hair, blood, urine etc.
DEBAL	Serum manganese, Mineral analysis, Laboratory, Laboratory and office procedures	Measurement of Serum Manganese level. Mineral analyses can be performed on a variety of physical substances such as hair, blood, urine etc.
DEBAM	Zinc, Mineral analysis, Laboratory, Laboratory and office procedures	Measurement of Zinc level. Mineral analyses can be performed on a variety of physical substances such as hair, blood, urine etc.
DEBAN	Copper, Mineral analysis, Laboratory, Laboratory and office procedures	Measurement of Copper level. Mineral analyses can be performed on a variety of physical substances such as hair, blood, urine etc.

Mineral analysis

ABC Code	Procedure Description	Expanded Definition
DEBAO	Electrolyte panel, complete, Mineral analysis, Laboratory, Laboratory and office procedures	Analysis of electrolyte levels, used to evaluate acid-base balance. Mineral analyses can be performed on a variety of physical substances such as hair, blood, urine etc.
DEBAP	Manganese, Mineral analysis, Laboratory, Laboratory and office procedures	Measurement of Manganese level. Mineral analyses can be performed on a variety of physical substances such as hair, blood, urine etc.
DEBAQ	Arsenic, Mineral analysis, Laboratory, Laboratory and office procedures	Measurement of Arsenic level, to assess toxicity. Mineral analyses can be performed on a variety of physical substances such as hair, blood, urine etc.
DEBAR	Lead, Mineral analysis, Laboratory, Laboratory and office procedures	Measurement of Lead level, to assess toxicity. Mineral analyses can be performed on a variety of physical substances such as hair, blood, urine etc.
DEBAS	Mercury, Mineral analysis, Laboratory, Laboratory and office procedures	Measurement of Mercury level, to assess toxicity. Mineral analyses can be performed on a variety of physical substances such as hair, blood, urine etc.
DEBAT	Cadmium, Mineral analysis, Laboratory, Laboratory and office procedures	Measurement of Cadmium level, to assess toxicity. Mineral analyses can be performed on a variety of physical substances such as hair, blood, urine, etc.
DEBAU	Calcium, ionized, Mineral analysis, Laboratory, Laboratory and office procedures	Measurement of biologically active calcium. Mineral analyses can be performed on a variety of physical substances such as hair, blood, urine, etc.
DEBAV	Chromium, Mineral analysis, Laboratory, Laboratory and office procedures	Measurement of Chromium level. Mineral analyses can be performed on a variety of physical substances such as hair, blood, urine, etc.
DEBAW	ELISA ACT LRA diagnostic benzoate test block, Mineral analysis, Laboratory, Laboratory and office procedures	Testing for 74 items including Benzene, Phthalates, Phthalide and toxic minerals.
DEBAX	ELISA ACT LRA diagnostic sulfite test block, Mineral analysis, Laboratory, Laboratory and office procedures	Testing for 40 items including food coloring, saccharine, sulfite, metabusulfite, additives, preservatives, crustaceans, dairy, cheese, fish and fowl.
DEBAY	ELISA ACT LRA screening toxic mineral and or metal block 8, Mineral analysis, Laboratory, Laboratory and office procedures	Testing for Aluminum, Arsenic, Cadmium, Gold, Lead, Mercury, Nickel (II) Chloride, Silver.
DEBAZ	Magnesium, ionized, Mineral analysis, Laboratory, Laboratory and office procedures	Measurement of biologically active magnesium. Mineral analyses can be performed on a variety of physical substances such as hair, blood, urine, etc.

Mineral analysis

ABC Code	Procedure Description	Expanded Definition
DEBBA	Molybdenum, Mineral analysis, Laboratory, Laboratory and office procedures	Measurement of Molybdenum level. Mineral analyses can be performed on a variety of physical substances such as hair, blood, urine, etc.
DEBBB	Nickel, Mineral analysis, Laboratory, Laboratory and office procedures	Measurement of Nickel level, to assess toxicity. Mineral analyses can be performed on a variety of physical substances such as hair, blood, urine, etc.
DEBBC	Silver, Mineral analysis, Laboratory, Laboratory and office procedures	Measurement of Silver level, to assess toxicity. Mineral analyses can be performed on a variety of physical substances such as hair, blood, urine, etc.
DEBBD	Strontium, Mineral analysis, Laboratory, Laboratory and office procedures	Measurement of Strontium level, to assess toxicity. Mineral analyses can be performed on a variety of physical substances such as hair, blood, urine, etc.
DEBBE	Vanadium, Mineral analysis, Laboratory, Laboratory and office procedures	Measurement of Vanadium level. Mineral analyses can be performed on a variety of physical substances such as hair, blood, urine, etc.
DEBZZ	Undefined, narrative required, Mineral analysis, Laboratory, Laboratory and office procedures	Anywhere else undefined Mineral Analysis.

Nutritional analysis

ABC Code	Procedure Description	Expanded Definition
DECAA	Elemental analysis hair, 34 elements plus 4 ratios, Nutritional analysis, Laboratory, Laboratory and office procedures	Analysis of hair for levels of 34 elements, using certain comparisons that commonly include sodium and potassium, calcium and magnesium, zinc and copper, among others.
DECAB	Elemental analysis urine, 18 elements, random, timed or 24 hour, Nutritional analysis, Laboratory, Laboratory and office procedures	Analysis of urine for levels of 18 elements, using random or timed samples or samples collected over a 24-hour period.
DECAC	Elemental analysis urine, provocative pre and post challenge, Nutritional analysis, Laboratory, Laboratory and office procedures	Analysis of urine for elemental levels, using an agent (such as penicillamine or other complexing agents) to mobilize elements into urine to assess tissue mineral status.
DECAD	Elemental analysis packed erythrocytes, Nutritional analysis, Laboratory, Laboratory and office procedures	Analyzing packed erythrocytes on an elemental and quantitative basis.
DECAE	Amino acid analysis, qualitative, 44 metabolites, urine, Nutritional analysis, Laboratory, Laboratory and office procedures	An assessment of an increase or decrease of the protein building block categories in a blood sample.

Nutritional analysis

ABC Code	Procedure Description	Expanded Definition
DECAF	Amino acid analysis, quantitative, 44 metabolites, urine, Nutritional analysis, Laboratory, Laboratory and office procedures	Measures the levels of 44 metabolites to analyze amino acids in urine.
DECAG	Amino acid analysis, 44 metabolites, plasma, Nutritional analysis, Laboratory, Laboratory and office procedures	Measures the levels of 44 metabolites to analyze amino acids in plasma.
DECAH	Comprehensive vitamin profile, 17 vitamins, Nutritional analysis, Laboratory, Laboratory and office procedures	Measures the levels of 16 vitamins in a comprehensive vitamin screen.
DECAI	Vitamin profile, 12 vitamins, Nutritional analysis, Laboratory, Laboratory and office procedures	Measures the levels of 12 vitamins in a vitamin screen.
DECAJ	Essential and metabolic fatty acid analysis, 44 metabolites, Nutritional analysis, Laboratory, Laboratory and office procedures	Measures the levels of 44 metabolites to analyze essential and metabolic fatty acids.
DECAK	Intestinal permeability, urine, Nutritional analysis, Laboratory, Laboratory and office procedures	Directly measures the ability of two nonmetabolized sugar molecules, mannitol and lactulose to enter the intestinal mucosa as markers of permeability. After ingesting, they are recovered in the urine over the following 6 hours.
DECAL	Heidelberg test, Nutritional analysis, Laboratory, Laboratory and office procedures	Measurement of stomach acid by telemetry.
DECZZ	Undefined, narrative required, Nutritional analysis, Laboratory, Laboratory and office procedures	Anywhere else undefined nutritional analysis. Narrative required.

Metabolic analysis

ABC Code	Procedure Description	Expanded Definition
DEDAA	Comprehensive detoxification profile, Metabolic analysis, Laboratory, Laboratory and office procedures	Detailed metabolic analysis for a comprehensive detoxification profile.
DEDAB	Basic detoxification profile, Metabolic analysis, Laboratory, Laboratory and office procedures	Basic metabolic analysis for a detoxification profile.
DEDAC	Oxidative stress, Metabolic analysis, Laboratory, Laboratory and office procedures	Use of peroxide or other oxidants to determine resistance to oxidation.

Metabolic analysis

ABC Code	Procedure Description	Expanded Definition
DEDAD	Oxidative stress, blood and urine, Metabolic analysis, Laboratory, Laboratory and office procedures	Use of peroxide or other oxidants to determine resistance to oxidation in blood and/or urine.
DEDAE	Antioxidant defense profile, Metabolic analysis, Laboratory, Laboratory and office procedures	Assessment of levels of multiple free-radical protectors.
DEDAF	Cotinine analysis, Metabolic analysis, Laboratory, Laboratory and office procedures	Measurement of Cotinine level, a by-product of cigarette smoking.
DEDZZ	Undefined, narrative required, Metabolic analysis, Laboratory, Laboratory and office procedures	Anywhere else undefined Metabolic Analysis.

Blood vitamin analysis

ABC Code	Procedure Description	Expanded Definition
DEEAA	Vitamin A, Blood vitamin analysis, Laboratory, Laboratory and office procedures	Analysis of Vitamin A level in blood, for diagnostic and therapeutic purposes.
DEEAB	Biotin, each report, Blood vitamin analysis, Laboratory, Laboratory and office procedures	Analysis of Biotin level in blood, for diagnostic and therapeutic purposes.
DEEAC	Niacin, each report, Blood vitamin analysis, Laboratory, Laboratory and office procedures	Analysis of Niacin level in blood, for diagnostic and therapeutic purposes.
DEEAD	Vitamin B-2, Blood vitamin analysis, Laboratory, Laboratory and office procedures	Analysis of Vitamin B-2 level in blood, for diagnostic and therapeutic purposes.
DEEAE	Vitamin B-12, Blood vitamin analysis, Laboratory, Laboratory and office procedures	Analysis of Vitamin B-12 level in blood, for diagnostic and therapeutic purposes.
DEEAF	Vitamin C, Blood vitamin analysis, Laboratory, Laboratory and office procedures	Analysis of Vitamin C level in blood, for diagnostic and therapeutic purposes.
DEEAG	Choline, free, Blood vitamin analysis, Laboratory, Laboratory and office procedures	Analysis of Free Choline level in blood, for diagnostic and therapeutic purposes.
DEEAH	Choline, total, Blood vitamin analysis, Laboratory, Laboratory and office procedures	Analysis of Total Choline level in blood, for diagnostic and therapeutic purposes.
DEEAI	Carnitine, Blood vitamin analysis, Laboratory, Laboratory and office procedures	Analysis of Carnitine level in blood, for diagnostic and therapeutic purposes.
DEEAJ	Vitamin E, Blood vitamin analysis, Laboratory, Laboratory and office procedures	Analysis of Vitamin E level in blood, for diagnostic and therapeutic purposes.

Laboratory

Blood vitamin analysis

ABC Code	Procedure Description	Expanded Definition
DEEAK	Folate serum, Blood vitamin analysis, Laboratory, Laboratory and office procedures	Analysis of Folate Serum level in blood, for diagnostic and therapeutic purposes.
DEEAL	Vitamin B 6, Blood vitamin analysis, Laboratory, Laboratory and office procedures	Analysis of Vitamin B-6 level in blood, for diagnostic and therapeutic purposes.
DEEAM	Vitamin B 1, Blood vitamin analysis, Laboratory, Laboratory and office procedures	Analysis of Vitamin B-1 level in blood, for diagnostic and therapeutic purposes.
DEEAN	Vitamin D, Blood vitamin analysis, Laboratory, Laboratory and office procedures	Analysis of Vitamin D level in blood, for diagnostic and therapeutic purposes.
DEEAO	Biopterin, Blood vitamin analysis, Laboratory, Laboratory and office procedures	Analysis of Biopterin level in blood, for diagnostic and therapeutic purposes.
DEEAP	Inositol, Blood vitamin analysis, Laboratory, Laboratory and office procedures	Analysis of Inositol level in blood, for diagnostic and therapeutic purposes.
DEEAQ	Pantothenic acid, Blood vitamin analysis, Laboratory, Laboratory and office procedures	Analysis of Pantothenic acid level in blood, for diagnostic and therapeutic purposes.
DEEZY	Undefined, narrative required, Blood vitamin analysis, Laboratory, Laboratory and office procedures	Anywhere else undefined blood vitamin analysis. Narrative required.

Saliva analysis

ABC Code	Procedure Description	Expanded Definition
DEFAA	Adrenocortex stress profile, Saliva analysis, Laboratory, Laboratory and office procedures	The evaluation of the bioactive levels of the stress hormones, cortisol and DHEA of the body over a 24 hour period.
DEFAB	Antigliadin or gluten antibodies, Saliva analysis, Laboratory, Laboratory and office procedures	A test for the reactivity or sensitivity of a person to the gliadin or gluten in wheat and other grains.
DEFZZ	Undefined, narrative required, Saliva analysis, Laboratory, Laboratory and office procedures	Anywhere else undefined saliva analysis. Narrative required.

Stool analysis

ABC Code	Procedure Description	Expanded Definition
DEGAA	Comprehensive ovum and parasite, 1 test, Stool analysis, Laboratory, Laboratory and office procedures	Microscopic analysis of stool sample for various stages of development of parasites, ova or larvae to diagnose parasitic infestation of the intestinal tract.

Stool analysis

ABC Code	Procedure Description	Expanded Definition
DEGAB	Comprehensive parasitology, two tests, Stool analysis, Laboratory, Laboratory and office procedures	Parasitology profile evaluates stool for presence of parasites and levels of beneficial flora, imbalanced flora, pathogenic bacteria, and yeast. For patients with abdominal pain, chronic diarrhea, and other GI-related symptoms.
DEGAC	Comprehensive parasitology, 3 tests, Stool analysis, Laboratory, Laboratory and office procedures	Parasitology profile evaluates stool for presence of parasites and levels of beneficial flora, imbalanced flora, pathogenic bacteria, and yeast. For patients with abdominal pain, chronic diarrhea, and other GI-related symptoms.
DEGAD	Comprehensive digestive stool analysis, without parasitology, Stool analysis, Laboratory, Laboratory and office procedures	Analysis of the stool to assess the digestion and absorption, bacterial balance and metabolism, yeast and immune status.
DEGAE	Comprehensive parasitology profile, with microbial and yeast, 1 sample, Stool analysis, Laboratory, Laboratory and office procedures	Determines stool, parasites, pathogens and yeasts. 1 sample.
DEGAF	Comprehensive parasitology profile, with microbial and yeast, 2 samples, Stool analysis, Laboratory, Laboratory and office procedures	Determines stool parasites, pathogens and yeasts. 2 samples.
DEGAG	Comprehensive parasitology profile, with microbial and yeast, 3 samples, Stool analysis, Laboratory, Laboratory and office procedures	Determines stool parasites, pathogens and yeasts. 3 samples.
DEGAH	Comprehensive bacteriology, Stool analysis, Laboratory, Laboratory and office procedures	Stool analysis of bacterial content.
DEGAI	Candida culture, Stool analysis, Laboratory, Laboratory and office procedures	Stool culture which determines type and quantity of candida albicans.
DEGAJ	Digestive function, Stool analysis, Laboratory, Laboratory and office procedures	Analysis of the quantity and effectiveness of the digestive enzymes, gastric excretions, gallbladder and liver function that breakdown of fats, protiens and sugars into absorbable nutrients in the GI tract.
DEGAK	EIA procedure, Stool analysis, Laboratory, Laboratory and office procedures	Stool enzyme immunoassay.
DEGAL	Fecal fatty acids, short chain, Stool analysis, Laboratory, Laboratory and office procedures	Stool analysis of short chain fatty acid content.
DEGAM	Fecal fat, 24, 48 or 72 hours, Stool analysis, Laboratory, Laboratory and office procedures	Stool analysis of the fecal fat content of the specimen taken at 24, 48 and 72 hours.

Stool analysis

ABC Code	Procedure Description	Expanded Definition
DEGAN	Fecal Sig A, Stool analysis, Laboratory, Laboratory and office procedures	Analysis of the stool immune-antibody status.
DEGAO	Giardia, specific, each report, Stool analysis, Laboratory, Laboratory and office procedures	Parasitology test specific for Giardia Lamblia inhabitants in the stool.
DEGAP	Hemoccult, blood stool analysis, 1 to 3 tests, Stool analysis, Laboratory, Laboratory and office procedures	Stool occult blood analysis.
DEGAQ	Microbiology analysis, Stool analysis, Laboratory, Laboratory and office procedures	Extensive analysis and identification of the micro-organisms found in a stool culture.
DEGAR	Parasitology, one sample, Stool analysis, Laboratory, Laboratory and office procedures	Determination of the stool content of parasites and their eggs.
DEGAS	Parasitology, 2 samples, Stool analysis, Laboratory, Laboratory and office procedures	Stool parasites, two samples.
DEGAT	Parasitology, 3 samples, Stool analysis, Laboratory, Laboratory and office procedures	Stool parasites, three samples.
DEGAU	Urobilinogen, quantitative, Stool analysis, Laboratory, Laboratory and office procedures	Analysis of the amount of stool urobilinogen indicating pathogen overgrowth.
DEGAV	Bilirubin, Stool analysis, Laboratory, Laboratory and office procedures	Measurement of the stool bilirubin content.
DEGAW	Trypsin, qualitative, Stool analysis, Laboratory, Laboratory and office procedures	Stool enzyme screen.
DEGAX	Trypsin, quantitative, Stool analysis, Laboratory, Laboratory and office procedures	Stool enzyme, quantitative measurement.
DEGAY	Carbohydrates, Stool analysis, Laboratory, Laboratory and office procedures	Stool carbohydrate management.
DEGBA	Fecal or body fluid pH, Stool analysis, Laboratory, Laboratory and office procedures	Stool acid/alkaline (pH) measurement.
DEGBB	Bowel transit times, Stool analysis, Laboratory, Laboratory and office procedures	Measurement of the time for food or test material to transit through the complete gastro-intestinal tract.
DEGBC	Colitis toxins, type A and B, Stool analysis, Laboratory, Laboratory and office procedures	Analysis of type A and B toxins associated with the occurance of colitis.
DEGBD	Cryptosporidium antigen, Stool analysis, Laboratory, Laboratory and office procedures	Immuno Assay for Cryptosporidium antigen.

Laboratory

Stool analysis

ABC Code	Procedure Description	Expanded Definition
DEGBE	Total intestinal secretory IgA, Stool analysis, Laboratory, Laboratory and office procedures	Quantitative assay of Intestinal mucosa levels of secretory IgA.
DEGBF	Intestinal Alpha Anti-Chymotripsin, Stool analysis, Laboratory, Laboratory and office procedures	Determination of the intestinal levels of Alpha Anti-Chymotripsin.
DEGBG	Intestinal Lysozyme, Stool analysis, Laboratory, Laboratory and office procedures	Determination of fecal levels of intestinal lysozymal content.
DEGBH	CSA II, with 1 parasitology test, Stool analysis, Laboratory, Laboratory and office procedures	Digestive tests and one parasite microscopy.
DEGBI	CSA II, with 2 parasitology tests, Stool analysis, Laboratory, Laboratory and office procedures	Digestive tests and 2 parasite microscopies.
DEGZZ	Undefined, narrative required, Stool analysis, Laboratory, Laboratory and office procedures	Anywhere else undefined stool analysis. Narrative required.

Urinalysis

ABC Code	Procedure Description	Expanded Definition
DEIAJ	Urinalysis, routine with microscopy, Urinalysis, Laboratory, Laboratory and office procedures	Routine analysis of urine, using visual inspection, strip-stick chemical analysis for protein, sugar and ketones and also microscopic techniques to identify cells, casts and crystals.
DEIAK	Urinalysis, routine without microscopy, Urinalysis, Laboratory, Laboratory and office procedures	Routine analysis of urine, using visual inspection and strip-stick chemical analysis for protein, sugar and ketones.
DEIZZ	Undefined, narrative required, Urinalysis, Laboratory, Laboratory and office procedures	Anywhere else undefined urinalysis. Narrative required.

General laboratory services

ABC Code	Procedure Description	Expanded Definition
DEJAD	Wet mount, General laboratory services, Laboratory, Laboratory and office procedures	Microscopic determination of micro-organisms present.
DEJAE	Tuberculosis, tine test, General laboratory services, Laboratory, Laboratory and office procedures	TB tine test is an intradermal skin test to stimulate an antibody reaction to tuberulosis therefore indicating exposure or infection.
DEJAF	Strep screen, each report, General laboratory services, Laboratory, Laboratory and office procedures	Screening test for bacteria of the streptococcus group, each report.

General laboratory services

ABC Code	Procedure Description	Expanded Definition
DEJAG	Epstein Barr panel, viral capsid, General laboratory services, Laboratory, Laboratory and office procedures	Measures presence of viral capsid associated with Epstein Barr virus, a high specificity determination.
DEJAH	Candida antibodies, IgG only, General laboratory services, Laboratory, Laboratory and office procedures	Measures IgG antibody response to Candida organism.
DEJAI	Candida intensive culture, blood and stool analysis, General laboratory services, Laboratory, Laboratory and office procedures	Identifies microbiological growth of Candida organisms in blood or stool sample.
DEJAJ	Bacterial overgrowth of small intestine, breath, General laboratory services, Laboratory, Laboratory and office procedures	Breath analysis to determine bacterial overgrowth in small intestine.
DEJAK	Helicobacter pylori antibodies, blood or saliva analysis, General laboratory services, Laboratory, Laboratory and office procedures	Measure of antibody response to helicobacter pylori organism.
DEJAL	HIV, antigen, each report, General laboratory services, Laboratory, Laboratory and office procedures	Introduction of substance to incite the formation of antibodies to HIV, thus identifying the presence if the human immunodeficiency virus, per report.
DEJAM	HIV1, with analysis, General laboratory services, Laboratory, Laboratory and office procedures	Identifies the specific sub type, HIV-1, of the human immunodeficiency virus.
DEJAN	HTLV1, with analysis and antibody detection, General laboratory services, Laboratory, Laboratory and office procedures	Identifies the specific sub type, HTLV-1 (human T-cell lymphotropic virus), of the human immunodeficiency virus.
DEJAO	HTLV and HIV antibody, Western Blot, with analysis, General laboratory services, Laboratory, Laboratory and office procedures	Analysis of HTLV (human T-cell lymphotropic virus) and human immunodeficiency virus with Western Blot method.
DEJAP	Epstein Barr panel, early antigen, General laboratory services, Laboratory, Laboratory and office procedures	Identifies recent infection of Epstein Barr virus (see also DEJAQ).
DEJAQ	Epstein Barr panel, nuclear antigen, General laboratory services, Laboratory, Laboratory and office procedures	Identifies long-standing infection of the Epstein Barr virus (see also DEJAP).
DEJAS	Candida antibodies, IgA only, General laboratory services, Laboratory, Laboratory and office procedures	Measures IgA antibody response to candida organism.

Laboratory

General laboratory services

ABC Code	Procedure Description	Expanded Definition
DEJAT	Candida antibodies, IgM only, General laboratory services, Laboratory, Laboratory and office procedures	Measures IgM antibody response to candida organism.
DEJAU	Candida, cell mediated immune response, General laboratory services, Laboratory, Laboratory and office procedures	Measures cell mediated immune response to candida organism.
DEJZZ	Undefined, narrative required, General laboratory services, Laboratory, Laboratory and office procedures	Anywhere else undefined general laboratory services. Narrative required.

Chemical screening

ABC Code	Procedure Description	Expanded Definition
DELAA	Heavy metal screening, with arsenic, barium, beryllium, bismuth, antimony, mercury, Chemical screening, Laboratory, Laboratory and office procedures	Assesses levels of 7 toxic metals.
DELAB	Heavy metal, quantitative, each, Chemical screening, Laboratory, Laboratory and office procedures	Quantitates toxic metals.
DELAC	Hair analysis, heavy metal screening, Chemical screening, Laboratory, Laboratory and office procedures	Assesses 7 toxic metals in hair sample.
DELAD	Aluminum, Chemical screening, Laboratory, Laboratory and office procedures	Measurement of aluminum levels to assess toxicity.
DELAF	ELISA ACT LRA screening additive and preservative Block 15, Chemical screening, Laboratory, Laboratory and office procedures	Testing for 15 additives and preservatives.
DELAG	ELISA ACT LRA screening additive and preservative Block 28, Chemical screening, Laboratory, Laboratory and office procedures	Testing for 28 additives and preservatives, including Block 15.
DELAH	ELISA ACT LRA screening environmental chemical Block 15, Chemical screening, Laboratory, Laboratory and office procedures	Testing for 15 environmental chemicals.
DELAI	ELISA ACT LRA screening environmental chemical Block 30, Chemical screening, Laboratory, Laboratory and office procedures	Testing for 30 environmental chemicals.

Chemical screening

ABC Code	Procedure Description	Expanded Definition
DELAJ	ELISA ACT LRA screening environmental chemical Block 59, Chemical screening, Laboratory, Laboratory and office procedures	Testing for 59 environmental chemicals.
DELAK	ELISA ACT LRA screening food coloring Block 14, Chemical screening, Laboratory, Laboratory and office procedures	Testing for 14 food colorings.
DELAL	ELISA ACT LRA screening medication Block 17, Chemical screening, Laboratory, Laboratory and office procedures	Testing for 17 medications.
DELZZ	Undefined, narrative required, Chemical screening, Laboratory, Laboratory and office procedures	Anywhere else undefined chemical screening. Narrative required.

Male testing

ABC Code	Procedure Description	Expanded Definition
DEMAB	Comprehensive hormone profile, Male testing, Laboratory, Laboratory and office procedures	Measures testosterone and other anabolic hormones.
DEMAC	Hormone profile, Male testing, Laboratory, Laboratory and office procedures	Measures key anabolic metabolites.
DEMAI	Prostatic acid phosphate panel, Male testing, Laboratory, Laboratory and office procedures	Measures enzymes (acid phosphatase) associated with prostrate activity.
DEMAL	Prostate specific antigen, free percentage, Male testing, Laboratory, Laboratory and office procedures	Highly predictive of prostate cancer versus prostate inflammation and/or infection.
DEMZZ	Undefined, narrative required, Male testing, Laboratory, Laboratory and office procedures	Anywhere else undefined male testing. Narrative required.

Female Testing

ABC Code	Procedure Description	Expanded Definition
DEOAA	Hormone Profile, Female Testing, Laboratory, Laboratory and office procedures	Measures key female (estrogen) hormones.
DEOAB	Comprehensive Hormone Profile, Female Testing, Laboratory, Laboratory and office procedures	Measures important estrogen-related compounds.
DEOAC	Post Menopause Profile, Female Testing, Laboratory, Laboratory and office procedures	Assesses hormone activity in women after menopause.

Female Testing

ABC Code	Procedure Description	Expanded Definition
DEOAD	Comprehensive Post Menopause Profile, Female Testing, Laboratory, Laboratory and office procedures	Complete measurement of estrogen-related compounds in women after menopause.
DEOAK	Vaginal Culture, Female Testing, Laboratory, Laboratory and office procedures	Analysis of vaginal smear to detect infection.
DEOAL	Pap smear, Female Testing, Laboratory, Laboratory and office procedures	Analysis of cervical smear or scraping from which to detect abnormal changes in the cells that may implicate pre-cancer or cancer.
DEOAM	Cervical Smear, Female Testing, Laboratory, Laboratory and office procedures	Analysis of cervical smear (see DEOAL) to also detect viral infections of the cervix and to assess the level of hormones in the body, particularly estrogen and progesterone.
DEOZZ	Undefined, narrative required, Female Testing, Laboratory, Laboratory and office procedures	Anywhere else undefined female testing. Narrative required.

Allergy

ABC Code	Procedure Description	Expanded Definition
DEPAA	Allergy Profile, 1 to 8 Items, Allergy, Laboratory, Laboratory and office procedures	Analysis of 1 - 8 allergen antigens to determine allergic response.
DEPAB	Food Allergy Profile, 1 to 8 Items, Allergy, Laboratory, Laboratory and office procedures	Analysis of 1 - 8 food allergen antigens to determine allergic response.
DEPAC	24 Spice Profile, with Separate IgE Profiles, Allergy, Laboratory, Laboratory and office procedures	Measures acute reacting allergens (alimentary).
DEPAD	24 Spice Profile, with Separate IgG4 Profiles, Allergy, Laboratory, Laboratory and office procedures	Measures antibody subtype.
DEPAG	Inhalants Profile, with IgE for 47 Inhalants,, Allergy, Laboratory, Laboratory and office procedures	Measures acute reactive allergens (breathed).
DEPAH	Candida Antigen, Immune Complex, with IgG, IgM, IgA, Allergy, Laboratory, Laboratory and office procedures	Measures response to Candida Albicans.

Allergy

ABC Code	Procedure Description	Expanded Definition
DEPAI	Anti Chemical Antibodies Profile, with Formaldehyde, Trimellitic Anhydride, Toluene Diisoganate, Phthalic Anhydride, Benzene Ring, Allergy, Laboratory, Laboratory and office procedures	Measures humoral immune response to 5 chemical groups.
DEPAJ	Autoimmune Panel, Allergy, Laboratory, Laboratory and office procedures	Assesses chronic inflammatory state.
DEPAK	Allergy Management, Allergy, Laboratory, Laboratory and office procedures	Identification, treatment, and prevention of allergic responses to food, medications, insect bites, contrast material, blood, or others substances.
DEPAL	Testing, Intracutaneous, Allergy, Laboratory, Laboratory and office procedures	Skin test for immune reactivity.
DEPAM	Testing, Intracutaneous with Allergenic Extracts, Immediate Type Reaction, Allergy, Laboratory, Laboratory and office procedures	Skin test for acute/immediate allergenic reactions.
DEPAN	Testing, Intracutaneous, Sequential and Incremental, Allergy, Laboratory, Laboratory and office procedures	Test for immune reactivity by titration within the skin.
DEPAO	Testing, Percutaneous with Allergenic Extracts, Immediate Type Reaction, each test, Allergy, Laboratory, Laboratory and office procedures	Test for acute/immediate allergenic reaction through the skin.
DEPAP	Testing, Percutaneous, Sequential and Incremental, Allergy, Laboratory, Laboratory and office procedures	Test for immune reactivity by titration through the skin.
DEPAQ	Testing, Skin End Point Titration, Allergy, Laboratory, Laboratory and office procedures	Clinical therapy determination of reactive dosage.
DEPAR	Allergy profile, 1 to 16 items, Allergy, Laboratory, Laboratory and office procedures	Analysis of 1 to 16 allergen antigens to determine allergic response.
DEPAS	Allergy profile, 1 to 24 items, Allergy, Laboratory, Laboratory and office procedures	Analysis of 1 to 24 allergen antigens to determine allergic response.
DEPAT	ELISA ACT LRA diagnostic candida albicans test block, Allergy, Laboratory, Laboratory and office procedures	Testing for 78 items.
DEPAU	ELISA ACT LRA diagnostic gluten test block, Allergy, Laboratory, Laboratory and office procedures	Testing for 73 items.

Allergy

ABC Code	Procedure Description	Expanded Definition
DEPAV	ELISA ACT LRA diagnostic lectin test block, Allergy, Laboratory, Laboratory and office procedures	Testing for 37 items.
DEPAW	ELISA ACT LRA diagnostic poke weed mitogen test block, Allergy, Laboratory, Laboratory and office procedures	Testing for 42 items.
DEPAX	ELISA ACT LRA diagnostic trichophyton test block, Allergy, Laboratory, Laboratory and office procedures	Testing for 49 items.
DEPAY	ELISA ACT LRA screening combination Block A, Allergy, Laboratory, Laboratory and office procedures	Testing for 271 total items in categories that include 142 Food, 59 Environmental, 28 Mold, 28 Additive and 14 Food Coloring.
DEPAZ	ELISA/ACT LRA screening combination Block B, Allergy, Laboratory, Laboratory and office procedures	Testing for 212 total items in categories that include 112 Food, 30 Environmental, 28 Mold, 28 Additive and 14 Food Coloring.
DEPBA	ELISA ACT LRA screening combination Block C, Allergy, Laboratory, Laboratory and office procedures	Testing for 101 total items in categories that include 46 Food, 15 Environmental, 11 Mold, 15 Additive and 14 Food Coloring.
DEPBB	ELISA ACT LRA screening combination Block D, Allergy, Laboratory, Laboratory and office procedures	Testing for 70 total items in categories that include 26 Food, 15 Environmental, 15 Additive and 14 Food Coloring.
DEPBC	ELISA ACT LRA screening comprehensive combination block, Allergy, Laboratory, Laboratory and office procedures	Testing for 375 total items in categories that include 228 Food, 59 Environmental, 28 Mold, 28 Additive, 14 Food Coloring, 8 Toxic Minerals and Metals, and 10 Danders, Hair and Feathers.
DEPBD	ELISA ACT LRA screening dander, hair, feather Block 10, Allergy, Laboratory, Laboratory and office procedures	Testing for 10 Dander, Hair and Feathers including Cat, Dog, Duck, Goat, Goose, Guinea Pig, Horse, Rabbit, Sheep and Turkey.
DEPBE	ELISA ACT LRA screening expanded combination Block A, Allergy, Laboratory, Laboratory and office procedures	Testing for 357 total items in categories that include 228 Food, 59 Environmental, 28 Mold, 28 Additive and 14 Food Coloring.
DEPBF	ELISA ACT LRA screening food Block 11, Allergy, Laboratory, Laboratory and office procedures	Testing for 11 food items.
DEPBG	ELISA ACT LRA screening food Block 26, Allergy, Laboratory, Laboratory and office procedures	Testing for 26 food items.

Allergy

ABC Code	Procedure Description	Expanded Definition
DEPBH	ELISA ACT LRA screening food Block 46, Allergy, Laboratory, Laboratory and office procedures	Testing for 46 food items.
DEPBI	ELISA ACT LRA screening food Block 112, Allergy, Laboratory, Laboratory and office procedures	Testing for 112 food items.
DEPBJ	ELISA ACT LRA screening food Block 142, Allergy, Laboratory, Laboratory and office procedures	Testing for 142 food items.
DEPBK	ELISA ACT LRA screening food Block 228, Allergy, Laboratory, Laboratory and office procedures	Testing for 228 food items.
DEPBL	ELISA ACT LRA screening mold Block 11, Allergy, Laboratory, Laboratory and office procedures	Testing for 11 molds.
DEPBM	ELISA ACT LRA screening mold Block 28, Allergy, Laboratory, Laboratory and office procedures	Testing for 28 molds.
DEPBN	ELISA ACT LRA screening self designed block, base test only when used for up to 10 test items, Allergy, Laboratory, Laboratory and office procedures	Any selected ELISA/ACT LRA Screening Test Blocks. Use this code for base fee ONLY. Use code DEPAB for each test item up to 10.
DEPBO	ELISA ACT LRA screening self designed block, per item up to 10, Allergy, Laboratory, Laboratory and office procedures	Any selected ELISA/ACT LRA Screening Test Blocks, per test item. Use code DEPAA for base test.
DEPBP	ELISA ACT LRA screening self designed block, base test only when used for 11 or more test items, Allergy, Laboratory, Laboratory and office procedures	Any selected ELISA/ACT LRA Screening Test Blocks. Use this code for base fee ONLY. Use code DEPAD for each test item over 10.
DEPBQ	ELISA ACT LRA screening self designed block, per item for 11 or more, Allergy, Laboratory, Laboratory and office procedures	Any selected ELISA/ACT LRA Screening Test Blocks, per test item. Use code DEPAC for base test.
DEPBR	Food allergy profile, 1 to 16 items, Allergy, Laboratory, Laboratory and office procedures	Analysis of 1 to 16 food allergen antigens to determine allergic response.
DEPBS	Food allergy profile, 1 to 24 items, Allergy, Laboratory, Laboratory and office procedures	Analysis of 1 to 24 food allergen antigens to determine allergic response.

Laboratory

Allergy

ABC Code	Procedure Description	Expanded Definition
DEPZZ	Undefined, narrative required, Allergy, Laboratory, Laboratory and office procedures	Anywhere else undefined allergy procedures. Narrative required.

Sample Collection

ABC Code	Procedure Description	Expanded Definition
DEZAA	Collection of Autogenous Material, Blood Sample, Sample Collection, Laboratory, Laboratory and office procedures	Collection of blood sample of an individual patient to be used for diagnostic or therapeutic purposes on or by the same individual patient.
DEZAB	Collection of Autogenous Material, Other, Sample Collection, Laboratory, Laboratory and office procedures	Collection of body material, other than blood, from an individual patient to be used for diagnostic of therapeutic purposes on or by the same individual patient.
DEZAC	Arterial Blood Sample, Phlebotomy, Sample Collection, Laboratory, Laboratory and office procedures	Obtaining a blood sample from an uncannulated artery to assess oxygen and carbon dioxide levels and acid-base balance.
DEZAD	Blood Unit Acquisition, Phlebotomy, Sample Collection, Laboratory, Laboratory and office procedures	Procuring blood and blood products from a donor.
DEZAE	Venous Blood Sample, Phlebotomy, Sample Collection, Laboratory, Laboratory and office procedures	Removal of a sample of venous blood from an uncannulated vein.
DEZAF	Handling and or conveyance of laboratory specimen, Sample Collection, Laboratory, Laboratory and office procedures	The handling and/or conveyance of a laboratory specimen from an office or place of procedure to the lab.
DEZAG	Heel or finger stick, Sample Collection, Laboratory, Laboratory and office procedures	Piercing of the skin of a digit or heel of the foot with a sterile pointed object to obtain a sample of blood for analysis.
DEZZZ	Undefined, in office sample collection only, narrative required, Sample Collection, Laboratory, Laboratory and office procedures	Anywhere else undefined sample collection. Narrative required.

Radiology

General

ABC Code	Procedure Description	Expanded Definition
DFAZZ	Undefined, narrative required, General, Radiology, Laboratory and office procedures	Anywhere else undefined radiology procedures. Narrative required. Only use this code if the appropriate radiology service is not coded in CPT (TM).

Spectroscopy

ABC Code	Procedure Description	Expanded Definition
DHAAA	Electromagnetic resonance spectroscopy, Spectroscopy, General procedures and services, Laboratory and office procedures	Combination of magnet, gradient coils and radiofrequency (RF) coils for use in a machine to provide electromagnetic analysis for diagnostic purposes. Also known as MRI.
DHAZZ	Undefined, narrative required, Spectroscopy, General procedures and services, Laboratory and office procedures	Anywhere else undefined use of electromagnetic radiation, X-rays, and their arrangement according to frequency or wavelength for diagnostic purposes. Narrative required.

Thermography

ABC Code	Procedure Description	Expanded Definition
DHCAA	Upper body, includes upper extremities, Thermography, General procedures and services, Laboratory and office procedures	Examining the upper body and upper extremities with thermographic techniques portraying surface temperatures of the body for diagnostic purposes.
DHCAB	Lower body, include lower extremities, Thermography, General procedures and services, Laboratory and office procedures	Examining the lower body and lower extremities with thermographic techniques using heat sensitive film that portrays D440 surface temperatures of the body for diagnostic purposes.
DHCAC	Upper body, includes upper extremities, liquid crystal, contact, Thermography, General procedures and services, Laboratory and office procedures	Examining the upper body and upper extremities with thermograph techniques, using temperature-sensitive liquid crystals applied to the skin, which portray surface temperatures of the body in different colors for diagnostic purposes.
DHCAD	Lower body, includes lower extremities, liquid crystal, contact, Thermography, General procedures and services, Laboratory and office procedures	Examining the lower body and lower extremities with thermograph techniques, using temperature-sensitive liquid crystals applied to the skin, which portray surface temperatures of the body in different colors for diagnostic purposes.
DHCAE	Total body, with report, liquid crystal, contact, Thermography, General procedures and services, Laboratory and office procedures	Examining the total body with thermograph techniques, using temperature-sensitive liquid crystals applied to the skin, which portray surface temperatures of the body in different colors for diagnostic purposes.
DHCAF	Neurodermothermograph, handheld, Thermography, General procedures and services, Laboratory and office procedures	A handheld device that measures heat gradiations through the skin, used to see how the heat build-up relates to neurologic transmission and resistance build-up to indicate stress in related organs.
DHCZZ	Undefined, narrative required, Thermography, General procedures and services, Laboratory and office procedures	Anywhere else undefined use of thermography. Narrative required.

Instructions

The following subsections are contained in Section E:

Physical devices
General

Topical applicants
General

Solution
Allergens
General

Any practitioner, if appropriately trained or certified, may use codes in this section if the scope of practice laws for their state or region allow them to use or order the supply. HCPCS Level II codes contain extensive supply items. Either coding system may be used to report supplies.

Do **not** add modifiers to the codes in Section E. See codes in Section A and choose the appropriate reference code to precede codes in this section or for HCPCS Level II codes.

Each subsection contains an "undefined" code that should only be used when the supply used is not accurately described by another more specific code. If an "undefined" code is used on the claims form, attach a report that provides a detailed narrative about that supply and why it was needed.

Supplies

Physical devices

General

ABC Code	Procedure Description	Expanded Definition
EAAAA	Abdominal binders and support, General, Physical devices, Supplies	
EAAAB	Acupuncture needles, disposable, General, Physical devices, Supplies	
EAAAC	Ankle canvass splint, General, Physical devices, Supplies	
EAAAD	Arm and shoulder immobilizer, General, Physical devices, Supplies	
EAAAE	Back frame support, General, Physical devices, Supplies	
EAAAF	Bandages and wraps, General, Physical devices, Supplies	
EAAAG	Casting materials, General, Physical devices, Supplies	
EAAAH	Cervical collar, fitted, General, Physical devices, Supplies	
EAAAI	Cervical exerciser, home use, General, Physical devices, Supplies	
EAAAJ	Cervical pillow, therapeutic, General, Physical devices, Supplies	
EAAAK	Cervical roll, General, Physical devices, Supplies	
EAAAL	Colema board, General, Physical devices, Supplies	
EAAAM	Compresses, General, Physical devices, Supplies	
EAAAN	Cryotherapy, cervical contour, General, Physical devices, Supplies	

ABC Code	Procedure Description	Expanded Definition
EAAAO	Cryotherapy, home use, eye, General, Physical devices, Supplies	
EAAAP	Cryotherapy, home use, large, General, Physical devices, Supplies	
EAAAQ	Cryotherapy, home use, medium, General, Physical devices, Supplies	
EAAAR	Cryotherapy, home use, small, General, Physical devices, Supplies	
EAAAS	Elastic bandages, General, Physical devices, Supplies	
EAAAT	Fomentel, General, Physical devices, Supplies	
EAAAU	Hand grip exerciser, home use, General, Physical devices, Supplies	
EAAAV	Holster arm sling, General, Physical devices, Supplies	
EAAAW	Hot pack, large, General, Physical devices, Supplies	
EAAAX	Hot pack, small, General, Physical devices, Supplies	
EAAAY	Ice pack, large, General, Physical devices, Supplies	
EAAAZ	OB delivery tray, General, Physical devices, Supplies	Contains a minimum of but not limited to sterile gloves, non-sterile gloves, sterile cord clamps, infant cover and hat, sterile 4x4 gauze pads, 4 packets of sutures, infant eye ointment, bulb syringe, delee, maternity kotex and chux pads.
EAABA	Ice pack, small, General, Physical devices, Supplies	
EAABB	Knee brace, General, Physical devices, Supplies	
EAABC	Knee cage brace, General, Physical devices, Supplies	
EAABD	Motorized cervical traction unit, home use, General, Physical devices, Supplies	

General

ABC Code	Procedure Description	Expanded Definition
EAABE	Orthopedic back support cushion, General, Physical devices, Supplies	
EAABF	Orthopedic elevator leg rest, General, Physical devices, Supplies	
EAABG	Orthopedic lift shoes, General, Physical devices, Supplies	
EAABH	Orthopedic lumbosacral support, molded, General, Physical devices, Supplies	
EAABI	Orthopedic pillow, cervical spine, small, General, Physical devices, Supplies	
EAABJ	Orthopedic stabilizers, pelvic, General, Physical devices, Supplies	
EAABK	Orthopedic support, knee, General, Physical devices, Supplies	
EAABL	Orthopedic support, wrist, General, Physical devices, Supplies	
EAABM	Orthotic heel lift, General, Physical devices, Supplies	
EAABN	Orthotics, General, Physical devices, Supplies	
EAABO	Over-the-door cervical traction unit, home use, General, Physical devices, Supplies	
EAABP	Over-the-door shoulder and arm exerciser, home use, General, Physical devices, Supplies	
EAABQ	Rib belt, General, Physical devices, Supplies	
EAABR	Spinal muscle massager, home use, General, Physical devices, Supplies	
EAABS	Stretch bands, resistive, General, Physical devices, Supplies	
EAABT	Taping supplies, General, Physical devices, Supplies	
EAABU	Tennis elbow support, General, Physical devices, Supplies	

General

ABC Code	Procedure Description	Expanded Definition
EAABV	TENS unit purchase for home use, General, Physical devices, Supplies	
EAABW	TENS unit replacement pads, General, Physical devices, Supplies	
EAABX	Tension reliever, General, Physical devices, Supplies	
EAABY	Therapeutic exercise ball, General, Physical devices, Supplies	
EAABZ	Moxa, General, Physical devices, Supplies	
EAACA	Therapeutic putty for finger, wrist and hand exercises, General, Physical devices, Supplies	
EAACB	Traction device, simple, General, Physical devices, Supplies	
EAACC	Wedges, supports, cushions, General, Physical devices, Supplies	
EAACD	Wrist brace with palm splint, General, Physical devices, Supplies	
EAACE	Orthotic insoles, General, Physical devices, Supplies	
EAACF	Braces, hinged, General, Physical devices, Supplies	
EAACG	Splints, rigid, General, Physical devices, Supplies	
EAACH	Slings, General, Physical devices, Supplies	
EAACI	Vaginal depletion packs, General, Physical devices, Supplies	
EAACJ	Cupping supplies, General, Physical devices, Supplies	
EAACK	Electro needles, General, Physical devices, Supplies	
EAACL	Pellets, General, Physical devices, Supplies	Pellets for auricular acupuncture, also called ear seeds.

Physical devices

General

ABC Code	Procedure Description	Expanded Definition
EAACM	Urine dip stick, General, Physical devices, Supplies	Urine dip stick for protein and glucose analysis.
EAACN	Intravenous supplies, General, Physical devices, Supplies	
EAACO	Hemoglobinometer, General, Physical devices, Supplies	
EAACP	Cervical cap. diaphragm, General, Physical devices, Supplies	
EAACQ	TDP Heat lamp, General, Physical devices, Supplies	
EAACR	Seven star Plum Blossom hammer needles, General, Physical devices, Supplies	Plastic type hammer with flexible handle and disposable seven-needle head.
EAAZZ	Undefined, narrative required, General, Physical devices, Supplies	Anywhere else undefined physical device. Narrative required.

Topical applicants

General

ABC Code	Procedure Description	Expanded Definition
EBAAA	Mineral ice, General, Topical applicants, Supplies	
EBAAB	Ophthalmic prophylaxis ointment, General, Topical applicants, Supplies	
EBAZZ	Undefined, narrative required, General, Topical applicants, Supplies	Anywhere else undefined topical applicant. Narrative required.

Solution

Allergen

ABC Code	Procedure Description	Expanded Definition
ECAAA	24 spice profile, with separate IgE profiles, Allergen, Solution, Supplies	
ECAAB	24 spice profile, with separate IgG4 profiles, Allergen, Solution, Supplies	
ECAAC	Additives or preservatives hypersensitivity, up to 15 items, Allergen, Solution, Supplies	

Allergen

ABC Code	Procedure Description	Expanded Definition
ECAAD	Additives or preservatives hypersensitivity, 16 to 30 items, Allergen, Solution, Supplies	
ECAAE	Alpha-1 Antitrypsin, Allergen, Solution, Supplies	
ECAAF	Autoimmune panel, Allergen, Solution, Supplies	
ECAAG	Benzoate hypersensitivity, Allergen, Solution, Supplies	
ECAAH	Candida antigen, Allergen, Solution, Supplies	
ECAAI	Danders, hair, feathers, up to 15 items, Allergen, Solution, Supplies	
ECAAJ	Environmental chemicals, up to 15 items, Allergen, Solution, Supplies	
ECAAK	Environmental chemicals, 16 to 30 items, Allergen, Solution, Supplies	
ECAAL	Environmental chemicals, 31 to 60 items, Allergen, Solution, Supplies	
ECAAM	Epstein Barr, early antigen, Allergen, Solution, Supplies	
ECAAN	Epstein Barr, nuclear antigen, Allergen, Solution, Supplies	
ECAAO	Stinging insect venoms, 5 items, Allergen, Solution, Supplies	
ECAAP	Food and inhalants, Allergen, Solution, Supplies	
ECAAQ	Food dyes and colors, up to 12 items, Allergen, Solution, Supplies	
ECAAR	Stinging insect venoms, 4 items, Allergen, Solution, Supplies	
ECAAS	Gut mucosal immunity, Allergen, Solution, Supplies	

Allergen

ABC Code	Procedure Description	Expanded Definition
ECAAT	Haptens, toxic mineral hypersensitivity, up to 12 items, Allergen, Solution, Supplies	
ECAAU	IgE for 100 vegetarian foods, Allergen, Solution, Supplies	
ECAAV	IgE for 96 general foods, Allergen, Solution, Supplies	
ECAAW	IgG4 for 100 vegetarian foods, Allergen, Solution, Supplies	
ECAAX	IgG4 for 96 general foods, Allergen, Solution, Supplies	
ECAAY	Individual antibody, Allergen, Solution, Supplies	
ECABA	Individual antigen, Allergen, Solution, Supplies	
ECABB	Inhalants profile, with IgE for 47 inhalants, Allergen, Solution, Supplies	
ECABC	Lecithin hypersensitivity, Allergen, Solution, Supplies	
ECABD	Lymphocyte transformation, Allergen, Solution, Supplies	
ECABE	Lymphocyte, tissue and blood distinction, Allergen, Solution, Supplies	
ECABF	Lymphocytes, B-cell study, Allergen, Solution, Supplies	
ECABG	Medications hypersensitivity, up to 15 items, Allergen, Solution, Supplies	
ECABH	Medications hypersensitivity, 16 to 30 items, Allergen, Solution, Supplies	
ECABI	Mold hypersensitivity, up to 15 items, Allergen, Solution, Supplies	
ECABJ	Mold hypersensitivity, 16 to 30 items, Allergen, Solution, Supplies	

Allergen

ABC Code	Procedure Description	Expanded Definition
ECABK	Pokeweed mitogen hypersensitivity, Allergen, Solution, Supplies	
ECABL	Stinging insect venom, 1 item, Allergen, Solution, Supplies	
ECABM	Stinging insect venoms, 2 items, Allergen, Solution, Supplies	
ECABN	Stinging insect venoms, 3 items, Allergen, Solution, Supplies	
ECABO	Total Salivary Sig A, Allergen, Solution, Supplies	
ECABP	Tricophyton hypersensitivity, Allergen, Solution, Supplies	
ECABQ	Sulfite hypersensitivity, Allergen, Solution, Supplies	
ECAZZ	Undefined, narrative required, Allergen, Solution, Supplies	

General

ABC Code	Procedure Description	Expanded Definition
ECBAA	A-Acetylcysteine, per cc, General, Solution, Supplies	
ECBAB	Adrenal cortical extract, General, Solution, Supplies	
ECBAC	Antibiotic, per cc, General, Solution, Supplies	
ECBAD	Aredia, per cc, General, Solution, Supplies	
ECBAE	Calcium bersonate and additives, per cc, General, Solution, Supplies	
ECBAF	Calcium, magnesium, per cc, General, Solution, Supplies	
ECBAG	Chromium, per cc, General, Solution, Supplies	
ECBAH	CMBZM, per cc, General, Solution, Supplies	

Solution

General

ABC Code	Procedure Description	Expanded Definition
ECBAI	Copper, per cc, General, Solution, Supplies	
ECBAJ	Deferoximine mesylate, per cc, General, Solution, Supplies	
ECBAK	Dimeracaprol, 1% procaine, per cc, General, Solution, Supplies	
ECBAL	EDTA, per 3 grams, General, Solution, Supplies	
ECBAM	Folic acid, per cc, General, Solution, Supplies	
ECBAN	Germanium, per cc, General, Solution, Supplies	
ECBAO	Glutathione, per cc, General, Solution, Supplies	
ECBAP	Heparin, per cc, General, Solution, Supplies	
ECBAQ	Hepatitis A vaccine, per cc, General, Solution, Supplies	
ECBAR	Hepatitis B vaccine, per cc, General, Solution, Supplies	
ECBAS	Hydrochloric acid, per cc, General, Solution, Supplies	
ECBAT	Hydrocortisone with additives, per cc, General, Solution, Supplies	
ECBAU	Hydrogen peroxide, per cc, General, Solution, Supplies	
ECBAV	Hydrogen peroxide with additives, per cc, General, Solution, Supplies	
ECBAW	Kutapressin, per cc, General, Solution, Supplies	
ECBAX	Laetrile, per cc, General, Solution, Supplies	
ECBAY	Lasix, per cc, General, Solution, Supplies	
ECBAZ	Methergine (R), per cc, General, Solution, Supplies	
ECBBA	Magnesium, per cc, General, Solution, Supplies	

General

ABC Code	Procedure Description	Expanded Definition
ECBBB	Manganese, per cc, General, Solution, Supplies	
ECBBC	Mineral build up, per cc, General, Solution, Supplies	
ECBBD	Molybdenum iodide, per cc, General, Solution, Supplies	
ECBBE	Ozone, per cc, General, Solution, Supplies	
ECBBF	Potassium, per cc, General, Solution, Supplies	
ECBBG	Saline, per cc, General, Solution, Supplies	
ECBBH	Selenium, per cc, General, Solution, Supplies	
ECBBI	Sodium bicarbonate, per cc, General, Solution, Supplies	
ECBBJ	Sodium iodide, per cc, General, Solution, Supplies	
ECBBK	Sterile water, per cc, General, Solution, Supplies	
ECBBL	Testosterone, per cc, General, Solution, Supplies	
ECBBM	Trace minerals 7, per cc, General, Solution, Supplies	
ECBBN	Tri-ox, per cc, General, Solution, Supplies	
ECBBO	Vitamin B complex, per cc, General, Solution, Supplies	
ECBBP	Vitamin B 12, per cc, General, Solution, Supplies	
ECBBQ	Vitamin B 5, per cc, General, Solution, Supplies	
ECBBR	Vitamin B 6, per cc, General, Solution, Supplies	
ECBBS	Vitamin C, per cc, General, Solution, Supplies	
ECBBT	Zinc, per cc, General, Solution, Supplies	

Solution

General

ABC Code	Procedure Description	Expanded Definition
ECBBU	Oxytocin, per cc, General, Solution, Supplies	
ECBBV	RhoGam, per cc, General, Solution, Supplies	
ECBBW	Vitamin K, per cc, General, Solution, Supplies	
ECBBX	Xylocaine, per cc, General, Solution, Supplies	
ECBZZ	Undefined, narrative required, General, Solution, Supplies	

Section F: Nutritional Supplements

Instructions

The following subsections are contained in Section F:

Amino acids
General (undefined code)

Enzymes
General (undefined code)

Minerals
General (undefined code)

Other
General

Oral chelation with natural agents
General (undefined)

Oxidative
General (undefined)

Vitamins
General (undefined)

Any practitioner, if appropriately trained or certified, may use codes in this section if the scope of practice laws for their state or region allows them to use or order the nutritional supplement.

Do **not** add modifiers to the codes in Section F. Use codes in Section A (ADXAA, ADZAA, ADZAR) followed by a modifier and choose the appropriate reference code to precede codes in this section.

Use the ADYAA - ADYAE codes for ordering a supplement followed by an undefined code in this section if the nutritional supplement is not included in ABC codes™ or CPT™. If an "undefined" code is used on the claims form, attach a report that provides a detailed narrative about that supply and why it was needed.

Nutritional supplements

Amino acids

General

ABC Code	Procedure Description	Expanded Definition
FAAZZ	Undefined, narrative required, General, Amino acids, Nutritional supplements	Anywhere else undefined Amino Acid. Narrative required.

Enzymes

General

ABC Code	Procedure Description	Expanded Definition
FBAZZ	Undefined, narrative required, General, Enzymes, Nutritional supplements	Anywhere else undefined Enzyme. Narrative required.

Minerals

General

ABC Code	Procedure Description	Expanded Definition
FCAZZ	Undefined, narrative required, General, Minerals, Nutritional supplements	Anywhere else undefined Mineral. Narrative required.

Other

General

ABC Code	Procedure Description	Expanded Definition
FDAAA	Himalaya ProSelect (TM) Gasex 120, 450 mg tablets, General, Other, Nutritional supplements	UPC Code 605069112017. Prescribed as a natural, simple and gentle approach to maintaining a balanced digestive function.
FDAAB	Himalaya ProSelect (TM) Glucosim 120, 500 mg tablets, General, Other, Nutritional supplements	UPC Code 605069109017. Prescribed to offer gentle and safe glycemic control and also help reduce serum triglycerides and cholesterol.
FDAAC	Himalaya ProSelect (TM) Kilose 60, 500 mg capsules, General, Other, Nutritional supplements	UPC Code 605069120012. Prescribed to regulate the metabolism of fats, protect overweight people against possible consequences of excess lipids.
FDAAD	Himalaya ProSelect (TM) Koflet 200 ml liquid, General, Other, Nutritional supplements	UPC Code 605069121316. Prescribed for bronchial support. Assists in increasing the watery bronchial secretions, reducing mucosal irritability and susceptibility to cough, and assist in building up defense mechanisms against common allergens.

General

ABC Code	Procedure Description	Expanded Definition
FDAAE	Himalaya ProSelect (TM) Koflet 24 lozenges, General, Other, Nutritional supplements	UPC Code 605069121590. Prescribed for bronchial support. Assists in increasing the watery bronchial secretions, reducing mucosal irritability and susceptibility to cough, and assist in building up defense mechanisms against common allergens.
FDAAF	Himalaya ProSelect (TM) Koflet sugar free 200 ml liquid, General, Other, Nutritional supplements	UPC Code 605069121415. Prescribed for bronchial support. Assists in increasing the watery bronchial secretions, reducing mucosal irritability and susceptibility to cough, and assist in building up defense mechanisms against common allergens.
FDAAG	Himalaya ProSelect (TM) Menstrim 200 ml liquid, General, Other, Nutritional supplements	UPC Code 605069113311.
FDAAH	Himalaya ProSelect (TM) Pilexim 100, 570 mg tablets, General, Other, Nutritional supplements	UPC Code 605069111010. Prescribed to provide herbal and mineral components essential for maintaining healthy veins.
FDAAI	Himalaya ProSelect (TM) Prostane 100, 630 mg tablets, General, Other, Nutritional supplements	UPC Code 605069110013. Prescribed to maintain a healthy prostate.
FDAAJ	Himalaya ProSelect (TM) Rumalaya 80, 820 mg tablets, General, Other, Nutritional supplements	UPC Code 605069107013. Prescribed to support the connective tissue structure and attenuate discomfort caused by impaired movement.
FDAAK	Himalaya ProSelect (TM) Septilin 200 ml liquid, General, Other, Nutritional supplements	UPC Code 605069108317. Prescribed to support the immune function, ensuring that the immune response works efficiently.
FDAAL	Himalaya ProSelect (TM) Septilin 80, 820 mg, General, Other, Nutritional supplements	UPC Code 605069108010. Prescribed to support the immune function, ensuring that the immune response works efficiently.
FDAAM	Himalaya ProSelect (TM) Septilin JR 120, 425 mg tablets, General, Other, Nutritional supplements	UPC Code 605069108218. Prescribed to support the immune function, ensuring that the immune response works efficiently.
FDAAN	Himalaya ProSelect (TM) Speman 100, 630 mg tablets, General, Other, Nutritional supplements	UPC Code 605069110112.
FDAAO	Himalaya ProSelect (TM) Styplon 80, 670 mg tablets, General, Other, Nutritional supplements	UPC Code 605069129015.
FDAAP	Himalaya ProSelect (TM) Tentex Forte 90, 500 mg tablets, General, Other, Nutritional supplements	UPC Code 605069115018. Prescribed for a normal sex life and function, non-hormonal.

General

ABC Code	Procedure Description	Expanded Definition
FDAAQ	Himalaya ProSelect (TM), Abana 60, 720 mg tablets, General, Other, Nutritional supplements	UPC Code 605069101011. Prescribed as a cardiac tonic that supports heart function and maintains the balance between supply and demand of myocardial oxygen.
FDAAR	Himalaya ProSelect (TM), Cystone 100, 620 mg tablets, General, Other, Nutritional supplements	UPC Code 605069102018. Prescribed to support the urinary tract function, controlling urine composition directed at correcting imbalances.
FDAAS	Himalaya ProSelect (TM), Geriforte 60, 920 mg tablets, General, Other, Nutritional supplements	UPC Code 605069103015. Prescribed to regulate and balance all the organs and systems of the body for comprehensive health maintenance.
FDAAT	Himalaya ProSelect (TM), Geriforte liquid, 200 ml, General, Other, Nutritional supplements	UPC Code 605069103312. Prescribed to regulate and balance all the organs and systems of the body for comprehensive health maintenance.
FDAAU	Himalaya ProSelect (TM), Liv 52, 120 tablets 515 mg, General, Other, Nutritional supplements	UPC Code 605069105019. Prescribed to ensure optimum liver function. Antioxidant properties act as a powerful detoxification agent.
FDAAV	Himalaya ProSelect (TM), Liv 52, 200 ml liquid, General, Other, Nutritional supplements	UPC Code 605069105316. Prescribed to ensure optimum liver function. Antioxidant properties act as a powerful detoxification agent.
FDAAW	Himalaya ProSelect (TM), Mentat 200 ml liquid, General, Other, Nutritional supplements	UPC Code 605069106313. Prescribed to support brain function in normal situations and when facing mental and emotional pressures.
FDAAX	Himalaya ProSelect (TM), Mentat 60, 490 mg tablets, General, Other, Nutritional supplements	UPC Code 605069106016. Prescribed to support brain function in normal situations and when facing mental and emotional pressures.
FDAAY	Himalaya ProSelect (TM), Mentat JR 120, 490 mg tablets, General, Other, Nutritional supplements	UPC Code 605069106214. Prescribed to support brain function in normal situations and when facing mental and emotional pressures.
FDAAZ	Himalaya ProSelect (TM), Vegelax 50, 800 mg capsules, General, Other, Nutritional supplements	UPC Code 605069104012. Prescribed as gentle support of the bowel function in cases of improper diet, low fluid consumption, stress and consumption of certain types of medicines.
FDABA	Perque (TM) 1, Lipotropic and Amino Acid, 180 tablets, General, Other, Nutritional supplements	UPC Code 791760016003.
FDABB	Perque (TM) 1, Lipotropic and Amino Acid, 60 tablets, General, Other, Nutritional supplements	UPC Code 791760015907.

General

ABC Code	Procedure Description	Expanded Definition
FDABC	Perque (TM) 2 without PABA or Folic Acid, 270 tablets, General, Other, Nutritional supplements	UPC Code 791760026200.
FDABD	Perque (TM) 2 without PABA or Folic Acid, 90 tablets, General, Other, Nutritional supplements	UPC Code 791760026101.
FDABE	Perque (TM) 2, Multiple, 180 tablets, General, Other, Nutritional supplements	UPC Code 791760016201.
FDABF	Perque (TM) 2, Multiple, 60 tablets, General, Other, Nutritional supplements	UPC Code 791760016102.
FDABG	Perque (TM) A/02 Antioxidant Formula ,120 tablets, General, Other, Nutritional supplements	UPC Code 791760014900. High effect antioxidant formula containing Vitamin A as beta carotine 20,000 IU, natural mixed tocopherols Vitamin E 150 IU, Zinc Citrate 10 mg, L-selenomethionine 50 mcg, pure crystalline ubiquinone Coenzyme Q-10 5 mg, L-Methionine 40 mg, glutathione 60 mg, Silymarin with 88.5% flavonoid activity 200 mg.
FDABH	Perque (TM) A/02 Antioxidant Formula, 60 tablets, General, Other, Nutritional supplements	UPC Code 791760014801. High effect antioxidant formula containing Vitamin A as beta carotine 20,000 IU, natural mixed tocopherols Vitamin E 150 IU, Zinc Citrate 10 mg, L-selenomethionine 50 mcg, pure crystalline ubiquinone Coenzyme Q-10 5 mg, L-Methionine 40 mg, glutathione 60 mg, Silymarin with 88.5% flavonoid activity 200 mg.
FDABI	Perque (TM) B 12 units, General, Other, Nutritional supplements	UPC Code 791760028006.
FDABJ	Perque (TM) Bio-Quercitin Forte, 100 tablets, General, Other, Nutritional supplements	UPC Code 791760013408. High potency non-citrus flavonol complex containing water soluble 50 mg. quercetin and OPC 85+ 5 mg., the patented trade name for extracted proanthocyiadins from grape seeds.
FDABK	Perque (TM) Bio-Quercitin Forte, 250 tablets, General, Other, Nutritional supplements	UPC Code 791760013507. High potency non-citrus flavonol complex containing water soluble 50 mg. quercetin and OPC 85+ 5 mg., the patented trade name for extracted proanthocyiadins from grape seeds.
FDABL	Perque (TM) Bone Guard, 100 tablets, General, Other, Nutritional supplements	UPC Code 791760021601.

General

ABC Code	Procedure Description	Expanded Definition
FDABM	Perque (TM) Bone Guard, 250 tablets, General, Other, Nutritional supplements	UPC Code 791760021700.
FDABN	Perque (TM) Buffered C Powder, 16 ounces, General, Other, Nutritional supplements	UPC Code 791760025302.
FDABO	Perque (TM) Buffered C Powder, 8 ounces, General, Other, Nutritional supplements	UPC Code 791760025203.
FDABP	Perque (TM) Buffered C Tablets 1,000 mg, 100 tablets, General, Other, Nutritional supplements	UPC Code 791760013804. Hypoallergenic, fully buffered, pH balanced and reduced vitamin C ascorbates of potassium, calcium, magnesium and zinc, containing cofactors, metabolites and transporters to facilitate absorption and prolonged tissue retention. The ascorbic acid powder is put through a triple recrystallization process to remove any source material antigens. No fillers or excipients.
FDABQ	Perque (TM) Buffered C Tablets 1,000 mg, 250 tablets, General, Other, Nutritional supplements	UPC Code 791760013903. Hypoallergenic, fully buffered, pH balanced and reduced vitamin C ascorbates of potassium, calcium, magnesium and zinc, containing cofactors, metabolites and transporters to facilitate absorption and prolonged tissue retention. The ascorbic acid powder is put through a triple recrystallization process to remove any source material antigens. No fillers or excipients.
FDABR	Perque (TM) C strips, General, Other, Nutritional supplements	UPC Code 791760014009. Chemically treated test papers used for measuring the Vitamin C content of urine. Acids will turn the strips pink. Only Vitamin C will turn the blue strips white.
FDABS	Perque (TM) Choline Citrate 7.86 oz, General, Other, Nutritional supplements	UPC Code 791760014108. Liquid form of Choline Citrate 1300 mg. and Vegetable Glycerine 1300 mg. per teaspoon. 7.86 oz container.
FDABT	Perque (TM) Co Q 10 Plus, 100 mg, 30 gelcaps, General, Other, Nutritional supplements	UPC Code 791760016508. 100 mg solubilized Co Q10 with bioactive lipids, Vitamin E d-alpha from mixed tocopherols 30 IU, Rice Bran Oil 226 mg, Gamma Oryzanol 2599 mcg.
FDABU	Perque (TM) Co Q 10 Plus, 30 mg, 60 gelcaps, General, Other, Nutritional supplements	UPC Code 791760016300. 30 mg solubilized Co Q10 with bioactive lipids, Vitamin E d-alpha from mixed tocopherols 30 IU, Rice Bran Oil 226 mg, Gamma Oryzanol 2599 mcg.
FDABV	Perque (TM) Co Q 10 Plus, 60 mg, 60 gelcaps, General, Other, Nutritional supplements	UPC Code 791760016409. 60 mg solubilized Co Q10 with bioactive lipids, Vitamin E d-alpha from mixed tocopherols 30 IU, Rice Bran Oil 226 mg, Gamma Oryzanol 2599 mcg.

General

ABC Code	Procedure Description	Expanded Definition
FDABW	Perque (TM) Co Enzyme Q 10, 100 mg, 30 caplets, General, Other, Nutritional supplements	UPC Code 791760015501.
FDABX	Perque (TM) Co Enzyme Q 10, 30 mg, 60 caplets, General, Other, Nutritional supplements	UPC Code 791760015600.
FDABY	Perque (TM) Co Enzyme Q 10, 60 mg, 60 caplets, General, Other, Nutritional supplements	UPC Code 791760015709.
FDABZ	Perque (TM) Dophilus Regular, 100 caplets, General, Other, Nutritional supplements	UPC Code 791760015808.
FDACA	Perque (TM) Double Zinc, 100 tablets, General, Other, Nutritional supplements	UPC Code 791760022004.
FDACB	Perque (TM) Hematin, New Formulation, 25 mg, General, Other, Nutritional supplements	UPC Code 791760022509.
FDACC	Perque (TM) L Glutamine and PAK, General, Other, Nutritional supplements	UPC Code 791760016805.
FDACD	Perque (TM) L Methionine, Glycine, Mg L Aspartate, General, Other, Nutritional supplements	UPC Code 791760025609.
FDACE	Perque (TM) Magnesium Plus, 650 mg, 180 caplets, General, Other, Nutritional supplements	UPC Code 791760029102.
FDACF	Perque (TM) Magnesium Plus, 650 mg, 60 caplets, General, Other, Nutritional supplements	UPC Code 791760029003.
FDACG	Perque (TM) Osteo 4 Restore, bone and joint formula, General, Other, Nutritional supplements	UPC Code 791760029601.
FDACH	Perque (TM) Perkies, Cherry Raspberry, 270 tablets, General, Other, Nutritional supplements	UPC Code 791760030306.
FDACI	Perque (TM) Perkies, Cherry Raspberry, 90 tablets, General, Other, Nutritional supplements	UPC Code 791760030504.
FDACJ	Perque (TM) Perkies, Honey malt, 270 tablets, General, Other, Nutritional supplements	UPC Code 79176003080.
FDACK	Perque (TM) Perkies, Honey Malt, 90 tablets, General, Other, Nutritional supplements	UPC Code 79176003070.

Other

General

ABC Code	Procedure Description	Expanded Definition
FDACL	Perque (TM) pH Hydrion Papers, measures pH 4.5 to 7.5, General, Other, Nutritional supplements	UPC Code 791760014207.
FDACM	Perque (TM) Pro 4 Abate, Prostate Formula, General, Other, Nutritional supplements	UPC Code 791760029508.
FDACN	Perque (TM) Zinc plus Lozenges, Cherry Raspberry, General, Other, Nutritional supplements	UPC Code 791760030009.
FDACO	Perque (TM) Zinc plus Lozenges, Orange, General, Other, Nutritional supplements	UPC Code 79176003010.
FDAZZ	Undefined, narrative required, General, Other, Nutritional supplements	Anywhere else undefined other Dietary Supplement. Narrative required.

Oral chelation with natural agents

General

ABC Code	Procedure Description	Expanded Definition
FEAZZ	Undefined, narrative required, General, Oral chelation with natural agents, Nutritional supplements	Anywhere else undefined Oral Chelation with Natural Agents. Narrative required.

Oxidative

General

ABC Code	Procedure Description	Expanded Definition
FFAZZ	Undefined, narrative required, General, Oxidative, Nutritional supplements	Anywhere else undefined Oxidative Dietary Supplement. Narrative required.

Vitamins

General

ABC Code	Procedure Description	Expanded Definition
FGAZZ	Undefined, narrative required, General, Vitamins, Nutritional supplements	Anywhere else undefined Vitamin. Narrative required.

Section G: Herbs and Botanicals

Instructions

The following subsections are in Section G:

Oriental

Latin name A – Z (scientific names in Supply & Product Index)

Western

Latin name A – Z (scientific names in Supply & Product Index)

General

Flower essences

Any practitioner, if appropriately trained or certified, may use codes in this section if the scope of practice laws for their state or region allows them to use or order herbs or botanicals.

Do **not** add modifiers to the codes in Section G. See codes in Section A and choose the appropriate reference code to precede codes in this section. Reference codes include prescription services (ADZAA – ADZAG), dispensing services (ADZAI – ADZAK, and ADZAP – ADZAT), compounding services (ADZAL – ADZAO), and general counseling on herbal or other remedies (AEAAL and AEAAM).

Each subsection contains an '**undefined**' code that should only be used when the supply used is not accurately described by another more specific code in this manual. If an '**undefined**' code is used on the claims form, attach a report that provides a detailed narrative about that supply and why it was needed.

Herbs and botanicals

Oriental

Scientific name A

ABC Code	Procedure Description	Expanded Definition
GAAAA	Acanthopanacis, wu jia pi, Scientific name A, Oriental, Herbs and botanicals	wu jia pi
GAAAB	Achyranthis bidentatae, huai niu xi, Scientific name A, Oriental, Herbs and botanicals	huai niu xi
GAAAC	Aconitum, fu zi, Scientific name A, Oriental, Herbs and botanicals	fu zi
GAAAD	Acorus, shi chang pu, Scientific name A, Oriental, Herbs and botanicals	shi chang pu
GAAAE	Actinolitum, yang qi shi, Scientific name A, Oriental, Herbs and botanicals	yang qi shi
GAAAF	Agastache rugosa, huo xiang, Scientific name A, Oriental, Herbs and botanicals	huo xiang
GAAAG	Agrimoniae, xian he cao, Scientific name A, Oriental, Herbs and botanicals	xian he cao
GAAAH	Akebia, mu tong, Scientific name A, Oriental, Herbs and botanicals	mu tong
GAAAI	Ailanthi, bai chun pi, Scientific name A, Oriental, Herbs and botanicals	bai chun pi
GAAAJ	Albizziae, he huan pi, Scientific name A, Oriental, Herbs and botanicals	he huan pi
GAAAK	Alismatis, ze xie, Scientific name A, Oriental, Herbs and botanicals	ze xie
GAAAL	Alli tuberosi, jiu zi, Scientific name A, Oriental, Herbs and botanicals	jiu zi
GAAAM	Allium macrostemona, jiu bai, Scientific name A, Oriental, Herbs and botanicals	jiu bai
GAAAN	Aloe vera, lu hui, Scientific name A, Oriental, Herbs and botanicals	lu hui

Scientific name A

ABC Code	Procedure Description	Expanded Definition
GAAAO	Alpiniae, gao liang jiang, Scientific name A, Oriental, Herbs and botanicals	gao liang jiang
GAAAP	Amomi cardamomi, bai dou kou, Scientific name A, Oriental, Herbs and botanicals	bai dou kou
GAAAQ	Amomum, cao guo, sha ren, Scientific name A, Oriental, Herbs and botanicals	cao guo, sha ren
GAAAR	Amydae, bie jia, Scientific name A, Oriental, Herbs and botanicals	bie jia
GAAAS	Anemarrhenae rhizoma, zhi mu, Scientific name A, Oriental, Herbs and botanicals	zhi mu
GAAAT	Angelica dahurica, bai zhi, Scientific name A, Oriental, Herbs and botanicals	bai zhi
GAAAU	Angelica pubescens, du huo, Scientific name A, Oriental, Herbs and botanicals	du huo
GAAAV	Angelica sinensis, dang gui, Scientific name A, Oriental, Herbs and botanicals	dang gui
GAAAW	Aquilariae, chen xiang, Scientific name A, Oriental, Herbs and botanicals	chen xiang
GAAAX	Arcae, wa leng zi, Scientific name A, Oriental, Herbs and botanicals	wa leng zi
GAAAY	Arctii lappae, niu bang zi, Scientific name A, Oriental, Herbs and botanicals	niu bang zi
GAABA	Areca, bing lang, da fu pi, Scientific name A, Oriental, Herbs and botanicals	bing lang, da fu pi
GAABB	Arisaematis, tian nan xing, Scientific name A, Oriental, Herbs and botanicals	tian nan xing
GAABC	Aristolochiae, ma dou ling, qing mu xiang, Scientific name A, Oriental, Herbs and botanicals	ma dou ling, qing mu xiang
GAABD	Aristolochiae, seu cocculi, guang fang ji, Scientific name A, Oriental, Herbs and botanicals	seu cocculi, guang fang ji

Scientific name A

ABC Code	Procedure Description	Expanded Definition
GAABE	Artemisia anomolae, liu yi nu, Scientific name A, Oriental, Herbs and botanicals	liu yi nu
GAABF	Artemisia apiacea, qing hao, Scientific name A, Oriental, Herbs and botanicals	qing hao
GAABG	Artemisia capillaris, yin chen hao, Scientific name A, Oriental, Herbs and botanicals	yin chen hao
GAABH	Artemisiae, ai ye, Scientific name A, Oriental, Herbs and botanicals	ai ye
GAABI	Asarum, xi xin, Scientific name A, Oriental, Herbs and botanicals	xi xin
GAABJ	Asini gelatinum, ah jao, Scientific name A, Oriental, Herbs and botanicals	ah jao
GAABK	Asparagus, tian men dong, Scientific name A, Oriental, Herbs and botanicals	tian men dong
GAABL	Asterista, zi wan, Scientific name A, Oriental, Herbs and botanicals	zi wan
GAABM	Astragali complanati, sha yuan ji li, Scientific name A, Oriental, Herbs and botanicals	sha yuan ji li
GAABN	Astragali, huang qi, Scientific name A, Oriental, Herbs and botanicals	huang qi
GAABO	Atractylodes lancia, cang zhu, bai zhu, Scientific name A, Oriental, Herbs and botanicals	cang zhu, bai zhu
GAAZY	Other Oriental herb or botanical, narrative required, Scientific name A, Oriental, Herbs and botanicals	Other Oriental herb or botanical with scientific name A. Narrative required.

Scientific name B

ABC Code	Procedure Description	Expanded Definition
GABAA	Bambusae, zhu ru, Scientific name B, Oriental, Herbs and botanicals	zhu ru
GABAB	Baphicacanthus, da qing ye, Scientific name B, Oriental, Herbs and botanicals	da qing ye

Scientific name B

ABC Code	Procedure Description	Expanded Definition
GABAC	Belamcandae, she gan, Scientific name B, Oriental, Herbs and botanicals	she gan
GABAD	Benincasae, don gua ren, Scientific name B, Oriental, Herbs and botanicals	don gua ren
GABAE	Biota orientalis, bai zi ren, Scientific name B, Oriental, Herbs and botanicals	bai zi ren
GABAF	Bletilla, bai ji, Scientific name B, Oriental, Herbs and botanicals	bai ji
GABAG	Bombyx, jiang can, Scientific name B, Oriental, Herbs and botanicals	jiang can
GABAH	Borax, peng sha, Scientific name B, Oriental, Herbs and botanicals	peng sha
GABAI	Boswellia, ru xiang, Scientific name B, Oriental, Herbs and botanicals	ru xiang
GABAJ	Brucea javanica, ya dan zi, Scientific name B, Oriental, Herbs and botanicals	ya dan zi
GABAK	Buddleia, mi meng hua, Scientific name B, Oriental, Herbs and botanicals	mi meng hua
GABAL	Bupleurum, chai hu, Scientific name B, Oriental, Herbs and botanicals	chai hu
GABZZ	Other Oriental herb or botanical, narrative required, Scientific name B, Oriental, Herbs and botanicals	Other Oriental herb or botanical with scientific name B. Narrative required.

Scientific name C

ABC Code	Procedure Description	Expanded Definition
GACAA	Calcitum, han shui shi, Scientific name C, Oriental, Herbs and botanicals	han shui shi
GACAB	Callicarpa, zi zhu, Scientific name C, Oriental, Herbs and botanicals	zi zhu
GACAC	Camphora, zhang nao, Scientific name C, Oriental, Herbs and botanicals	zhang nao
GACAE	Carpesium abrotanoides, he shi, Scientific name C, Oriental, Herbs and botanicals	he shi

Scientific name C

ABC Code	Procedure Description	Expanded Definition
GACAF	Carthamus, hong hua, Scientific name C, Oriental, Herbs and botanicals	hong hua
GACAG	Caryophylli, ding xiang, Scientific name C, Oriental, Herbs and botanicals	ding xiang
GACAH	Cassiae torae, jue ming zi, Scientific name C, Oriental, Herbs and botanicals	jue ming zi
GACAI	Cubebae, bi cheng qie, Scientific name C, Oriental, Herbs and botanicals	bi cheng qie
GACAJ	Cephalanopios, xiao ji, Scientific name C, Oriental, Herbs and botanicals	xiao ji
GACAK	Chaenomelis, mu gua, Scientific name C, Oriental, Herbs and botanicals	mu gua
GACAL	Chebula, ke zi rou, Scientific name C, Oriental, Herbs and botanicals	ke zi rou
GACAM	Chrysanthemum, ju hua, Scientific name C, Oriental, Herbs and botanicals	ju hua
GACAN	Cibotium, gou ji, Scientific name C, Oriental, Herbs and botanicals	gou ji
GACAO	Cicadae, chan tui, Scientific name C, Oriental, Herbs and botanicals	chan tui
GACAP	Cimicifuga foetida, sheng ma, Scientific name C, Oriental, Herbs and botanicals	sheng ma
GACAQ	Cnidium monnieri, she chuang zi, Scientific name C, Oriental, Herbs and botanicals	she chuang zi
GACAR	Cinnabaris, zhu sha, Scientific name C, Oriental, Herbs and botanicals	zhu sha
GACAS	Cinnamomum, gui zhi, rou gui, Scientific name C, Oriental, Herbs and botanicals	gui zhi, rou gui
GACAT	Cirsii japonica, da ji, Scientific name C, Oriental, Herbs and botanicals	da ji
GACAU	Cistanches, rou cong rong, Scientific name C, Oriental, Herbs and botanicals	rou cong rong

Scientific name C

ABC Code	Procedure Description	Expanded Definition
GACAV	Citri reticulatae, qing pi, Scientific name C, Oriental, Herbs and botanicals	qing pi
GACAW	Citri sarcodactylis, citrus medica, fo shou gan, Scientific name C, Oriental, Herbs and botanicals	fo shou gan
GACAX	Citrullus vulgaris, xi gua, Scientific name C, Oriental, Herbs and botanicals	xi gua
GACAY	Citrus aurantium, citri seu ponciri, zhi shi, Scientific name C, Oriental, Herbs and botanicals	zhi shi
GACBA	Clematidis, wei ling xiang, Scientific name C, Oriental, Herbs and botanicals	wei ling xiang
GACBB	Codonopsis, dang shen, Scientific name C, Oriental, Herbs and botanicals	dang shen
GACBC	Coicis lachryma, yi yi ren, Scientific name C, Oriental, Herbs and botanicals	yi yi ren
GACBD	Coptidis, huang lian, Scientific name C, Oriental, Herbs and botanicals	huang lian
GACBE	Cordyceps, dong chong xiao cao, Scientific name C, Oriental, Herbs and botanicals	dong chong xiao cao
GACBF	Corni, shan zhu yu, Scientific name C, Oriental, Herbs and botanicals	shan zhu yu
GACBG	Corydalis, yuanhusuo, Scientific name C, Oriental, Herbs and botanicals	yuanhusuo
GACBH	Crataegus, shan zha, Scientific name C, Oriental, Herbs and botanicals	shan zha
GACBJ	Cucurbitae, nan gua zi, Scientific name C, Oriental, Herbs and botanicals	nan gua zi
GACBK	Curculigo, xian mao, Scientific name C, Oriental, Herbs and botanicals	xian mao
GACBL	Curcumae, e zhu, jiang huan, yu jin, Scientific name C, Oriental, Herbs and botanicals	e zhu, jiang huan, yu jin

Scientific name C

ABC Code	Procedure Description	Expanded Definition
GACBM	Cuscutae, tu si zi, Scientific name C, Oriental, Herbs and botanicals	tu si zi
GACBN	Cyathulae, chuan niu xi, Scientific name C, Oriental, Herbs and botanicals	chuan niu xi
GACBO	Cynanchum stautoni, bai qian, Scientific name C, Oriental, Herbs and botanicals	bai qian
GACBP	Cynomorii, suo yang, Scientific name C, Oriental, Herbs and botanicals	suo yang
GACBQ	Cyperus, xhiang fu, Scientific name C, Oriental, Herbs and botanicals	xhiang fu
GACZZ	Other Oriental herb or botanical, narrative required, Scientific name C, Oriental, Herbs and botanicals	Other Oriental herb or botanical with scientific name C. Narrative required.

Scientific name D

ABC Code	Procedure Description	Expanded Definition
GADAA	Dalbergiae odoriferae, jiang xiang, Scientific name D, Oriental, Herbs and botanicals	jiang xiang
GADAB	Daphne genkwa, yuan hua, Scientific name D, Oriental, Herbs and botanicals	yuan hua
GADAC	Dendrobium, shi hu, Scientific name D, Oriental, Herbs and botanicals	shi hu
GADAD	Dianthi, qu mai, Scientific name D, Oriental, Herbs and botanicals	qu mai
GADAE	Dichroae febrifugae, chang shan, Scientific name D, Oriental, Herbs and botanicals	chang shan
GADAF	Dictamni, bai xian pi, Scientific name D, Oriental, Herbs and botanicals	bai xian pi
GADAG	Dioscoreae bulbiferae, huang yao zi, Scientific name D, Oriental, Herbs and botanicals	huang yao zi
GADAH	Dioscoreae, bei xie, Scientific name D, Oriental, Herbs and botanicals	bei xie
GADAI	Dioscoreae oppositae, shan yao, Scientific name D, Oriental, Herbs and botanicals	shan yao

Scientific name D

ABC Code	Procedure Description	Expanded Definition
GADAJ	Diospyros kaki, shi di, Scientific name D, Oriental, Herbs and botanicals	shi di
GADAK	Dipsacus, xu duan, Scientific name D, Oriental, Herbs and botanicals	xu duan
GADAL	Dolichoris, bai bian dou, Scientific name D, Oriental, Herbs and botanicals	bai bian dou
GADAM	Drynaria, gu sui bu, Scientific name D, Oriental, Herbs and botanicals	gu sui bu
GADZZ	Other Oriental herb or botanical, narrative required, Scientific name D, Oriental, Herbs and botanicals	Other Oriental herb or botanical with scientific name D. Narrative required.

Scientific name E

ABC Code	Procedure Description	Expanded Definition
GAEAA	Ecliptae, han lian cao, Scientific name E, Oriental, Herbs and botanicals	han lian cao
GAEAB	Elsholtziae, xiang ru, Scientific name E, Oriental, Herbs and botanicals	xiang ru
GAEAC	Ephedra, ma huang, Scientific name E, Oriental, Herbs and botanicals	ma huang
GAEAD	Epimedium, yin yang huo, Scientific name E, Oriental, Herbs and botanicals	yin yang huo
GAEAE	Equisetii, mu zei, Scientific name E, Oriental, Herbs and botanicals	mu zei
GAEAF	Eriobotrya, pi pa ye, Scientific name E, Oriental, Herbs and botanicals	pi pa ye
GAEAG	Eriocaulis buergeriana, eriocaulis sieboldianus, gu jiang cao, Scientific name E, Oriental, Herbs and botanicals	gu jiang cao
GAEAH	Erythrinae, hai tong pi, Scientific name E, Oriental, Herbs and botanicals	hai tong pi
GAEAI	Eucommia, du zhong, Scientific name E, Oriental, Herbs and botanicals	du zhong

Scientific name E

ABC Code	Procedure Description	Expanded Definition
GAEAJ	Eupatorii fortunei, pei lan, Scientific name E, Oriental, Herbs and botanicals	pei lan
GAEAK	Euphorbia helioscopia, ze qi, Scientific name E, Oriental, Herbs and botanicals	ze qi
GAEAL	Euphoria longana, long yan rou, Scientific name E, Oriental, Herbs and botanicals	long yan rou
GAEAM	Euphorbia, gan sui, Scientific name E, Oriental, Herbs and botanicals	gan sui
GAEAN	Euryales ferox, qian shi, Scientific name E, Oriental, Herbs and botanicals	qian shi
GAEAO	Evodia, wu zhu yu, Scientific name E, Oriental, Herbs and botanicals	wu zhu yu
GAEZZ	Other Oriental herb or botanical, narrative required, Scientific name E, Oriental, Herbs and botanicals	Other Oriental herb or botanical with scientific name E. Narrative required.

Scientific name F

ABC Code	Procedure Description	Expanded Definition
GAFAA	Fagopyrii, qiao mai, Scientific name F, Oriental, Herbs and botanicals	qiao mai
GAFAB	Foeniculum, xiao hui xiang, Scientific name F, Oriental, Herbs and botanicals	xiao hui xiang
GAFAC	Forsythia, lian qiao, Scientific name F, Oriental, Herbs and botanicals	lian qiao
GAFAD	Fraxini, qin pi, Scientific name F, Oriental, Herbs and botanicals	qin pi
GAFAE	Fritillariae cirrhosae, chuan bei mu, Scientific name F, Oriental, Herbs and botanicals	chuan bei mu
GAFAF	Fritillariae thunbergii, zhe bei mu, Scientific name F, Oriental, Herbs and botanicals	zhe bei mu
GAFZZ	Other Oriental herb or botanical, narrative required, Scientific name F, Oriental, Herbs and botanicals	Other Oriental herb or botanical with scientific name F. Narrative required.

Scientific Name G

ABC Code	Procedure Description	Expanded Definition
GAGAA	Ganoderma lucidum, lin zhi, Scientific Name G, Oriental, Herbs and botanicals	lin zhi
GAGAB	Gardeniae, zhi zi, Scientific Name G, Oriental, Herbs and botanicals	zhi zi
GAGAC	Gastrodiae, tian ma, Scientific Name G, Oriental, Herbs and botanicals	tian ma
GAGAD	Gentiana macrophylla, qin jiao, Scientific Name G, Oriental, Herbs and botanicals	qin jiao
GAGAE	Gentiana scabra, long dan, Scientific Name G, Oriental, Herbs and botanicals	long dan
GAGAF	Ginkgo, yin guo, ying xing ye, Scientific Name G, Oriental, Herbs and botanicals	yin guo, ying xing ye
GAGAG	Ginseng, ren shen, xi yan she, Scientific Name G, Oriental, Herbs and botanicals	ren shen, xi yan she
GAGAH	Gleditsia, zao jiao ci, Scientific Name G, Oriental, Herbs and botanicals	zao jiao ci
GAGAI	Glehniae littoralis, bei sha shen, Scientific Name G, Oriental, Herbs and botanicals	bei sha shen
GAGAJ	Glycyrrhiza, gan cao, Scientific Name G, Oriental, Herbs and botanicals	gan cao
GAGZZ	Other Oriental herb or botanical, narrative required, Scientific Name G, Oriental, Herbs and botanicals	Other Oriental herb or botanical with scientific name G. Narrative required.

Scientific name H

ABC Code	Procedure Description	Expanded Definition
GAHAA	Haliotis, shi jue ming, Scientific name H, Oriental, Herbs and botanicals	shi jue ming
GAHAB	Halloysitum, chi shi zhi, Scientific name H, Oriental, Herbs and botanicals	chi shi zhi
GAHAC	Homalomenae, qian nian jian, Scientific name H, Oriental, Herbs and botanicals	qian nian jian
GAHAD	Hordeum germinatus, mai ya, Scientific name H, Oriental, Herbs and botanicals	mai ya

Scientific name H

ABC Code	Procedure Description	Expanded Definition
GAHAE	Houttuynia, yu xing cao, Scientific name H, Oriental, Herbs and botanicals	yu xing cao
GAHAF	Hydnocarpi, da feng zi, Scientific name H, Oriental, Herbs and botanicals	da feng zi
GAHAG	Hypoglaucae dioscoreae, bie xie, Scientific name H, Oriental, Herbs and botanicals	bie xie
GAHZZ	Other Oriental herb or botanical, narrative required, Scientific name H, Oriental, Herbs and botanicals	Other Oriental herb or botanical with scientific name H. Narrative required.

Scientific name I

ABC Code	Procedure Description	Expanded Definition
GAIAA	Imperata cylindrica, bai mao gen, Scientific name I, Oriental, Herbs and botanicals	bai mao gen
GAIAB	Inulae, xuan fu hua, Scientific name I, Oriental, Herbs and botanicals	xuan fu hua
GAIAC	Isatidis baphicacanthi, ban lan gen, Scientific name I, Oriental, Herbs and botanicals	ban lan gen
GAIZZ	Other Oriental herb or botanical, narrative required, Scientific name I, Oriental, Herbs and botanicals	Other Oriental herb or botanical with scientific name I. Narrative required.

Scientific name J

ABC Code	Procedure Description	Expanded Definition
GAJAA	Juglandis regiae, hu tao ren, Scientific name J, Oriental, Herbs and botanicals	hu tao ren
GAJAB	Juncii, deng xin cao, Scientific name J, Oriental, Herbs and botanicals	deng xin cao
GAJZZ	Other Oriental herb or botanical, narrative required, Scientific name J, Oriental, Herbs and botanicals	Other Oriental herb or botanical with scientific name J. Narrative required.

Scientific name K

ABC Code	Procedure Description	Expanded Definition
GAKAA	Kaempferia, san nai, Scientific name K, Oriental, Herbs and botanicals	san nai

Scientific name K

ABC Code	Procedure Description	Expanded Definition
GAKAB	Kochiae scopariae, di fu zi, Scientific name K, Oriental, Herbs and botanicals	di fu zi
GAKZZ	Other Oriental herb or botanical, narrative required, Scientific name K, Oriental, Herbs and botanicals	Other Oriental herb or botanical with scientific name K. Narrative required.

Scientific name L

ABC Code	Procedure Description	Expanded Definition
GALAA	Laminaria japonica, alga, kun bu, Scientific name L, Oriental, Herbs and botanicals	alga, kun bu
GALAB	Laminaria, hai dai, Scientific name L, Oriental, Herbs and botanicals	hai dai
GALAC	Lasiospharae, ma bo, Scientific name L, Oriental, Herbs and botanicals	ma bo
GALAD	Ledebouriella seseloides, fang feng, Scientific name L, Oriental, Herbs and botanicals	fang feng
GALAE	Lemnae seu spirodelae, fu ping, Scientific name L, Oriental, Herbs and botanicals	fu ping
GALAF	Leonuri heterophylli, yi mu cao, Scientific name L, Oriental, Herbs and botanicals	yi mu cao
GALAG	Lepidium, ting li zi, Scientific name L, Oriental, Herbs and botanicals	ting li zi
GALAH	Ligustici wallichii, chuan xiong, Scientific name L, Oriental, Herbs and botanicals	chuan xiong
GALAI	Ligustici, gao ben, Scientific name L, Oriental, Herbs and botanicals	gao ben
GALAJ	Ligustrum, nu zhen zi, Scientific name L, Oriental, Herbs and botanicals	nu zhen zi
GALAK	Lillii, bai he, Scientific name L, Oriental, Herbs and botanicals	bai he
GALAL	Linderae strychnifolia, wu yao, Scientific name L, Oriental, Herbs and botanicals	wu yao
GALAM	Liquidambaris, lu lu tong, Scientific name L, Oriental, Herbs and botanicals	lu lu tong

Scientific name L

ABC Code	Procedure Description	Expanded Definition
GALAN	Lithospermum, zi cao gen, Scientific name L, Oriental, Herbs and botanicals	zi cao gen
GALAO	Litsea, dou chi jiang, Scientific name L, Oriental, Herbs and botanicals	dou chi jiang
GALAP	Lobelia, ban bian lian, Scientific name L, Oriental, Herbs and botanicals	ban bian lian
GALAQ	Lonicera japonica, ren dong teng, Scientific name L, Oriental, Herbs and botanicals	ren dong teng
GALAR	Longanae, long yen, Scientific name L, Oriental, Herbs and botanicals	long yen
GALAS	Lonicerae japonica, jin yin hua, Scientific name L, Oriental, Herbs and botanicals	jin yin hua
GALAT	Lophatheri gracilis, dan zhu ye, Scientific name L, Oriental, Herbs and botanicals	dan zhu ye
GALAU	Loranthi seu visci, sang ji sheng, Scientific name L, Oriental, Herbs and botanicals	sang ji sheng
GALAV	Lumbricus, di long, Scientific name L, Oriental, Herbs and botanicals	di long
GALAW	Lycium chinense, di gu pi, gou qi zi, Scientific name L, Oriental, Herbs and botanicals	di gu pi, gou qi zi
GALAX	Lycoperdon, ma po, Scientific name L, Oriental, Herbs and botanicals	ma po
GALAY	Lycopi lucidi, ze lan, Scientific name L, Oriental, Herbs and botanicals	ze lan
GALBA	Lycopodii, shen jin cao, Scientific name L, Oriental, Herbs and botanicals	shen jin cao
GALBB	Lycopodium serratum, jin bu huan, Scientific name L, Oriental, Herbs and botanicals	jin bu huan
GALBC	Lygodii japonici, hai jin sha, jin sha teng, Scientific name L, Oriental, Herbs and botanicals	hai jin sha, jin sha teng
GALBD	Lysimachia, jin qian cao, Scientific name L, Oriental, Herbs and botanicals	jin qian cao

Scientific name L

ABC Code	Procedure Description	Expanded Definition
GALZZ	Other Oriental herb or botanical, narrative required, Scientific name L, Oriental, Herbs and botanicals	Other Oriental herb or botanical with scientific name L. Narrative required.

Scientific name M

ABC Code	Procedure Description	Expanded Definition
GAMAA	Macacae, hou zao, Scientific name M, Oriental, Herbs and botanicals	hou zao
GAMAB	Magnolia, hou po, xin yi, Scientific name M, Oriental, Herbs and botanicals	hou po, xin yi
GAMAC	Maidis stigma, yu mi xu, Scientific name M, Oriental, Herbs and botanicals	yu mi xu
GAMAD	Manitis, chuan shan jia, Scientific name M, Oriental, Herbs and botanicals	chuan shan jia
GAMAE	Massa fermentata, shen qu, Scientific name M, Oriental, Herbs and botanicals	shen qu
GAMAF	Matteuccia struthiopteris, guan zhong, Scientific name M, Oriental, Herbs and botanicals	guan zhong
GAMAG	Mazus, ding jin cao, Scientific name M, Oriental, Herbs and botanicals	ding jin cao
GAMAH	Meliae radicis, chuan lian zi, Scientific name M, Oriental, Herbs and botanicals	chuan lian zi
GAMAI	Mentha, bo he, Scientific name M, Oriental, Herbs and botanicals	bo he
GAMAJ	Millettia, ji xue teng, Scientific name M, Oriental, Herbs and botanicals	ji xue teng
GAMAK	Minium, qian dan, Scientific name M, Oriental, Herbs and botanicals	qian dan
GAMAL	Moghaniae, yi tiao gen, Scientific name M, Oriental, Herbs and botanicals	yi tiao gen
GAMAM	Momordicae, luo han guo, luo han ye, mu bie zi, Scientific name M, Oriental, Herbs and botanicals	luo han guo, luo han ye, mu bie zi

Scientific name M

ABC Code	Procedure Description	Expanded Definition
GAMAN	Mori albae, sang bai pi, sang shen, sang ye, sang zhi, Scientific name M, Oriental, Herbs and botanicals	sang bai pi, sang shen, sang ye, sang zhi
GAMAO	Morindae, ba ji tian, Scientific name M, Oriental, Herbs and botanicals	ba ji tian
GAMAP	Moutan radicis, mu dan pi, Scientific name M, Oriental, Herbs and botanicals	mu dan pi
GAMAQ	Mucunae, ji xue teng, Scientific name M, Oriental, Herbs and botanicals	ji xue teng
GAMAR	Myristicae, rou dou kou, Scientific name M, Oriental, Herbs and botanicals	rou dou kou
GAMAS	Myrrha, mo yao, Scientific name M, Oriental, Herbs and botanicals	mo yao
GAMZZ	Other Oriental herb or botanical, narrative required, Scientific name M, Oriental, Herbs and botanicals	Other Oriental herb or botanical with scientific name M. Narrative required.

Scientific name N

ABC Code	Procedure Description	Expanded Definition
GANAA	Naemorhedis, shan yang, Scientific name N, Oriental, Herbs and botanicals	shan yang
GANAB	Nelumbo, he ye, liang fan, lian geng, lian xin, lian xu, lian zi, ou lie, Scientific name N, Oriental, Herbs and botanicals	he ye, liang fan, lian geng, lian xin, lian xu, lian zi, ou lie
GANZZ	Other Oriental herb or botanical, narrative required, Scientific name N, Oriental, Herbs and botanicals	Other Oriental herb or botanical with scientific name N. Narrative required.

Scientific name O

ABC Code	Procedure Description	Expanded Definition
GAOAA	Oldenlandiae, bai hua she, Scientific name O, Oriental, Herbs and botanicals	bai hua she
GAOAB	Olibanum, ru xiang, Scientific name O, Oriental, Herbs and botanicals	ru xiang
GAOAC	Ophiopogonis, mai men dong, Scientific name O, Oriental, Herbs and botanicals	mai men dong

Scientific name O

ABC Code	Procedure Description	Expanded Definition
GAOAD	Oroxyli, gu zhi hua, Scientific name O, Oriental, Herbs and botanicals	gu zhi hua
GAOAE	Orthosiphon, hu shi cao, Scientific name O, Oriental, Herbs and botanicals	hu shi cao
GAOAF	Oryzae sativa, gu ya, Scientific name O, Oriental, Herbs and botanicals	gu ya
GAOAG	Oryzae, nuo dao gen, Scientific name O, Oriental, Herbs and botanicals	nuo dao gen
GAOZZ	Other Oriental herb or botanical, narrative required, Scientific name O, Oriental, Herbs and botanicals	Other Oriental herb or botanical with scientific name O. Narrative required.

Scientific name P

ABC Code	Procedure Description	Expanded Definition
GAPAA	Paeonia, bai shao yao, chi shao yao, dan pi, mu dan pi, Scientific name P, Oriental, Herbs and botanicals	bai shao yao, chi shao yao, dan pi, mu dan pi
GAPAB	Panacis quinquefolii, xi yang shen, Scientific name P, Oriental, Herbs and botanicals	xi yang shen
GAPAC	Papaveris, ying su ke, Scientific name P, Oriental, Herbs and botanicals	ying su ke
GAPAD	Patriniae seu thlaspi, bai jiang cao, Scientific name P, Oriental, Herbs and botanicals	bai jiang cao
GAPAE	Perillae, zi su ye, Scientific name P, Oriental, Herbs and botanicals	zi su ye
GAPAF	Persicae, tao ren, Scientific name P, Oriental, Herbs and botanicals	tao ren
GAPAG	Peucedani, qian hu, Scientific name P, Oriental, Herbs and botanicals	qian hu
GAPAH	Pharbitidis, qian niu zi, Scientific name P, Oriental, Herbs and botanicals	qian niu zi
GAPAI	Phaseoli radiati, lu dou, Scientific name P, Oriental, Herbs and botanicals	lu dou

Scientific name P

ABC Code	Procedure Description	Expanded Definition
GAPAJ	Phaseoli, chi xiao dou, Scientific name P, Oriental, Herbs and botanicals	chi xiao dou
GAPAK	Phellodendri, huang bai, Scientific name P, Oriental, Herbs and botanicals	huang bai
GAPAL	Phragmatis, lu gen, Scientific name P, Oriental, Herbs and botanicals	lu gen
GAPAM	Phytolaccae, shang lu, Scientific name P, Oriental, Herbs and botanicals	shang lu
GAPAN	Picrorhiza, hu huang, Scientific name P, Oriental, Herbs and botanicals	hu huang
GAPAO	Pinellia ternatae, ban xia, Scientific name P, Oriental, Herbs and botanicals	ban xia
GAPAP	Pini nodi, song jie, Scientific name P, Oriental, Herbs and botanicals	song jie
GAPAQ	Piperis longi, bi bo, Scientific name P, Oriental, Herbs and botanicals	bi bo
GAPAR	Piperis nigri, hu jiao, Scientific name P, Oriental, Herbs and botanicals	hu jiao
GAPAS	Piperis, hai feng, Scientific name P, Oriental, Herbs and botanicals	hai feng
GAPAT	Plantaginis, che qian, che qian zi, Scientific name P, Oriental, Herbs and botanicals	che qian, che qian zi
GAPAU	Platycodi grandifolii, jie geng, Scientific name P, Oriental, Herbs and botanicals	jie geng
GAPAV	Polygalae, yuan zhi, Scientific name P, Oriental, Herbs and botanicals	yuan zhi
GAPAW	Polygonati, huang jing, yu zhu, Scientific name P, Oriental, Herbs and botanicals	huang jing, yu zhu
GAPAX	Polygoni mylittae, lei wan, Scientific name P, Oriental, Herbs and botanicals	lei wan
GAPAY	Polygoni, bian bu, he shou wu, ye jiao teng, Scientific name P, Oriental, Herbs and botanicals	bian bu, he shou wu, ye jiao teng

Scientific name P

ABC Code	Procedure Description	Expanded Definition
GAPBA	Polypori umbellati, zhu ling, Scientific name P, Oriental, Herbs and botanicals	zhu ling
GAPBB	Poriae cocos, chi fu ling, fu ling, fu shen, Scientific name P, Oriental, Herbs and botanicals	chi fu ling, fu ling, fu shen
GAPBC	Portulacae, ma ci jian, Scientific name P, Oriental, Herbs and botanicals	ma ci jian
GAPBD	Prunellae, xia ku cao, Scientific name P, Oriental, Herbs and botanicals	xia ku cao
GAPBE	Pruni armeniacae, xing ren, Scientific name P, Oriental, Herbs and botanicals	xing ren
GAPBF	Pruni mume, wu mei, Scientific name P, Oriental, Herbs and botanicals	wu mei
GAPBG	Pruni, yu li ren, Scientific name P, Oriental, Herbs and botanicals	yu li ren
GAPBH	Pseudoginseng, san qi, Scientific name P, Oriental, Herbs and botanicals	san qi
GAPBI	Pseudostellariae, hai er shen, Scientific name P, Oriental, Herbs and botanicals	hai er shen
GAPBJ	Psoraleae, bu gu zhi, Scientific name P, Oriental, Herbs and botanicals	bu gu zhi
GAPBK	Pteris, feng wei cao, Scientific name P, Oriental, Herbs and botanicals	feng wei cao
GAPBL	Puerariae, ge gen, ge hua, Scientific name P, Oriental, Herbs and botanicals	ge gen, ge hua
GAPBM	Pulsatillae, bai tou weng, Scientific name P, Oriental, Herbs and botanicals	bai tou weng
GAPBN	Punicae granati, shi liu pi, Scientific name P, Oriental, Herbs and botanicals	shi liu pi
GAPBO	Punicae, shi liu gen pi, Scientific name P, Oriental, Herbs and botanicals	shi liu gen pi
GAPBP	Pyrrosiae, shi wei, Scientific name P, Oriental, Herbs and botanicals	shi wei

Scientific name P

ABC Code	Procedure Description	Expanded Definition
GAPZZ	Other Oriental herb or botanical, narrative required, Scientific name P, Oriental, Herbs and botanicals	Other Oriental herb or botanical with scientific name P. Narrative required.

Scientific name Q

ABC Code	Procedure Description	Expanded Definition
GAQAA	Quisqualis indicae, shi jun zi, Scientific name Q, Oriental, Herbs and botanicals	shi jun zi
GAQZZ	Other Oriental herb or botanical, narrative required, Scientific name Q, Oriental, Herbs and botanicals	Other Oriental herb or botanical with scientific name Q. Narrative required.

Scientific name R

ABC Code	Procedure Description	Expanded Definition
GARAA	Raphni, lai fu zi, Scientific name R, Oriental, Herbs and botanicals	lai fu zi
GARAB	Rehmanniae, sheng di, shu di huang, Scientific name R, Oriental, Herbs and botanicals	sheng di, shu di huang
GARAC	Rhapontici seu, lou lu, Scientific name R, Oriental, Herbs and botanicals	lou lu
GARAD	Rhei, da huang, Scientific name R, Oriental, Herbs and botanicals	da huang
GARAE	Rhi chinensis, wu bei zi, Scientific name R, Oriental, Herbs and botanicals	wu bei zi
GARAF	Rosae chinensis, yue ji hua, Scientific name R, Oriental, Herbs and botanicals	yue ji hua
GARAG	Rosae cymosae, xiao jin ying, Scientific name R, Oriental, Herbs and botanicals	xiao jin ying
GARAH	Rosae laevigatae, jin ying zi, Scientific name R, Oriental, Herbs and botanicals	jin ying zi
GARAI	Rosae rugosae, mei gui hua, Scientific name R, Oriental, Herbs and botanicals	mei gui hua
GARAJ	Rubiae, qian cao, Scientific name R, Oriental, Herbs and botanicals	qian cao

Scientific name R

ABC Code	Procedure Description	Expanded Definition
GARAK	Rubus, fu pen zi, Scientific name R, Oriental, Herbs and botanicals	fu pen zi
GARZZ	Other Oriental herb or botanical, narrative required, Scientific name R, Oriental, Herbs and botanicals	Other Oriental herb or botanical with scientific name R. Narrative required.

Scientific name S

ABC Code	Procedure Description	Expanded Definition
GASAA	Saccharum granorum, yi tang, Scientific name S, Oriental, Herbs and botanicals	yi tang
GASAB	Salvia, dan shen, Scientific name S, Oriental, Herbs and botanicals	dan shen
GASAC	Sanguisorba, di yu, hei di yu, Scientific name S, Oriental, Herbs and botanicals	di yu, hei di yu
GASAD	Santali albi, tan xiang, Scientific name S, Oriental, Herbs and botanicals	tan xiang
GASAE	Sappan, su mu, Scientific name S, Oriental, Herbs and botanicals	su mu
GASAF	Sargassi, hai zao, Scientific name S, Oriental, Herbs and botanicals	hai zao
GASAG	Saussureae, mu xiang, Scientific name S, Oriental, Herbs and botanicals	mu xiang
GASAH	Schisandrae chinensis, wu wei zi, Scientific name S, Oriental, Herbs and botanicals	wu wei zi
GASAI	Schizonepetae, jin jie, Scientific name S, Oriental, Herbs and botanicals	jin jie
GASAJ	Scrophulariae, yuan shen, Scientific name S, Oriental, Herbs and botanicals	yuan shen
GASAK	Scutellariae, ban zhi lian, huang qin, Scientific name S, Oriental, Herbs and botanicals	ban zhi lian, huang qin
GASAL	Selaginella tamariscina, juan bai, Scientific name S, Oriental, Herbs and botanicals	juan bai
GASAM	Selaginellae, shi shang bai, Scientific name S, Oriental, Herbs and botanicals	shi shang bai

Scientific name S

ABC Code	Procedure Description	Expanded Definition
GASAN	Senna, fan xie yeh, Scientific name S, Oriental, Herbs and botanicals	fan xie yeh
GASAO	Sesami, hu ma ren, Scientific name S, Oriental, Herbs and botanicals	hu ma ren
GASAP	Siegesbeckiae, xi qian cao, Scientific name S, Oriental, Herbs and botanicals	xi qian cao
GASAQ	Sielris, fan feng, Scientific name S, Oriental, Herbs and botanicals	fan feng
GASAR	Sinapis alba, Scientific name S, Oriental, Herbs and botanicals	sinapis alba
GASAS	Smilacis glabrae, tu fu ling, Scientific name S, Oriental, Herbs and botanicals	tu fu ling
GASAT	Sojae, dan dou chi, Scientific name S, Oriental, Herbs and botanicals	dan dou chi
GASAU	Sophorae japonica, huai hua, huai jiao, Scientific name S, Oriental, Herbs and botanicals	huai hua, huai jiao
GASAV	Sophorae, ku shen, shan dougen, Scientific name S, Oriental, Herbs and botanicals	ku shen, shan dougen
GASAW	Sparganium, san leng, Scientific name S, Oriental, Herbs and botanicals	san leng
GASAX	Stellariae, yin chai hu, Scientific name S, Oriental, Herbs and botanicals	yin chai hu
GASAY	Stemona, bai bu, Scientific name S, Oriental, Herbs and botanicals	bai bu
GASBA	Stephania, han fang ji, Scientific name S, Oriental, Herbs and botanicals	han fang ji
GASBB	Sterculiae, pang da hai, Scientific name S, Oriental, Herbs and botanicals	pang da hai
GASBC	Strychnotis, ma qian zi, Scientific name S, Oriental, Herbs and botanicals	ma qian zi
GASBD	Succinum, hu po, Scientific name S, Oriental, Herbs and botanicals	hu po

Scientific name S

ABC Code	Procedure Description	Expanded Definition
GASZZ	Other Oriental herb or botanical, narrative required, Scientific name S, Oriental, Herbs and botanicals	Other Oriental herb or botanical with scientific name S. Narrative required.

Scientific name T

ABC Code	Procedure Description	Expanded Definition
GATAA	Taraxacum, pu gong ying, Scientific name T, Oriental, Herbs and botanicals	pu gong ying
GATAB	Terminaliae, ke zi rou, Scientific name T, Oriental, Herbs and botanicals	ke zi rou
GATAC	Testudinis, gui ban, Scientific name T, Oriental, Herbs and botanicals	gui ban
GATAD	Tetrapanacis, tong cao, Scientific name T, Oriental, Herbs and botanicals	tong cao
GATAE	Tinosporae, kuan jin teng, Scientific name T, Oriental, Herbs and botanicals	kuan jin teng
GATAF	Torreyae, fei zi, Scientific name T, Oriental, Herbs and botanicals	fei zi
GATAG	Trachelospermi, luo shi teng, Scientific name T, Oriental, Herbs and botanicals	luo shi teng
GATAH	Tremellae, bai mu er, Scientific name T, Oriental, Herbs and botanicals	bai mu er
GATAI	Tribuli, ji li, Scientific name T, Oriental, Herbs and botanicals	ji li
GATAJ	Trichosanthis, gua lou pi, gua lou ren, gua lou shi, tian hua fen, Scientific name T, Oriental, Herbs and botanicals	gua lou pi, gua lou ren, gua lou shi, tian hua fen
GATAK	Trigonellae, hu lu ba, Scientific name T, Oriental, Herbs and botanicals	hu lu ba
GATAL	Tritici, fu xiao mai, Scientific name T, Oriental, Herbs and botanicals	fu xiao mai
GATAM	Trogopterorum, wu ling zhi, Scientific name T, Oriental, Herbs and botanicals	wu ling zhi

Scientific name T

ABC Code	Procedure Description	Expanded Definition
GATAN	Tussilago farfara, kuan dong hua, Scientific name T, Oriental, Herbs and botanicals	kuan dong hua
GATAO	Typhae, hei pu huang, pu huang, Scientific name T, Oriental, Herbs and botanicals	hei pu huang, pu huang
GATAP	Typhonii gigantei, bai fu zi, Scientific name T, Oriental, Herbs and botanicals	bai fu zi
GATZZ	Other Oriental herb or botanical, narrative required, Scientific name T, Oriental, Herbs and botanicals	Other Oriental herb or botanical with scientific name T. Narrative required.

Scientific name U

ABC Code	Procedure Description	Expanded Definition
GAUAA	Ulmi macrocarpi, wu yi, Scientific name U, Oriental, Herbs and botanicals	wu yi
GAUAB	Uncaria rhynchophylla, gou teng, Scientific name U, Oriental, Herbs and botanicals	gou teng
GAUZZ	Other Oriental herb or botanical, narrative required, Scientific name U, Oriental, Herbs and botanicals	Other Oriental herb or botanical with scientific name U. Narrative required.

Scientific name V

ABC Code	Procedure Description	Expanded Definition
GAVAA	Vaccariae, wang buliuxing, Scientific name V, Oriental, Herbs and botanicals	wang buliuxing
GAVAB	Vascularis luffae, si gua luo, Scientific name V, Oriental, Herbs and botanicals	si gua luo
GAVAC	Verpertilii, ye ming sha, Scientific name V, Oriental, Herbs and botanicals	ye ming sha
GAVAD	Vespae, lu feng fang, Scientific name V, Oriental, Herbs and botanicals	lu feng fang
GAVAE	Viola, zi hua di, Scientific name V, Oriental, Herbs and botanicals	zi hua di
GAVAF	Viticis, man jing zi, Scientific name V, Oriental, Herbs and botanicals	man jing zi

Scientific name V

ABC Code	Procedure Description	Expanded Definition
GAVZZ	Other Oriental herb or botanical, narrative required, Scientific name V, Oriental, Herbs and botanicals	Other Oriental herb or botanical with scientific name V. Narrative required.

Scientific name W

ABC Code	Procedure Description	Expanded Definition
GAWZZ	Other Oriental herb or botanical, narrative required, Scientific name W, Oriental, Herbs and botanicals	Other Oriental herb or botanical with scientific name W. Narrative required.

Scientific name X

ABC Code	Procedure Description	Expanded Definition
GAXAA	Xanthium, cang erci, Scientific name X, Oriental, Herbs and botanicals	cang erci
GAXZZ	Other Oriental herb or botanical, narrative required, Scientific name X, Oriental, Herbs and botanicals	Other Oriental herb or botanical with scientific name X. Narrative required.

Scientific name Y

ABC Code	Procedure Description	Expanded Definition
GAYZZ	Other Oriental herb or botanical, narrative required, Scientific name Y, Oriental, Herbs and botanicals	Other Oriental herb or botanical with scientific name Y. Narrative required.

Scientific name Z

ABC Code	Procedure Description	Expanded Definition
GAZAA	Zanthoxyli, chuan jiao, chuan jiao zi, Scientific name Z, Oriental, Herbs and botanicals	chuan jiao, chuan jiao zi
GAZAB	Zeae mays, yu mi xu, Scientific name Z, Oriental, Herbs and botanicals	yu mi xu
GAZAC	Zingiberis siccatum, gan jiang, Scientific name Z, Oriental, Herbs and botanicals	gan jiang
GAZAD	Zingiber, pao jiang, sheng jiang, Scientific name Z, Oriental, Herbs and botanicals	pao jiang, sheng jiang
GAZAE	Zizyphus, hong zao, suan zaoren, Scientific name Z, Oriental, Herbs and botanicals	hong zao, suan zaoren

Oriental

Scientific name Z

ABC Code	Procedure Description	Expanded Definition
GAZZZ	Other Oriental herb or botanical, narrative required, Scientific name Z, Oriental, Herbs and botanicals	Other Oriental herb or botanical with scientific name Z. Narrative required.

Western

Scientific name A

ABC Code	Procedure Description	Expanded Definition
GBAAA	Acer rubrum, red maple, sugar maple, swamp maple, Scientific name A, Western, Herbs and botanicals	Red maple, sugar maple, swamp maple.
GBAAB	Achillea millefolium, yarrow flower, Scientific name A, Western, Herbs and botanicals	Yarrow flower.
GBAAC	Acorus calamus, calamus root, Scientific name A, Western, Herbs and botanicals	Calamus root.
GBAAD	Adiantum capillus veneris, maidenhair fern, Scientific name A, Western, Herbs and botanicals	Maidenhair fern.
GBAAE	Agrimonia eupatoria, agrimony herb, Scientific name A, Western, Herbs and botanicals	Agrimony herb.
GBAAF	Agropyrum repens, couch grass, Scientific name A, Western, Herbs and botanicals	Couch grass.
GBAAG	Aletris farinosa, star grass, true unicorn grass, Scientific name A, Western, Herbs and botanicals	Star grass, true unicorn grass.
GBAAH	Allium cepa, everlasting onion, onion tree, Scientific name A, Western, Herbs and botanicals	Everlasting onion, onion tree.
GBAAI	Aloe socotrina, Bombay aloe, turkey aloe, Scientific name A, Western, Herbs and botanicals	Bombay aloe, turkey aloe.
GBAAJ	Amaranthus hypochondriacus, princes feather, Scientific name A, Western, Herbs and botanicals	Princes feather.
GBAAK	Angelica atropurpurea, American angelica, Scientific name A, Western, Herbs and botanicals	American angelica.

Scientific name A

ABC Code	Procedure Description	Expanded Definition
GBAAL	Apium graveolens, smallage, Scientific name A, Western, Herbs and botanicals	Smallage.
GBAAM	Apocynum androsaemifolium, milk weed, Western wall, Scientific name A, Western, Herbs and botanicals	Milk weed, Western wall.
GBAAN	Apocynum cannabinum, Canadian hemp, dog bane, Scientific name A, Western, Herbs and botanicals	Canadian hemp, dog bane.
GBAAO	Aralia nudicaulis, wild sarsaparilla, Scientific name A, Western, Herbs and botanicals	Wild sarsaparilla.
GBAAP	Aralia racemosa, American spikenard, life of man, Scientific name A, Western, Herbs and botanicals	American spikenard, life of man.
GBAAQ	Arctium lappa, burdock root, Scientific name A, Western, Herbs and botanicals	Burdock root.
GBAAR	Arctostaphylos uva ursi, uva ursi leaf, Scientific name A, Western, Herbs and botanicals	Uva ursi leaf.
GBAAS	Aristolochia serpentaria, Virginia snakeroot, Scientific name A, Western, Herbs and botanicals	Virginia snakeroot.
GBAAT	Arnica montana, arnica flower, Scientific name A, Western, Herbs and botanicals	Arnica flower.
GBAAU	Artemisia absinthium, wormwood herb, Scientific name A, Western, Herbs and botanicals	Wormwood herb.
GBAAV	Artemisia vulgaris, mugwort herb, Scientific name A, Western, Herbs and botanicals	Mugwort herb.
GBAAW	Arum triphyllum, dragons root, wake robin, Scientific name A, Western, Herbs and botanicals	Dragons root, wake robin.
GBAAX	Asarum canadense, wild ginger, Scientific name A, Western, Herbs and botanicals	Wild ginger.

Scientific name A

ABC Code	Procedure Description	Expanded Definition
GBAAY	Asclepias syriaca, emetic root, milk ipecac, snake milk, Scientific name A, Western, Herbs and botanicals	Emetic root, milk ipecac, snake milk.
GBABA	Asclepias tuberosa, pleurisy root, Scientific name A, Western, Herbs and botanicals	Pleurisy root.
GBABB	Avena sativa, oatstraw, Scientific name A, Western, Herbs and botanicals	Oatstraw.
GBAZY	Other Western herb or botanical, narrative required, Scientific name A, Western, Herbs and botanicals	Other Western herb or botanical with scientific name A. Narrative required.

Scientific name B

ABC Code	Procedure Description	Expanded Definition
GBBAA	Baptisia tinctoria, wild indigo, Scientific name B, Western, Herbs and botanicals	Wild indigo.
GBBAB	Berberis vulgaris, barberry bark, Scientific name B, Western, Herbs and botanicals	Barberry bark.
GBBAC	Betula alba, silver birch, Scientific name B, Western, Herbs and botanicals	Silver birch.
GBBAD	Bidens connata, beggars tick, cockhold herb, Spanish needles, Scientific name B, Western, Herbs and botanicals	Beggars tick, cockhold herb, Spanish needles.
GBBZZ	Other Western herb or botanical, narrative required, Scientific name B, Western, Herbs and botanicals	Other Western herb or botanical with scientific name B. Narrative required.

Scientific name C

ABC Code	Procedure Description	Expanded Definition
GBCAA	Capsella bursa pastoris, shepherds purse, Scientific name C, Western, Herbs and botanicals	Shepherds purse.
GBCAB	Capsicum frutescens, hot pepper, tabasco pepper, Scientific name C, Western, Herbs and botanicals	Hot pepper, tabasco pepper.
GBCAC	Cassia marilandica, wild senna, Scientific name C, Western, Herbs and botanicals	Wild senna.

Scientific name C

ABC Code	Procedure Description	Expanded Definition
GBCAD	Castanea dentata, horse chestnut, Spanish chestnut, sweet chestnut, Scientific name C, Western, Herbs and botanicals	Horse chestnut, Spanish chestnut, sweet chestnut.
GBCAE	Caulophyllum thalictroides, blue cohosh root, Scientific name C, Western, Herbs and botanicals	Blue cohosh root.
GBCAF	Ceanothus americanus, New Jersey tea, Scientific name C, Western, Herbs and botanicals	New Jersey tea.
GBCAG	Chelidonium majus, celandine herb, Scientific name C, Western, Herbs and botanicals	Celandine herb.
GBCAH	Chelone glabra, balmony, turtlehead, Scientific name C, Western, Herbs and botanicals	Balmony, turtlehead .
GBCAI	Chenopodium anthelminticum, American wormseed, Mexican tea, Scientific name C, Western, Herbs and botanicals	American wormseed, Mexican tea.
GBCAJ	Chicorium intybus, chicory root, Scientific name C, Western, Herbs and botanicals	Chicory root.
GBCAK	Chimaphila umbellata, pipsissewa, princes pine, Scientific name C, Western, Herbs and botanicals	Pipsissewa, princes pine.
GBCAL	Chionanthus virginica, fringe tree, Scientific name C, Western, Herbs and botanicals	Fringe tree.
GBCAM	Cimicifuga racemosa, black cohosh root, Scientific name C, Western, Herbs and botanicals	Black cohosh root.
GBCAN	Cochlearia armoracia, horseradish, Scientific name C, Western, Herbs and botanicals	Horseradish.
GBCAO	Collinsonia canadensis, horse balm, stone root, Scientific name C, Western, Herbs and botanicals	Horse balm, stone root.
GBCAP	Convolvulus jalapa, jalap, Scientific name C, Western, Herbs and botanicals	Jalap.

Scientific name C

ABC Code	Procedure Description	Expanded Definition
GBCAQ	Coptis groenlandica, canker root, goldthread, Scientific name C, Western, Herbs and botanicals	Canker root, goldthread.
GBCAR	Corallorhiza odontorhiza, coralroot, dragons claw, Scientific name C, Western, Herbs and botanicals	Coralroot, dragons claw.
GBCAS	Cornus florida, flowering dogwood, Scientific name C, Western, Herbs and botanicals	Flowering dogwood.
GBCAT	Corydalis canadensis, stagger weed, wild turkey corn, Scientific name C, Western, Herbs and botanicals	Stagger weed, wild turkey corn.
GBCAU	Cupressus macrocarpa, Monterey cypress, Scientific name C, Western, Herbs and botanicals	Monterey cypress.
GBCAV	Cynoglossum officinale, hounds tongue, Scientific name C, Western, Herbs and botanicals	Hounds tongue.
GBCAW	Cypripedium pubescens, yellow ladys slipper, Scientific name C, Western, Herbs and botanicals	Yellow ladys slipper.
GBCZZ	Other Western herb or botanical, narrative required, Scientific name C, Western, Herbs and botanicals	Other Western herb or botanical with scientific name C. Narrative required.

Scientific name D

ABC Code	Procedure Description	Expanded Definition
GBDAA	Datura stramonium, thorn apple, Scientific name D, Western, Herbs and botanicals	Thorn apple.
GBDAB	Daucus carota, Queen Anns lace, Scientific name D, Western, Herbs and botanicals	Queen Anns lace.
GBDAC	Delphinium consolida, larkspur, Scientific name D, Western, Herbs and botanicals	Larkspur.
GBDAD	Dioscorea villosa, wild yam, Scientific name D, Western, Herbs and botanicals	Wild yam.

Scientific name D

ABC Code	Procedure Description	Expanded Definition
GBDAE	Drosera rotundifolia, dew plant, round leafed sundew, Scientific name D, Western, Herbs and botanicals	Dew plant, round leafed sundew.
GBDZZ	Other Western herb or botanical, narrative required, Scientific name D, Western, Herbs and botanicals	Other Western herb or botanical with scientific name D. Narrative required.

Scientific name E

ABC Code	Procedure Description	Expanded Definition
GBEAA	Echinacea angustifolia, purple coneflower, black sampson, Scientific name E, Western, Herbs and botanicals	Purple coneflower, black sampson.
GBEAB	Epigaea repens, mayflower, trailing arbutus, Scientific name E, Western, Herbs and botanicals	Mayflower, trailing arbutus.
GBEAC	Equisetum arvense, horsetail, Scientific name E, Western, Herbs and botanicals	Horsetail
GBEAD	Erechthites hieracifolia, pile wort, Scientific name E, Western, Herbs and botanicals	Pile wort.
GBEAE	Eriodictyon californicum, yerba santa leaf, Scientific name E, Western, Herbs and botanicals	Yerba santa leaf.
GBEAF	Eryngium aquaticum, button snakeroot, Scientific name E, Western, Herbs and botanicals	Button snakeroot.
GBEAG	Erythronium americanum, adders tongue, Scientific name E, Western, Herbs and botanicals	Adders tongue.
GBEAH	Eucalyptus globulus, eucalyptus leaf, Scientific name E, Western, Herbs and botanicals	Eucalyptus leaf.
GBEAI	Euonymus atropurpureus, burning bush, wahoo, Scientific name E, Western, Herbs and botanicals	Burning bush, wahoo.
GBEAJ	Eupatorium perfoliatum, boneset, thoroughwort, Scientific name E, Western, Herbs and botanicals	Boneset, thoroughwort.

Scientific name E

ABC Code	Procedure Description	Expanded Definition
GBEAK	Eupatorium purpureum, gravel root, Scientific name E, Western, Herbs and botanicals	Gravel root.
GBEZZ	Other Western herb or botanical, narrative required, Scientific name E, Western, Herbs and botanicals	Other Western herb or botanical with scientific name E. Narrative required.

Scientific name F

ABC Code	Procedure Description	Expanded Definition
GBFAA	Fagus sylvatica, European beech, Scientific name F, Western, Herbs and botanicals	European beech.
GBFAB	Fragaria americana, strawberry, Scientific name F, Western, Herbs and botanicals	Strawberry.
GBFAC	Fraxinus excelsior, common ash, Scientific name F, Western, Herbs and botanicals	Common ash.
GBFAD	Fragaria vesca, wood strawberry leaf, Scientific name F, Western, Herbs and botanicals	Wood strawberry leaf.
GBFZZ	Other Western herb or botanical, narrative required, Scientific name F, Western, Herbs and botanicals	Other Western herb or botanical with scientific name F. Narrative required.

Scientific name G

ABC Code	Procedure Description	Expanded Definition
GBGAA	Galium aparine, cleavers herb, Scientific name G, Western, Herbs and botanicals	Cleavers herb.
GBGAB	Gaultheria procumbens, winter green, Scientific name G, Western, Herbs and botanicals	Winter green.
GBGAC	Gelsemium sempervirens, false jasmine, Scientific name G, Western, Herbs and botanicals	False jasmine.
GBGAD	Geranium maculatum, cranesbill root, Scientific name G, Western, Herbs and botanicals	Cranesbill root.
GBGAE	Gerardia pedicularis, American foxglove, fever weed, Scientific name G, Western, Herbs and botanicals	American foxglove, fever weed.

Scientific name G

ABC Code	Procedure Description	Expanded Definition
GBGAF	Gillenia trifoliata, Bowmans root, Scientific name G, Western, Herbs and botanicals	Bowmans root.
GBGAG	Glehoma hederacea, ground ivy, Scientific name G, Western, Herbs and botanicals	Ground ivy.
GBGAH	Glycyrrhiza glabra, licorice, Scientific name G, Western, Herbs and botanicals	Licorice.
GBGAI	Gossypium herbaceum, cotton, levant cotton, Scientific name G, Western, Herbs and botanicals	Cotton, levant cotton.
GBGAJ	Grindelia squarrosa, gum weed, sticky heads, tar weed, Scientific name G, Western, Herbs and botanicals	Gum weed, sticky heads, tar weed.
GBGZZ	Other Western herb or botanical, narrative required, Scientific name G, Western, Herbs and botanicals	Other Western herb or botanical with scientific name G. Narrative required.

Scientific name H

ABC Code	Procedure Description	Expanded Definition
GBHAA	Hamamelis virginica, snapping hazelnut, spotted alder, winter bloom, witch hazel, Scientific name H, Western, Herbs and botanicals	Snapping hazelnut, spotted alder, winter bloom, witch hazel.
GBHAB	Hedeoma pulegioides, American pennyroyal, squaw mint, Scientific name H, Western, Herbs and botanicals	American pennyroyal, squaw mint
GBHAC	Helianthemum canadense, frost plant, frost weed, rock rose, Scientific name H, Western, Herbs and botanicals	Frost plant, frost weed, rock rose.
GBHAD	Helianthus annuus, sunflower, Scientific name H, Western, Herbs and botanicals	Sunflower.
GBHAE	Hepatica americana, liver leaf, noble liver wort, Scientific name H, Western, Herbs and botanicals	Liver leaf, noble liver wort.
GBHAF	Heuchera americana, alumroot, Scientific name H, Western, Herbs and botanicals	Alumroot.

Scientific name H

ABC Code	Procedure Description	Expanded Definition
GBHAG	Hordeum vulgare, barley grass, Scientific name H, Western, Herbs and botanicals	Barley grass.
GBHAH	Humulus lupulus, common hop, Scientific name H, Western, Herbs and botanicals	Common hop.
GBHAI	Hydrangea arborescens, seven barks, wild hydrangea, Scientific name H, Western, Herbs and botanicals	Seven barks, wild hydrangea.
GBHAJ	Hydrastis canadensis, goldenseal, Scientific name H, Western, Herbs and botanicals	Goldenseal.
GBHAK	Hyoscyamus niger, henbane, Scientific name H, Western, Herbs and botanicals	Henbane.
GBHAL	Hypericum perforatum, Saint Johns wort, Scientific name H, Western, Herbs and botanicals	St. Johns wort.
GBHAM	Hyssopus officinalis, hyssop leaf, Scientific name H, Western, Herbs and botanicals	Hyssop leaf.
GBHZZ	Other Western herb or botanical, narrative required, Scientific name H, Western, Herbs and botanicals	Other Western herb or botanical with scientific name H. Narrative required.

Scientific name I

ABC Code	Procedure Description	Expanded Definition
GBIAA	Inonotus obliquus, birch mushroom, chaga, Scientific name I, Western, Herbs and botanicals	Birch mushroom, chaga.
GBIAB	Inula helenium, elecampane root, Scientific name I, Western, Herbs and botanicals	Elecampane root.
GBIAC	Iris versicolor, blue fiag root, Scientific name I, Western, Herbs and botanicals	Blue fiag root.
GBIZZ	Other Western herb or botanical, narrative required, Scientific name I, Western, Herbs and botanicals	Other Western herb or botanical with scientific name I. Narrative required.

Scientific name J

ABC Code	Procedure Description	Expanded Definition

Scientific name J

ABC Code	Procedure Description	Expanded Definition
GBJAA	Juglans cinerea, butternut, white walnut, Scientific name J, Western, Herbs and botanicals	Butternut, white walnut.
GBJAB	Juglans nigra, black walnut hull, Scientific name J, Western, Herbs and botanicals	Black walnut hull.
GBJAC	Juniperus communis, juniper berries, Scientific name J, Western, Herbs and botanicals	Juniper berries.
GBJZZ	Other Western herb or botanical, narrative required, Scientific name J, Western, Herbs and botanicals	Other Western herb or botanical with scientific name J. Narrative required.

Scientific name K

ABC Code	Procedure Description	Expanded Definition
GBKAA	Kalmia latifolia, calico bush, mountain laurel, Scientific name K, Western, Herbs and botanicals	Calico bush, mountain laurel.
GBKZZ	Other Western herb or botanical, narrative required, Scientific name K, Western, Herbs and botanicals	Other Western herb or botanical with scientific name K. Narrative required.

Scientific name L

ABC Code	Procedure Description	Expanded Definition
GBLAA	Larix americana, American larch, black larch, Scientific name L, Western, Herbs and botanicals	American larch, black larch.
GBLAB	Larrea divaricata, chaparral, creosote bush, Scientific name L, Western, Herbs and botanicals	Chaparral, creosote bush.
GBLAC	Laurus sassafras, saloop, saxifrax, Scientific name L, Western, Herbs and botanicals	Saloop, saxifrax.
GBLAD	Ledum latifolium, Labrador tea, Scientific name L, Western, Herbs and botanicals	Labrador tea.
GBLAE	Leontodon taraxacum, dandelion root, Scientific name L, Western, Herbs and botanicals	Dandelion root.
GBLAF	Leonurus cardiaca, motherwort herb, Scientific name L, Western, Herbs and botanicals	Motherwort herb.

Scientific name L

ABC Code	Procedure Description	Expanded Definition
GBLAG	Leptandra virginica, black root, Culvers root, Scientific name L, Western, Herbs and botanicals	Black root, Culvers root.
GBLAH	Ligustrum vulgare, common privet, Scientific name L, Western, Herbs and botanicals	Common privet.
GBLAI	Lippia dulcis, cimarron, Scientific name L, Western, Herbs and botanicals	Cimarron.
GBLAJ	Liquidambar styraciflua, sweet gum, Scientific name L, Western, Herbs and botanicals	Sweet gum.
GBLAK	Lobelia inflata, common lobelia, Indian tobacco, Scientific name L, Western, Herbs and botanicals	Common lobelia, Indian tobacco.
GBLZZ	Other Western herb or botanical, narrative required, Scientific name L, Western, Herbs and botanicals	Other Western herb or botanical with scientific name L. Narrative required.

Scientific name M

ABC Code	Procedure Description	Expanded Definition
GBMAA	Magnolia virginiana, beaver tree, white bay, Scientific name M, Western, Herbs and botanicals	Beaver tree, white bay.
GBMAB	Malva sylvestris, common mallow, Scientific name M, Western, Herbs and botanicals	Common mallow.
GBMAC	Marrubium vulgare, horehound herb, Scientific name M, Western, Herbs and botanicals	Horehound herb.
GBMAD	Matricaria chamomilla, Roman camomile, Scientific name M, Western, Herbs and botanicals	Roman camomile.
GBMAE	Medicago sativa, alfalfa leaf, Scientific name M, Western, Herbs and botanicals	Alfalfa leaf.
GBMAF	Menispermum canadense, moon seed, vine maple, Scientific name M, Western, Herbs and botanicals	Moon seed, vine maple.
GBMAG	Mentha piperita, peppermint leaf, Scientific name M, Western, Herbs and botanicals	Peppermint leaf.

Scientific name M

ABC Code	Procedure Description	Expanded Definition
GBMAH	Mitchella repens, partridge berry, squaw vine, Scientific name M, Western, Herbs and botanicals	Partridge berry, squaw vine.
GBMAI	Monotropa uniflora, fit plant, ice plant, Scientific name M, Western, Herbs and botanicals	Fit plant, ice plant.
GBMAJ	Myrica cerifera, bayberry bark, Scientific name M, Western, Herbs and botanicals	Bayberry bark.
GBMZZ	Other Western herb or botanical, narrative required, Scientific name M, Western, Herbs and botanicals	Other Western herb or botanical with scientific name M. Narrative required.

Scientific name N

ABC Code	Procedure Description	Expanded Definition
GBNAA	Nabalus serpentaria, rattlesnakeroot, white lettuce, Scientific name N, Western, Herbs and botanicals	Rattlesnakeroot, white lettuce.
GBNAB	Nasturtium officinale, watercress, Scientific name N, Western, Herbs and botanicals	Watercress.
GBNAC	Nepeta cataria, catnip, Scientific name N, Western, Herbs and botanicals	Catnip.
GBNAD	Nymphaea odorata, water cabbage, white pond lily, Scientific name N, Western, Herbs and botanicals	Water cabbage, white pond lily.
GBNZZ	Other Western herb or botanical, narrative required, Scientific name N, Western, Herbs and botanicals	Other Western herb or botanical with scientific name N. Narrative required.

Scientific name O

ABC Code	Procedure Description	Expanded Definition
GBOAA	Oenothera biennis, evening primrose, Scientific name O, Western, Herbs and botanicals	Evening primrose.
GBOAB	Oleum ricini, castor oil, palma christie, Scientific name O, Western, Herbs and botanicals	Castor oil, palma christie.
GBOAC	Orobanche virginiana, cancer root, Scientific name O, Western, Herbs and botanicals	Cancer root.

Scientific name O

ABC Code	Procedure Description	Expanded Definition
GBOAD	Ostria virginiana, deer wood, hop horn beam, ironwood, Scientific name O, Western, Herbs and botanicals	Deer wood, hop horn beam, ironwood.
GBOZZ	Other Western herb or botanical, narrative required, Scientific name O, Western, Herbs and botanicals	Other Western herb or botanical with scientific name O. Narrative required.

Scientific name P

ABC Code	Procedure Description	Expanded Definition
GBPAA	Panax quinquefolium, North American ginseng, Scientific name P, Western, Herbs and botanicals	North American ginseng.
GBPAB	Passiflora incarnata, maypops, passionflower, Scientific name P, Western, Herbs and botanicals	Maypops, passionflower.
GBPAC	Persicaria maculata, dead arssmare, Scientific name P, Western, Herbs and botanicals	Dead arssmare.
GBPAD	Petroselinum sativum, parsley, Scientific name P, Western, Herbs and botanicals	Parsley.
GBPAE	Phytolacca decandra, pokeroot, pokeweed, Scientific name P, Western, Herbs and botanicals	Pokeroot, pokeweed.
GBPAF	Pinus strobus, white pine, Scientific name P, Western, Herbs and botanicals	White Pine.
GBPAG	Plantago major, plantain, Scientific name P, Western, Herbs and botanicals	Plantain.
GBPAH	Podophyllum peltatum, mandrake root, Scientific name P, Western, Herbs and botanicals	Mandrake root.
GBPAI	Polygala senega, rattlesnakeroot, Scientific name P, Western, Herbs and botanicals	Rattlesnakeroot.
GBPAJ	Polygonatum commutatum, dropberry, sealwort, Scientific name P, Western, Herbs and botanicals	Dropberry, sealwort.

Scientific name P

ABC Code	Procedure Description	Expanded Definition
GBPAK	Polygonum hydropiper, smartweed, water pepper, Scientific name P, Western, Herbs and botanicals	Smartweed, water pepper.
GBPAL	Polygonum punctatum, American water smartweed, Scientific name P, Western, Herbs and botanicals	American water smartweed.
GBPAM	Polymnia uvedalia, balsam resin, leafcup, Scientific name P, Western, Herbs and botanicals	Balsam resin, leafcup.
GBPAN	Polypodium vulgare, polypody, Scientific name P, Western, Herbs and botanicals	Polypody.
GBPAO	Polytrichum juniperium, ground moss, robins eye, Scientific name P, Western, Herbs and botanicals	Ground moss, robins eye.
GBPAP	Populus balsamifera, balsam poplar, Scientific name P, Western, Herbs and botanicals	Balsam poplar.
GBPAQ	Populus tremuloides, American aspen, Scientific name P, Western, Herbs and botanicals	American aspen.
GBPAR	Potentilla tormentilla, bloodroot, Scientific name P, Western, Herbs and botanicals	Bloodroot.
GBPAS	Primula officinalis, paigles, palsywort, Scientific name P, Western, Herbs and botanicals	Paigles, palsywort.
GBPAT	Prinos verticillatus, American black alder, Scientific name P, Western, Herbs and botanicals	American black alder.
GBPAU	Prunus virginiana, choke cherry, wild black cherry, Scientific name P, Western, Herbs and botanicals	Choke cherry, wild black cherry .
GBPAV	Ptelea trifoliata, hop tree, wafer ash, Scientific name P, Western, Herbs and botanicals	Hop tree, wafer ash.
GBPAW	Pulmonaria officinalis, lungwort, Scientific name P, Western, Herbs and botanicals	Lungwort.

Scientific name P

ABC Code	Procedure Description	Expanded Definition
GBPAX	Pyrethrum parthenium, feather few, Scientific name P, Western, Herbs and botanicals	Feather few.
GBPAY	Pyrola rotundifolia, false wintergreen, shin leaf, Scientific name P, Western, Herbs and botanicals	False wintergreen, shin leaf.
GBPZZ	Other Western herb or botanical, narrative required, Scientific name P, Western, Herbs and botanicals	Other Western herb or botanical with scientific name P. Narrative required.

Scientific name Q

ABC Code	Procedure Description	Expanded Definition
GBQAA	Quercus robur, English oak, Scientific name Q, Western, Herbs and botanicals	English oak.
GBQZZ	Other Western herb or botanical, narrative required, Scientific name Q, Western, Herbs and botanicals	Other Western herb or botanical with scientific name Q. Narrative required.

Scientific name R

ABC Code	Procedure Description	Expanded Definition
GBRAA	Ranunculus bulbosus, buttercup, crowfoot, Scientific name R, Western, Herbs and botanicals	Buttercup, crowfoot.
GBRAB	Rhamnus purshiana, cascara sagrada, Scientific name R, Western, Herbs and botanicals	Cascara sagrada.
GBRAC	Rhus glabra, smooth sumac, Scientific name R, Western, Herbs and botanicals	Smooth sumac.
GBRAD	Rubus idaeus, red raspberry leaf, Scientific name R, Western, Herbs and botanicals	Red raspberry leaf.
GBRAE	Rubus villosus, American blackberry, Scientific name R, Western, Herbs and botanicals	American blackberry.
GBRAF	Rumex acetosa, broadleaf sorrel, Scientific name R, Western, Herbs and botanicals	Broadleaf sorrel.
GBRAG	Rumex crispus, yellowdock root, Scientific name R, Western, Herbs and botanicals	Yellowdock root.

Scientific name R

ABC Code	Procedure Description	Expanded Definition
GBRZZ	Other Western herb or botanical, narrative required, Scientific name R, Western, Herbs and botanicals	Other Western herb or botanical with scientific name R. Narrative required.

Scientific name S

ABC Code	Procedure Description	Expanded Definition
GBSAA	Sabbatia angularis, bitter bloom, bitter clover, rose pink, Scientific name S, Western, Herbs and botanicals	Bitter bloom, bitter clover, rose pink.
GBSAB	Salix nigra, black willow, Scientific name S, Western, Herbs and botanicals	Black willow.
GBSAC	Salvia officinalis, sage, Scientific name S, Western, Herbs and botanicals	Sage.
GBSAD	Sambucus canadensis, elderberry, Scientific name S, Western, Herbs and botanicals	Elderberry.
GBSAE	Sanguinaria canadensis, bloodroot, red puccoon, Scientific name S, Western, Herbs and botanicals	Bloodroot, red puccoon.
GBSAF	Sanicula marilandica, black snakeroot, poolroot, Scientific name S, Western, Herbs and botanicals	Black snakeroot, poolroot.
GBSAG	Scutellaria lateriflora, Virginia skullcap, Scientific name S, Western, Herbs and botanicals	Virginia skullcap.
GBSAH	Senecio aureus, golden ragwort, liferoot, squaw weed, Scientific name S, Western, Herbs and botanicals	Golden ragwort, liferoot, squaw weed.
GBSAI	Serenoa serrulata, saw palmetto, Scientific name S, Western, Herbs and botanicals	Saw palmetto.
GBSAJ	Silphium perfoliatum, Indian cup plant, Indian gum, Scientific name S, Western, Herbs and botanicals	Indian cup plant, Indian gum.
GBSAK	Solanum dulcamara, bittersweet, deadly nightshade, Scientific name S, Western, Herbs and botanicals	Bittersweet, deadly nightshade.

Scientific name S

ABC Code	Procedure Description	Expanded Definition
GBSAL	Solanum nigrum, black nightshade, Scientific name S, Western, Herbs and botanicals	Black nightshade.
GBSAM	Solidago canadensis, Canada goldenrod, Scientific name S, Western, Herbs and botanicals	Canada goldenrod.
GBSAN	Spigelia marilandica, Carolina pink, Indian pink, worm grass, Scientific name S, Western, Herbs and botanicals	Carolina pink, Indian pink, worm grass.
GBSAO	Stellaria media, chickweed, Scientific name S, Western, Herbs and botanicals	Chickweed.
GBSAP	Stillingia sylvatica, stillingia root, Scientific name S, Western, Herbs and botanicals	Stillingia root.
GBSAQ	Stigmata maydis, Indian corn, jugnog, sea mays, Scientific name S, Western, Herbs and botanicals	Indian corn, jugnog, sea mays.
GBSAR	Symphytum officinale, comfrey leaf, comfrey root, Scientific name S, Western, Herbs and botanicals	Comfrey leaf, comfrey root.
GBSAS	Symplocarpus foetidus, skunk cabbage, Scientific name S, Western, Herbs and botanicals	Skunk cabbage.
GBSZZ	Other Western herb or botanical, narrative required, Scientific name S, Western, Herbs and botanicals	Other Western herb or botanical with scientific name S. Narrative required.

Scientific name T

ABC Code	Procedure Description	Expanded Definition
GBTAA	Tanacetum vulgare, tansey herb, Scientific name T, Western, Herbs and botanicals	Tansey herb.
GBTAB	Terebinthine canadesis, Christmas tree, Scientific name T, Western, Herbs and botanicals	Christmas tree.
GBTAC	Thuja occidentalis, Eastern arbor vitae, Scientific name T, Western, Herbs and botanicals	Eastern arbor vitae.

Scientific name T

ABC Code	Procedure Description	Expanded Definition
GBTAD	Thymus vulgaris, common thyme, Scientific name T, Western, Herbs and botanicals	Common thyme.
GBTAE	Tilia cordata, small leafed linden, Scientific name T, Western, Herbs and botanicals	Small leafed linden.
GBTAF	Trifolium pratense, red clover blossom, Scientific name T, Western, Herbs and botanicals	Red clover blossom.
GBTAG	Trillium edectum, birth root, wake robin, Scientific name T, Western, Herbs and botanicals	Birth root, wake robin.
GBTAH	Turnera aphrodisiaca, damiana leaf, Scientific name T, Western, Herbs and botanicals	Damiana leaf.
GBTAI	Tussilago farfara, coltsfoot leaf, Scientific name T, Western, Herbs and botanicals	Coltsfoot leaf.
GBTAJ	Trillium pendulum, beth root, Scientific name T, Western, Herbs and botanicals	Beth root.
GBTZZ	Other Western herb or botanical, narrative required, Scientific name T, Western, Herbs and botanicals	Other Western herb or botanical with scientific name T. Narrative required.

Scientific name U

ABC Code	Procedure Description	Expanded Definition
GBUAA	Ulmus fulva, red elm, slippery elm, Scientific name U, Western, Herbs and botanicals	Red elm, slippery elm.
GBUAB	Urtica dioica, nettle, stinging nettle, Scientific name U, Western, Herbs and botanicals	Nettle, stinging nettle.
GBUZZ	Other Western herb or botanical, narrative required, Scientific name U, Western, Herbs and botanicals	Other Western herb or botanical with scientific name U. Narrative required.

Scientific name V

ABC Code	Procedure Description	Expanded Definition
GBVAA	Vaccinium myrtillus, bilberry leaf, Scientific name V, Western, Herbs and botanicals	Bilberry leaf.

Scientific name V

ABC Code	Procedure Description	Expanded Definition
GBVAB	Valerian officinalis, common valerian, garden heliotrope, Scientific name V, Western, Herbs and botanicals	Common valerian, garden heliotrope.
GBVAC	Veratrum viride, hellebore, Indian poke, itch weed, Scientific name V, Western, Herbs and botanicals	Hellebore, Indian poke, itch weed.
GBVAD	Verbascum blattaria, verbascum flower, Scientific name V, Western, Herbs and botanicals	Verbascum flower.
GBVAE	Verbena hastata, blue vervain herb, Scientific name V, Western, Herbs and botanicals	Blue vervain herb.
GBVAF	Vernonia noveboracenis, iron weed, Scientific name V, Western, Herbs and botanicals	Iron weed.
GBVAG	Viburnum opulus, crampbark, Scientific name V, Western, Herbs and botanicals	Crampbark.
GBVAH	Viburnum prunifolium, black haw, stagbush, Scientific name V, Western, Herbs and botanicals	Black haw, stagbush.
GBVAI	Viola odorata, blue violet, Scientific name V, Western, Herbs and botanicals	Blue violet.
GBVAJ	Vitis quinquefolia, Virginia creeper, woodbine, Scientific name V, Western, Herbs and botanicals	Virginia creeper, woodbine.
GBVAK	Verbascum thaspus, white mullein leaf, Scientific name V, Western, Herbs and botanicals	White mullein leaf.
GBVZZ	Other Western herb or botanical, narrative required, Scientific name V, Western, Herbs and botanicals	Other Western herb or botanical with scientific name V. Narrative required.

Scientific name W

ABC Code	Procedure Description	Expanded Definition
GBWZZ	Other Western herb or botanical, narrative required, Scientific name W, Western, Herbs and botanicals	Other Western herb or botanical with scientific name W. Narrative required.

Western

Scientific name X

ABC Code	Procedure Description	Expanded Definition
GBXAA	Xanthoxylum fraxineum, prickly ash, suterberry, yellow wood, Scientific name X, Western, Herbs and botanicals	Prickly ash, suterberry, yellow wood.
GBXZZ	Other Western herb or botanical, narrative required, Scientific name X, Western, Herbs and botanicals	Other Western herb or botanical with scientific name X. Narrative required.

Scientific name Y

ABC Code	Procedure Description	Expanded Definition
GBYZZ	Other Western herb or botanical, narrative required, Scientific name Y, Western, Herbs and botanicals	Other Western herb or botanical with scientific name Y. Narrative required.

Scientific name Z

ABC Code	Procedure Description	Expanded Definition
GBZZZ	Other Western herb or botanical, narrative required, Scientific name Z, Western, Herbs and botanicals	Other Western herb or botanical with scientific name Z. Narrative required.

General

Flower essences

ABC Code	Procedure Description	Expanded Definition
GCAAA	Achillea filipendulina, golden yarrow, Flower essences, General, Herbs and botanicals	Golden yarrow.
GCAAB	Achillea millefolium, yarrow, Flower essences, General, Herbs and botanicals	Yarrow.
GCAAC	Achillea millefolium, pink yarrow, Flower essences, General, Herbs and botanicals	Pink yarrow.
GCAAD	Achillea millefolium, yarrow special formula, Flower essences, General, Herbs and botanicals	Yarrow special formula (in a sea salt water base).
GCAAE	Aesculus carnea, red chestnut, Flower essences, General, Herbs and botanicals	Red chestnut.
GCAAF	Aesculus hippocastanum, white chestnut, Flower essences, General, Herbs and botanicals	White chestnut.
GCAAG	Aesculus hippocastanum, chestnut bud, Flower essences, General, Herbs and botanicals	Chestnut bud.

Flower essences

ABC Code	Procedure Description	Expanded Definition
GCAAH	Agrimonia eupatoria, agrimony, Flower essences, General, Herbs and botanicals	Agrimony.
GCAAI	Allium sativum, garlic, Flower essences, General, Herbs and botanicals	Garlic.
GCAAJ	Aloe vera, aloe plant, Flower essences, General, Herbs and botanicals	Aloe plant.
GCAAK	Amaranthus caudatus, Love lies bleeding, Flower essences, General, Herbs and botanicals	Love lies bleeding.
GCAAL	Anethum graveolens, dill, Flower essences, General, Herbs and botanicals	Dill.
GCAAM	Angelica archangelica, angelica, Flower essences, General, Herbs and botanicals	Angelica.
GCAAN	Antirrhinum majus, snapdragon, Flower essences, General, Herbs and botanicals	Snapdragon.
GCAAO	Arctostaphylos viscida, manzanita, Flower essences, General, Herbs and botanicals	Manzanita.
GCAAP	Arnica mollis, arnica, Flower essences, General, Herbs and botanicals	Arnica.
GCAAQ	Artemisia douglasiana, mugwort, Flower essences, General, Herbs and botanicals	Mugwort.
GCAAR	Artemisia tridentata, sagebrush, Flower essences, General, Herbs and botanicals	Sagebrush.
GCAAS	Asclepias cordifolia, milkweed, Flower essences, General, Herbs and botanicals	Milkweed.
GCAAT	Berberis aquifolium, Oregon grape, Flower essences, General, Herbs and botanicals	Oregon grape.
GCAAU	Borago officinalis, borage, Flower essences, General, Herbs and botanicals	Borage.
GCAAV	Briza maxima, quaking grass, Flower essences, General, Herbs and botanicals	Quaking grass.
GCAAW	Bromus ramosus, wild oat, Flower essences, General, Herbs and botanicals	Wild oat.

Flower essences

ABC Code	Procedure Description	Expanded Definition
GCAAX	Calendula officinalis, calendula, Flower essences, General, Herbs and botanicals	Calendula.
GCAAY	Calluna vulgaris, heather, Flower essences, General, Herbs and botanicals	Heather.
GCABA	Calochortus leichtlinii, mariposa lily, Flower essences, General, Herbs and botanicals	Mariposa lily.
GCABB	Calochortus monophyllus, yellow star tulip, Flower essences, General, Herbs and botanicals	Yellow star tulip.
GCABC	Calochortus tolmiei, star tulip, Flower essences, General, Herbs and botanicals	Star tulip.
GCABD	Campsis tagliabuana, trumpet vine, Flower essences, General, Herbs and botanicals	Trumpet vine.
GCABE	Capsium annuum, cayenne pepper, Flower essences, General, Herbs and botanicals	Cayenne pepper.
GCABF	Carpinus betulus, hornbeam, Flower essences, General, Herbs and botanicals	Hornbeam.
GCABG	Castanea sativa, sweet chestnut, Flower essences, General, Herbs and botanicals	Sweet chestnut.
GCABH	Castilleja miniata, Indian paintbrush, Flower essences, General, Herbs and botanicals	Indian paintbrush.
GCABI	Ceanothus integerrimus, deerbrush, Flower essences, General, Herbs and botanicals	Deerbrush.
GCABJ	Centaurea solstitialis, star thistle, Flower essences, General, Herbs and botanicals	Star thistle.
GCABK	Centaurium erythraea, centaury, Flower essences, General, Herbs and botanicals	Centaury.
GCABL	Ceratostigma willmottiana, cerato, Flower essences, General, Herbs and botanicals	Cerato.
GCABM	Cereus giganteus, saguaro, Flower essences, General, Herbs and botanicals	Saguaro.
GCABN	Chaenomeles speciosa, quince, Flower essences, General, Herbs and botanicals	Quince.

Flower essences

ABC Code	Procedure Description	Expanded Definition
GCABO	Chrysanthemum maximum, shasta daisy, Flower essences, General, Herbs and botanicals	Shasta daisy.
GCABP	Chrysanthemum morifolium, chrysanthemum, Flower essences, General, Herbs and botanicals	Chrysanthemum.
GCABQ	Chrysothamnus nauseosus, rubber rabbitbrush, Flower essences, General, Herbs and botanicals	Rubber rabbitbrush.
GCABR	Cichorium intybus, chicory, Flower essences, General, Herbs and botanicals	Chicory.
GCABS	Cimicifuga racemosa, black cohosh, Flower essences, General, Herbs and botanicals	Black cohosh.
GCABT	Clematis vitalba, clematis, Flower essences, General, Herbs and botanicals	Clematis.
GCABU	Calochortus albus, white fairy lantern, Flower essences, General, Herbs and botanicals	White fairy lantern.
GCABV	Cornus nuttallii, Pacific dogwood, Flower essences, General, Herbs and botanicals	Pacific dogwood.
GCABW	Cosmos bipinnatus, cosmos, Flower essences, General, Herbs and botanicals	Cosmos.
GCABX	Cynoglossum grande, hounds tongue, Flower essences, General, Herbs and botanicals	Hounds tongue.
GCABY	Cypripedium parviflorum, yellow ladys slipper, Flower essences, General, Herbs and botanicals	Yellow ladys slipper.
GCACA	Cypripedium reginae, showy ladys slipper, Flower essences, General, Herbs and botanicals	Showy ladys slipper.
GCACB	Cytisus scoparius, Scotch broom, Flower essences, General, Herbs and botanicals	Scotch broom.
GCACC	Darlingtonia californica, California pitcher plant, Flower essences, General, Herbs and botanicals	California pitcher plant.
GCACD	Datura candida, angels trumpet, Flower essences, General, Herbs and botanicals	Angels trumpet.
GCACE	Daucus carota, Queen Annes Lace, Flower essences, General, Herbs and botanicals	Queen Annes Lace.

Flower essences

ABC Code	Procedure Description	Expanded Definition
GCACF	Delphinium nuttallianum, larkspur, Flower essences, General, Herbs and botanicals	Larkspur.
GCACG	Dicentra chrysantha, golden ear drops, Flower essences, General, Herbs and botanicals	Golden ear drops.
GCACH	Dicentra formosa, bleeding heart, Flower essences, General, Herbs and botanicals	Bleeding heart.
GCACI	Dodecatheon hendersonii, shooting star, Flower essences, General, Herbs and botanicals	Shooting star.
GCACJ	Dudleya cymosa, canyon dudleya, Flower essences, General, Herbs and botanicals	Canyon dudleya.
GCACK	Echinacea purpurea, purple coneflower, Flower essences, General, Herbs and botanicals	Purple coneflower.
GCACL	Eriodictyon californicum, yerba santa, Flower essences, General, Herbs and botanicals	Yerba santa.
GCACM	Erodium cicutarium, filaree, Flower essences, General, Herbs and botanicals	Filaree.
GCACN	Erythronium purpurea, fawn lily, Flower essences, General, Herbs and botanicals	Fawn lily.
GCACO	Eschscholzia californica, California poppy, Flower essences, General, Herbs and botanicals	California poppy.
GCACP	Fagus sylvatica, beech, Flower essences, General, Herbs and botanicals	Beech.
GCACQ	Five flower formula, rescue remedy, Flower essences, General, Herbs and botanicals	Five flower formula, rescue remedy.
GCACR	Fuchsia hybrida, fuchsia, Flower essences, General, Herbs and botanicals	Fuchsia.
GCACS	Gentiana amarella, gentian, Flower essences, General, Herbs and botanicals	Gentian.
GCACT	Helianthemum nummularium, rock rose, Flower essences, General, Herbs and botanicals	Rock rose.
GCACU	Helianthus annuus, sunflower, Flower essences, General, Herbs and botanicals	Sunflower.

Flower essences

ABC Code	Procedure Description	Expanded Definition
GCACV	Hibiscus rosa sinensis, hibiscus, Flower essences, General, Herbs and botanicals	Hibiscus.
GCACW	Hottonia palustris, water violet, Flower essences, General, Herbs and botanicals	Water violet.
GCACX	Hypericum perforatum, Saint Johns wort, Flower essences, General, Herbs and botanicals	Saint Johns wort.
GCACY	Ilex aquifolium, holly, Flower essences, General, Herbs and botanicals	Holly.
GCADA	Impatiens gladulifera, impatiens, Flower essences, General, Herbs and botanicals	Impatiens.
GCADB	Ipomoea purpurea, morning glory, Flower essences, General, Herbs and botanicals	Morning glory.
GCADC	Iris douglasiana, iris, Flower essences, General, Herbs and botanicals	Iris.
GCADD	Juglans regia, walnut, Flower essences, General, Herbs and botanicals	Walnut.
GCADE	Larix decidua, larch, Flower essences, General, Herbs and botanicals	Larch.
GCADF	Larrea tridentata, chaparral, Flower essences, General, Herbs and botanicals	Chaparral.
GCADG	Lathyrus latifolius, sweet pea, Flower essences, General, Herbs and botanicals	Sweet pea.
GCADH	Lavandula officinalis, lavender, Flower essences, General, Herbs and botanicals	Lavender.
GCADI	Lilium humboldtii, tiger lily, Flower essences, General, Herbs and botanicals	Tiger lily.
GCADJ	Lilium longiflorum, Easter lily, Flower essences, General, Herbs and botanicals	Easter lily.
GCADK	Lilium parvum, alpine lily, Flower essences, General, Herbs and botanicals	Alpine lily.
GCADL	Lonicera caprifolium, honeysuckle, Flower essences, General, Herbs and botanicals	Honeysuckle.

Flower essences

ABC Code	Procedure Description	Expanded Definition
GCADM	Madia elegans, common madia, Flower essences, General, Herbs and botanicals	Common madia.
GCADN	Malus sylvestris, wild apple, Flower essences, General, Herbs and botanicals	Wild apple.
GCADO	Matricaria chamomilla, chamomile, Flower essences, General, Herbs and botanicals	Chamomile.
GCADP	Mentha piperita, peppermint, Flower essences, General, Herbs and botanicals	Peppermint.
GCADQ	Mimulus aurantiacus, bush musk, Flower essences, General, Herbs and botanicals	Bush musk.
GCADR	Mimulus cardinalis, scarlet monkeyflower, Flower essences, General, Herbs and botanicals	Scarlet monkeyflower.
GCADS	Mimulus guttatus, figwort, Flower essences, General, Herbs and botanicals	Figwort.
GCADT	Mimulus kelloggii, purple monkeyflower, Flower essences, General, Herbs and botanicals	Purple monkeyflower.
GCADU	Mimulus lewisii, rose colored musk, Flower essences, General, Herbs and botanicals	Rose colored musk.
GCADV	Monardella odoratissima, mountain pennyroyal, Flower essences, General, Herbs and botanicals	Mountain pennyroyal.
GCADW	Myosotis sylvatica, forget me not, Flower essences, General, Herbs and botanicals	Forget-me-not.
GCADX	Nelumbo nucifera, lotus, Flower essences, General, Herbs and botanicals	Lotus.
GCADY	Nemophila menziesii, baby blue eyes, Flower essences, General, Herbs and botanicals	Baby blue eyes.
GCAEA	Nicotiana alata, nicotiana, Flower essences, General, Herbs and botanicals	Nicotiana.
GCAEB	Ocimum basilicum, basil, Flower essences, General, Herbs and botanicals	Basil.
GCAEC	Olea europaea, olive, Flower essences, General, Herbs and botanicals	Olive.

Flower essences

ABC Code	Procedure Description	Expanded Definition
GCAED	Oenothera wolfii, Wolfs evening primrose, Flower essences, General, Herbs and botanicals	Wolfs evening primrose.
GCAEE	Ornithogalum umbellatum, star of Bethlehem, Flower essences, General, Herbs and botanicals	Star of Bethlehem.
GCAEF	Penstemon davidsonii, penstemon, Flower essences, General, Herbs and botanicals	Penstemon.
GCAEG	Penstemon newberryi, mountain pride, Flower essences, General, Herbs and botanicals	Mountain pride.
GCAEH	Pinus sylvestris, pine, Flower essences, General, Herbs and botanicals	Pine.
GCAEI	Populus tremula, aspen, Flower essences, General, Herbs and botanicals	Aspen.
GCAEJ	Prunella vulgaris, self heal, Flower essences, General, Herbs and botanicals	Self heal.
GCAEK	Prunus cerasifera, flowering plum, Flower essences, General, Herbs and botanicals	Flowering plum.
GCAEL	Punica granatum, pomegranate, Flower essences, General, Herbs and botanicals	Pomegranate.
GCAEM	Quercus robur, English oak, Flower essences, General, Herbs and botanicals	English oak.
GCAEN	Ranunculus acris, buttercup, Flower essences, General, Herbs and botanicals	Buttercup.
GCAEO	Rhus diversiloba, poison oak, Flower essences, General, Herbs and botanicals	Poison oak.
GCAEP	Rosa californica, California wild rose, Flower essences, General, Herbs and botanicals	California wild rose.
GCAEQ	Rosa canina, wild rose, Flower essences, General, Herbs and botanicals	Wild rose.
GCAER	Rosmarinus officinalis, rosemary, Flower essences, General, Herbs and botanicals	Rosemary.
GCAES	Rubus ursinus, California blackberry, Flower essences, General, Herbs and botanicals	California blackberry.

Flower essences

ABC Code	Procedure Description	Expanded Definition
GCAET	Rudbeckia hirta, black eyed Susan, Flower essences, General, Herbs and botanicals	Black eyed Susan.
GCAEU	Salix vitellina, willow, Flower essences, General, Herbs and botanicals	Willow.
GCAEV	Salvia officinalis, common sage, Flower essences, General, Herbs and botanicals	Common sage.
GCAEW	Scleranthus annuus, scleranthus, Flower essences, General, Herbs and botanicals	Scleranthus.
GCAEX	Sidalcea glaucescens, mallow, Flower essences, General, Herbs and botanicals	Mallow.
GCAEY	Silene californica, Indian pink, Flower essences, General, Herbs and botanicals	Indian pink.
GCAFA	Sinapis arvensis, yellow mustard, Flower essences, General, Herbs and botanicals	Yellow mustard.
GCAFB	Solarized spring water, rock water, Flower essences, General, Herbs and botanicals	Solarized spring water, rock water.
GCAFC	Solidago californica, goldenrod, Flower essences, General, Herbs and botanicals	Goldenrod.
GCAFD	Tanacetum vulgare, tansy, Flower essences, General, Herbs and botanicals	Tansy.
GCAFE	Taraxacum officinale, dandelion, Flower essences, General, Herbs and botanicals	Dandelion.
GCAFF	Trifolium pratense, red clover, Flower essences, General, Herbs and botanicals	Red clover.
GCAFG	Trillium chloropetalum, wake robin, Flower essences, General, Herbs and botanicals	Wake robin.
GCAFH	Triteleia ixioides, prettyface, golden brodiaea, Flower essences, General, Herbs and botanicals	Prettyface, golden brodiaea.
GCAFI	Tropaeolum majus, nasturtium, Flower essences, General, Herbs and botanicals	Nasturtium.
GCAFJ	Ulex europaeus, gorse, Flower essences, General, Herbs and botanicals	Gorse.

Flower essences

ABC Code	Procedure Description	Expanded Definition
GCAFK	Ulmus procera, elm, Flower essences, General, Herbs and botanicals	Elm.
GCAFL	Verbascum thapsus, mullein, Flower essences, General, Herbs and botanicals	Mullein.
GCAFM	Verbena officinalis, verbena, Flower essences, General, Herbs and botanicals	Verbena.
GCAFN	Viola odorata, violet, Flower essences, General, Herbs and botanicals	Violet.
GCAFO	Vitis vinifera, vine, Flower essences, General, Herbs and botanicals	Vine.
GCAFP	Zantedeschia aethiopica, lily of the Nile, white arum lily, Flower essences, General, Herbs and botanicals	Lily of the Nile, white arum lily.
GCAFQ	Zea mays, corn, Flower essences, General, Herbs and botanicals	Corn.
GCAFR	Zinnia elegans, zinnia, Flower essences, General, Herbs and botanicals	Zinnia.
GCAZY	Other flower essence, narrative required, Flower essences, General, Herbs and botanicals	Other flower essence. Narrative required.

Section H: Homeopathic Preparations

Instructions

The following subsections are included in Section H:

General

Latin name A – Z (scientific names are found in the Supply & Product Index)

Any practitioner, if appropriately trained or certified, may use codes in this section if the scope of practice laws for their state or region allows them to use or order homeopathic preparations.

Do **not** add specific provider modifiers to the codes in Section H. See codes in Section A and choose the appropriate reference code to precede codes in this section. Use reference codes for prescribing (ADZAA – ADZAG), dispensing services (ADZAI – ADZAK, and ADZAP – ADZAT), compounding services (ADZAL – ADZAO), and general counseling on homeopathic remedies (AEAAO and AEAAS) prior to reporting homeopathic preparations.

Each subsection contains an '**undefined**' code that should only be used when the homeopathic remedy is not accurately described by another more specific code. If an '**undefined**' code is used on the claims form, attach a report that provides a detailed narrative about that supply and why it was needed.

Homeopathic preparations

General

Scientific name A

ABC Code	Procedure Description	Expanded Definition
HAAAA	Abelmoschus moschatus, musk seed, Scientific name A, General, Homeopathic preparations	Musk seed
HAAAB	Abies canadensis, Hemlock spruce, Scientific name A, General, Homeopathic preparations	Hemlock spruce
HAAAC	Abies nigra, black spruce, Scientific name A, General, Homeopathic preparations	Black spruce
HAAAD	Artemisia abrotanum, southernwood, Scientific name A, General, Homeopathic preparations	Southernwood
HAAAE	Abrus precatorius, carbs eye vine, Scientific name A, General, Homeopathic preparations	Carbs eye vine
HAAAF	Artemisia absinthium, common wormwood, Scientific name A, General, Homeopathic preparations	Common wormwood
HAAAG	Acalypha indica, Indian nettle, Scientific name A, General, Homeopathic preparations	Indian nettle
HAAAH	Acetanilidum, antifebrinum, Scientific name A, General, Homeopathic preparations	Antifebrinum
HAAAI	Aceticum acidum, glacial acetic acid, Scientific name A, General, Homeopathic preparations	Glacial acetic acid
HAAAJ	Achyranthes aspera, prickly chaff flower, Scientific name A, General, Homeopathic preparations	Prickly-chaff flower
HAAAK	Aconite napellus, monkshood, Scientific name A, General, Homeopathic preparations	Monkshood
HAAAL	Aconitinum, aconite, Scientific name A, General, Homeopathic preparations	Aconite
HAAAM	Aconitum cammarum, aconite cammarum, Scientific name A, General, Homeopathic preparations	Aconite cammarum

ABC Code	Procedure Description	Expanded Definition
HAAAN	Aconitum ferox, Indian aconite, Scientific name A, General, Homeopathic preparations	Indian aconite
HAAAO	Aconitum lycotonum, great yellow wolfsbane, Scientific name A, General, Homeopathic preparations	Great yellow wolfsbane
HAAAP	Actea spicata, baneberry, Scientific name A, General, Homeopathic preparations	Baneberry
HAAAQ	Adelheidsquelle aqua, water from the mineral springs Adelheidsquelle, Scientific name A, General, Homeopathic preparations	Water from the mineral springs Adelheidsquelle
HAAAR	Adonis vernalis, pheasants eye, Scientific name A, General, Homeopathic preparations	Pheasants eye
HAAAS	Adoxa moschatellina, common moschatel, Scientific name A, General, Homeopathic preparations	Common moschatel
HAAAT	Adrenalinum, internal secretion of the suprarenal glands, Scientific name A, General, Homeopathic preparations	Internal secretion of the suprarenal glands
HAAAU	Aethiops mercurialis, trituration sulfuret of antiomony and quicksilver, Scientific name A, General, Homeopathic preparations	Trituration sulfuret of antiomony and quicksilver
HAAAV	Aesculus glabra, Ohio buckeye, Scientific name A, General, Homeopathic preparations	Ohio buckeye
HAAAW	Aesculus hippocastanum, horse chestnut, Scientific name A, General, Homeopathic preparations	Horse chestnut
HAAAX	Aethiops antimonialis, trituration of aethiops mineralis and antimonium crudum, Scientific name A, General, Homeopathic preparations	Trituration of aethiops mineralis and antimonium crudum
HAAAY	Aethusa cynapium, fools parsley, Scientific name A, General, Homeopathic preparations	Fools parsley
HAAAZ	Antimonium sulphuratum, golden sulphuret of antimony, Scientific name A, General, Homeopathic preparations	Golden sulphuret of antimony

Scientific name A

ABC Code	Procedure Description	Expanded Definition
HAABA	Agaricus emeticus, russula emetica, the sickener, Scientific name A, General, Homeopathic preparations	The sickener
HAABB	Agaricus muscarius, amanita, Scientific name A, General, Homeopathic preparations	Amanita
HAABC	Agaricus pantherinus, spotted amanita, Scientific name A, General, Homeopathic preparations	Spotted amanita
HAABD	Agaricus phalloides, amanita bulbosa, deathcap, Scientific name A, General, Homeopathic preparations	Deathcap
HAABE	Agave americana, century plant, Scientific name A, General, Homeopathic preparations	Century plant
HAABF	Agave tequilana, blue agave, Scientific name A, General, Homeopathic preparations	Blue agave
HAABG	Agnus castus, chaste tree, Scientific name A, General, Homeopathic preparations	Chaste tree
HAABH	Agraphis nutans, bluebell, Scientific name A, General, Homeopathic preparations	Bluebell
HAABI	Agrostemma githago, corn cockle, Scientific name A, General, Homeopathic preparations	Corn cockle
HAABJ	Ailanthus altissima, tree of heaven, Scientific name A, General, Homeopathic preparations	Tree of heaven
HAABK	Alchemilla arvensis, parsley piert, Scientific name A, General, Homeopathic preparations	Parsley piert
HAABL	Alchemilla vulgaris, ladys mantle, Scientific name A, General, Homeopathic preparations	Ladys mantle
HAABM	Alcohol, ethyl alcohol, Scientific name A, General, Homeopathic preparations	Ethyl alcohol
HAABN	Aletris farinosa, stargrass, Scientific name A, General, Homeopathic preparations	Stargrass
HAABO	Allium cepa, red onion, Scientific name A, General, Homeopathic preparations	Red onion

Scientific name A

ABC Code	Procedure Description	Expanded Definition
HAABP	Allium sativum, garlic, Scientific name A, General, Homeopathic preparations	Garlic
HAABQ	Alloxanum, alloxan, Scientific name A, General, Homeopathic preparations	Alloxan
HAABR	Alnus rubra, red alder, Scientific name A, General, Homeopathic preparations	Red alder
HAABS	Aloe socotrina, socotrine aloe, Scientific name A, General, Homeopathic preparations	Socotrine aloe
HAABT	Aloe Vera, Scientific name A, General, Homeopathic preparations	Aloe vera
HAABU	Alstonia constricta, bitter bark, Scientific name A, General, Homeopathic preparations	Bitter bark
HAABV	Alumen, potash alum, Scientific name A, General, Homeopathic preparations	Potash alum
HAABW	Alumina silicata, kaolin, Scientific name A, General, Homeopathic preparations	Kaolin
HAABX	Alumina, oxide of aluminum, Scientific name A, General, Homeopathic preparations	Oxide of aluminum
HAABY	Aluminum acetate, aluminum acetate solution, Scientific name A, General, Homeopathic preparations	Aluminum acetate solution
HAABZ	Arundo mauritanica, reed, Italian grass, Scientific name A, General, Homeopathic preparations	Reed, Italian grass
HAACA	Ambra grisea, ambergris, Scientific name A, General, Homeopathic preparations	Ambergris
HAACB	Ambrosia artemisiifolia, ragweed, Scientific name A, General, Homeopathic preparations	Ragweed
HAACD	Ammonium aceticum, acetate of ammonia, Scientific name A, General, Homeopathic preparations	Acetate of ammonia
HAACE	Ammonium benzoicum, benzoate of ammonia, Scientific name A, General, Homeopathic preparations	Benzoate of ammonia

Scientific name A

ABC Code	Procedure Description	Expanded Definition
HAACF	Ammonium bromatum, bromide of ammonia, Scientific name A, General, Homeopathic preparations	Bromide of ammonia
HAACG	Ammonium carbonicum, carbonate of ammonia, sal volatile, Scientific name A, General, Homeopathic preparations	Carbonate of ammonia, sal volatile
HAACH	Ammonium causticum, spirits of hartshorn, hydrate of ammonia, Scientific name A, General, Homeopathic preparations	Spirits of hartshorn, hydrate of ammonia
HAACI	Ammonium iodatum, iodide of ammonia, Scientific name A, General, Homeopathic preparations	Iodide of ammonia
HAACJ	Ammonium muriaticum, ammon chloride, sal ammoniac, Scientific name A, General, Homeopathic preparations	Ammon chloride, sal ammoniac
HAACK	Ammonium phosphoricum, phosphate of ammonia, Scientific name A, General, Homeopathic preparations	Phosphate of ammonia
HAACL	Ammonium picricum, picrate of ammonia, Scientific name A, General, Homeopathic preparations	Picrate of ammonia
HAACM	Ammonium valerianicum, valerianate of ammonia, Scientific name A, General, Homeopathic preparations	Valerianate of ammonia
HAACN	Amorphophallus rivieri, Chinese umbel, Scientific name A, General, Homeopathic preparations	Chinese umbel
HAACO	Ampelopsis quinquefolia, Virginia creeper, Scientific name A, General, Homeopathic preparations	Virginia creeper
HAACQ	Amygdalus amara aqua, bitter almond, Scientific name A, General, Homeopathic preparations	Bitter almond
HAACR	Amygdalus persica, peach tree, Scientific name A, General, Homeopathic preparations	Peach tree
HAACS	Amylenum nitrosum, amyl nitrate, Scientific name A, General, Homeopathic preparations	Amyl nitrate

ABC Code	Procedure Description	Expanded Definition
HAACT	Anacardium occidentale, cashew nut, Scientific name A, General, Homeopathic preparations	Cashew nut
HAACU	Anacardium orientale, marking nut, Scientific name A, General, Homeopathic preparations	Marking nut
HAACV	Anagallis arvensis, scarlet pimpernel, Scientific name A, General, Homeopathic preparations	Scarlet pimpernel
HAACX	Anemopsis californica, yerba manza, Scientific name A, General, Homeopathic preparations	Yerba manza
HAACY	Angelica atropurpurea, angelica, Scientific name A, General, Homeopathic preparations	Angelica
HAACZ	Achillea millefolium, yarrow, Scientific name A, General, Homeopathic preparations	Yarrow
HAADA	Angelica sinensis, dong quay, Scientific name A, General, Homeopathic preparations	Dong quay
HAADB	Angophora lanceolata, red gum, Scientific name A, General, Homeopathic preparations	Red gum
HAADC	Angustura vera, bark of galipea cusparia, Scientific name A, General, Homeopathic preparations	Bark of galipea cusparia
HAADD	Anhalonium lewinii, peyote cactus, Scientific name A, General, Homeopathic preparations	Peyote cactus
HAADE	Anilinum, amidobenzene, Scientific name A, General, Homeopathic preparations	Amidobenzene
HAADF	Anise stellatum, star anise, Scientific name A, General, Homeopathic preparations	Star anise
HAADG	Anthemis nobilis, Roman chamomile, Scientific name A, General, Homeopathic preparations	Roman chamomile
HAADH	Anthoxanthum odoratum, sweet scented vernal grass, Scientific name A, General, Homeopathic preparations	Sweet scented vernal grass
HAADI	Anthracinum, nosode of anthrax, Scientific name A, General, Homeopathic preparations	Nosode of anthrax

Scientific name A

ABC Code	Procedure Description	Expanded Definition
HAADJ	Anthrakokali, anthracite coal, Scientific name A, General, Homeopathic preparations	Anthracite coal
HAADK	Antimonium arsenicosum, arsenite of antimony, Scientific name A, General, Homeopathic preparations	Arsenite of antimony
HAADL	Antimonium crudum, sulphide of antimony, Scientific name A, General, Homeopathic preparations	Sulphide of antimony
HAADM	Antimonium iodatum, teriodide of antimony, Scientific name A, General, Homeopathic preparations	Teriodide of antimony
HAADN	Antimonium muriaticum, butter of antimony, Scientific name A, General, Homeopathic preparations	Butter of antimony
HAADO	Antimonium tartaricum, tartrate of antimony and potash, Scientific name A, General, Homeopathic preparations	Tartrate of antimony and potash
HAADP	Antipyrinum, phenazone, Scientific name A, General, Homeopathic preparations	Phenazone
HAADQ	Aphis chenopodii glauci, aphids, Scientific name A, General, Homeopathic preparations	Aphids
HAADR	Apis mellifica, honey bee, Scientific name A, General, Homeopathic preparations	Honey bee
HAADS	Apium graveolens, common celery, Scientific name A, General, Homeopathic preparations	Common celery
HAADT	Apocynum andros, spreading dogbane, Scientific name A, General, Homeopathic preparations	Spreading dogbane
HAADU	Apocynum cannabinum, Indian hemp, Scientific name A, General, Homeopathic preparations	Indian hemp
HAADV	Apomorphinum, alkaloid of morphine, Scientific name A, General, Homeopathic preparations	Alkaloid of morphine

Scientific name A

ABC Code	Procedure Description	Expanded Definition
HAADW	Aqua marina, sea water, Scientific name A, General, Homeopathic preparations	Sea water
HAADX	Aqua pura, alchemical water, Scientific name A, General, Homeopathic preparations	Alchemical water
HAADY	Aquilegia vulgaris, columbine, Scientific name A, General, Homeopathic preparations	Columbine
HAADZ	Acer negundo, box elder, Scientific name A, General, Homeopathic preparations	Box elder
HAAEA	Aragallus lamberti, white loco weed, rattle weed, Scientific name A, General, Homeopathic preparations	White loco weed, rattle weed
HAAEB	Aralia hispida, wild elder, Scientific name A, General, Homeopathic preparations	Wild elder
HAAEC	Aralia racemosa, American spikenard, Scientific name A, General, Homeopathic preparations	American spikenard
HAAED	Aranea diadema, papal cross spider, Scientific name A, General, Homeopathic preparations	Papal cross spider
HAAEE	Aranea ixobola, cross spider, Scientific name A, General, Homeopathic preparations	Cross spider
HAAEF	Aranea scinencia, gray spider, Scientific name A, General, Homeopathic preparations	Gray spider
HAAEG	Arbutus andrachne, strawberry tree, Scientific name A, General, Homeopathic preparations	Strawberry tree
HAAEH	Areca catechu, betel nut, Scientific name A, General, Homeopathic preparations	Betel nut
HAAEI	Argentum nitricum, silver nitrate, Scientific name A, General, Homeopathic preparations	Silver nitrate
HAAEJ	Argemone mexicana, prickly poppy, Scientific name A, General, Homeopathic preparations	Prickly poppy
HAAEK	Argentum cyanatum, silver cyanide, Scientific name A, General, Homeopathic preparations	Silver cyanide

Scientific name A

ABC Code	Procedure Description	Expanded Definition
HAAEL	Argentum iodatum, silver iodide, Scientific name A, General, Homeopathic preparations	Silver iodide
HAAEM	Argentum metallicum, silver, Scientific name A, General, Homeopathic preparations	Silver
HAAEN	Aristolochia clematitis, aristolochic acid from subterranean parts of plant, Scientific name A, General, Homeopathic preparations	Aristolochic acid from subterranean parts of plant
HAAEO	Aristolochia milhomens, Brazilian snake root, Scientific name A, General, Homeopathic preparations	Brazilian snake root
HAAEP	Aristolochia serpentaria, Virginia snake root, Scientific name A, General, Homeopathic preparations	Virginia snake root
HAAEQ	Arnica montana, leopards bane, Scientific name A, General, Homeopathic preparations	Leopards bane
HAAER	Arsenicum album, white oxide of arsenic, Scientific name A, General, Homeopathic preparations	White oxide of arsenic
HAAES	Arsenicum bromatum, bromide of arsenic, Scientific name A, General, Homeopathic preparations	Bromide of arsenic
HAAET	Arsenicum hydrogenisatum, arseniuretted hydrogen, Scientific name A, General, Homeopathic preparations	Arseniuretted hydrogen
HAAEU	Arsenicum iodatum, iodide of arsenic, Scientific name A, General, Homeopathic preparations	Iodide of arsenic
HAAEV	Arsenicum metallicum, arsenic, Scientific name A, General, Homeopathic preparations	Arsenic
HAAEW	Arsenicum sulfuratum flavum, arsenious sulphide, arsenic trisulphate, piment, Scientific name A, General, Homeopathic preparations	Arsenious sulphide, arsenic trisulphate, piment
HAAEX	Arsenicum sulfuratum rubrum, arsenic sulphide, arsenic disulphide, realgar, Scientific name A, General, Homeopathic preparations	Arsenic sulphide, arsenic disulphide, realgar

Scientific name A

ABC Code	Procedure Description	Expanded Definition
HAAEY	Artemisia vulgaris, mugwort, wormwood, Scientific name A, General, Homeopathic preparations	Mugwort, wormwood
HAAEZ	Aqua fortis, nitric acid, Scientific name A, General, Homeopathic preparations	Nitric acid
HAAFA	Arum dracontium, green dragon, Scientific name A, General, Homeopathic preparations	Green dragon
HAAFB	Arum dracunculus, dracunculus vulgarus, dragon lily, Scientific name A, General, Homeopathic preparations	Dragon lily
HAAFC	Arum italicum, arum of Italy, Scientific name A, General, Homeopathic preparations	Arum of Italy
HAAFD	Arum maculatum, cuckoo pint, Scientific name A, General, Homeopathic preparations	Cuckoo pint
HAAFE	Arum triphyllum, Jack in the pulpit, Scientific name A, General, Homeopathic preparations	Jack in the pulpit
HAAFG	Asarum canadense, wild ginger, Scientific name A, General, Homeopathic preparations	Wild ginger
HAAFH	Asarum europaeum, European sanke root, Scientific name A, General, Homeopathic preparations	European sanke root
HAAFI	Asclepias cornuti, milkweed, silkweed, Scientific name A, General, Homeopathic preparations	Milkweed, silkweed
HAAFJ	Asclepias incarnata, swamp milkweed, Scientific name A, General, Homeopathic preparations	Swamp milkweed
HAAFK	Asclepias tuberosa, pleurisy root, butterfly weed, Scientific name A, General, Homeopathic preparations	Pleurisy root, butterfly weed
HAAFL	Asclepias vincetoxicum, swallow wort, vince, Scientific name A, General, Homeopathic preparations	Swallow wort, vince
HAAFM	Asimina triloba, American papaw, Scientific name A, General, Homeopathic preparations	American papaw

Scientific name A

ABC Code	Procedure Description	Expanded Definition
HAAFN	Asparagus officinalis, garden asparagus, Scientific name A, General, Homeopathic preparations	Garden asparagus
HAAFO	Astacus fluviatilis, crawfish, river crab, Scientific name A, General, Homeopathic preparations	Crawfish, river crab
HAAFP	Asterias rubens, red starfish, Scientific name A, General, Homeopathic preparations	Red starfish
HAAFQ	Astragalus excapus, huang qi, Scientific name A, General, Homeopathic preparations	Huang qi
HAAFS	Astragalus mollissimus, purple loco weed, Scientific name A, General, Homeopathic preparations	Purple loco weed
HAAFT	Athamanta oreoselium, peucedanum oreoselium, athamanta, Scientific name A, General, Homeopathic preparations	Athamanta
HAAFU	Atrax robustus, Australian spider, Scientific name A, General, Homeopathic preparations	Australian spider
HAAFV	Atropinum, atropine, Scientific name A, General, Homeopathic preparations	Atropine
HAAFW	Aurum arsenicum, arseniate of gold, Scientific name A, General, Homeopathic preparations	Arseniate of gold
HAAFX	Aurum bromatum, bromide of gold, Scientific name A, General, Homeopathic preparations	Bromide of gold
HAAFY	Aurum iodatum, iodide of gold, Scientific name A, General, Homeopathic preparations	Iodide of gold
HAAFZ	Anemone pulsatilla, pasque flower, Scientific name A, General, Homeopathic preparations	Pasque flower
HAAGA	Aurum metallicum, gold, Scientific name A, General, Homeopathic preparations	Gold
HAAGB	Aurum muriaticum kalinatum, double chloride of potassium and gold, potassium chloroaurate, Scientific name A, General, Homeopathic preparations	Double chloride of potassium and gold, potassium chloroaurate

Scientific name A

ABC Code	Procedure Description	Expanded Definition
HAAGC	Aurum muriaticum natronatum, double chloride of gold and sodium, sodium chloroaurate, Scientific name A, General, Homeopathic preparations	Double chloride of gold and sodium, sodium chloroaurate
HAAGD	Aurum muriaticum, chloride of gold, Scientific name A, General, Homeopathic preparations	Chloride of gold
HAAGE	Aurum sulphuratum, gold sulphide, Scientific name A, General, Homeopathic preparations	Gold sulphide
HAAGF	Avena sativa, oatstraw, Scientific name A, General, Homeopathic preparations	Oatstraw
HAAGG	Azadirachta indica, margosa bark, Scientific name A, General, Homeopathic preparations	Margosa bark
HAAGH	Antiaris toxicaria, bohun upas, toxin of the bausor tree, Scientific name A, General, Homeopathic preparations	Bohun upas, toxin of the bausor tree
HAAGI	Atropa belladonna, deadly nightshade, Scientific name A, General, Homeopathic preparations	Deadly nightshade
HAAGJ	Agkistrodon contortrix, cenchris contortrix, copperhead snake, Scientific name A, General, Homeopathic preparations	Copperhead snake
HAAGK	Andira araroba, chrysarobinum, chrysophan, goa powder, Scientific name A, General, Homeopathic preparations	Chrysarobinum, chrysophan, goa powder
HAAZZ	Other homeopathic preparation, narrative required, Scientific name A, General, Homeopathic preparations	Other homeopathic preparation with scientific name A. Narrative required.

Scientific name B

ABC Code	Procedure Description	Expanded Definition
HABAA	Bacillinum, nosode of tuberculosis, Scientific name B, General, Homeopathic preparations	Nosode of tuberculosis
HABAB	Bacillinum testium, nosode of tuberculosis testicle, Scientific name B, General, Homeopathic preparations	Nosode of tuberculosis testicle

Scientific name B

ABC Code	Procedure Description	Expanded Definition
HABAC	Bacillus number ten, tenth non lactose fermenting type of bacillus, Scientific name B, General, Homeopathic preparations	Tenth non lactose fermenting type of bacillus
HABAD	Bacillus number seven, seventh non lactose fermenting type of bacillus, Scientific name B, General, Homeopathic preparations	Seventh non lactose fermenting type of bacillus
HABAF	Balsamum peruvianum, Peruvian balsam, Scientific name B, General, Homeopathic preparations	Peruvian balsam
HABAG	Balsamum tolutanum, balsam of myroxylon toluifera, Scientific name B, General, Homeopathic preparations	Balsam of myroxylon toluifera
HABAH	Baptisia confusa acetica, Australian baptisia, Scientific name B, General, Homeopathic preparations	Australian baptisia
HABAI	Baptisia tinctoria, wild indigo, Scientific name B, General, Homeopathic preparations	Wild indigo
HABAJ	Barosma crenulatum, buchu, Scientific name B, General, Homeopathic preparations	Buchu
HABAK	Baryta acetica, acetate of barium, Scientific name B, General, Homeopathic preparations	Acetate of barium
HABAL	Baryta carbonica, carbonate of barium, Scientific name B, General, Homeopathic preparations	Carbonate of barium
HABAM	Baryta iodata, iodide of barium, Scientific name B, General, Homeopathic preparations	Iodide of barium
HABAN	Baryta muriatica, barium chloride, Scientific name B, General, Homeopathic preparations	Barium chloride
HABAP	Bellis perennis, daisy, Scientific name B, General, Homeopathic preparations	Daisy
HABAR	Benzinum nitricum, nitro benzene, Scientific name B, General, Homeopathic preparations	Nitro benzene
HABAS	Benzinum dinitricum, benzinum, benzol, coal naphtha, Scientific name B, General, Homeopathic preparations	Benzinum, benzol, coal naphtha

ABC Code	Procedure Description	Expanded Definition
HABAT	Benzoicum acidum, benzoic acid, Scientific name B, General, Homeopathic preparations	Benzoic acid
HABAU	Benzoinum odoriferum, spicebush, Scientific name B, General, Homeopathic preparations	Spicebush
HABAV	Berberis aquifolium, Oregon grape, Scientific name B, General, Homeopathic preparations	Oregon grape
HABAW	Berberis vulgaris, barberry, Scientific name B, General, Homeopathic preparations	Barberry
HABAX	Beryllium metallicum, metallic beryllium, Scientific name B, General, Homeopathic preparations	Betallic beryllium
HABAY	Beta vulgaris, beet root, Scientific name B, General, Homeopathic preparations	Beet root
HABAZ	Bad Kissingen aqua, water of springs in Bad Kissingen in Bavaria, Scientific name B, General, Homeopathic preparations	Water of springs in Bad Kissingen in Bavaria
HABBA	Betonica stachys, wood betony, Scientific name B, General, Homeopathic preparations	Wood betony
HABBB	Bismuthum, sub nitrate of bismuth, Scientific name B, General, Homeopathic preparations	Sub nitrate of bismuth
HABBC	Bixa orellana, lipstick tree, Scientific name B, General, Homeopathic preparations	Lipstick tree
HABBD	Blatta americana, American cockroach, Scientific name B, General, Homeopathic preparations	American cockroach
HABBE	Blatta orientalis, Indian cockroach, Scientific name B, General, Homeopathic preparations	Indian cockroach
HABBF	Boldoa fragrans, peumus boldus, boldo, Scientific name B, General, Homeopathic preparations	Boldo
HABBH	Boletus laricis, white agaric, Scientific name B, General, Homeopathic preparations	White agaric

Scientific name B

ABC Code	Procedure Description	Expanded Definition
HABBI	Boletus luridus, boletus nigrescens, red pored bolete, Scientific name B, General, Homeopathic preparations	Red-pored bolete
HABBJ	Boletus satanas, satans cap, Scientific name B, General, Homeopathic preparations	Satans cap
HABBK	Bombyx processionea, procession moth, Scientific name B, General, Homeopathic preparations	Procession moth
HABBL	Borax, borate of sodium, Scientific name B, General, Homeopathic preparations	Borate of sodium
HABBM	Boric acidum, boric acid, Scientific name B, General, Homeopathic preparations	Boric acid
HABBN	Bothriechis schlegeli, eyelash viper, yellow viper, Scientific name B, General, Homeopathic preparations	Eyelash viper, yellow viper
HABBO	Botulinum toxinum, botulinum toxin, Scientific name B, General, Homeopathic preparations	Botulinum toxin
HABBP	Bovista gigantea, puff ball, warted puff ball, Scientific name B, General, Homeopathic preparations	Puff ball, warted puff ball
HABBQ	Brachyglottis monroi, rangiora, Scientific name B, General, Homeopathic preparations	Rangiora
HABBR	Brassica napus, cole seed, Scientific name B, General, Homeopathic preparations	Cole seed
HABBS	Bromium, bromine, Scientific name B, General, Homeopathic preparations	Bromine
HABBT	Brucea antidysenterica, angustura spuria, bitter barked tree, Scientific name B, General, Homeopathic preparations	Bitter-barked tree
HABBU	Brucinum, brucine, Scientific name B, General, Homeopathic preparations	Brucine
HABBV	Bryonia alba, wild hops, Scientific name B, General, Homeopathic preparations	Wild hops

Scientific name B

ABC Code	Procedure Description	Expanded Definition
HABBW	Bufo rana, poison of the toad, Scientific name B, General, Homeopathic preparations	Poison of the toad
HABBX	Bunias orientalis, warty cabbage, hill mustard, Scientific name B, General, Homeopathic preparations	Warty cabbage, hill mustard
HABBY	Buthus australis, scorpion venom, Scientific name B, General, Homeopathic preparations	Scorpion venom
HABBZ	Brayera anthelmintica, hagenia abyssinica, kousso, Scientific name B, General, Homeopathic preparations	Kousso
HABCA	Butyricum acidum, butyric acid, Scientific name B, General, Homeopathic preparations	Butyric acid
HABCB	Bad Lippspringe aqua, water of the mineral springs in Bad Lippspringe in Westphalia, Scientific name B, General, Homeopathic preparations	Water of the mineral springs in Bad Lippspringe in Westphalia
HABCC	Boiron oscillococcinum, anas barbariae hepatis et cordis extractum, oscillococcinum, Scientific name B, General, Homeopathic preparations	Oscillococcinum
HABZZ	Other homeopathic preparation, narrative required, Scientific name B, General, Homeopathic preparations	Other homeopathic preparation with scientific name B. Narrative required.

Scientific name C

ABC Code	Procedure Description	Expanded Definition
HACAB	Cactus grandiflorus, night blooming cereus, Scientific name C, General, Homeopathic preparations	Night-blooming cereus
HACAC	Cadmium bromatum, cadmium bromide, Scientific name C, General, Homeopathic preparations	Cadmium bromide
HACAD	Cadmium fluorata, cadmium fluoride, Scientific name C, General, Homeopathic preparations	Cadmium fluoride
HACAE	Cadmium iodatum, cadmium iodine, Scientific name C, General, Homeopathic preparations	Cadmium iodine

Scientific name C

ABC Code	Procedure Description	Expanded Definition
HACAF	Cadmium metallicum, cadmium, Scientific name C, General, Homeopathic preparations	Cadmium
HACAG	Cadmium sulphuricum, cadmium sulphate, Scientific name C, General, Homeopathic preparations	Cadmium sulphate
HACAH	Caffeine, coffee alkaloid, Scientific name C, General, Homeopathic preparations	Coffee alkaloid
HACAI	Chiococca racemosa, cahinca root, snowberry, Scientific name C, General, Homeopathic preparations	Cahinca-root, snowberry
HACAK	Caladium seguinum, American arum, Scientific name C, General, Homeopathic preparations	American arum
HACAL	Calcarea arsenicosa, arsenite of lime, Scientific name C, General, Homeopathic preparations	Arsenite of lime
HACAM	Calcarea acetica, acetate of lime, Scientific name C, General, Homeopathic preparations	Acetate of lime
HACAN	Calcarea bromata, bromide of calcium, Scientific name C, General, Homeopathic preparations	Bromide of calcium
HACAO	Calcarea carbonica, carbonate of lime, Scientific name C, General, Homeopathic preparations	Carbonate of lime
HACAP	Calcarea caustica, lime water, Scientific name C, General, Homeopathic preparations	Lime water
HACAQ	Calcarea chlorinata, chlorinated lime, Scientific name C, General, Homeopathic preparations	Chlorinated lime
HACAR	Calcarea fluorica, fluoride of lime, Scientific name C, General, Homeopathic preparations	Fluoride of lime
HACAS	Calcarea hypophosphorosa, hypophosphite of lime, Scientific name C, General, Homeopathic preparations	Hypophosphite of lime
HACAT	Calcarea iodata, iodide of lime, Scientific name C, General, Homeopathic preparations	Iodide of lime

ABC Code	Procedure Description	Expanded Definition
HACAU	Calcarea muriatica, chloride of lime, Scientific name C, General, Homeopathic preparations	Chloride of lime
HACAV	Calcarea ovi testae, egg shell, Scientific name C, General, Homeopathic preparations	Egg shell
HACAW	Calcarea phosphorica, calcium phosphate, Scientific name C, General, Homeopathic preparations	Calcium phosphate
HACAX	Calcarea picrica, picrate of calcium, Scientific name C, General, Homeopathic preparations	Picrate of calcium
HACAY	Calcarea renalis, kidney stone, Scientific name C, General, Homeopathic preparations	Kidney stone
HACAZ	Citrullus colocynthis, bitter apple, bitter cucumber, Scientific name C, General, Homeopathic preparations	Bitter apple, bitter cucumber
HACBA	Calcarea silicata, silicate of lime, Scientific name C, General, Homeopathic preparations	Silicate of lime
HACBB	Calcarea sulphurica, gypsum, sulphate of calcium, Scientific name C, General, Homeopathic preparations	Gypsum, sulphate of calcium
HACBC	Calendula officinalis, pot marigold, Scientific name C, General, Homeopathic preparations	Pot marigold
HACBD	Calotropis gigantea, madar bark, Scientific name C, General, Homeopathic preparations	Madar bark
HACBE	Caltha palustris, cowslip, Scientific name C, General, Homeopathic preparations	Cowslip
HACBF	Camphora bromata, monobromide of camphor, Scientific name C, General, Homeopathic preparations	Monobromide of camphor
HACBG	Cinnamomum camphora, camphor, Scientific name C, General, Homeopathic preparations	Camphor
HACBI	Cannabis indica, marijuana, hashish, Scientific name C, General, Homeopathic preparations	Marijuana, hashish

Scientific name C

ABC Code	Procedure Description	Expanded Definition
HACBJ	Cannabis sativa, American hemp, European hemp, marijuana, Scientific name C, General, Homeopathic preparations	American hemp, European hemp, marijuana
HACBK	Cantharis vesicatoria, Spanish fly, Scientific name C, General, Homeopathic preparations	Spanish fly
HACBL	Capsicum minimum, cayenne pepper, Scientific name C, General, Homeopathic preparations	Cayenne pepper
HACBM	Carbo animalis, animal charcoal, Scientific name C, General, Homeopathic preparations	Animal charcoal
HACBN	Carbo vegetabilis, vegetable charcoal, Scientific name C, General, Homeopathic preparations	Vegetable charcoal
HACBO	Carbolicum acidum, carbolic acid, Scientific name C, General, Homeopathic preparations	Carbolic acid
HACBP	Carbon tetrachloride, Scientific name C, General, Homeopathic preparations	Carbon tetrachloride
HACBQ	Carboneum hydrogen, carburetted hydrogen, Scientific name C, General, Homeopathic preparations	Carburetted hydrogen
HACBR	Carboneum oxygen, carbonous oxide, Scientific name C, General, Homeopathic preparations	Carbonous oxide
HACBS	Carboneum sulphuratum, bisulphide of carbon, Scientific name C, General, Homeopathic preparations	Bisulphide of carbon
HACBT	Carboneum, lamp black, Scientific name C, General, Homeopathic preparations	Lamp black
HACBU	Carcinosin, nosode of cancer, Scientific name C, General, Homeopathic preparations	Nosode of cancer
HACBV	Carduus benedictus, blessed thistle, Scientific name C, General, Homeopathic preparations	Blessed thistle
HACBW	Carduus marianus, Saint Marys thistle, Scientific name C, General, Homeopathic preparations	Saint Marys thistle

Scientific name C

ABC Code	Procedure Description	Expanded Definition
HACBX	Carlsbad aqua, water of Muehlbrunnen springs, Scientific name C, General, Homeopathic preparations	Water of Muehlbrunnen springs
HACBY	Carya alba, shell bark, Scientific name C, General, Homeopathic preparations	Shell bark
HACBZ	Cornus circinata, roundleafed dogwood, Scientific name C, General, Homeopathic preparations	Roundleafed dogwood
HACCA	Cascara sagrada, sacred bark, Scientific name C, General, Homeopathic preparations	Sacred bark
HACCB	Croton eleuteria, cascarilla, amber kabug, sweet bark, Scientific name C, General, Homeopathic preparations	Cascarilla, amber kabug, sweet bark
HACCC	Castanea vesca, chestnut leafs, Scientific name C, General, Homeopathic preparations	Chestnut leafs
HACCD	Castor equi, horse hoof, Scientific name C, General, Homeopathic preparations	Horse hoof
HACCE	Castoreum, beaver secretion, Scientific name C, General, Homeopathic preparations	Beaver secretion
HACCF	Cataria nepeta, catnip, Scientific name C, General, Homeopathic preparations	Catnip
HACCG	Caulophyllum thalictroides, blue cohosh, Scientific name C, General, Homeopathic preparations	Blue cohosh
HACCH	Causticum, potassium hydrate, Scientific name C, General, Homeopathic preparations	Potassium hydrate
HACCI	Ceanothus americanus, red root, Scientific name C, General, Homeopathic preparations	Red root
HACCK	Cement, cement rock, Scientific name C, General, Homeopathic preparations	Cement rock
HACCM	Centaurea tagana, cornflower, Scientific name C, General, Homeopathic preparations	Cornflower

ABC Code	Procedure Description	Expanded Definition
HACCN	Cephalanthus, crane willow, button bush, Scientific name C, General, Homeopathic preparations	Crane willow, button bush
HACCP	Cereus serpentinus, nyctocereus serpentinus, snake cactus, Scientific name C, General, Homeopathic preparations	Snake cactus
HACCQ	Cerium oxalicum, oxalate of cerium, Scientific name C, General, Homeopathic preparations	Oxalate of cerium
HACCR	Cervus campestris, Brazilian deer, Scientific name C, General, Homeopathic preparations	Brazilian deer
HACCS	Cetraria islandica, Iceland moss, Scientific name C, General, Homeopathic preparations	Iceland moss
HACCT	Chamomilla matricaria, German chamomile, Scientific name C, General, Homeopathic preparations	German chamomile
HACCU	Chaparro amargoso, goat bush, Scientific name C, General, Homeopathic preparations	Goat bush
HACCV	Chaulmoogra, taraktogenos, Scientific name C, General, Homeopathic preparations	Taraktogenos
HACCW	Cheiranthus cheiri, wallflower, Scientific name C, General, Homeopathic preparations	Wallflower
HACCX	Chelidonium majus, greater celandine, swallow wort, Scientific name C, General, Homeopathic preparations	Greater celandine, swallow wort
HACCY	Chelone glabra, snakehead, Scientific name C, General, Homeopathic preparations	Snakehead
HACCZ	Cuprum oxydatum nigrum, Scientific name C, General, Homeopathic preparations	
HACDA	Chenopodium vulvaria, stinkender, Scientific name C, General, Homeopathic preparations	Stinkender
HACDB	Chenopodium olidum, epazote, stinking motherwort, wild arrach, Jerusalem oak, Scientific name C, General, Homeopathic preparations	Epazote, stinking motherwort, wild arrach, Jerusalem oak

ABC Code	Procedure Description	Expanded Definition
HACDC	Chimaphila maculata, spotted wintergreen, Scientific name C, General, Homeopathic preparations	Spotted wintergreen
HACDD	Chimaphila umbellata, pipsissewa, Scientific name C, General, Homeopathic preparations	Pipsissewa
HACDE	China arsenicosum, arsenite of quinine, Scientific name C, General, Homeopathic preparations	Arsenite of quinine
HACDF	Cinchona boliviana, Jesuits bark, Scientific name C, General, Homeopathic preparations	Jesuits bark
HACDG	Cinchona officinalis, Peruvian bark, Scientific name C, General, Homeopathic preparations	Peruvian bark
HACDH	China salicylicum, salicylate of quinine, Scientific name C, General, Homeopathic preparations	Salicylate of quinine
HACDI	China sulphuricum, sulphate of quinine, Scientific name C, General, Homeopathic preparations	Sulphate of quinine
HACDJ	Chininum muriaticum, muriate of quinine, Scientific name C, General, Homeopathic preparations	Muriate of quinine
HACDK	Chionanthus virginica, fringe tree, Scientific name C, General, Homeopathic preparations	Fringe tree
HACDL	Chloralum hydratum, chloral hydrate, Scientific name C, General, Homeopathic preparations	Chloral hydrate
HACDM	Chloramphenicol palmitate, chloramphenicol succinate, chloramphenicol, Scientific name C, General, Homeopathic preparations	Chloramphenicol
HACDN	Chloroformum, chloroform, Scientific name C, General, Homeopathic preparations	Chloroform
HACDO	Chlorpromazine, largactil, Scientific name C, General, Homeopathic preparations	Largactil
HACDP	Chlorum aqua, chlorine water, Scientific name C, General, Homeopathic preparations	Chlorine water

Scientific name C

ABC Code	Procedure Description	Expanded Definition
HACDR	Cholesterinum, cholesterine, Scientific name C, General, Homeopathic preparations	Cholesterine
HACDS	Chromicum acidum, chromic acid, Scientific name C, General, Homeopathic preparations	Chromic acid
HACDT	Chromium kali sulphuratum, potassic chrome alum, Scientific name C, General, Homeopathic preparations	Potassic chrome alum
HACDU	Chrysanthemum leucanthemum, oxeye daisy, Scientific name C, General, Homeopathic preparations	Oxeye daisy
HACDW	Chrysophanicum acidum, chrysophanic acid, Scientific name C, General, Homeopathic preparations	Chrysophanic acid
HACDX	Cichorium intybus, chicory, Scientific name C, General, Homeopathic preparations	Chicory
HACDY	Cicuta maculata, spotted cowbane, Scientific name C, General, Homeopathic preparations	Spotted cowbane
HACDZ	Centella asiatica, gotu kola, Scientific name C, General, Homeopathic preparations	Gotu kola
HACEA	Cicuta virosa, water hemlock, Scientific name C, General, Homeopathic preparations	Water hemlock
HACEB	Cimex lectularius, bedbug, Scientific name C, General, Homeopathic preparations	Bedbug
HACEC	Cimicifuga racemosa, black cohosh, Scientific name C, General, Homeopathic preparations	Black cohosh
HACED	Cina artemisia, wormseed, Scientific name C, General, Homeopathic preparations	Wormseed
HACEE	Cephaelis ipecacuanha, ipecac root and rhizome, Scientific name C, General, Homeopathic preparations	Ipecac root and rhizome
HACEF	Cineraria maritima, dusty miller, Scientific name C, General, Homeopathic preparations	Dusty miller
HACEG	Cinnabaris, red mercuric sulphide, Scientific name C, General, Homeopathic preparations	Red mercuric sulphide

Scientific name C

ABC Code	Procedure Description	Expanded Definition
HACEH	Cinnamonum ceylanicum, cinnamon, Scientific name C, General, Homeopathic preparations	Cinnamon
HACEI	Cistus canadensis, rock rose, Scientific name C, General, Homeopathic preparations	Rock rose
HACEJ	Citricum acidum, citric acid, Scientific name C, General, Homeopathic preparations	Citric acid
HACEK	Citrus decumana, grapefruit, Scientific name C, General, Homeopathic preparations	Grapefruit
HACEL	Citrus limon, lemon, Scientific name C, General, Homeopathic preparations	Lemon
HACEM	Citrus vulgaris, bitter orange, Scientific name C, General, Homeopathic preparations	Bitter orange
HACEN	Clematis erecta, virgins bower, Scientific name C, General, Homeopathic preparations	Virgins bower
HACEO	Cobaltum metallicum, cobalt, Scientific name C, General, Homeopathic preparations	Cobalt
HACEP	Cobaltum nitricum, nitrate of cobalt, Scientific name C, General, Homeopathic preparations	Nitrate of cobalt
HACER	Cocaine, alkaloid of cocaine, Scientific name C, General, Homeopathic preparations	Alkaloid of cocaine
HACES	Coccinella septempunctata, ladybug, Scientific name C, General, Homeopathic preparations	Ladybug
HACET	Cocculus indicus, Indian cockle, Scientific name C, General, Homeopathic preparations	Indian cockle
HACEU	Coccus cacti, cochineal, Scientific name C, General, Homeopathic preparations	Cochineal
HACEV	Cochlearia armoracia, horseradish, Scientific name C, General, Homeopathic preparations	Horseradish
HACEW	Codeine, alkaloid of opium, Scientific name C, General, Homeopathic preparations	Alkaloid of opium
HACEX	Coffea cruda, unroasted coffee, Scientific name C, General, Homeopathic preparations	Unroasted coffee

ABC Code	Procedure Description	Expanded Definition
HACEY	Coffea tosta, roasted coffee, Scientific name C, General, Homeopathic preparations	Roasted coffee
HACEZ	Corynocarpus laevigatus, karaka, kopi tree, Scientific name C, General, Homeopathic preparations	Karaka, kopi tree
HACFA	Colchicine, alkaloid of colchicum, Scientific name C, General, Homeopathic preparations	Alkaloid of colchicum
HACFB	Colchicum autumnale, meadow saffron, Scientific name C, General, Homeopathic preparations	Meadow saffron
HACFC	Collinsonia canadensis, stone root, Scientific name C, General, Homeopathic preparations	Stone root
HACFE	Colostrum, Scientific name C, General, Homeopathic preparations	Colostrum
HACFF	Comocladia dentata, guao, Scientific name C, General, Homeopathic preparations	Guao
HACFG	Conchiolinum, mother of pearl, Scientific name C, General, Homeopathic preparations	Mother of pearl
HACFH	Conium maculatum, poison hemlock, Scientific name C, General, Homeopathic preparations	Poison hemlock
HACFI	Convallaria majalis, lilly of the valley, Scientific name C, General, Homeopathic preparations	Lilly of the valley
HACFJ	Convolvulus arvensis, bind weed, Scientific name C, General, Homeopathic preparations	Bind weed
HACFK	Convolvulus duartinus, morning glory, Scientific name C, General, Homeopathic preparations	Morning glory
HACFL	Copaifera langsdorffii, copaiva, copaiba, balsam of copaiva, Scientific name C, General, Homeopathic preparations	Copaiva, copaiba, balsam of copaiva
HACFM	Corallium rubrum, red coral, Scientific name C, General, Homeopathic preparations	Red coral

Scientific name C

ABC Code	Procedure Description	Expanded Definition
HACFN	Corallorhiza ondotorhiza, crawley root, Scientific name C, General, Homeopathic preparations	Crawley root
HACFO	Cordyceps sinensis, caterpillar fungus, Scientific name C, General, Homeopathic preparations	Caterpillar fungus
HACFP	Coriaria ruscifolia, toot berry, Scientific name C, General, Homeopathic preparations	Toot berry
HACFQ	Cornus alternifolia, swamp walnut, Scientific name C, General, Homeopathic preparations	Swamp walnut
HACFR	Cornus florida, dogwood, Scientific name C, General, Homeopathic preparations	Dogwood
HACFS	Cortisone, cortisone, steroid produced by the adrenal glands, Scientific name C, General, Homeopathic preparations	Cortisone, steroid produced by the adrenal glands
HACFT	Corydalis formosa, turkey pea, Scientific name C, General, Homeopathic preparations	Turkey pea
HACFV	Cotyledon umbilicus, pennywort, Scientific name C, General, Homeopathic preparations	Pennywort
HACFW	Crataegus oxyacantha, hawthorne berry, Scientific name C, General, Homeopathic preparations	Hawthorne berry
HACFX	Cresylolum, cresol, Scientific name C, General, Homeopathic preparations	Cresol
HACFY	Crocus sativa, saffron, Scientific name C, General, Homeopathic preparations	Saffron
HACFZ	Cyanea capillata, medusa, jellyfish, Scientific name C, General, Homeopathic preparations	Medusa, jellyfish
HACGA	Crotalus cascavella, Brazilian rattlesnake, Scientific name C, General, Homeopathic preparations	Brazilian rattlesnake
HACGB	Crotalus horridus, rattlesnake, Scientific name C, General, Homeopathic preparations	Rattlesnake

Scientific name C

ABC Code	Procedure Description	Expanded Definition
HACGC	Croton tiglium, croton oil, Scientific name C, General, Homeopathic preparations	Croton oil
HACGD	Cubeba officinalis, cubeba, cubebs, Scientific name C, General, Homeopathic preparations	Cubeba, cubebs
HACGE	Citrullus lanatus citroides, citronmellon, Scientific name C, General, Homeopathic preparations	Citronmellon
HACGF	Culex musca, mosquito, Scientific name C, General, Homeopathic preparations	Mosquito
HACGH	Cuphea viscosissima, flux weed, Scientific name C, General, Homeopathic preparations	Flux weed
HACGI	Cupressus australis, Australian cypress, Scientific name C, General, Homeopathic preparations	Australian cypress
HACGJ	Cupressus lawsoniana, lawsons cypress, Scientific name C, General, Homeopathic preparations	Lawsons cypress
HACGK	Cuprum aceticum, acetate of copper, Scientific name C, General, Homeopathic preparations	Acetate of copper
HACGL	Cuprum arsenicosum, arsenite of copper, Scientific name C, General, Homeopathic preparations	Arsenite of copper
HACGM	Cuprum metallicum, copper, Scientific name C, General, Homeopathic preparations	Copper
HACGN	Cuprum sulphuricum, sulphate of copper, Scientific name C, General, Homeopathic preparations	Sulphate of copper
HACGO	Curare, arrow poison, Scientific name C, General, Homeopathic preparations	Arrow poison
HACGP	Curcurbita pepo, pumpkin seed, Scientific name C, General, Homeopathic preparations	Pumpkin seed
HACGQ	Cyclamen hederaefolium, sow bread, Scientific name C, General, Homeopathic preparations	Sow bread

Scientific name C

ABC Code	Procedure Description	Expanded Definition
HACGR	Cynodon dactylon, doorba, Scientific name C, General, Homeopathic preparations	Doorba
HACGS	Cypripedium calceolus, yellow ladys slipper, Scientific name C, General, Homeopathic preparations	Yellow ladys slipper
HACGU	Commiphora myrrha, myrrh, Scientific name C, General, Homeopathic preparations	Myrrh
HACGV	Cassia acutifolia, senna, Scientific name C, General, Homeopathic preparations	Senna
HACGW	Coryanthe yohimbe, yohimbe bark, Scientific name C, General, Homeopathic preparations	Yohimbe bark
HACGX	Capsella bursa pastoris, shepherds purse, Scientific name C, General, Homeopathic preparations	Shepherds purse
HACZZ	Other homeopathic preparation, narrative required, Scientific name C, General, Homeopathic preparations	Other homeopathic preparation with scientific name C. Narrative required.

Scientific name D

ABC Code	Procedure Description	Expanded Definition
HADAB	Daphne indica, spurge laurel, Scientific name D, General, Homeopathic preparations	Spurge laurel
HADAC	Datura aborea, datura flower, Scientific name D, General, Homeopathic preparations	Datura flower
HADAD	Datura ferox, Chinese datura, Scientific name D, General, Homeopathic preparations	Chinese datura
HADAE	Datura metel, Indian datura, Scientific name D, General, Homeopathic preparations	Indian datura
HADAF	Derris pinnata, member of the leguminosa family, Scientific name D, General, Homeopathic preparations	Member of the leguminosa family
HADAG	Dichapetalum cymosum, gifblaar, Scientific name D, General, Homeopathic preparations	Gifblaar
HADAH	Dictamnus albus, burning bush, Scientific name D, General, Homeopathic preparations	Burning bush

Scientific name D

ABC Code	Procedure Description	Expanded Definition
HADAI	Digitalis purpurea, foxglove, Scientific name D, General, Homeopathic preparations	Foxglove
HADAK	Digitoxinum, digitalis disolved in chloroform, Scientific name D, General, Homeopathic preparations	Digitalis disolved in chloroform
HADAL	Dioscorea villosa, wild yam, Scientific name D, General, Homeopathic preparations	Wild yam
HADAM	Diosma lincaris, buku, Scientific name D, General, Homeopathic preparations	Buku
HADAN	Diphtheria, pertussis tetanus, DPT vaccine, Scientific name D, General, Homeopathic preparations	DPT vaccine
HADAO	Diphtherinum, nosode of diphtheria, Scientific name D, General, Homeopathic preparations	Nosode of diphtheria
HADAP	Dirca palustris, leatherwood, Scientific name D, General, Homeopathic preparations	Leatherwood
HADAQ	DNA, desoxyribonucleic acid, Scientific name D, General, Homeopathic preparations	Desoxyribonucleic acid
HADAS	Doryphora decemlineata, Colorado potato beetle, Scientific name D, General, Homeopathic preparations	Colorado potato beetle
HADAT	Drosera rotundifolia, sundew, Scientific name D, General, Homeopathic preparations	Sundew
HADAU	Duboisia myoporoides, corkwood tree, Scientific name D, General, Homeopathic preparations	Corkwood tree
HADAW	Dysentery bacillus, disentery, Scientific name D, General, Homeopathic preparations	Disentery
HADAX	Duboisinum, alkaloid of corkwood tree, Scientific name D, General, Homeopathic preparations	Alkaloid of corkwood tree
HADAY	Daphne mezereum, dwarf laurel, wild pepper, Scientific name D, General, Homeopathic preparations	Dwarf laurel, wild pepper

Scientific name D

ABC Code	Procedure Description	Expanded Definition
HADAZ	Delphinium staphisagria, Eurasian larkspur, stavesacre, Scientific name D, General, Homeopathic preparations	Eurasian larkspur, stavesacre
HADBA	Datura stramonium, jimson weed, Scientific name D, General, Homeopathic preparations	Jimson weed
HADBB	Dipteryx odorata, coumarouna odorata, tonka bean, tonco bean, Scientific name D, General, Homeopathic preparations	Tonka bean, tonco bean
HADBC	Dorema ammoniacum, resin and balsam of gum ammoniac, Scientific name D, General, Homeopathic preparations	Resin and balsam of gum ammoniac
HADZZ	Other homeopathic preparation, narrative required, Scientific name D, General, Homeopathic preparations	Other homeopathic preparation with scientific name D. Narrative required.

Scientific name E

ABC Code	Procedure Description	Expanded Definition
HAEAA	Echinacea angustifolia, purple coneflower, Scientific name E, General, Homeopathic preparations	Purple coneflower
HAEAB	Echinacea purpurea, black sampson, Scientific name E, General, Homeopathic preparations	Black sampson
HAEAC	Elaeis guineensis, African oil plant, Scientific name E, General, Homeopathic preparations	African oil plant
HAEAD	Elaps corallinus, coral snake, Scientific name E, General, Homeopathic preparations	Coral snake
HAEAE	Echallium elaterium, squirting cucumber, Scientific name E, General, Homeopathic preparations	Squirting cucumber
HAEAF	Electricitas, electricity, Scientific name E, General, Homeopathic preparations	Electricity
HAEAG	Emetine, alkaloid of ipecac, Scientific name E, General, Homeopathic preparations	Alkaloid of ipecac
HAEAH	Eosinum, eosin, Scientific name E, General, Homeopathic preparations	Eosin

Scientific name E

ABC Code	Procedure Description	Expanded Definition
HAEAI	Ephedra vulgaris, ephedra, Scientific name E, General, Homeopathic preparations	Ephedra
HAEAJ	Epigea repens, gravel weed, Scientific name E, General, Homeopathic preparations	Gravel weed
HAEAK	Epilobium palustre, willow herb, Scientific name E, General, Homeopathic preparations	Willow herb
HAEAL	Epiphegus virginiana, beech drop, Scientific name E, General, Homeopathic preparations	Beech drop
HAEAM	Epiphysterinum, nosode of epiphysterinum, Scientific name E, General, Homeopathic preparations	Nosode of epiphysterinum
HAEAN	Equisetum hyemale, scouring rush, horsetail, Scientific name E, General, Homeopathic preparations	Scouring-rush, horsetail
HAEAO	Erechthites hieracifolia, fire weed, Scientific name E, General, Homeopathic preparations	Fire weed
HAEAP	Ergotinum, ergot, Scientific name E, General, Homeopathic preparations	Ergot
HAEAQ	Erigeron canadense, fleabane, Scientific name E, General, Homeopathic preparations	Fleabane
HAEAR	Eriodictyon californicum, yerba santa, Scientific name E, General, Homeopathic preparations	Yerba santa
HAEAS	Erodium cicutarium, hemlock storks bill, Scientific name E, General, Homeopathic preparations	Hemlock storks bill
HAEAT	Eryngium aquaticum, button snake root, Scientific name E, General, Homeopathic preparations	Button snake root
HAEAU	Eryngium maritimum, sea holly, Scientific name E, General, Homeopathic preparations	Sea holly
HAEAV	Erythrinus erythrinus, red mullet fish, Scientific name E, General, Homeopathic preparations	Red mullet fish

Scientific name E

ABC Code	Procedure Description	Expanded Definition
HAEAW	Eschscholzia californica, California goldpoppy, Scientific name E, General, Homeopathic preparations	California goldpoppy
HAEAX	Eserinum, eserine, Scientific name E, General, Homeopathic preparations	Eserine
HAEAY	Etherum, ether, Scientific name E, General, Homeopathic preparations	Ether
HAEAZ	Erythraea chilensis, canchalagua, Chilian centaury, Scientific name E, General, Homeopathic preparations	Chilian centaury, canchalagua
HAEBA	Eucalyptus globulus, blue gum tree, Scientific name E, General, Homeopathic preparations	Blue gum tree
HAEBB	Eugenia jambos, rose apple, Scientific name E, General, Homeopathic preparations	Rose apple
HAEBC	Euphorbia peplus, petty spurge, Scientific name E, General, Homeopathic preparations	Petty spurge
HAEBD	Euonymus americanus, strawberry bush, Scientific name E, General, Homeopathic preparations	Strawberry bush
HAEBE	Euonymus atropurpurea, wahoo, Scientific name E, General, Homeopathic preparations	Wahoo
HAEBF	Euonymus europaea, spindle tree, Scientific name E, General, Homeopathic preparations	Spindle tree
HAEBG	Eupatorium aromaticum, white snake root, Scientific name E, General, Homeopathic preparations	White snake root
HAEBH	Eupatorium perfoliatum, boneset, Scientific name E, General, Homeopathic preparations	Boneset
HAEBI	Eupatorium purpureum, gravel root, Scientific name E, General, Homeopathic preparations	Gravel root
HAEBJ	Euphorbia amygdaloides, wood spurge, Scientific name E, General, Homeopathic preparations	Wood spurge

Scientific name E

ABC Code	Procedure Description	Expanded Definition
HAEBK	Euphorbia corollata, large flowering spurge, Scientific name E, General, Homeopathic preparations	Large flowering spurge
HAEBL	Euphorbia cyparissias, cypress spurge, Scientific name E, General, Homeopathic preparations	Cypress spurge
HAEBM	Euphorbia heterodoxa, aveloz, Scientific name E, General, Homeopathic preparations	Aveloz
HAEBN	Euphorbia hypericifolia, large spotted spurge, Scientific name E, General, Homeopathic preparations	Large spotted spurge
HAEBO	Euphorbia ipecacuanhae, ipecacuan spurge, Scientific name E, General, Homeopathic preparations	Ipecacuan spurge
HAEBP	Euphorbia lathyris, gopher plant, Scientific name E, General, Homeopathic preparations	Gopher plant
HAEBQ	Euphorbia officinarum, gum euphorbium, Scientific name E, General, Homeopathic preparations	Gum euphorbium
HAEBR	Euphorbia pilulifera, pill bearing spurge, Scientific name E, General, Homeopathic preparations	Pill-bearing spurge
HAEBS	Euphorbia polycarpa, golondrina, Scientific name E, General, Homeopathic preparations	Golondrina
HAEBT	Euphrasia officinalis, eyebright, Scientific name E, General, Homeopathic preparations	Eyebright
HAEBU	Eupionum, wood tar, Scientific name E, General, Homeopathic preparations	Wood tar
HAEBV	Eysenhardtia polystachia, orteaga, Scientific name E, General, Homeopathic preparations	Orteaga
HAEBW	Erythroxylon coca, coca, the divine plant of the Incas, Scientific name E, General, Homeopathic preparations	Coca, the divine plant of the Incas

Scientific name E

ABC Code	Procedure Description	Expanded Definition
HAEZZ	Other homeopathic preparation, narrative required, Scientific name E, General, Homeopathic preparations	Other homeopathic preparation with scientific name E. Narrative required.

Scientific name F

ABC Code	Procedure Description	Expanded Definition
HAFAA	Fabiana imbricata, pichi pichi, Scientific name F, General, Homeopathic preparations	Pichi pichi
HAFAB	Fagopyrum, buckwheat, Scientific name F, General, Homeopathic preparations	Buckwheat
HAFAC	Fagus sylvatica, beech nuts, Scientific name F, General, Homeopathic preparations	Beech nuts
HAFAD	Fel tauri, ox gall, Scientific name F, General, Homeopathic preparations	Ox gall
HAFAE	Ferrum aceticum, acetate of iron, Scientific name F, General, Homeopathic preparations	Acetate of iron
HAFAF	Ferrum arsenicosum, arseniate of iron, Scientific name F, General, Homeopathic preparations	Arseniate of iron
HAFAG	Ferrum bromatum, bromide of iron, Scientific name F, General, Homeopathic preparations	Bromide of iron
HAFAH	Ferrum iodatum, iodide of iron, Scientific name F, General, Homeopathic preparations	Iodide of iron
HAFAI	Ferrum magneticum, loadstone, Scientific name F, General, Homeopathic preparations	Loadstone
HAFAJ	Ferrum metallicum, iron, Scientific name F, General, Homeopathic preparations	Iron
HAFAK	Ferrum muriaticum, iron chloride, Scientific name F, General, Homeopathic preparations	Iron chloride
HAFAL	Ferrum pernitricum, pernitrate of iron, Scientific name F, General, Homeopathic preparations	Pernitrate of iron
HAFAM	Ferrum phosphoricum, phosphate of iron, Scientific name F, General, Homeopathic preparations	Phosphate of iron

Scientific name F

ABC Code	Procedure Description	Expanded Definition
HAFAN	Ferrum picricum, picrate of iron, Scientific name F, General, Homeopathic preparations	Picrate of iron
HAFAO	Ferrum sulphuricum, sulphate of iron, Scientific name F, General, Homeopathic preparations	Sulphate of iron
HAFAP	Ferrum tartaricum, iron tartrate, Scientific name F, General, Homeopathic preparations	Iron tartrate
HAFAQ	Ferula communis glauca, ferula neapolitana, giant fennel, Scientific name F, General, Homeopathic preparations	Giant fennel
HAFAR	Ferrum cyanatum, cyanide of iron, Scientific name F, General, Homeopathic preparations	Cyanide of iron
HAFAS	Ficus religiosa, ashwathya, Scientific name F, General, Homeopathic preparations	Ashwathya
HAFAT	Filix mas, male fern, Scientific name F, General, Homeopathic preparations	Male fern
HAFAW	Fluoricum acidum, hydrofluoric acid, Scientific name F, General, Homeopathic preparations	Hydrofluoric acid
HAFAX	Folliculinum, ovarian follicle, Scientific name F, General, Homeopathic preparations	Ovarian follicle
HAFAY	Formalinum, formaldehyde, Scientific name F, General, Homeopathic preparations	Formaldehyde
HAFAZ	Ferula foetida, asafoetida, gum of the stinkasand, Scientific name F, General, Homeopathic preparations	Asafoetida, gum of the stinkasand
HAFBA	Formicum acidum, formic acid, Scientific name F, General, Homeopathic preparations	Formic acid
HAFBB	Formica rufa, red ant, Scientific name F, General, Homeopathic preparations	Red ant
HAFBC	Fragaria vesca, wood strawberry, Scientific name F, General, Homeopathic preparations	Wood strawberry
HAFBD	Franciscea uniflora, Brazilian manaca root, Scientific name F, General, Homeopathic preparations	Brazilian manaca root

Scientific name F

ABC Code	Procedure Description	Expanded Definition
HAFBE	Franzenbad aqua, spring water of Franzenbad, Scientific name F, General, Homeopathic preparations	Spring water of Franzenbad
HAFBF	Fraxinus americana, white ash, Scientific name F, General, Homeopathic preparations	White ash
HAFBG	Fraxinus excelsior, European ash, Scientific name F, General, Homeopathic preparations	European ash
HAFBH	Fuchsia triphylla, fuchsia, Scientific name F, General, Homeopathic preparations	Fuchsia
HAFBI	Fucus vesiculosus, sea kelp, Scientific name F, General, Homeopathic preparations	Sea kelp
HAFBJ	Fuligo ligni, soot, Scientific name F, General, Homeopathic preparations	Soot
HAFZZ	Other homeopathic preparation, narrative required, Scientific name F, General, Homeopathic preparations	Other homeopathic preparation with scientific name F. Narrative required.

Scientific name G

ABC Code	Procedure Description	Expanded Definition
HAGAA	Gadus morrhua, cod fish, Scientific name G, General, Homeopathic preparations	Cod fish
HAGAB	Gaertner bacillus, nosode of bowel, Scientific name G, General, Homeopathic preparations	Nosode of bowel
HAGAC	Galanthus nivalis, snow drop, Scientific name G, General, Homeopathic preparations	Snow drop
HAGAD	Galega officinalis, goats rue, Scientific name G, General, Homeopathic preparations	Goats rue
HAGAE	Galium aparine, goose grass, Scientific name G, General, Homeopathic preparations	Goose grass
HAGAF	Gallicum acidum, gallic acid, Scientific name G, General, Homeopathic preparations	Gallic acid
HAGAG	Galphimia glauca, thyrallis, rain of gold, Scientific name G, General, Homeopathic preparations	Thyrallis, rain of gold

Scientific name G

ABC Code	Procedure Description	Expanded Definition
HAGAH	Garcinia morella, gambogia, Scientific name G, General, Homeopathic preparations	Gambogia
HAGAI	Gastein aqua, water of hot springs in Wildbad Gastein, Scientific name G, General, Homeopathic preparations	Water of hot springs in Wildbad Gastein
HAGAJ	Gaultheria procumbens, wintergreen, Scientific name G, General, Homeopathic preparations	Wintergreen
HAGAK	Gelsemium sempervirens, yellow jasmine, Scientific name G, General, Homeopathic preparations	Yellow jasmine
HAGAL	Genista tinctoria, dyers weed, Scientific name G, General, Homeopathic preparations	Dyers weed
HAGAM	Gentiana cruciata, cross leaved gentian, Scientific name G, General, Homeopathic preparations	Cross-leaved gentian
HAGAN	Gentiana lutea, yellow gentian, Scientific name G, General, Homeopathic preparations	Yellow gentian
HAGAO	Gentiana quinqueflora, five flowered gentian, Scientific name G, General, Homeopathic preparations	Five-flowered gentian
HAGAP	Geranium maculatum, cranes bill, Scientific name G, General, Homeopathic preparations	Cranes bill
HAGAQ	Gettysburg aqua, salt of mineral spring at Gettysburg, Scientific name G, General, Homeopathic preparations	Salt of mineral spring at Gettysburg
HAGAR	Geum rivale, water avens, Scientific name G, General, Homeopathic preparations	Water avens
HAGAS	Ginkgo biloba, ginkgo leaf, Scientific name G, General, Homeopathic preparations	Ginkgo leaf
HAGAU	Galvanismus, galvanism, Scientific name G, General, Homeopathic preparations	Galvanism
HAGAV	Glonoine, nitroglycerine, Scientific name G, General, Homeopathic preparations	Nitroglycerine

Scientific name G

ABC Code	Procedure Description	Expanded Definition
HAGAW	Glycerinum, glycerine, Scientific name G, General, Homeopathic preparations	Glycerine
HAGAX	Gnaphalium sylvaticum, cudweed, old balsam, Scientific name G, General, Homeopathic preparations	Cudweed, old balsam
HAGAY	Gossypium hirsutum, cotton plant, Scientific name G, General, Homeopathic preparations	Cotton plant
HAGAZ	Gonolobus cundurango, cundurango, condor plant, Scientific name G, General, Homeopathic preparations	Cundurango, condor plant
HAGBB	Granitum, granite, Scientific name G, General, Homeopathic preparations	Granite
HAGBC	Graphites, black lead, Scientific name G, General, Homeopathic preparations	Black lead
HAGBD	Gratiola heterosepala, hedge hyssop, Scientific name G, General, Homeopathic preparations	Hedge hyssop
HAGBE	Grindelia robusta, rosin wood, Scientific name G, General, Homeopathic preparations	Rosin wood
HAGBG	Guaiacum, resin of lignum vitae, Scientific name G, General, Homeopathic preparations	Resin of lignum vitae
HAGBI	Guarea trichiloides, ballwood, Scientific name G, General, Homeopathic preparations	Ballwood
HAGBJ	Guatteria foliosa, majagua, Scientific name G, General, Homeopathic preparations	Majagua
HAGBK	Gunpowder, blackpowder, Scientific name G, General, Homeopathic preparations	Gunpowder, blackpowder
HAGBL	Gymnocladus dioica, American coffee tree, Scientific name G, General, Homeopathic preparations	American coffee tree
HAGZZ	Other homeopathic preparation, narrative required, Scientific name G, General, Homeopathic preparations	Other homeopathic preparation with scientific name G. Narrative required.

Scientific name H

ABC Code	Procedure Description	Expanded Definition

Scientific name H

ABC Code	Procedure Description	Expanded Definition
HAHAA	Haematoxylon campechianum, kampeche, logwood, Scientific name H, General, Homeopathic preparations	Kampeche, logwood
HAHAB	Hall Aqua, salt of springs of Hall in upper Australia, Scientific name H, General, Homeopathic preparations	Salt of springs of Hall in upper Australia
HAHAC	Haldol decanoate, haloperidol, Scientific name H, General, Homeopathic preparations	Haloperidol
HAHAD	Hamamelis virginiana, witch hazel, Scientific name H, General, Homeopathic preparations	Witch hazel
HAHAE	Hecla lava, volcanic ash, Scientific name H, General, Homeopathic preparations	Volcanic ash
HAHAF	Hedeoma pulegioides, pennyroyal, Scientific name H, General, Homeopathic preparations	Pennyroyal
HAHAG	Hedra helix, common ivy, Scientific name H, General, Homeopathic preparations	Common ivy
HAHAH	Hedysarum desmodium, Brazilian burdock, carapicho, Scientific name H, General, Homeopathic preparations	Brazilian burdock, carapicho
HAHAI	Helleborus viridis, green hellebore, Scientific name H, General, Homeopathic preparations	Green hellebore
HAHAJ	Helianthus annuus, sunflower, Scientific name H, General, Homeopathic preparations	Sunflower
HAHAK	Heliotropinum, heliotrophe, Scientific name H, General, Homeopathic preparations	Heliotrophe
HAHAL	Helix tosta, toasted snail, Scientific name H, General, Homeopathic preparations	Toasted snail
HAHAM	Helleborus fetidus, bears foot, Scientific name H, General, Homeopathic preparations	Bears foot
HAHAN	Helleborus niger, snow rose, Scientific name H, General, Homeopathic preparations	Snow rose
HAHAO	Helleborus orientalis, lenten rose, crowfoot, Scientific name H, General, Homeopathic preparations	Lenten rose, crowfoot

ABC Code	Procedure Description	Expanded Definition
HAHAP	Heloderma suspectum, gila monster, Scientific name H, General, Homeopathic preparations	Gila monster
HAHAQ	Helonias dioica, unicorn root, Scientific name H, General, Homeopathic preparations	Unicorn root
HAHAR	Hepar sulphuris, calcium sulphide, Scientific name H, General, Homeopathic preparations	Calcium sulphide
HAHAS	Hepatica triloba, liver wort, Scientific name H, General, Homeopathic preparations	Liver wort
HAHAT	Heracleum sphondylium, hogweed, Scientific name H, General, Homeopathic preparations	Hogweed
HAHAU	Hippomanes, horse meconium, Scientific name H, General, Homeopathic preparations	Horse meconium
HAHAV	Hippozaeninum, nosode of glanders, Scientific name H, General, Homeopathic preparations	Nosode of glanders
HAHAW	Hippuricum acidum, hippuric acid, Scientific name H, General, Homeopathic preparations	Hippuric acid
HAHAX	Hirudo medicinalis, leech, Scientific name H, General, Homeopathic preparations	Leech
HAHAY	Histamine, imidazolethylamine, Scientific name H, General, Homeopathic preparations	Imidazolethylamine
HAHAZ	Humulus lupulus, hops, Scientific name H, General, Homeopathic preparations	Hops
HAHBA	Hoitzia coccinea, colibri flower, Scientific name H, General, Homeopathic preparations	Colibri flower
HAHBB	Homarus americanus, digestive fluid of the lobster, Scientific name H, General, Homeopathic preparations	Lobster digestive fluid
HAHBC	Homeria collina, cape tulip, Scientific name H, General, Homeopathic preparations	Cape tulip
HAHBD	Hura brasiliensis, assacu, Scientific name H, General, Homeopathic preparations	Assacu
HAHBE	Hura crepitans, monkeys dinner bell, Scientific name H, General, Homeopathic preparations	Monkeys dinner bell

Scientific name H

ABC Code	Procedure Description	Expanded Definition
HAHBF	Hydrangea aborescens, seven barks, smooth hydrangea, Scientific name H, General, Homeopathic preparations	Seven barks, smooth hydrangea
HAHBG	Hydrastinum muriaticum, muriate of hydrastia, Scientific name H, General, Homeopathic preparations	Muriate of hydrastia
HAHBH	Hydrastis canadensis, golden seal root, Scientific name H, General, Homeopathic preparations	Golden seal root
HAHBI	Hydrobromicum acidum, hydrobromic acid, Scientific name H, General, Homeopathic preparations	Hydrobromic acid
HAHBK	Hydrocyanicum acidum, prussic acid, Scientific name H, General, Homeopathic preparations	Prussic acid
HAHBL	Hydrogen, Scientific name H, General, Homeopathic preparations	Hydrogen
HAHBM	Hydrophis cyanocinctus, sea serpent, Scientific name H, General, Homeopathic preparations	Sea serpent
HAHBN	Hydrophyllum virginianum, Virginia waterleaf, Scientific name H, General, Homeopathic preparations	Virginia waterleaf
HAHBO	Hyoscyamine, alkaloid of hyoscyamus, Scientific name H, General, Homeopathic preparations	Alkaloid of hyoscyamus
HAHBP	Hyoscyamus niger, henbane, Scientific name H, General, Homeopathic preparations	Henbane
HAHBQ	Hypericum perforatum, Saint Johns wort, Scientific name H, General, Homeopathic preparations	St. Johns wort
HAHBR	Hypothalamus, hypothalamus gland, Scientific name H, General, Homeopathic preparations	Hypothalamus gland
HAHBS	Hippomane mancinella, manchineel, manganeel apple, Scientific name H, General, Homeopathic preparations	Manchineel, manganeel apple

Scientific name H

ABC Code	Procedure Description	Expanded Definition
HAHZZ	Other homeopathic preparation, narrative required, Scientific name H, General, Homeopathic preparations	Other homeopathic preparation with scientific name H. Narrative required.

Scientific name I

ABC Code	Procedure Description	Expanded Definition
HAIAA	Iberis amara, bitter candytuff, Scientific name I, General, Homeopathic preparations	Bitter candytuff
HAIAB	Ichthyolum, ammonium ichthyol sulphonate, Scientific name I, General, Homeopathic preparations	Ammonium ichthyol sulphonate
HAIAC	Ictodes foetidus, skunk cabbage, Scientific name I, General, Homeopathic preparations	Skunk cabbage
HAIAD	Ignatia amara, strychnos ignatii, Saint Ignatius bean, Scientific name I, General, Homeopathic preparations	St. Ignatius bean
HAIAE	Ilex aquifolium, American holly, Scientific name I, General, Homeopathic preparations	American holly
HAIAF	Ilex paraguayensis, yerba mate, Scientific name I, General, Homeopathic preparations	Yerba mate
HAIAG	Ilex vomitoria, yaupon, Scientific name I, General, Homeopathic preparations	Yaupon
HAIAH	Imperatoria ostruthium, peucedanum ostruthium, masterwort, Scientific name I, General, Homeopathic preparations	Masterwort
HAIAI	Indigofera tinctoria, Indian maddar, Scientific name I, General, Homeopathic preparations	Indian maddar
HAIAJ	Indium, Scientific name I, General, Homeopathic preparations	Indium
HAIAK	Indolum, indol, Scientific name I, General, Homeopathic preparations	Indol
HAIAL	Influenza, nosode of influenza, Scientific name I, General, Homeopathic preparations	Nosode of influenza
HAIAM	Insulinum, insulin, Scientific name I, General, Homeopathic preparations	Insulin

Scientific name I

ABC Code	Procedure Description	Expanded Definition
HAIAN	Inula helenium, scabwort, Scientific name I, General, Homeopathic preparations	Scabwort
HAIAO	Iodium, iodine, Scientific name I, General, Homeopathic preparations	Iodine
HAIAP	Iodoformum, iodoform, Scientific name I, General, Homeopathic preparations	Iodoform
HAIAR	Ipomoea purpurea, morning glory, Scientific name I, General, Homeopathic preparations	Morning glory
HAIAS	Iridium, Scientific name I, General, Homeopathic preparations	Iridium
HAIAT	Iridium chloride, Scientific name I, General, Homeopathic preparations	Iridium chloride
HAIAU	Iris foetidissima, Gladwin iris, Scientific name I, General, Homeopathic preparations	Gladwin iris
HAIAV	Iris germanica var florentina, bearded iris, Scientific name I, General, Homeopathic preparations	Bearded iris
HAIAW	Iris germanica, bearded iris, Scientific name I, General, Homeopathic preparations	Bearded iris
HAIAX	Iris tenax, pacific coast iris hybrid, Scientific name I, General, Homeopathic preparations	Pacific coast iris hybrid
HAIAY	Iris versicolor, Blue flag iris, Scientific name I, General, Homeopathic preparations	Blue flag iris
HAIAZ	Illecebrum paronychia, coral necklace, Scientific name I, General, Homeopathic preparations	Coral necklace
HAIZZ	Other homeopathic preparation, narrative required, Scientific name I, General, Homeopathic preparations	Other homeopathic preparation with scientific name I. Narrative required.

Scientific name J

ABC Code	Procedure Description	Expanded Definition
HAJAB	Jacaranda caroba, Brazilian caroba tree, Scientific name J, General, Homeopathic preparations	Brazilian caroba tree

Scientific name J

ABC Code	Procedure Description	Expanded Definition
HAJAC	Jacaranda gualandai, palisander, Scientific name J, General, Homeopathic preparations	Palisander
HAJAE	Jasminum officinale, white jasmine, Scientific name J, General, Homeopathic preparations	White jasmine
HAJAF	Jatropha curcas, purging nut, Scientific name J, General, Homeopathic preparations	Purging nut
HAJAG	Jatropha urens, spurge nettle, Scientific name J, General, Homeopathic preparations	Spurge nettle
HAJAI	Juglans cinerea, butternut, Scientific name J, General, Homeopathic preparations	Butternut
HAJAJ	Juglans regia, walnut, Scientific name J, General, Homeopathic preparations	Walnut
HAJAK	Juncus effusus, soft rush, Scientific name J, General, Homeopathic preparations	Soft rush
HAJAL	Juniperus communis, juniper berries, Scientific name J, General, Homeopathic preparations	Juniper berries
HAJAM	Juniperus virginianus, red cedar, Scientific name J, General, Homeopathic preparations	Red cedar
HAJAN	Justicia adhatoda, Indian shrub, Scientific name J, General, Homeopathic preparations	Indian shrub
HAJAO	Juniperus sabina, savine, Scientific name J, General, Homeopathic preparations	Savine
HAJZZ	Other homeopathic preparation, narrative required, Scientific name J, General, Homeopathic preparations	Other homeopathic preparation with scientific name J. Narrative required.

Scientific name K

ABC Code	Procedure Description	Expanded Definition
HAKAA	Kali aceticum, acetate of potash, Scientific name K, General, Homeopathic preparations	Acetate of potash
HAKAB	Kali arsenicosum, potassium arseniate, fowlers solution, Scientific name K, General, Homeopathic preparations	Potassium arseniate, fowlers solution

Scientific name K

ABC Code	Procedure Description	Expanded Definition
HAKAC	Kali bichromicum, bichromate of potash, Scientific name K, General, Homeopathic preparations	Bichromate of potash
HAKAD	Kali carbonicum, carbonate of potassium, Scientific name K, General, Homeopathic preparations	Carbonate of potassium
HAKAE	Kali chloricum, chlorate of potassium, Scientific name K, General, Homeopathic preparations	Chlorate of potassium
HAKAF	Kali chlorosum, javelle water, bleaching fluid, Scientific name K, General, Homeopathic preparations	Javelle water, bleaching fluid
HAKAG	Kali citricum, potassium citrate, Scientific name K, General, Homeopathic preparations	Potassium citrate
HAKAH	Kali cyanatum, potassium cyanide, Scientific name K, General, Homeopathic preparations	Potassium cyanide
HAKAI	Kali ferrocyanatum, Prussian blue, Scientific name K, General, Homeopathic preparations	Prussian blue
HAKAJ	Kali hypophosphoricum, hypophosphate of potassium, Scientific name K, General, Homeopathic preparations	Hypophosphate of potassium
HAKAK	Kali iodatum, iodide of potassium, Scientific name K, General, Homeopathic preparations	Iodide of potassium
HAKAL	Kali muriaticum, chloride of potassium, Scientific name K, General, Homeopathic preparations	Chloride of potassium
HAKAM	Kali nitricum, saltpeter, Scientific name K, General, Homeopathic preparations	Saltpeter
HAKAN	Kali oxalicum, potassium bioxalate, Scientific name K, General, Homeopathic preparations	Potassium bioxalate
HAKAO	Kali permanganicum, permanganate of potassium, Scientific name K, General, Homeopathic preparations	Permanganate of potassium

Scientific name K

ABC Code	Procedure Description	Expanded Definition
HAKAP	Kali phosphoricum, phosphate of potassium, Scientific name K, General, Homeopathic preparations	Phosphate of potassium
HAKAQ	Kali silicicum, silicate of potash, Scientific name K, General, Homeopathic preparations	Silicate of potash
HAKAR	Kali sulphuricum, potassium sulphate, Scientific name K, General, Homeopathic preparations	Potassium sulphate
HAKAS	Kali tartaricum, tartrate of potash, Scientific name K, General, Homeopathic preparations	Tartrate of potash
HAKAT	Kali telluricum, potassium tellurate, Scientific name K, General, Homeopathic preparations	Potassium tellurate
HAKAU	Kalmia latifolia, mountain laurel, Scientific name K, General, Homeopathic preparations	Mountain laurel
HAKAX	Karwinskia humboldtiana, coyoyillo, Scientific name K, General, Homeopathic preparations	Coyotillo
HAKAY	Kerosolenum, kerosene, Scientific name K, General, Homeopathic preparations	Kerosene
HAKAZ	Kali bromatum, bromide of potassium, Scientific name K, General, Homeopathic preparations	Bromide of potassium
HAKBC	Kreosotum, beechwood kreosote, Scientific name K, General, Homeopathic preparations	Beechwood kreosote
HAKZZ	Other homeopathic preparation, narrative required, Scientific name K, General, Homeopathic preparations	Other homeopathic preparation with scientific name K. Narrative required.

Scientific name L

ABC Code	Procedure Description	Expanded Definition
HALAA	Lac caninum, dog milk, Scientific name L, General, Homeopathic preparations	Dog milk
HALAB	Lac defloratum, skimmed milk, Scientific name L, General, Homeopathic preparations	Skimmed milk
HALAC	Lac felinum, cat milk, Scientific name L, General, Homeopathic preparations	Cat milk

Scientific name L

ABC Code	Procedure Description	Expanded Definition
HALAD	Lac humanum, human breast milk, Scientific name L, General, Homeopathic preparations	Human breast milk
HALAE	Lac vaccinum, cow milk, Scientific name L, General, Homeopathic preparations	Cow milk
HALAF	Lac vaccinum coagulatum, milk curds, Scientific name L, General, Homeopathic preparations	Milk curds
HALAG	Lacerta agilis, green lizard, Scientific name L, General, Homeopathic preparations	Green lizard
HALAH	Lachesus mutus, bushmaster snake, Scientific name L, General, Homeopathic preparations	Bushmaster snake
HALAI	Lachnanthes tinctoria, spirit weed, paint root, Scientific name L, General, Homeopathic preparations	Spirit weed, paint root
HALAJ	Lacticum acidum, Lactic Acid, Scientific name L, General, Homeopathic preparations	Lactic Acid
HALAK	Lactis vaccini floc, milk cream, Scientific name L, General, Homeopathic preparations	Milk cream
HALAL	Latrodectus mactans, black widow spider, Scientific name L, General, Homeopathic preparations	Black widow spider
HALAM	Lactuca virosa, wild lettuce, Scientific name L, General, Homeopathic preparations	Wild lettuce
HALAN	Lamium album, white nettle, Scientific name L, General, Homeopathic preparations	White nettle
HALAO	Lapathum sylvestris, common dock, Scientific name L, General, Homeopathic preparations	Common dock
HALAP	Lapis albus, silico fluoride of calcium, Scientific name L, General, Homeopathic preparations	Silico fluoride of calcium
HALAQ	Lappa arctium, burdock, Scientific name L, General, Homeopathic preparations	Burdock
HALAR	Lapsana communis, nipple wort, Scientific name L, General, Homeopathic preparations	Nipple wort

Scientific name L

ABC Code	Procedure Description	Expanded Definition
HALAS	Lathyrus sativus, chickpea, Scientific name L, General, Homeopathic preparations	Chickpea
HALAT	Latrodectus hasselti, black spider, Scientific name L, General, Homeopathic preparations	Black spider
HALAU	Latrodectus kalipo, New Zealand spider, Scientific name L, General, Homeopathic preparations	New Zealand spider
HALAW	Lycopersicum esculentum, tomato, Scientific name L, General, Homeopathic preparations	Tomato
HALAX	Lecithinum, lecithin, Scientific name L, General, Homeopathic preparations	Lecithin
HALAY	Ledum palustre, marsh tea, wild rosemary, Scientific name L, General, Homeopathic preparations	Marsh tea, wild rosemary
HALBA	Lemna minor, duckweed, Scientific name L, General, Homeopathic preparations	Duckweed
HALBB	Leonurus cardiaca, motherwort, Scientific name L, General, Homeopathic preparations	Motherwort
HALBC	Lepidium bonariense, Brazilian cress, Scientific name L, General, Homeopathic preparations	Brazilian cress
HALBD	Leptandra virginica, veronica virginica, Culvers root, black root, Scientific name L, General, Homeopathic preparations	Culvers root, black root
HALBE	Levico aqua, arsenical mineral water Levico in South Tyrol, Scientific name L, General, Homeopathic preparations	Arsenical mineral water Levico in South Tyrol
HALBF	Levomepromazine, methotrimeprazine, Scientific name L, General, Homeopathic preparations	Levomepromazine, methotrimeprazine
HALBG	Liatris spicata, colic root, Scientific name L, General, Homeopathic preparations	Colic root
HALBH	Lilium tigrinum, tiger lily, Scientific name L, General, Homeopathic preparations	Tiger lily

Scientific name L

ABC Code	Procedure Description	Expanded Definition
HALBI	Limulus cyclops, king crab, Scientific name L, General, Homeopathic preparations	King crab
HALBJ	Linaria vulgaris, snap dragon, Scientific name L, General, Homeopathic preparations	Snap dragon
HALBK	Linum catharticum, purging flax, Scientific name L, General, Homeopathic preparations	Purging flax
HALBL	Linum usitatissimum, common flax, Scientific name L, General, Homeopathic preparations	Common flax
HALBM	Lippia dulcis, Mexican lippia, Scientific name L, General, Homeopathic preparations	Mexican lippia
HALBO	Lithium benzoicum, benzoate of lithium, Scientific name L, General, Homeopathic preparations	Benzoate of lithium
HALBP	Lithium bromatum, bromide of lithium, Scientific name L, General, Homeopathic preparations	Bromide of lithium
HALBQ	Lithium carbonicum, carbonate of lithium, Scientific name L, General, Homeopathic preparations	Carbonate of lithium
HALBR	Lithium lacticum, lactate of lithium, Scientific name L, General, Homeopathic preparations	Lactate of lithium
HALBS	Lithium muriaticum, muriate of lithium, Scientific name L, General, Homeopathic preparations	Muriate of lithium
HALBT	Lobelia dortmanna, water lobelia, Scientific name L, General, Homeopathic preparations	Water lobelia
HALBU	Lobelia erinus, trailing lobelia, Scientific name L, General, Homeopathic preparations	Trailing lobelia
HALBV	Lobelia inflata, Indian tobacco, Scientific name L, General, Homeopathic preparations	Indian tobacco
HALBW	Lobelia purpurascens, purple lobelia, Scientific name L, General, Homeopathic preparations	Purple lobelia

Scientific name L

ABC Code	Procedure Description	Expanded Definition
HALBX	Lobelia syphilitica, great blue lobelia, Scientific name L, General, Homeopathic preparations	Great blue lobelia
HALBY	Lobelia cardinalis, red lobelia, Scientific name L, General, Homeopathic preparations	Red lobelia
HALBZ	Laburnum anagyroides, cystisus laburnum, common laburnum, Scientific name L, General, Homeopathic preparations	Common laburnum
HALCA	Loleum temulentum, darnel, Scientific name L, General, Homeopathic preparations	Darnel
HALCB	Lonicera pericylmenum, woodbine, Scientific name L, General, Homeopathic preparations	Woodbine
HALCC	Lonicera xylosteum, fly woodbine, Scientific name L, General, Homeopathic preparations	Fly woodbine
HALCD	Luffa operculata, ball luffa, Scientific name L, General, Homeopathic preparations	Ball luffa
HALCE	Luna, moonlight, Scientific name L, General, Homeopathic preparations	Moonlight
HALCG	Lycopodium inundatum, club moss, Scientific name L, General, Homeopathic preparations	Club moss
HALCH	Lycopus virginicus, bugle weed, Scientific name L, General, Homeopathic preparations	Bugle weed
HALCI	Lysidinum, trituration of ethylene ethenyl diamine, Scientific name L, General, Homeopathic preparations	Trituration of Ethylene-Ethenyl-diamine
HALCJ	Lyssin, nosode of rabies, Scientific name L, General, Homeopathic preparations	Nosode of rabies
HALCK	Lophophytum leandri, flor de piedra, Scientific name L, General, Homeopathic preparations	Flor de piedra
HALCL	Larrea tridentata, chapparal, gobernadora, Scientific name L, General, Homeopathic preparations	Chapparal, gobernadora

Scientific name L

ABC Code	Procedure Description	Expanded Definition
HALZZ	Other homeopathic preparation, narrative required, Scientific name L, General, Homeopathic preparations	Other homeopathic preparation with scientific name L. Narrative required.

Scientific name M

ABC Code	Procedure Description	Expanded Definition
HAMAB	Macrotinum, trituration of resin of actaea racemosa, macrotyn, Scientific name M, General, Homeopathic preparations	Trituration of resin of actaea racemosa, macrotyn
HAMAC	Magnesia carbonica, carbonate of magnesia, Scientific name M, General, Homeopathic preparations	Carbonate of magnesia
HAMAD	Magnesia fluoride, fluoride of magnesia, Scientific name M, General, Homeopathic preparations	Fluoride of magnesia
HAMAE	Magnesia muriatica, chloride of magnesia, Scientific name M, General, Homeopathic preparations	Chloride of magnesia
HAMAF	Magnesia phosphorica, phosphate of magnesia, Scientific name M, General, Homeopathic preparations	Phosphate of magnesia
HAMAG	Magnesia sulphurica, epsom salt, Scientific name M, General, Homeopathic preparations	Epsom salt
HAMAH	Magnetis poli ambo, magnet, Scientific name M, General, Homeopathic preparations	Magnet
HAMAI	Magnetis polus articus, north pole of magnet, Scientific name M, General, Homeopathic preparations	North pole of magnet
HAMAJ	Magnetis polus australis, south pole of magnet, Scientific name M, General, Homeopathic preparations	South pole of magnet
HAMAK	Magnolia glauca, sweet magnolia, Scientific name M, General, Homeopathic preparations	Sweet magnolia
HAMAL	Magnolia grandiflora, southern magnolia, Scientific name M, General, Homeopathic preparations	Southern magnolia

ABC Code	Procedure Description	Expanded Definition
HAMAM	Malandrinum, grease of horses, Scientific name M, General, Homeopathic preparations	Grease of horses
HAMAN	Malaria officinalis, decomposed vegetable matter, Scientific name M, General, Homeopathic preparations	Decomposed vegetable matter
HAMAO	Mandragora officinalis, mandrake, Scientific name M, General, Homeopathic preparations	Mandrake
HAMAP	Manganum aceticum, manganese acetate, Scientific name M, General, Homeopathic preparations	Manganese acetate
HAMAQ	Manganum muriaticum, chloride of manganese, Scientific name M, General, Homeopathic preparations	Chloride of manganese
HAMAR	Manganum oxydatum, managnese oxide, Scientific name M, General, Homeopathic preparations	Managnese oxide
HAMAS	Manganum sulphuricum, sulphate of manganese, Scientific name M, General, Homeopathic preparations	Sulphate of manganese
HAMAT	Mangifera indica, mango tree, Scientific name M, General, Homeopathic preparations	Mango tree
HAMAU	Mercurius sulphocyanatus, pharoahs serpents, Scientific name M, General, Homeopathic preparations	Pharoahs serpents
HAMAV	Marrubium vulgare, horehound, Scientific name M, General, Homeopathic preparations	Horehound
HAMAW	Matthiola graeca, giliflower, Scientific name M, General, Homeopathic preparations	Giliflower
HAMAX	Medicago sativa, alfalfa, California clover, Scientific name M, General, Homeopathic preparations	Alfalfa, California clover
HAMAY	Medorrhinum, nosode of gonorrhea, Scientific name M, General, Homeopathic preparations	Nosode of gonorrhea
HAMAZ	Momordica charantia, kalara, oriya, Scientific name M, General, Homeopathic preparations	Kalara, oriya

Scientific name M

ABC Code	Procedure Description	Expanded Definition
HAMBB	Mel cum sale, honey with salt, Scientific name M, General, Homeopathic preparations	Honey with salt
HAMBC	Melaleuca alternifolia, tea tree oil, Scientific name M, General, Homeopathic preparations	Tea tree oil
HAMBD	Melastoma ackermanni, lesandra, Scientific name M, General, Homeopathic preparations	Lesandra
HAMBE	Melilotus officinalis, yellow sweet clover, Scientific name M, General, Homeopathic preparations	Yellow sweet clover
HAMBF	Melissa officinalis, lemon balm, Scientific name M, General, Homeopathic preparations	Lemon balm
HAMBG	Melitagrinum, nosode of eczema capitis, Scientific name M, General, Homeopathic preparations	Nosode of eczema capitis
HAMBH	Melus, honey, Scientific name M, General, Homeopathic preparations	Honey
HAMBI	Menispermum canadense, moonseed, Scientific name M, General, Homeopathic preparations	Moonseed
HAMBJ	Mentha piperita, peppermint, Scientific name M, General, Homeopathic preparations	Peppermint
HAMBK	Mentha pulegium, English pennyroyal, Scientific name M, General, Homeopathic preparations	English pennyroyal
HAMBL	Menthol, oil of mentha piperita, Scientific name M, General, Homeopathic preparations	Oil of mentha piperita
HAMBM	Menyanthes trifoliata, buckbean, Scientific name M, General, Homeopathic preparations	Buckbean
HAMBN	Mephitis, skunk secretion, Scientific name M, General, Homeopathic preparations	Skunk secretion
HAMBO	Mercurialis perennis, dog mercury, Scientific name M, General, Homeopathic preparations	Dog mercury
HAMBP	Mercurius aceticus, mercury acetate, Scientific name M, General, Homeopathic preparations	Mercury acetate

ABC Code	Procedure Description	Expanded Definition
HAMBQ	Mercurius praecipitatus albus, mercuric ammonium chloride, Scientific name M, General, Homeopathic preparations	Mercuric ammonium chloride
HAMBR	Mercurius corrosivus, corrosive sublimate, Scientific name M, General, Homeopathic preparations	Corrosive sublimate
HAMBS	Mercurius cyanatus, cyanide of mercury, Scientific name M, General, Homeopathic preparations	Cyanide of mercury
HAMBT	Mercurius dulcis, calomel, Scientific name M, General, Homeopathic preparations	Calomel
HAMBU	Mercurius iodatus flavus, proto iodide of mercury, Scientific name M, General, Homeopathic preparations	Proto-iodide of mercury
HAMBV	Mercurius iodatus ruber, bin iodide of mercury, Scientific name M, General, Homeopathic preparations	Bin-iodide of mercury
HAMBW	Mercurius nitrosus, mercury nitrate, Scientific name M, General, Homeopathic preparations	Mercury nitrate
HAMBX	Mercurius precipitatus ruber, red oxide of mercury, Scientific name M, General, Homeopathic preparations	Red oxide of mercury
HAMBY	Mercurius sulphuricus, yellow sulphate of mercury, Scientific name M, General, Homeopathic preparations	Yellow sulphate of mercury
HAMBZ	Mirabilis jalapa, marvel of Peru, Scientific name M, General, Homeopathic preparations	Marvel of Peru
HAMCA	Mercurius vivus, mercury, quicksilver, Scientific name M, General, Homeopathic preparations	Mercury, quicksilver
HAMCB	Methylene blue, member of the aniline dye family, Scientific name M, General, Homeopathic preparations	Member of the aniline dye family
HAMCD	Micromeria douglasii, yerba buena, Scientific name M, General, Homeopathic preparations	Yerba buena

Scientific name M

ABC Code	Procedure Description	Expanded Definition
HAMCF	Mimosa humilis, Brazilian mimosa, sensitive plant, Scientific name M, General, Homeopathic preparations	Brazilian mimosa, sensitive plant
HAMCG	Mimosa pudica, sensitive plant, modest princess, Scientific name M, General, Homeopathic preparations	Sensitive plant, modest princess
HAMCH	Mitchella repens, partridge berry, Scientific name M, General, Homeopathic preparations	Partridge berry
HAMCI	Momordica balsamica, balsam apple, Scientific name M, General, Homeopathic preparations	Balsam apple
HAMCJ	Morbillinum, nosode of measles, Scientific name M, General, Homeopathic preparations	Nosode of measles
HAMCK	Morgan bacillus, nosode of bowel, Scientific name M, General, Homeopathic preparations	Nosode of bowel
HAMCL	Morphine, alkaloid of opium, Scientific name M, General, Homeopathic preparations	Alkaloid of opium
HAMCM	Moschus, deer musk, Scientific name M, General, Homeopathic preparations	Deer musk
HAMCN	Mucuna urens, horse eye, Scientific name M, General, Homeopathic preparations	Horse eye
HAMCO	Murex trunculus, mollusk secreting tyrean purple, Scientific name M, General, Homeopathic preparations	Mollusk secreting tyrean purple
HAMCP	Muriaticum acidum, hydrochloric acid, Scientific name M, General, Homeopathic preparations	Hydrochloric acid
HAMCQ	Musa sapientum, banana, Scientific name M, General, Homeopathic preparations	Banana
HAMCR	Muscarine, alkaloid of agaricus muscarius, Scientific name M, General, Homeopathic preparations	Alkaloid of agaricus muscarius
HAMCT	Mygale lasiodora, black Cuban spider, Scientific name M, General, Homeopathic preparations	Black Cuban spider

Scientific name M

ABC Code	Procedure Description	Expanded Definition
HAMCU	Myosotis arvensis, forget me not, Scientific name M, General, Homeopathic preparations	Forget-me-not
HAMCV	Myrica cerifera, bayberry, Scientific name M, General, Homeopathic preparations	Bayberry
HAMCW	Myristica sebifera, Brazilian ucuba, Scientific name M, General, Homeopathic preparations	Brazilian ucuba
HAMCY	Myrtus chekan, eugenia cheken, cheken, Scientific name M, General, Homeopathic preparations	Cheken
HAMCZ	Mallotus philippinensis, kamala, spoonwood, Scientific name M, General, Homeopathic preparations	Kamala, spoonwood
HAMDA	Myrtus communis, common myrtle, Scientific name M, General, Homeopathic preparations	Common myrtle
HAMDB	Mucuna pruriens, dolichos pruriens, cowhage, Scientific name M, General, Homeopathic preparations	Cowhage
HAMDC	Mikania cordifolia, guaco, climbing hemp weed, Scientific name M, General, Homeopathic preparations	Guaco, climbing hemp weed
HAMZZ	Other homeopathic preparation, narrative required, Scientific name M, General, Homeopathic preparations	Other homeopathic preparation with scientific name M. Narrative required.

Scientific name N

ABC Code	Procedure Description	Expanded Definition
HANAA	Nabalus serpentaria, white lettuce, Scientific name N, General, Homeopathic preparations	White lettuce
HANAB	Naja atra, cytotoxin 3, Chinese cobra venom, Scientific name N, General, Homeopathic preparations	Cytotoxin 3, Chinese cobra venom
HANAC	Naphthaline, tar camphor, Scientific name N, General, Homeopathic preparations	Tar camphor
HANAD	Narcissus pseudonarcissus, yellow daffodil, Scientific name N, General, Homeopathic preparations	Yellow daffodil

Scientific name N

ABC Code	Procedure Description	Expanded Definition
HANAE	Narcotinum, alkaloid of opium, Scientific name N, General, Homeopathic preparations	Alkaloid of opium
HANAG	Natrium arsenicosum, arseniate of sodium, Scientific name N, General, Homeopathic preparations	Arseniate of sodium
HANAH	Natrium cacodylicum, cacodylate of soda, Scientific name N, General, Homeopathic preparations	Cacodylate of soda
HANAI	Natrium carbonicum, carbonate of sodium, Scientific name N, General, Homeopathic preparations	Carbonate of sodium
HANAJ	Natrium fluoratum, sodium fluoride, Scientific name N, General, Homeopathic preparations	Sodium fluoride
HANAK	Natrium hypochlorosum, Labarraques solution, Scientific name N, General, Homeopathic preparations	Labarraques solution
HANAL	Natrium iodatum, sodium iodide, Scientific name N, General, Homeopathic preparations	Sodium iodide
HANAM	Natrium lacticum, sodium lactate, Scientific name N, General, Homeopathic preparations	Sodium lactate
HANAN	Natrium muriaticum, common salt, Scientific name N, General, Homeopathic preparations	Common salt
HANAO	Natrium nitricum, nitrate of sodium, cubic nitre, Scientific name N, General, Homeopathic preparations	Nitrate of sodium, cubic nitre
HANAP	Natrium nitrosum, nitrate of sodium, trituration, Scientific name N, General, Homeopathic preparations	Nitrate of sodium, trituration
HANAQ	Natrium phosphoricum, phosphate of sodium, Scientific name N, General, Homeopathic preparations	Phosphate of sodium
HANAR	Natrium salicylicum, salicylate of sodium, Scientific name N, General, Homeopathic preparations	Salicylate of sodium

ABC Code	Procedure Description	Expanded Definition
HANAS	Natrium selenicum, selenate of sodium, Scientific name N, General, Homeopathic preparations	Selenate of sodium
HANAT	Natrium silicofluoricum, sulphate of sodium, Scientific name N, General, Homeopathic preparations	Sulphate of sodium
HANAU	Natrium sulphuricum, sulphate of sodium, Glauber salt, Scientific name N, General, Homeopathic preparations	Sulphate of sodium, Glauber salt
HANAV	Natrium sulphurosum, sulphite of sodium, Scientific name N, General, Homeopathic preparations	Sulphite of sodium
HANAW	Nectrianinum, nosode of tree cancer, Scientific name N, General, Homeopathic preparations	Nosode of tree cancer
HANAY	Nepenthes distillatoria, pitcher plant, Scientific name N, General, Homeopathic preparations	Pitcher Plant
HANAZ	Nerium oleander, rose bay, Scientific name N, General, Homeopathic preparations	Rose bay
HANBA	Niccolum metallicum, nickel, Scientific name N, General, Homeopathic preparations	Nickel
HANBB	Niccolum sulphuricum, sulphate of nickel, Scientific name N, General, Homeopathic preparations	Sulphate of nickel
HANBC	Nicotinum, nicotine, Scientific name N, General, Homeopathic preparations	Nicotine
HANBD	Nigella sativa, black cumin, Scientific name N, General, Homeopathic preparations	Black cumin
HANBE	Nitri spiritus dulcis, sweet spirits of nitre, Scientific name N, General, Homeopathic preparations	Sweet spirits of nitre
HANBG	Nitro muriatic acid, Scientific name N, General, Homeopathic preparations	Nitro-muriatic acid
HANBH	Nitrogenium oxygenatum, nitrous oxide, Scientific name N, General, Homeopathic preparations	Nitrous oxide

Scientific name N

ABC Code	Procedure Description	Expanded Definition
HANBI	Nuphar luteum, yellow pond lily, Scientific name N, General, Homeopathic preparations	Yellow pond lily
HANBJ	Nux moschata, nutmeg, Scientific name N, General, Homeopathic preparations	Nutmeg
HANBK	Nux vomica, poison nut, Scientific name N, General, Homeopathic preparations	Poison nut
HANBL	Nyctanthes arbortristis, sad tree, parijat, Scientific name N, General, Homeopathic preparations	Sad tree, parijat
HANBM	Nymphea odorata, sweet water lily, Scientific name N, General, Homeopathic preparations	Sweet water lily
HANBN	Nicotiana tabacum, tobacco, Scientific name N, General, Homeopathic preparations	Tobacco
HANZZ	Other homeopathic preparation, narrative required, Scientific name N, General, Homeopathic preparations	Other homeopathic preparation with scientific name N. Narrative required.

Scientific name O

ABC Code	Procedure Description	Expanded Definition
HAOAA	Ocimum canum, Brazilian alfavaca, Scientific name O, General, Homeopathic preparations	Brazilian alfavaca
HAOAB	Oenanthe aquatica, water dropwart, Scientific name O, General, Homeopathic preparations	Water dropwart
HAOAC	Oenothera biennis, large evening primrose, Scientific name O, General, Homeopathic preparations	Large evening primrose
HAOAE	Oleum animale, Dippels animal oil, Scientific name O, General, Homeopathic preparations	Dippels animal oil
HAOAF	Oleum jecoris aselli, cod liver oil, Scientific name O, General, Homeopathic preparations	Cod liver oil
HAOAG	Oniscus asellus, wood louse, Scientific name O, General, Homeopathic preparations	Wood louse
HAOAH	Ononis spinosa , rest harrow, Scientific name O, General, Homeopathic preparations	Rest harrow

ABC Code	Procedure Description	Expanded Definition
HAOAI	Onosmodium molle, false gromwell, Scientific name O, General, Homeopathic preparations	False gromwell
HAOAJ	Operculina turpenthium, nishope, Scientific name O, General, Homeopathic preparations	Nishope
HAOAL	Opuntia vulgaris, prickly pear, Scientific name O, General, Homeopathic preparations	Prickly pear
HAOAM	Orchitinum, testes extract, Scientific name O, General, Homeopathic preparations	Testes extract
HAOAN	Oreodaphne californica, umbellularia californica, California Laurel, Scientific name O, General, Homeopathic preparations	California Laurel
HAOAO	Origanum majorana, marjoram, Scientific name O, General, Homeopathic preparations	Marjoram
HAOAP	Ornithogalum umbellatum, star of Bethlehem, Scientific name O, General, Homeopathic preparations	Star of Bethlehem
HAOAR	Osmium metallicum, osmium, Scientific name O, General, Homeopathic preparations	Osmium
HAOAS	Osteo arthritic nosode, synovial fluid of arthritic joints, Scientific name O, General, Homeopathic preparations	Nosode of osteo-arthritis, synovial fluid of arthritic joints
HAOAT	Ostrya virginica, ironwood, Scientific name O, General, Homeopathic preparations	Ironwood
HAOAU	Oophorinum, potentised ovary gland, Scientific name O, General, Homeopathic preparations	Potentised ovary gland
HAOAV	Ovi gallinae pellicula, membrane of egg shell, Scientific name O, General, Homeopathic preparations	Membrane of egg shell
HAOAW	Oxalicum acidum, oxalic acid, sorrel acid, Scientific name O, General, Homeopathic preparations	Oxalic acid, sorrel acid
HAOAX	Oxydendron arboreum, sorrel tree, sourwood, Scientific name O, General, Homeopathic preparations	Sorrel tree, sourwood

Scientific name O

ABC Code	Procedure Description	Expanded Definition
HAOAY	Oxygenium, oxygen, ozone, Scientific name O, General, Homeopathic preparations	Oxygen, ozone
HAOAZ	Oleum wittnebianum, cajuputum, cajuput oil, Scientific name O, General, Homeopathic preparations	Cajuput oil, cajuputum
HAOBA	Oxytropis lambertii, Lambert loco weed, Scientific name O, General, Homeopathic preparations	Lambert loco weed
HAOZZ	Other homeopathic preparation, narrative required, Scientific name O, General, Homeopathic preparations	Other homeopathic preparation with scientific name O. Narrative required.

Scientific name P

ABC Code	Procedure Description	Expanded Definition
HAPAA	Paeonia officinalis, paeony, Scientific name P, General, Homeopathic preparations	Paeony
HAPAB	Palladium metallicum, palladium, Scientific name P, General, Homeopathic preparations	Palladium
HAPAD	Pancreatinum, pancreatic glands of ox or sheep, Scientific name P, General, Homeopathic preparations	Pancreatic glands of ox or sheep
HAPAE	Paraffinum, paraffine, purified paraffin, Scientific name P, General, Homeopathic preparations	Paraffine, purified paraffin
HAPAF	Parathyroid, parathyroid hormone, Scientific name P, General, Homeopathic preparations	Parathyroid hormone
HAPAG	Pareira brava, virgin vine, Scientific name P, General, Homeopathic preparations	Virgin vine
HAPAH	Parthenium integrifolia, parthenium root, Scientific name P, General, Homeopathic preparations	Parthenium root
HAPAI	Parietaria officinalis, pellitory of the wall, Scientific name P, General, Homeopathic preparations	Pellitory-of-the-wall
HAPAJ	Paris quadrifolia, one berry, Scientific name P, General, Homeopathic preparations	One berry

ABC Code	Procedure Description	Expanded Definition
HAPAL	Parotidinum, nosode of mumps, Scientific name P, General, Homeopathic preparations	Nosode of mumps
HAPAM	Passiflora incarnata, passionflower, Scientific name P, General, Homeopathic preparations	Passionflower
HAPAN	Pastinaca sativa, wild parsnip, Scientific name P, General, Homeopathic preparations	Wild parsnip
HAPAO	Pecten jacobaeus, scallop, Scientific name P, General, Homeopathic preparations	Scallop
HAPAP	Pediculus capitis, head louse, Scientific name P, General, Homeopathic preparations	Head louse
HAPAQ	Pelargonium reniforme, furry geranium, Scientific name P, General, Homeopathic preparations	Furry geranium
HAPAR	Penicillinum, penicillin, antibiotic drug, Scientific name P, General, Homeopathic preparations	Penicillin, antibiotic drug
HAPAS	Penthorum sedoides, Virginia stonecrop, Scientific name P, General, Homeopathic preparations	Virginia stonecrop
HAPAT	Pepsinum, digestive enzyme, Scientific name P, General, Homeopathic preparations	Digestive enzyme
HAPAU	Pertussin, nosode of whooping cough, Scientific name P, General, Homeopathic preparations	Nosode of whooping cough
HAPAV	Pestinum, nosode of plague, Scientific name P, General, Homeopathic preparations	nosode of plague
HAPAW	Phytolacca octandra, red ink plant, Scientific name P, General, Homeopathic preparations	Red ink plant
HAPAX	Petra oleum, petroleum, crude rock oil, Scientific name P, General, Homeopathic preparations	Crude rock oil, petroleum
HAPAY	Petroselinum crispum, parsley, Scientific name P, General, Homeopathic preparations	Parsley

Scientific name P

ABC Code	Procedure Description	Expanded Definition
HAPAZ	Prunus laurocerasus, cherry laurel, Scientific name P, General, Homeopathic preparations	Cherry laurel
HAPBA	Phallus impudicus, stinkhorn fungus, Scientific name P, General, Homeopathic preparations	Stinkhorn fungus
HAPBB	Phaseolus vulgaris, dwarf bean, Scientific name P, General, Homeopathic preparations	Dwarf bean
HAPBC	Phellandrium aquaticum, oenanthe phellandrium, water dropwort, horsebane, Scientific name P, General, Homeopathic preparations	Water dropwort, horsebane
HAPBD	Phenacetinum, para acetphenatidine, Scientific name P, General, Homeopathic preparations	Para-acetphenatidine
HAPBE	Phenobarbitalum, phenobarbital, Scientific name P, General, Homeopathic preparations	Phenobarbital
HAPBF	Phlorizinum, trituration of a substance discovered in the fresh bark of trees, phlorizin, Scientific name P, General, Homeopathic preparations	Trituration of a substance discovered in the fresh bark of trees, phlorizin
HAPBG	Phosphoricum acidum, phosphoric acid, Scientific name P, General, Homeopathic preparations	Phosphoric acid
HAPBH	Phosphorus hydrogenatus, hydrogenatted phosphorus, Scientific name P, General, Homeopathic preparations	Hydrogenatted phosphorus
HAPBI	Phosphorus muriaticus, phosphorus pentachloride, Scientific name P, General, Homeopathic preparations	Phosphorus pentachloride
HAPBJ	Phosphorus, Scientific name P, General, Homeopathic preparations	Phosphorus
HAPBK	Phytolacca americana, pokeroot, inkberry, Scientific name P, General, Homeopathic preparations	Pokeroot, inkberry
HAPBL	Phylum cnidaria, Portuguese man of war, Scientific name P, General, Homeopathic preparations	Portuguese-man-of-war

Scientific name P

ABC Code	Procedure Description	Expanded Definition
HAPBM	Physostigma venenosum, calabar bean, Scientific name P, General, Homeopathic preparations	Calabar bean
HAPBN	Picricum acidum, picric acid, Scientific name P, General, Homeopathic preparations	Picric acid
HAPBO	Picrotoxinum, picrotoxin, Scientific name P, General, Homeopathic preparations	Picrotoxin
HAPBP	Pilocarpine, alkaloid of jaborandi, Scientific name P, General, Homeopathic preparations	Alkaloid of jaborandi
HAPBQ	Pimenta officinalis, sweet spicy clove, Scientific name P, General, Homeopathic preparations	Sweet spicy clove
HAPBR	Pimpinella saxifraga, bibernell, pimpinella root, Scientific name P, General, Homeopathic preparations	Bibernell, pimpinella root
HAPBS	Pinus lambertina, sugar pine, Scientific name P, General, Homeopathic preparations	Sugar pine
HAPBT	Pinus sylvestris, Scotch pine, Scientific name P, General, Homeopathic preparations	Scotch pine
HAPBU	Piper methysticum, kava kava, Scientific name P, General, Homeopathic preparations	Kava kava
HAPBV	Piper nigrum, black pepper, Scientific name P, General, Homeopathic preparations	Black pepper
HAPBW	Piperazinum, piperazidine, Scientific name P, General, Homeopathic preparations	Piperazidine
HAPBX	Piscidia piscipula, Jamaica dogwood, Scientific name P, General, Homeopathic preparations	Jamaica dogwood
HAPBY	Pituitaria glandula, pituitary gland, Scientific name P, General, Homeopathic preparations	Pituitary gland
HAPBZ	Papapver somniferum, opium, dried latex of poppy, Scientific name P, General, Homeopathic preparations	Opium, dried latex of poppy
HAPCA	Pix liquida, pine tar, Scientific name P, General, Homeopathic preparations	Pine tar

Scientific name P

ABC Code	Procedure Description	Expanded Definition
HAPCB	Plantago major, plantain, Scientific name P, General, Homeopathic preparations	Plantain
HAPCC	Platanus racemosa, sycamore, planetree, Scientific name P, General, Homeopathic preparations	Sycamore, planetree
HAPCD	Platinum metallicum, platinum, Scientific name P, General, Homeopathic preparations	Platinum
HAPCE	Platinum muriaticum, chloride of platinum, Scientific name P, General, Homeopathic preparations	Chloride of platinum
HAPCF	Platinum muriaticum natronatum, chloroplatinate of sodium, Scientific name P, General, Homeopathic preparations	Chloroplatinate of sodium
HAPCG	Plectranthus fruticosus, Mexican mint, Scientific name P, General, Homeopathic preparations	Mexican mint
HAPCH	Plumbago litteralis, plumbago, Scientific name P, General, Homeopathic preparations	Plumbago
HAPCI	Plumbum aceticum, acetate of lead, Scientific name P, General, Homeopathic preparations	Acetate of lead
HAPCJ	Plumbum chromicum, chromate of lead, Scientific name P, General, Homeopathic preparations	Chromate of lead
HAPCK	Plumbum iodatum, iodide of lead, Scientific name P, General, Homeopathic preparations	Iodide of lead
HAPCL	Plumbum metallicum, lead, Scientific name P, General, Homeopathic preparations	Lead
HAPCM	Pneumococcinum, nosode of pneumococcus, Scientific name P, General, Homeopathic preparations	Nosode of pneumococcus
HAPCN	Podophyllum peltatum, mayapple, Scientific name P, General, Homeopathic preparations	Mayapple
HAPCO	Polygonum aviculare, knotgrass, Scientific name P, General, Homeopathic preparations	Knotgrass

ABC Code	Procedure Description	Expanded Definition
HAPCP	Polygonum punctatum, smartweed, Scientific name P, General, Homeopathic preparations	Smartweed
HAPCQ	Polygonum sagitatum, arrow leaved, Scientific name P, General, Homeopathic preparations	Arrow leaved
HAPCR	Polyporus pinicola, pine agaric, Scientific name P, General, Homeopathic preparations	Pine agaric
HAPCS	Populus candicans, balm of gilead, Scientific name P, General, Homeopathic preparations	Balm of gilead
HAPCT	Populus tremuloides, American aspen, Scientific name P, General, Homeopathic preparations	American aspen
HAPCV	Primula obconica, primrose, Scientific name P, General, Homeopathic preparations	Primrose
HAPCW	Primula veris, cowslip, Scientific name P, General, Homeopathic preparations	Cowslip
HAPCX	Primula vulgaris, common primrose, Scientific name P, General, Homeopathic preparations	Common primrose
HAPCY	Prinos verticillatus, black alder, Scientific name P, General, Homeopathic preparations	Black alder
HAPCZ	Polygala senega, snakewort, senega, Scientific name P, General, Homeopathic preparations	Snakewort, senega
HAPDA	Propylaminum, trimethylaminum, Scientific name P, General, Homeopathic preparations	Trimethylaminum
HAPDB	Proteus bacillus, proteus bacteria, Scientific name P, General, Homeopathic preparations	Proteus bacteria
HAPDC	Prunus padus, bird cherry, Scientific name P, General, Homeopathic preparations	Bird cherry
HAPDD	Prunus spinosa, black thorn, Scientific name P, General, Homeopathic preparations	Black thorn
HAPDE	Prunus virginiana, choke cherry, Scientific name P, General, Homeopathic preparations	Choke cherry
HAPDF	Psorinum, nosode of scabies, Scientific name P, General, Homeopathic preparations	Nosode of scabies

Scientific name P

ABC Code	Procedure Description	Expanded Definition
HAPDG	Ptelea trifoliata, common hop tree, Scientific name P, General, Homeopathic preparations	Common hop tree
HAPDH	Pulex irritans, common flea, Scientific name P, General, Homeopathic preparations	Common flea
HAPDI	Pulmo vulpis, foxs lung, Scientific name P, General, Homeopathic preparations	Foxs lung
HAPDJ	Pulsatilla nuttaliana, American pasque flower, Scientific name P, General, Homeopathic preparations	American pasque flower
HAPDL	Pyrethrum parthenium, chrysanthemum parthenium, feverfew, Scientific name P, General, Homeopathic preparations	Feverfew
HAPDM	Pyrogen, rotten meat pus, Scientific name P, General, Homeopathic preparations	Rotten meat pus
HAPDN	Pyrus americanus, mountain ash, Scientific name P, General, Homeopathic preparations	Mountain ash
HAPDO	Pilocarpus jaborandi, Indian hemp, jaborandi, Scientific name P, General, Homeopathic preparations	Indian hemp, jaborandi
HAPDP	Palicourea densiflors, coto bark, Scientific name P, General, Homeopathic preparations	Coto bark
HAPDQ	Panax quinquefolius, wild ginseng, Scientific name P, General, Homeopathic preparations	Wild ginseng
HAPDR	Punica granatum, pomegranate root bark, Scientific name P, General, Homeopathic preparations	Pomegranate root bark
HAPDS	Paullinia cupana, guarana, Brazilian cocoa, Scientific name P, General, Homeopathic preparations	Guarana, Brazilian coca
HAPZZ	Other homeopathic preparation, narrative required, Scientific name P, General, Homeopathic preparations	Other homeopathic preparation with scientific name P. Narrative required.

Scientific name Q

ABC Code	Procedure Description	Expanded Definition

Scientific name Q

ABC Code	Procedure Description	Expanded Definition
HAQAA	Quassia amara, quassia wood, Scientific name Q, General, Homeopathic preparations	Quassia wood
HAQAC	Quercus glandium spiritus, acorn kernel, Scientific name Q, General, Homeopathic preparations	Acorn kernel
HAQAD	Quillaya saponaria, Chile soap bark, Scientific name Q, General, Homeopathic preparations	Chile soap bark
HAQZZ	Other homeopathic preparation, narrative required, Scientific name Q, General, Homeopathic preparations	Other homeopathic preparation with scientific name Q. Narrative required.

Scientific name R

ABC Code	Procedure Description	Expanded Definition
HARAA	Radium bromatum, radium bromide, Scientific name R, General, Homeopathic preparations	Radium bromide
HARAC	Ranunculus acris, goldcup, Scientific name R, General, Homeopathic preparations	Goldcup
HARAD	Ranunculus bulbosus, buttercup, Scientific name R, General, Homeopathic preparations	Buttercup
HARAE	Ranunculus ficaria, lesser celandine, Scientific name R, General, Homeopathic preparations	Lesser celandine
HARAF	Ranunculus glacialis, reindeer flower, Scientific name R, General, Homeopathic preparations	Reindeer flower
HARAG	Ranunculus repens, creeping buttercup, Scientific name R, General, Homeopathic preparations	Creeping buttercup
HARAH	Ranunculus sceleratus, marsh buttercup, Scientific name R, General, Homeopathic preparations	Marsh buttercup
HARAI	Raphanus sativus niger, black garden radish, Scientific name R, General, Homeopathic preparations	Black garden radish
HARAJ	Ratanhia peruviana, krameria mapato, Scientific name R, General, Homeopathic preparations	Krameria mapato

Scientific name R

ABC Code	Procedure Description	Expanded Definition
HARAK	Rauwolfia serpentina, rauwolfia, sarpghanda, Scientific name R, General, Homeopathic preparations	Rauwolfia, sarpghanda
HARAL	Reserpine, alkaloid of rauwolfia serpentina, Scientific name R, General, Homeopathic preparations	Alkaloid of rauwolfia serpentina
HARAM	Rhamnus californica, california coffee tree, Scientific name R, General, Homeopathic preparations	California coffee tree
HARAN	Rhamnus catharticus, buckthorn, Scientific name R, General, Homeopathic preparations	Buckthorn
HARAO	Rhamnus frangula, alder buckthorn, Scientific name R, General, Homeopathic preparations	Alder buckthorn
HARAP	Rheum palmatum, turkey rhubarb, Scientific name R, General, Homeopathic preparations	Turkey rhubarb
HARAQ	Rhodium oxydatum nitricum, nitrate of rhodium oxide, Scientific name R, General, Homeopathic preparations	Nitrate of rhodium oxide
HARAR	Rhodium metallicum, rhodium, Scientific name R, General, Homeopathic preparations	Rhodium
HARAS	Rhododendron chrysanthum, yellow snow rose, Scientific name R, General, Homeopathic preparations	Yellow snow rose
HARAT	Rhus aromatica, fragrant sumach, Scientific name R, General, Homeopathic preparations	Fragrant sumach
HARAU	Rhus diversiloba, California poison oak, Scientific name R, General, Homeopathic preparations	California poison oak
HARAV	Rhus glabra, smooth sumach, Scientific name R, General, Homeopathic preparations	Smooth sumach
HARAW	Rhus toxicodendron, poison oak, Scientific name R, General, Homeopathic preparations	Poison oak
HARAX	Rhus venenata, poison elder, Scientific name R, General, Homeopathic preparations	Poison elder

Scientific name R

ABC Code	Procedure Description	Expanded Definition
HARAY	Ribonucleinicum acidum, ribonucleic acid, Scientific name R, General, Homeopathic preparations	Ribonucleic acid
HARAZ	Rorippa nasturtium aquaticum, water cress, Scientific name R, General, Homeopathic preparations	Water cress
HARBA	Ricinus communis, castor oil, Scientific name R, General, Homeopathic preparations	Castor oil
HARBB	Robinia pseudoacacia, yellow locust, Scientific name R, General, Homeopathic preparations	Yellow locust
HARBC	Rosa canina, dog rose, Scientific name R, General, Homeopathic preparations	Dog rose
HARBD	Rosa damascena, Damacus rose, Scientific name R, General, Homeopathic preparations	Damacus rose
HARBE	Rosmarinus officinalis, rosemary, Scientific name R, General, Homeopathic preparations	Rosemary
HARBF	Rubia tinctorum, madder, Scientific name R, General, Homeopathic preparations	Madder
HARBG	Rumex acetosa, sorrel, Scientific name R, General, Homeopathic preparations	Sorrel
HARBH	Rumex crispus, yellow dock, Scientific name R, General, Homeopathic preparations	Yellow dock
HARBI	Russula foetens, stinky russula, Scientific name R, General, Homeopathic preparations	Stinky russula
HARBJ	Ruta graveolens, garden rue, Scientific name R, General, Homeopathic preparations	Garden rue
HARBK	Resina itu, solution of the resin of itu in alcohol, Scientific name R, General, Homeopathic preparations	Solution of the resin of itu in alcohol
HARZZ	Other homeopathic preparation, narrative required, Scientific name R, General, Homeopathic preparations	Other homeopathic preparation with scientific name R. Narrative required.

Scientific name S

ABC Code	Procedure Description	Expanded Definition

Scientific name S

ABC Code	Procedure Description	Expanded Definition
HASAB	Sabal serrulata, saw palmetto, Scientific name S, General, Homeopathic preparations	Saw palmetto
HASAD	Saccharum lactis, lactose, milk sugar, Scientific name S, General, Homeopathic preparations	Lactose, milk sugar
HASAE	Saccharum officinale, sucrose, cane sugar, Scientific name S, General, Homeopathic preparations	Sucrose, cane sugar
HASAF	Salicylicum acidum, salicylic acid, Scientific name S, General, Homeopathic preparations	Salicylic acid
HASAG	Salix mollissima, willow hybrid of salix triandra x salix viminalis, Scientific name S, General, Homeopathic preparations	Willow hybrid of salix triandra x salix viminalis
HASAH	Salix nigra, black willow, Scientific name S, General, Homeopathic preparations	Black willow
HASAI	Salix purpurea, purple willow, red willow, Scientific name S, General, Homeopathic preparations	Purple willow, red willow
HASAJ	Salol, salicylate of phenol, Scientific name S, General, Homeopathic preparations	Salicylate of phenol
HASAK	Salvia officinalis, sage, Scientific name S, General, Homeopathic preparations	Sage
HASAL	Sambucus canadensis, elder bush, Scientific name S, General, Homeopathic preparations	Elder bush
HASAM	Sambucus nigra, black elder, Scientific name S, General, Homeopathic preparations	Black elder
HASAN	Sanguinaria canadensis, bloodroot, Scientific name S, General, Homeopathic preparations	Bloodroot
HASAO	Sanguinarinum nitricum, nitrate of sanguinarine, Scientific name S, General, Homeopathic preparations	Nitrate of sanguinarine
HASAP	Sanguinarinum tartaricum, tartrate of sanguinarine, Scientific name S, General, Homeopathic preparations	Tartrate of sanguinarine

ABC Code	Procedure Description	Expanded Definition
HASAQ	Sanguinarinum, sanguinarinum trituration, Scientific name S, General, Homeopathic preparations	Sanguinarinum trituration
HASAR	Sanicula aqua, water of the mineral springs in Sanicula in Ottawa, Scientific name S, General, Homeopathic preparations	Water of the mineral springs in Sanicula in Ottawa
HASAS	Santalum album, white sandalwood, Scientific name S, General, Homeopathic preparations	White sandalwood
HASAT	Santalum oleum, oil of sandalwood, Scientific name S, General, Homeopathic preparations	Oil of sandalwood
HASAU	Santoninum, santonin, Scientific name S, General, Homeopathic preparations	Santonin
HASAV	Saponaria officinalis, soap root, Scientific name S, General, Homeopathic preparations	Soap root
HASAW	Saponinum, saponin, glucosidal found in Quillaya, Yucca and Senega, Scientific name S, General, Homeopathic preparations	Saponin, glucosidal found in Quillaya, Yucca and Senega
HASAX	Sarcolacticum acidum, sarcolactic acid, Scientific name S, General, Homeopathic preparations	Sarcolactic acid
HASAY	Sarothamnus scoparius, broom, Scientific name S, General, Homeopathic preparations	Broom
HASAZ	Saraca asoca, saraca indica, ashoka, Scientific name S, General, Homeopathic preparations	Ashoka
HASBA	Sarracenia purpurea, pitcher plant, Scientific name S, General, Homeopathic preparations	Pitcher plant
HASBB	Sarsaparilla officinalis, wild liquorice, sarsaparilla, Scientific name S, General, Homeopathic preparations	Wild liquorice, sarsaparilla
HASBC	Saururus cernuus, lizards tail, Scientific name S, General, Homeopathic preparations	Lizards tail
HASBD	Scammonium, scammony, resin of convolvulus scammonia root, Scientific name S, General, Homeopathic preparations	Scammony, resin of convolvulus scammonia root

Scientific name S

ABC Code	Procedure Description	Expanded Definition
HASBE	Scarlatininum, nosode of scarlet fever, Scientific name S, General, Homeopathic preparations	Nosode of scarlet fever
HASBF	Schinus molle, Brazilian peppertree, Scientific name S, General, Homeopathic preparations	Brazilian peppertree
HASBG	Scirrhinum, nosode of cancer, Scientific name S, General, Homeopathic preparations	Nosode of cancer
HASBH	Scolopendra vilidicornis, centipede, Scientific name S, General, Homeopathic preparations	Centipede
HASBI	Scorpio europaeus, scorpion, Scientific name S, General, Homeopathic preparations	Scorpion
HASBJ	Scrophularia nodosa, knotted figwort, Scientific name S, General, Homeopathic preparations	Knotted figwort
HASBK	Scutellaria laterifolia, skullcap, Scientific name S, General, Homeopathic preparations	Skullcap
HASBL	Secale cornutum, claviceps purpurea, ergot of rye, Scientific name S, General, Homeopathic preparations	Ergot of rye
HASBM	Sedum acre, small houseleek, Scientific name S, General, Homeopathic preparations	Small houseleek
HASBN	Selenium metallicum, selenium, Scientific name S, General, Homeopathic preparations	Selenium
HASBO	Sempervivum tectorum, common houseleek, hens and chickens, Scientific name S, General, Homeopathic preparations	Common houseleek, hens and chickens
HASBP	Senecio aureus, golden ragwort, Scientific name S, General, Homeopathic preparations	Golden ragwort
HASBQ	Senecio jacobea, stinking Willie, Scientific name S, General, Homeopathic preparations	Stinking Willie
HASBT	Sepia officinalis, cuttlefish ink, Scientific name S, General, Homeopathic preparations	Cuttlefish ink

Scientific name S

ABC Code	Procedure Description	Expanded Definition
HASBU	Serum anguillar ichthyotoxin, eel serum, Scientific name S, General, Homeopathic preparations	Eel serum
HASBV	Silica marina, beach sand, Scientific name S, General, Homeopathic preparations	Beach sand
HASBW	Silicea terra, silica, pure flint, Scientific name S, General, Homeopathic preparations	Silica, pure flint
HASBX	Silphium lacinatum, rosin weed, Scientific name S, General, Homeopathic preparations	Rosin weed
HASBY	Simaruba amara, dysentery bark, mountain damson, Scientific name S, General, Homeopathic preparations	Dysentery bark, mountain damson
HASBZ	Schinopsis balansaei, red quebracho, Scientific name S, General, Homeopathic preparations	Red quebracho
HASCA	Sinapis nigra, black mustard, Scientific name S, General, Homeopathic preparations	Black mustard
HASCB	Sinapis alba, white mustard, Scientific name S, General, Homeopathic preparations	White mustard
HASCG	Sisyrinchium bellum, sisyrinchium atlanticum, blue eyed grass, Scientific name S, General, Homeopathic preparations	Blue-eyed grass
HASCH	Sium latifolium, water parsnip, Scientific name S, General, Homeopathic preparations	Water parsnip
HASCI	Skatolum, skatol, Scientific name S, General, Homeopathic preparations	Skatol
HASCJ	Skookum chuck aqua, water of Medical Lake in Washington, Scientific name S, General, Homeopathic preparations	Water of Medical Lake in Washington
HASCK	Slag, pulverized slag, agricultural liming material, Scientific name S, General, Homeopathic preparations	Pulverized slag, agricultural liming material
HASCL	Sol, sunlight, Scientific name S, General, Homeopathic preparations	Sunlight

Scientific name S

ABC Code	Procedure Description	Expanded Definition
HASCM	Solanium nigrum, Jerusalem cherry, Scientific name S, General, Homeopathic preparations	Jerusalem cherry
HASCN	Solanum aculeatissimus, arrebenta, Scientific name S, General, Homeopathic preparations	Arrebenta
HASCO	Solanum carolinense, horse nettle, Scientific name S, General, Homeopathic preparations	Horse nettle
HASCP	Solanum mammosum, apple of Sodom, Scientific name S, General, Homeopathic preparations	Apple of Sodom
HASCQ	Solanum nigrum, black nightshade, Scientific name S, General, Homeopathic preparations	Black nightshade
HASCR	Solanum oleraceum, juquerioba, Scientific name S, General, Homeopathic preparations	Juquerioba
HASCS	Solanum tuberosum aegrotans, decomposing potato, Scientific name S, General, Homeopathic preparations	Decomposing potato
HASCT	Solanum tuberosum, potato, Scientific name S, General, Homeopathic preparations	Potato
HASCU	Solidago virgaurea, goldenrod, Scientific name S, General, Homeopathic preparations	Goldenrod
HASCV	Sphingurus martini, porcupine tree, Scientific name S, General, Homeopathic preparations	Porcupine tree
HASCW	Spigelia anthelmia, pinkroot, Scientific name S, General, Homeopathic preparations	Pinkroot
HASCX	Spigelia marylandica, worm grass, Scientific name S, General, Homeopathic preparations	Worm grass
HASCY	Spiraea ulmaria, meadow sweet, Scientific name S, General, Homeopathic preparations	Meadow sweet
HASCZ	Spongilla badiaga, freshwater sponge, Scientific name S, General, Homeopathic preparations	Freshwater sponge
HASDA	Spiranthes autumnalis, ladys tresses, Scientific name S, General, Homeopathic preparations	Ladys tresses

Scientific name S

ABC Code	Procedure Description	Expanded Definition
HASDB	Spongia tosta, roasted sponge, Scientific name S, General, Homeopathic preparations	Roasted sponge
HASDC	Squilla maritima, sea onion, Scientific name S, General, Homeopathic preparations	Sea onion
HASDD	Stannum iodatum, iodide of tin, Scientific name S, General, Homeopathic preparations	Iodide of tin
HASDE	Stannum metallicum, tin, Scientific name S, General, Homeopathic preparations	Tin
HASDF	Staphylococcus bacteria, staph bacteria, Scientific name S, General, Homeopathic preparations	Staph bacteria
HASDH	Stellaria media, chickweed, Scientific name S, General, Homeopathic preparations	Chickweed
HASDI	Sterculia cola, kola tree, cola tree, Scientific name S, General, Homeopathic preparations	Kola tree, cola tree
HASDJ	Sticta pulmonaria, lungwort, Scientific name S, General, Homeopathic preparations	Lungwort
HASDK	Stigmata maydis, corn silk, Scientific name S, General, Homeopathic preparations	Corn silk
HASDL	Stillingia silvatica, queens root, Scientific name S, General, Homeopathic preparations	Queens root
HASDN	Streptococcinum bacteria, step bacteria, Scientific name S, General, Homeopathic preparations	Step bacteria
HASDO	Strontium bromatum, bromide of strontium, Scientific name S, General, Homeopathic preparations	Bromide of strontium
HASDP	Strontium carbonicum, carbonate of strontia, Scientific name S, General, Homeopathic preparations	Carbonate of strontia
HASDQ	Strontium nitricum, nitrate of strontium, Scientific name S, General, Homeopathic preparations	Nitrate of strontium

Scientific name S

ABC Code	Procedure Description	Expanded Definition
HASDR	Strophanthus hispidus, kombe seed, Scientific name S, General, Homeopathic preparations	Kombe-seed
HASDS	Strychnia phosphorica, phosphate of strychnine, Scientific name S, General, Homeopathic preparations	Phosphate of strychnine
HASDT	Strychnine, alkaloid of nux vomica, Scientific name S, General, Homeopathic preparations	Alkaloid of nux vomica
HASDU	Strychnos gaultheriana, tropical bind weed, hoang nan, Scientific name S, General, Homeopathic preparations	Tropical bind weed, hoang nan
HASDV	Succinum, succinite, amber, Scientific name S, General, Homeopathic preparations	Succinite, amber
HASDW	Sulfanilamide, anti infective agent used to treat candida albicans, Scientific name S, General, Homeopathic preparations	Sulfanilamide, anti-infective agent used to treat candida albicans
HASDX	Sulfonal, coal tar product, Scientific name S, General, Homeopathic preparations	Coal tar product
HASDY	Sulphur hydrogen, sulfurated hydrogen, Scientific name S, General, Homeopathic preparations	Sulfurated hydrogen
HASDZ	Simaruba ferroginea, cedron, rattlesnake bean, Scientific name S, General, Homeopathic preparations	Cedron, rattlesnake bean
HASEA	Sulphur iodatum, iodide of sulphur, Scientific name S, General, Homeopathic preparations	Iodide of sulphur
HASEB	Sulphur terebinthinatum, terebinthinated sulphur, Scientific name S, General, Homeopathic preparations	Terebinthinated sulphur
HASEC	Sulphur, sublimated sulphur, Scientific name S, General, Homeopathic preparations	Sublimated sulphur
HASED	Sulphuricum acidum, sulphuric acid, vitriol, Scientific name S, General, Homeopathic preparations	Sulphuric acid, vitriol

Scientific name S

ABC Code	Procedure Description	Expanded Definition
HASEE	Sulphurosum acidum, sulphur dioxide, Scientific name S, General, Homeopathic preparations	Sulphur dioxide
HASEF	Sumbulus moschatus, musk root, Scientific name S, General, Homeopathic preparations	Musk root
HASEG	Sycotic bacillus, causes sycotic miasm, Scientific name S, General, Homeopathic preparations	Sycotic bacillus, causes sycotic miasm, also expressed by ridged nails.
HASEH	Symphoricarpus racemosus, snowberry, Scientific name S, General, Homeopathic preparations	Snowberry
HASEI	Symphytum officinale, common comfrey, Scientific name S, General, Homeopathic preparations	Common comfrey
HASEJ	Syphilinum, nosode of syphilis, Scientific name S, General, Homeopathic preparations	Nosode of syphilis
HASEK	Syzygium jambolanum, jambul, jambol seed, Scientific name S, General, Homeopathic preparations	Jambul, jambol seed
HASEL	Solanum dulcamara, bittersweet, Scientific name S, General, Homeopathic preparations	Bittersweet
HASZZ	Other homeopathic preparation, narrative required, Scientific name S, General, Homeopathic preparations	Other homeopathic preparation with scientific name S. Narrative required.

Scientific name T

ABC Code	Procedure Description	Expanded Definition
HATAB	Tamus communis, ladies seal, Scientific name T, General, Homeopathic preparations	Ladies seal
HATAC	Tanacetum vulgare, common tansy, Scientific name T, General, Homeopathic preparations	Common tansy
HATAD	Tanghinia venenifera, cerbera tanghin, cerbera venenifera, ordeal tree, Scientific name T, General, Homeopathic preparations	Ordeal tree
HATAE	Tannicum acidum, tannic acid, Scientific name T, General, Homeopathic preparations	Tannic acid

Scientific name T

ABC Code	Procedure Description	Expanded Definition
HATAF	Taraxacum officinale, dandelion, Scientific name T, General, Homeopathic preparations	Dandelion
HATAG	Tarentula cubensis, Cuban spider, Scientific name T, General, Homeopathic preparations	Cuban spider
HATAH	Tarentula hispanica, Spanish spider, Scientific name T, General, Homeopathic preparations	Spanish spider
HATAI	Tartaricum acidum, tartaric acid, Scientific name T, General, Homeopathic preparations	Tartaric acid
HATAJ	Taxus baccata, yew, Scientific name T, General, Homeopathic preparations	Yew
HATAK	Tela aranearum, spiders web, Scientific name T, General, Homeopathic preparations	Spiders web
HATAL	Tellurium metallicum, tellurium, Scientific name T, General, Homeopathic preparations	Tellurium
HATAM	Teplitz aqua, mineral water of Teplitz in Bohemia, Scientific name T, General, Homeopathic preparations	Mineral water of Teplitz in Bohemia
HATAN	Terebinthiniae oleum, turpentine, Scientific name T, General, Homeopathic preparations	Turpentine
HATAO	Tetradymitum, tetradymite, Scientific name T, General, Homeopathic preparations	Tetradymite
HATAP	Teucrium marum, cat thyme, Scientific name T, General, Homeopathic preparations	Cat thyme
HATAQ	Teucrium scorodonia, wood sage, Scientific name T, General, Homeopathic preparations	Wood sage
HATAR	Thallium metallicum, thallium, Scientific name T, General, Homeopathic preparations	Thallium
HATAS	Thalamus, nerve hormonal tissue from the brain, Scientific name T, General, Homeopathic preparations	Nerve hormonal tissue from the brain
HATAT	Thea sinensis, tea, Scientific name T, General, Homeopathic preparations	Tea

Scientific name T

ABC Code	Procedure Description	Expanded Definition
HATAU	Theridion curassavicum, orange spider, Scientific name T, General, Homeopathic preparations	Orange spider
HATAV	Thevetia peruviana, thevetia neriifolia, cerbera peruviana, yellow oleander, Scientific name T, General, Homeopathic preparations	Yellow oleander
HATAW	Thiosinaminum, thiosinamin, oil of mustard seed, Scientific name T, General, Homeopathic preparations	Thiosinamin, oil of mustard seed
HATAY	Thuja lobbi, red cedar, Scientific name T, General, Homeopathic preparations	Red cedar
HATAZ	Turnera aphrodisiaca, damiana, Scientific name T, General, Homeopathic preparations	Damiana
HATBA	Thuja occidentalis, arbor vitae, Scientific name T, General, Homeopathic preparations	Arbor vitae
HATBB	Thymolum, thyme camphor, Scientific name T, General, Homeopathic preparations	Thyme camphor
HATBC	Thymus serpyllum, wild thyme, Scientific name T, General, Homeopathic preparations	Wild thyme
HATBD	Thyroidinum, thyroid gland, Scientific name T, General, Homeopathic preparations	Thyroid gland
HATBE	Thyroidinum, dried thyroid gland of the sheep, Scientific name T, General, Homeopathic preparations	Dried thyroid gland of the sheep
HATBF	Tilia americana, linden, Scientific name T, General, Homeopathic preparations	Linden
HATBG	Titanium metallicum, titanium, Scientific name T, General, Homeopathic preparations	Titanium
HATBI	Torula cerevisiae, yeast plant, Scientific name T, General, Homeopathic preparations	Yeast plant
HATBJ	Toxicophis pugnax, moccasin snake, Scientific name T, General, Homeopathic preparations	Moccasin snake
HATBK	Trachinus vipera, stingfish, teleostei, Scientific name T, General, Homeopathic preparations	Stingfish, teleostei

Scientific name T

ABC Code	Procedure Description	Expanded Definition
HATBL	Tradescantia diuretica, trapoeraba, Scientific name T, General, Homeopathic preparations	Trapoeraba
HATBM	Tribulus terrestris, ikshugandha, Scientific name T, General, Homeopathic preparations	Ikshugandha
HATBN	Trifolium pratense, red clover, Scientific name T, General, Homeopathic preparations	Red clover
HATBO	Trifolium repens, white clover, Scientific name T, General, Homeopathic preparations	White clover
HATBP	Trillium pendulum, lambs quarter, beth root, Scientific name T, General, Homeopathic preparations	Lambs quarter, beth root
HATBQ	Trinitrotoluenum, TNT, Scientific name T, General, Homeopathic preparations	TNT
HATBR	Triosteum perfoliatum, fever root, Scientific name T, General, Homeopathic preparations	Fever root
HATBS	Triticum repens, couch grass, Scientific name T, General, Homeopathic preparations	Couch grass
HATBT	Trombidium muscae, red acarus of the fly, Scientific name T, General, Homeopathic preparations	Red acarus of the fly
HATBU	Tropaeolum majus, Indian cress, Scientific name T, General, Homeopathic preparations	Indian cress
HATBV	Tuberculinum, nosode of tuberculosis, Scientific name T, General, Homeopathic preparations	Nosode of tuberculosis
HATBW	Tuberculinum aviare, chicken tuberculosis, Scientific name T, General, Homeopathic preparations	Chicken tuberculosis
HATBX	Tussilago fragrans, fragrant tussilage, Scientific name T, General, Homeopathic preparations	Fragrant tussilage
HATBY	Tussilago petasites, butter burr, Scientific name T, General, Homeopathic preparations	Butter burr
HATBZ	Theobroma cacao, cocoa, chocolate, Scientific name T, General, Homeopathic preparations	Cocoa, chocolate

Scientific name T

ABC Code	Procedure Description	Expanded Definition
HATCA	Tussilago farfara, coltsfoot, Scientific name T, General, Homeopathic preparations	Coltsfoot
HATZZ	Other homeopathic preparation, narrative required, Scientific name T, General, Homeopathic preparations	Other homeopathic preparation with scientific name T. Narrative required.

Scientific name U

ABC Code	Procedure Description	Expanded Definition
HAUAA	Ulmus campestris, slippery elm, Scientific name U, General, Homeopathic preparations	Slippery elm
HAUAB	Uncaria tomentosa, cats claw, Scientific name U, General, Homeopathic preparations	Cats claw
HAUAD	Upas tiente, strychnos tiente, upas tree, Scientific name U, General, Homeopathic preparations	Upas tree, strychnos tiente
HAUAE	Uranium nitricum, nitrate of uranium, Scientific name U, General, Homeopathic preparations	Nitrate of uranium
HAUAF	Urea pura, carbamide, Scientific name U, General, Homeopathic preparations	Carbamide
HAUAG	Uricum acidum, uric acid, Scientific name U, General, Homeopathic preparations	Uric acid
HAUAH	Urinum humanum, human urine, Scientific name U, General, Homeopathic preparations	Human urine
HAUAI	Urtica urens, stinging nettle, Scientific name U, General, Homeopathic preparations	Stinging nettle
HAUAJ	Usnea barbata, tree moss, Scientific name U, General, Homeopathic preparations	Tree moss
HAUAK	Ustilago maydis, corn smut, Scientific name U, General, Homeopathic preparations	Corn smut
HAUAL	Uva ursi, bearberry, Scientific name U, General, Homeopathic preparations	Bearberry
HAUZZ	Other homeopathic preparation, narrative required, Scientific name U, General, Homeopathic preparations	Other homeopathic preparation with scientific name U. Narrative required.

Scientific name V

ABC Code	Procedure Description	Expanded Definition
HAVAA	Vaccinium myrtillus, bilberry, Scientific name V, General, Homeopathic preparations	Bilberry
HAVAB	Vaccininum, nosode made from vaccine matter, Scientific name V, General, Homeopathic preparations	Nosode made from vaccine matter
HAVAC	Valeriana officinalis, valerian, Scientific name V, General, Homeopathic preparations	Valerian
HAVAD	Vanadium metallicum, vanadium, Scientific name V, General, Homeopathic preparations	Vanadium
HAVAE	Vanilla aromatica, vanilla, Scientific name V, General, Homeopathic preparations	Vanilla
HAVAF	Variolinum, nosode of small pox, Scientific name V, General, Homeopathic preparations	Nosode of small pox
HAVAG	Venus mercenaria, American scallop, Scientific name V, General, Homeopathic preparations	American scallop
HAVAH	Veratrinum, alkaloid from seeds of sabadilla, Scientific name V, General, Homeopathic preparations	Alkaloid from seeds of sabadilla
HAVAI	Veratrum album, white hellebore, Scientific name V, General, Homeopathic preparations	White hellebore
HAVAJ	Veratrum nigrum, dark flowered veratrum, Scientific name V, General, Homeopathic preparations	Dark flowered veratrum
HAVAK	Veratrum viride, American hellebore, Scientific name V, General, Homeopathic preparations	American hellebore
HAVAL	Verbascum thapsus, mullein, Scientific name V, General, Homeopathic preparations	Mullein
HAVAM	Verbena hastata, blue vervain, Scientific name V, General, Homeopathic preparations	Blue vervain
HAVAN	Veronal, Scientific name V, General, Homeopathic preparations	Veronal
HAVAO	Vesicaria communis, vesicaria, tribe, Scientific name V, General, Homeopathic preparations	Vesicaria, tribe

ABC Code	Procedure Description	Expanded Definition
HAVAP	Vespa crabro, wasp, Scientific name V, General, Homeopathic preparations	Wasp
HAVAQ	Viburnum opulus, high cranberry, Scientific name V, General, Homeopathic preparations	High cranberry
HAVAR	Viburnum prunifolium, black haw, Scientific name V, General, Homeopathic preparations	Black haw
HAVAS	Viburnum tinus, laurustinus honeysuckle, Scientific name V, General, Homeopathic preparations	Laurustinus honeysuckle
HAVAT	Vichy aqua, water from the mineral springs at Vichy in France, Scientific name V, General, Homeopathic preparations	Water from the mineral springs at Vichy in France
HAVAU	Vinca minor, lesser periwinkle, Scientific name V, General, Homeopathic preparations	Lesser periwinkle
HAVAV	Viola odorata, violet, Scientific name V, General, Homeopathic preparations	Violet
HAVAW	Viola tricolor, pansy, Scientific name V, General, Homeopathic preparations	Pansy
HAVAX	Vipera berus, German viper, Scientific name V, General, Homeopathic preparations	German viper
HAVAY	Viscum album, mistletoe, Scientific name V, General, Homeopathic preparations	Mistletoe
HAVAZ	Veratrum sabadilla, cevadilla, Scientific name V, General, Homeopathic preparations	Cevadilla
HAVBA	Vitex trifolia, Indian arnica, Scientific name V, General, Homeopathic preparations	Indian arnica
HAVBB	Voeslau aqua, water from the mineral springs at Voeslau in Austria, Scientific name V, General, Homeopathic preparations	Water from the mineral springs at Voeslau in Austria
HAVBC	Vetiveria zizanioides, anatherum muricatum, vetiver, cuscus grass, Scientific name V, General, Homeopathic preparations	Cuscus grass

Scientific name V

ABC Code	Procedure Description	Expanded Definition
HAVZZ	Other homeopathic preparation, narrative required, Scientific name V, General, Homeopathic preparations	Other homeopathic preparation with scientific name V. Narrative required.

Scientific name W

ABC Code	Procedure Description	Expanded Definition
HAWAA	Wiesbaden aqua, water from the spring at Wiesbaden in Prussia, Scientific name W, General, Homeopathic preparations	Water from the spring at Wiesbaden in Prussia
HAWAB	Wildbad aqua, water from the springs at Wildbad in Wuerttemberg, Scientific name W, General, Homeopathic preparations	Water from the springs at Wildbad in Wuerttemberg
HAWAC	Wyethia helenoides, poison weed, Scientific name W, General, Homeopathic preparations	Poison weed
HAWZZ	Other homeopathic preparation, narrative required, Scientific name W, General, Homeopathic preparations	Other homeopathic preparation with scientific name W. Narrative required.

Scientific name X

ABC Code	Procedure Description	Expanded Definition
HAXAA	X-rays, Scientific name X, General, Homeopathic preparations	X-rays
HAXAB	Xanthorrhea arborea, grass tree, Scientific name X, General, Homeopathic preparations	Grass tree
HAXAC	Xanthorrhiza apifolia, shrub yellow root, Scientific name X, General, Homeopathic preparations	Shrub yellow root
HAXAD	Xanthoxylum fraxineum, prickley ash, Scientific name X, General, Homeopathic preparations	Prickley ash
HAXAE	Xerophyllum tenax, basket grass flower, tamalpais lily, Scientific name X, General, Homeopathic preparations	Basket grass flower, tamalpais lily
HAXZZ	Other homeopathic preparation, narrative required, Scientific name X, General, Homeopathic preparations	Other homeopathic preparation with scientific name X. Narrative required.

Scientific name Y

ABC Code	Procedure Description	Expanded Definition
HAYAB	Yucca filamentosa, bear grass, Scientific name Y, General, Homeopathic preparations	Bear grass
HAYZZ	Other homeopathic preparation, narrative required, Scientific name Y, General, Homeopathic preparations	Other homeopathic preparation with scientific name Y. Narrative required.

Scientific name Z

ABC Code	Procedure Description	Expanded Definition
HAZAA	Zea italica, corn silk, Scientific name Z, General, Homeopathic preparations	Corn silk
HAZAB	Zincum chromatum, chromate of zinc, Scientific name Z, General, Homeopathic preparations	Chromate of zinc
HAZAC	Zincum cyanatum, cyanide of zinc, Scientific name Z, General, Homeopathic preparations	Cyanide of zinc
HAZAD	Zincum iodatum, iodide of zinc, Scientific name Z, General, Homeopathic preparations	Iodide of zinc
HAZAE	Zincum muriaticum, chloride of zinc, Scientific name Z, General, Homeopathic preparations	Chloride of zinc
HAZAF	Zincum oxydatum, oxide of zinc, Scientific name Z, General, Homeopathic preparations	Oxide of zinc
HAZAG	Zincum phosphoricum, phosphide of zinc, Scientific name Z, General, Homeopathic preparations	Phosphide of zinc
HAZAH	Zincum picricum, picrate of zinc, Scientific name Z, General, Homeopathic preparations	Picrate of zinc
HAZAI	Zincum sulphuricum, sulphate of zinc, Scientific name Z, General, Homeopathic preparations	Sulphate of zinc
HAZAJ	Zincum valerianum, valerinate of zinc, Scientific name Z, General, Homeopathic preparations	Valerinate of zinc
HAZAK	Zingiber officinale, ginger, Scientific name Z, General, Homeopathic preparations	Ginger

Scientific name Z

ABC Code	Procedure Description	Expanded Definition
HAZAL	Zizia aurea, meadow parsnip, Scientific name Z, General, Homeopathic preparations	Meadow parsnip
HAZAM	Zincum aceticum, acetate of zinc, Scientific name Z, General, Homeopathic preparations	Acetate of zinc
HAZAN	Zincum arsenicosum, zinc arsenate, Scientific name Z, General, Homeopathic preparations	Zinc arsenate
HAZAO	Zincum bromatum, zinc bromide, Scientific name Z, General, Homeopathic preparations	Zinc bromide
HAZAP	Zincum metallicum, zinc, Scientific name Z, General, Homeopathic preparations	Zinc
HAZZZ	Other homeopathic preparation, narrative required, Scientific name Z, General, Homeopathic preparations	Other homeopathic preparation with scientific name Z. Narrative required.

Instructions

The following subsections are contained in the Nursing Section:

Interventions
General

Nursing education
Patient education and counseling
Public health
Communication disorders

Codes that pertain to additionasl nursing services are referenced throughout the book (e.g. midwifery, counseling, etc.). Nursing codes in this section are not always in a logical procedure order. Use the Index to look up procedures that are related.

Any practitioner, regardless of their practice specialty, may use codes in this section if the scope of practice laws for their state or region allows them to perform these services.

Add provider modifiers to the codes in Section N. For example, wound care (NAAKG) performed by a nurse practitioner would be coded as NAAKG-1H, or by a naturopathic doctor as NAAKG-1E.

Nursing practitioners are encouraged to read the nursing guidelines on page xxi of the introduction of this manual.

Nursing

Interventions

General

ABC Code	Procedure Description	Expanded Definition
NAAAA	Risk identification, General, Interventions, Nursing	Analyzing potential risk factors, determining health risks and prioritizing risk education strategies.
NAAAC	Chest tube care, General, Interventions, Nursing	Managing a patient with an external water-seal drainage device exiting the chest cavity.
NAAAD	Drainage tube care, General, Interventions, Nursing	Managing a patient with an external drainage device exiting the body.
NAAAL	Intracranial pressure monitoring, General, Interventions, Nursing	Measuring and interpreting patient data to regulate intracranial pressure.
NAAAO	Urinary tube care, General, Interventions, Nursing	Managing a patient with urinary drainage equipment. Also see codes NAAJX, NAAKA, NAAKB and NAAOC.
NAAAP	Ventriculostomy, lumbar drain tube care, General, Interventions, Nursing	Managing a patient with an external cerebrospinal fluid drainage system.
NAAAQ	Acid base management, initial stabilization, General, Interventions, Nursing	Initial promoting and preventing complications resulting from acid-base imbalance. For additional time, see code NAAAR.
NAAAR	Acid base management, each additional 15 minutes, General, Interventions, Nursing	Additional fifteen minute period of promoting and preventing complications resulting from acid-base imbalance. For initial time, see code NAAAQ.
NAAAS	Acid base management, metabolic acidosis, initial stabilization, General, Interventions, Nursing	Initial promoting acid-base balance and preventing complications resulting from serum HCO3 levels lower than desired. For additional time, see code NAAAT.
NAAAT	Acid base management, metabolic acidosis, each additional 15 minutes, General, Interventions, Nursing	Additional fifteen minute period of promoting acid-base balance and preventing complications resulting from serum HCO3 levels lower than desired. For initial time, see code NAAAS.
NAAAU	Acid base management, respiratory acidosis, initial stabilization, General, Interventions, Nursing	Initial promoting acid-base balance and preventing complications resulting from serum pCO2 levels higher than desired. For additional time, see code NAAAV.

Interventions

General

ABC Code	Procedure Description	Expanded Definition
NAAAV	Acid base management, respiratory acidosis, each additional 15 minutes, General, Interventions, Nursing	Additional fifteen minute period of promoting acid-base balance and preventing complications resulting from serum pCO2 levels higher than desired. For initial time, see code NAAAU.
NAAAW	Acid base monitoring, any type, General, Interventions, Nursing	Collecting and analyzing patient data to regulate acid-base balance.
NAAAY	Airway suctioning, General, Interventions, Nursing	Airway secretion removal by inserting a suction catheter into the patients oral airway and/or trachea.
NAAAZ	Fluid or electrolyte management, each additional 15 minutes, General, Interventions, Nursing	Additional fifteen minute period of promoting fluid balance and preventing complications resulting from abnormal or undesired fluid levels. For initial time, see code NAABZ.
NAABA	Amputation care, General, Interventions, Nursing	Promoting physical and psychological healing after amputation.
NAABB	Artificial airway management, General, Interventions, Nursing	Facilitating patency of air passages.
NAABC	Bathing, General, Interventions, Nursing	Cleaning the body for relaxation, cleanliness, and healing.
NAABD	Bed rest care, each repositioning and reassessment, General, Interventions, Nursing	Promoting comfort and safety and preventing complications for a bed-ridden patient.
NAABE	Bladder irrigation, General, Interventions, Nursing	Instilling a solution into the bladder to provide cleansing.
NAABF	Bleeding precautions, General, Interventions, Nursing	Reducing stimuli that induce bleeding or hemorrhage in at-risk patients.
NAABG	Bleeding reduction, gastrointestinal, initial stabilization, General, Interventions, Nursing	Initial limiting blood loss from the upper and lower gastrointestinal tract and related complications. For additional time, see code NAABH.
NAABH	Bleeding reduction, gastrointestinal, each additional 15 minutes, General, Interventions, Nursing	Additional fifteen minute period of limiting blood loss from the upper and lower gastrointestinal tract and related complications. For initial time, see code NAABG.
NAABI	Bleeding reduction, General, Interventions, Nursing	Limiting loss of blood volume during an episode of bleeding.
NAABJ	Bleeding reduction, nasal, General, Interventions, Nursing	Limiting nasal blood loss.

Interventions

General

ABC Code	Procedure Description	Expanded Definition
NAABK	Bleeding reduction, wound, General, Interventions, Nursing	Limiting blood loss from a wound that may be the result of a trauma, incision, or placement of a tube or catheter.
NAABL	Bowel incontinence care, encopresis, General, Interventions, Nursing	Promoting bowel continence in children.
NAABM	Bowel incontinence care, General, Interventions, Nursing	Promoting bowel continence and maintaining personal skin integrity.
NAABN	Bowel management, General, Interventions, Nursing	Establishing and maintaining a regular pattern of bowel elimination.
NAABO	Bowel training, General, Interventions, Nursing	Assisting training the bowel to evacuate at specific intervals.
NAABP	Calming technique, General, Interventions, Nursing	Reducing anxiety in patient experiencing acute distress.
NAABQ	Cardiac care, acute, initial hour, General, Interventions, Nursing	Initial limiting complications of an imbalance between myocardial oxygen supply and demand, resulting in impaired cardiac function. For additional time, see code NAABR.
NAABR	Cardiac care, acute, each additional 15 minutes, General, Interventions, Nursing	Additional fifteen minute period limiting complications of an imbalance between myocardial oxygen supply and demand, resulting in impaired cardiac function. For initial time, see code NAABQ.
NAABT	Cardiac care monitoring, General, Interventions, Nursing	Limiting complications resulting from an imbalance between myocardial oxygen supply and demand with symptoms of impaired cardiac function.
NAABU	Cardiac care, rehabilitative, General, Interventions, Nursing	Promoting maximum functional activity level for a patient who has suffered an episode of impaired cardiac function which resulted from an imbalance between myocardial oxygen supply and demand.
NAABV	Cardiac precautions, General, Interventions, Nursing	Preventing an acute episode of impaired cardiac function by minimizing myocardial oxygen consumption or increasing supply thereof.
NAABX	Cast care, maintenance, General, Interventions, Nursing	Care of a cast after the drying period.
NAABY	Cast care, wet, General, Interventions, Nursing	Care of a new cast during the drying period.

Interventions

General

ABC Code	Procedure Description	Expanded Definition
NAABZ	Fluid or electrolyte management, initial hour, General, Interventions, Nursing	Initial hour promoting fluid balance and preventing complications resulting from abnormal or undesired fluid levels. For additional time, see code NAAAZ.
NAACA	Cerebral edema management, initial hour, General, Interventions, Nursing	Initial hour limitating secondary cerebral injury resulting from brain tissue swelling. For additional time, see code NAACB.
NAACB	Cerebral edema management, each additional 15 minutes, General, Interventions, Nursing	Additional fifteen minute period limiting secondary cerebral injury resulting from brain tissue swelling. For initial time see, code NAACA.
NAACC	Cerebral perfusion promotion, initial hour, General, Interventions, Nursing	Initial hour promoting adequate perfusion and limitating complications for a patient experiencing or at-risk for inadequate perfusion. For additional time, see code NAACD.
NAACD	Cerebral perfusion promotion, each additional 15 minutes, General, Interventions, Nursing	Additional fifteen minute period promoting adequate perfusion and limitating complications for a patient experiencing or at-risk for inadequate perfusion. For initial time, see code NAACC.
NAACE	Chest physiotherapy, General, Interventions, Nursing	Assisting patient to move secretions from peripheral to central airways for expectoration and/or suctioning.
NAACF	Circulatory care, General, Interventions, Nursing	Promoting arterial and venous circulation.
NAACG	Circulatory care, mechanical assist device, initial hour, General, Interventions, Nursing	Initial hour of temporary circulation support mechanical devices or pumps. For additional time, see code NAACH.
NAACH	Circulatory care, mechanical assist device, additional 4 hours, General, Interventions, Nursing	Additional four hour period of temporary circulation support through mechanical devices or pumps. For initial time, see code NAACG.
NAACI	Circulatory precautions, General, Interventions, Nursing	Protecting a localized area with limited perfusion.
NAACJ	Cardiac arrest code management, initial hour, General, Interventions, Nursing	Initial hour of coordinating emergency measures to sustain life. For additional time, see code NAACK.
NAACK	Cardiac arrest code management, each additional 15 minutes, General, Interventions, Nursing	Additional fifteen minute period of coordinating emergency measures to sustain life. For initial time, see code NAACJ.
NAACL	Cognitive restructuring, General, Interventions, Nursing	Challenging to alter distorted thought patterns to view self and the world more realistically.

Interventions

General

ABC Code	Procedure Description	Expanded Definition
NAACM	Cognitive stimulation, General, Interventions, Nursing	Promoting awareness and comprehension of surroundings utilizing planned stimuli.
NAACN	Communication enhancement, hearing deficit, General, Interventions, Nursing	Working toward accepting and learning alternate methods for living with diminished hearing.
NAACO	Communication enhancement, speech deficit, General, Interventions, Nursing	Working toward accepting and learning alternate methods for living with diminished speech.
NAACP	Communication enhancement, visual deficit, General, Interventions, Nursing	Working toward accepting and learning alternate methods for living with diminished vision.
NAACR	Conscious sedation, initial 15 minutes, General, Interventions, Nursing	Initial fifteen minute period of administering sedatives, monitoring patient response and providing physiological support during a diagnostic or therapeutic procedure. For additional time, see code NAACS.
NAACS	Conscious sedation, each additional 15 minutes, General, Interventions, Nursing	Additional fifteen minute period of administering sedatives, monitoring patient response and providing physiological support during a diagnostic or therapeutic procedure. For initial time, see code NAACR.
NAACT	Constipation or impaction management, General, Interventions, Nursing	Prevention and alleviation of constipation and/or impaction.
NAACU	Contact lens care, General, Interventions, Nursing	Prevention of eye injury and lens damage by contact lense use.
NAACV	Cough enhancement, General, Interventions, Nursing	Deep inhalation with subsequent generation of high intrathoracic pressures and compression of underlying lung parenchyma for the forceful expulsion of air.
NAACX	Cutaneous stimulation, General, Interventions, Nursing	Stimulating the skin and underlying tissues thereby decreasing pain, muscle spasm, or inflammation.
NAACY	Delusion management, General, Interventions, Nursing	Promoting the safety, comfort, and reality orientation of a patient experiencing false, fixed beliefs that have little or no basis in reality.
NAACZ	Gastrointestinal tube care, General, Interventions, Nursing	Tube care that was previously placed into the gastrointestinal tract.
NAADA	Dementia management, General, Interventions, Nursing	Providing a modified environment for a patient experiencing a chronic confusional state.

Interventions

General

ABC Code	Procedure Description	Expanded Definition
NAADD	Diarrhea management, General, Interventions, Nursing	Preventing and alleviating diarrhea.
NAADE	Diet staging, General, Interventions, Nursing	Instituting diet restrictions with subsequent progression of diet as tolerated.
NAADF	Distraction, General, Interventions, Nursing	Purposeful re-focusing attention.
NAADG	Dressing, General, Interventions, Nursing	Choosing, putting on and removing clothes.
NAADJ	Dysreflexia management, General, Interventions, Nursing	Preventing and eliminating stimuli which cause hyperactive reflexes and inappropriate autonomous responses in a patient with a cervical or high thoracic cord lesion.
NAADK	Dysrhythmia management, initial hour, General, Interventions, Nursing	Initial hour preventing, recognizing, and facilitating treatment of abnormal cardiac rhythms. For additional time, see code NAADL.
NAADL	Dysrhythmia management, each additional four hours, General, Interventions, Nursing	Additional four hour period preventing, recognizing, and facilitating treatment of abnormal cardiac rhythms. For initial time, see code NAADK.
NAADM	Electrolyte management, each 4 hours, General, Interventions, Nursing	Four hour period promoting electrolyte balance preventing complications from abnormal or undesired serum electrolyte levels.
NAADN	Electrolyte monitoring, General, Interventions, Nursing	Collecting and analyzing patient data to regulate electrolyte balance.
NAADO	Elopement precautions, General, Interventions, Nursing	Patient risk minimization of leaving the treatment setting without authorization.
NAADP	Embolus precautions, General, Interventions, Nursing	Risk reduction of a patient embolus with thrombi or at risk for thrombus formation.
NAADQ	Emergency care, General, Interventions, Nursing	Providing life saving measures in life threatening situations.
NAADR	Emotional support, initial hour, General, Interventions, Nursing	Initial hour of providing reassurance, acceptance and encouragement during times of stress. For additional time, see code NAALE.
NAADS	Enuresis, urinary incontinence care, General, Interventions, Nursing	Promotion of urinary continence especially nocturnal bed wetting.
NAADT	Environmental management, patient comfort, General, Interventions, Nursing	Manipulating the surroundings for optimal comfort.

General

ABC Code	Procedure Description	Expanded Definition
NAADU	Examination assistance, General, Interventions, Nursing	Assisting the patient and another health care provider during a procedure or examination.
NAADW	Eye care, General, Interventions, Nursing	Preventing or minimizing threats to eye or visual integrity.
NAADX	Fall prevention, General, Interventions, Nursing	Instituting special precautions with patient at risk for injury from falling.
NAADY	Feeding, General, Interventions, Nursing	Nutritional intake for patient who is unable to feed self.
NAADZ	Invasive hemodynamic monitoring, General, Interventions, Nursing	Measurement and interpretation of invasive hemodynamic parameters to determine cardiovascular function and regulate therapy.
NAAEA	Fever treatment, General, Interventions, Nursing	Managing a patient with hyperpyrexia caused by non-environmental factors.
NAAEB	Fire setting precautions, General, Interventions, Nursing	Prevention of fire-setting behaviors.
NAAEC	First aid, initial hour, General, Interventions, Nursing	Initial hour of minor injury care. For additional time, see code NAAED.
NAAED	First aid, each additional 15 minutes, General, Interventions, Nursing	Additional fifteen minute period of minor injury care. For initial time, see code NAAEC.
NAAEE	Flatulence reduction, General, Interventions, Nursing	Prevention of flatus formation and facilitation of passage of excessive gas.
NAAEF	Fluid monitoring, General, Interventions, Nursing	Collection and analysis of patient data to regulate fluid balance.
NAAEG	Foot care, General, Interventions, Nursing	Cleansing and inspecting the feet for relaxation, cleanliness and healthy skin.
NAAEI	Hair care, General, Interventions, Nursing	Promoting neat, clean and attractive hair.
NAAEJ	Hallucination management, initial hour, General, Interventions, Nursing	Initial hour promoting safety, comfort and reality orientation of a patient experiencing hallucinations. For additional time, see code NAAEK.
NAAEK	Hallucination management, each additional 15 minutes, General, Interventions, Nursing	Additional fifteen minute period promoting safety, comfort and reality orientation of a patient experiencing hallucinations. For initial time, see code NAAEJ.

Interventions

General

ABC Code	Procedure Description	Expanded Definition
NAAEL	Heat exposure treatment, General, Interventions, Nursing	Management of patient overcome by heat due to environmental heat exposure.
NAAEM	Hemodialysis therapy, each additional hour, General, Interventions, Nursing	Additional hour of managing extracorporeal blood passage through a dialyzer. For initial time, see code NAAEN.
NAAEN	Hemodialysis therapy, initial hour, General, Interventions, Nursing	Initial hour of managing extracorporeal blood passage through a dialyzer. For additional time, see code NAAEM.
NAAEO	Hemodynamic regulation, each 45 minutes, General, Interventions, Nursing	Forty-five minute period of optimizing heart rate, preload, afterload, and contractility.
NAAEP	Hemorrhage control, initial 15 minutes, General, Interventions, Nursing	Initial fifteen minute period reducing and eliminating rapid and excessive blood loss. For additional time, see code NAALQ.
NAAEQ	Hope instillation, General, Interventions, Nursing	Facilitating a positive outlook in a particular situation.
NAAER	Electrolyte management, hypercalcemia, initial hour, General, Interventions, Nursing	Initial hour of promoting calcium balance and preventing complications resulting from serum calcium levels higher than desired. For additional time, see code NAAMC.
NAAEZ	Malignant hyperthermia precautions, General, Interventions, Nursing	Prevention or reduction of hypermetabolic response to pharmacological agents used during surgery.
NAAFA	Hypervolemia management, General, Interventions, Nursing	Reducing extracellular and/or intracellular fluid volume and preventing fluid overload complications.
NAAFK	Impulse control, General, Interventions, Nursing	Assisting to mediate impulsive behavior through problem solving strategies to social and interpersonal situations. Direct and timely patient-contact nursing intervention performed at site of care.
NAAFL	Incision site care, General, Interventions, Nursing	Cleansing, monitoring and promoting healing in a surgical wound that is closed with sutures, clips, or staples.
NAAFN	Intraoperative positioning, General, Interventions, Nursing	Moving the patient or body part to promote surgical exposure while reducing discomfort and complications.
NAAFP	Laboratory data interpretation, General, Interventions, Nursing	Interpreting patient laboratory data to assist with clinical decision-making.

General

ABC Code	Procedure Description	Expanded Definition
NAAFQ	Latex precautions, General, Interventions, Nursing	Reducing a systematic reaction to latex.
NAAFR	Leech therapy, each site, General, Interventions, Nursing	Application of medicinal leeches to drain replanted or transplanted tissue engorged with venous blood.
NAAFS	Limit setting, General, Interventions, Nursing	Establishing desirable and acceptable patient behavior.
NAAFT	Maggot therapy application, each site, General, Interventions, Nursing	Site specific placement of medicinal maggots, including bandaging. Application of medicinal maggots for cleaning non-healing wounds.
NAAFU	Maggot therapy removal, General, Interventions, Nursing	Removing medicinal maggots, including re-bandaging.
NAAFW	Mechanical ventilation, initial contact and setup, General, Interventions, Nursing	Initial hour using an artificial device assisting a patient to breath. For additional time, see code NAAFX.
NAAFX	Mechanical ventilation, each additional 15 minutes, General, Interventions, Nursing	Additional fifteen minute period of using an artificial device to assist a patient to breath. For initial time see code NAAFW.
NAAFY	Mechanical ventilatory weaning, General, Interventions, Nursing	Assisting a patient to breath without the aid of a mechanical ventilator.
NAAFZ	Peripherally inserted central catheter care, General, Interventions, Nursing	Insertion and maintenance of a peripherally inserted central catheter.
NAAGA	Medication management, General, Interventions, Nursing	Facilitation of safe and effective use of prescription and over-the-counter drugs. Also see codes NAANF and NBAAC.
NAAGB	Nail care, General, Interventions, Nursing	Promoting clean, neat, attractive nails and prevention of skin lesions related to improper nail care.
NAAGC	Neurologic monitoring, General, Interventions, Nursing	Collecting and analyzing patient data to prevent or minimize neurologic complications.
NAAGD	Neurologic positioning, General, Interventions, Nursing	Achieving optimal, appropriate body alignment for the patient experiencing or at risk for spinal cord injury or vertebral irritability.
NAAGE	Normalization promotion, General, Interventions, Nursing	Assisting parents and other family members of children families with chronic illnesses or disabilities in providing normal life experiences.

Interventions

General

ABC Code	Procedure Description	Expanded Definition
NAAGI	Oral health maintenance, General, Interventions, Nursing	Maintaining and promoting oral hygiene and dental care for a patient at risk for developing oral or dental lesions.
NAAGJ	Oral health promotion, General, Interventions, Nursing	Promoting oral hygiene and dental care for a patient with normal oral and dental health.
NAAGK	Oral health restoration, General, Interventions, Nursing	Promoting healing for a patient who has an oral mucosa or dental lesion.
NAAGL	Organ procurement, General, Interventions, Nursing	Guiding families through the donation process to ensure timely retrieval of vital organs and tissue for transplant.
NAAGM	Oxygen therapy, General, Interventions, Nursing	Administering measured amount of oxygen and monitoring its effectiveness.
NAAGN	Patient pain management, initial contact, first hour, General, Interventions, Nursing	Initial hour alleviating or reducing pain to the comfort level of the patient. For additional time, see code NAAGO.
NAAGO	Patient pain management, each additional 15 minutes, General, Interventions, Nursing	Additional fifteen minute period alleviating or reducing pain to the comfort level of the patient. For initial time, see code NAAGN.
NAAGP	Agreement contracting, General, Interventions, Nursing	Negotiation which reinforces a specific behavior change.
NAAGQ	Patient controlled analgesia (PCA) assistance, General, Interventions, Nursing	Facilitate patient control of analgesic administration and regulation.
NAAGS	Peripheral embolus care, General, Interventions, Nursing	Limiting complications for a patient experiencing or at risk for occlusion of peripheral circulation.
NAAGT	Peripheral sensation management, General, Interventions, Nursing	Preventing or minimizing injury or discomfort patient altered sensation.
NAAGU	Peritoneal dialysis therapy, initial contact and setup, General, Interventions, Nursing	Initial hour administering and monitoring dialysis solution into and out of the peritoneal cavity. For additional time, see code NAAGV.
NAAGV	Peritoneal dialysis therapy, each additional 15 minutes, General, Interventions, Nursing	Additional fifteen minute period administering and monitoring dialysis solution into and out of the peritoneal cavity. For initial time, see code NAAGU.
NAAGW	Physical restraint placement, General, Interventions, Nursing	Application and monitoring mechanical or manual restraints used to limit physical mobility.

General

ABC Code	Procedure Description	Expanded Definition
NAAGX	Physical restraint, each re-evaluation and or removal, General, Interventions, Nursing	Removal of mechanical or manual restraints used to limit oatient physical mobility.
NAAGY	Pneumatic tourniquet placement, General, Interventions, Nursing	Placement of a pneumatic tourniquet while minimizing the potential for patient injury from said use. For additional time, see code NAAHA.
NAAGZ	Allergic reaction care, individual, General, Interventions, Nursing	Actions or precautions to reduce symptoms or allergic reactions.
NAAHA	Pneumatic tourniquet precautions, General, Interventions, Nursing	Monitoring an applied pneumatic tourniquet while minimizing patient injury from said use. For initial time, see code NAAGY.
NAAHB	Patient positioning, General, Interventions, Nursing	Moving the patient or a body part to provide comfort, reduce the risk of skin breakdown, promote skin integrity and/or healing.
NAAHC	Postanesthesia care, initial contact, first hour, General, Interventions, Nursing	Initial hour monitoring and managing the patient who has recently undergone general or regional anesthesia. For additional time, see code NAAHD.
NAAHD	Postanesthesia care, each additional 15 minutes, General, Interventions, Nursing	Additional fifteen minute period monitoring and managing the patient who has recently undergone general or regional anesthesia. For initial time, see code NAAHC.
NAAHE	Postmortem care, initial contact, first hour, General, Interventions, Nursing	Initial hour providing physical care for an expired patient and support for the family. For additional time, see code NAAHF.
NAAHF	Postmortem care, each additional 15 minutes, General, Interventions, Nursing	Additional fifteen minute period of providing physical care of the body of an expired patient and support for the family viewing the body. For initial time see code NAAHE.
NAAHG	Preparatory sensory information, General, Interventions, Nursing	Describing the subjective and objective physical sensations associated with an upcoming stressful healthcare procedure and/or treatment.
NAAHH	Care provider presence, General, Interventions, Nursing	Being with another during times of need.
NAAHI	Pressure management, General, Interventions, Nursing	Minimizing pressure to body parts.
NAAHJ	Pressure ulcer care, General, Interventions, Nursing	Facilitating healing in pressure ulcers.

General

ABC Code	Procedure Description	Expanded Definition
NAAHK	Pressure ulcer prevention, General, Interventions, Nursing	Preventive pressure ulcers development.
NAAHL	Pulmonary embolus care, General, Interventions, Nursing	Limiting complications for a patient experiencing or at risk for occlusion of pulmonary circulation.
NAAHM	Radiation therapy management, General, Interventions, Nursing	Understanding and minimizing the side effects of radiation treatments.
NAAHN	Rape trauma treatment, initial contact, first hour, General, Interventions, Nursing	Initial hour of providing emotional and physical support immediately following an alleged rape. For additional time, see code NAAHO
NAAHO	Rape trauma treatment, each additional 15 minutes, General, Interventions, Nursing	Additional fifteen minute period of providing emotional and physical support immediately following an alleged rape. For initial time, see code NAAHN.
NAAHQ	Rectal prolapse management, General, Interventions, Nursing	Preventing and/or manually reducing rectal prolapse.
NAAHS	Respiratory monitoring, General, Interventions, Nursing	Collecting and analyzing patient data to ensure patency and adequate gas exchange.
NAAHT	Respite care, each hour, General, Interventions, Nursing	One hour period of short term care for relief of family caregiver.
NAAHU	Resuscitation, General, Interventions, Nursing	Emergency measures to sustain life.
NAAHW	Safety surveillance, General, Interventions, Nursing	Purposeful and ongoing collection and analysis of patient information and the environment for promoting and maintaining patient safety.
NAAHX	Self care assistance, dressing, grooming, General, Interventions, Nursing	Assisting with dressing and general grooming activities.
NAAHY	Self care assistance, feeding, General, Interventions, Nursing	Assisting with providing nutritional intake for patient who is unable to feed self.
NAAHZ	Anaphylaxis management, General, Interventions, Nursing	Promoting adequate ventilation and tissue perfusion for a patient with a severe allergic (antigen-antibody) reaction.
NAAIA	Self care assistance, toileting, General, Interventions, Nursing	Assisting with elimination.

General

ABC Code	Procedure Description	Expanded Definition
NAAIB	Shock management, sepsis, initial hour, General, Interventions, Nursing	Initial hour facilitating oxygen and nutrients delivery to systemic tissue with removal of cellular waste products in a patient with severe infection. For additional time, see code NAALO.
NAAIC	Shock management, cardiac, initial hour, General, Interventions, Nursing	Initial hour promoting adequate tissue perfusion for a patient with severely compromised heart pumping. For additional time, see code NAAID.
NAAID	Shock management, cardiac, each additional 15 minutes, General, Interventions, Nursing	Additional fifteen minute period promoting adequate tissue perfusion for a patient with severely compromised heart pumping. For initial time, see code NAAIC.
NAAIE	Shock management, vasogenic, initial hour, General, Interventions, Nursing	Initial hour promoting the adequate tissue perfusion for a patient with severe loss of vascular tone. For additional time, see code NAAIF.
NAAIF	Shock management, vasogenic, each additional 15 minutes, General, Interventions, Nursing	Additional fifteen minute period promoting the adequate tissue perfusion for a patient with severe loss of vascular tone. For initial time, see code NAAIE.
NAAIG	Shock management, volume, initial hour, General, Interventions, Nursing	Initial hour promoting adequate tissue perfusion for a patient with severely compromised intravascular volume. For additional time, see code NAAIH.
NAAIH	Shock management, volume, each additional 15 minutes, General, Interventions, Nursing	Additional fifteen minute period of promoting adequate tissue perfusion for a patient with severely compromised intravascular volume. For initial time see code NAAIG.
NAAII	Shock prevention, General, Interventions, Nursing	Detecting and treating a patient at risk for impending shock.
NAAIK	Skin care, topical treatments, General, Interventions, Nursing	Applying topical substances or manipulating devices for skin integrity to minimize skin breakdown.
NAAIL	Skin surveillance, General, Interventions, Nursing	Collecting and analyzing patient data to maintain skin and mucous membrane integrity.
NAAIM	Sleep enhancement, General, Interventions, Nursing	Facilitating regular sleep and wake cycles.
NAAIO	Environmental management, patient safety, General, Interventions, Nursing	Monitoring and manipulating the physical environment to promote safety.

Interventions

General

ABC Code	Procedure Description	Expanded Definition
NAAIP	Subarachnoid hemorrhage precautions, General, Interventions, Nursing	Reduction of external and internal stimuli or stressors to minimize risk or rebleeding prior to aneurysm surgery.
NAAIQ	Seclusion, initial hour, General, Interventions, Nursing	Initial hour of solitary containment in a protective environment with nursing staff surveillance for safety or behavior management. For additional time, see code NAAIS.
NAAIS	Seclusion, each reevaluation, General, Interventions, Nursing	Each re-evaluation for solitary containment in a protective environment with close nursing staff surveillance for safety or behavior management. For initial time, see code NAAIQ.
NAAIU	Security enhancement, General, Interventions, Nursing	Intensifying a patient towards physical and psychological safety.
NAAIW	Seizure management, General, Interventions, Nursing	Care during a seizure and the postictal state.
NAAIY	Seizure precautions, General, Interventions, Nursing	Preventing or minimizing potential injuries sustained by a patient with a known seizure disorder.
NAAIZ	Circulatory care, arterial insufficiency, General, Interventions, Nursing	Arterial circulation promotion.
NAAJB	Self care assistance, other, General, Interventions, Nursing	Assisting another to perform activities of daily living.
NAAJC	Substance use treatment, drug withdrawal, initial hour, General, Interventions, Nursing	Initial hour of supportive care with physical and psychosocial problems associated with alcohol or drug use. For additional time, see code NAALR.
NAAJD	Self care assistance, bathing, hygiene, General, Interventions, Nursing	Assisting patient to perform personal hygiene.
NAAJE	Substance use treatment, overdose, initial hour, General, Interventions, Nursing	Initial hour monitoring, treatment, and emotional support of a patient who has ingested prescription or over-the-counter drugs beyond the therapeutic range. For additional time, see code NAALS.
NAAJH	Suicide prevention, initial hour, General, Interventions, Nursing	Initial hour of direct patient interventions to reduce self-inflicted harm for a patient in crisis or severe depression. For additional time, see code NAAJI.
NAAJI	Suicide prevention, each additional hour, General, Interventions, Nursing	Additional one hour period of direct patient interventions to reduce self-inflicted harm for a patient in crisis or severe depression. For initial time, see code NAAJH.

General

ABC Code	Procedure Description	Expanded Definition
NAAJJ	Sustenance support, General, Interventions, Nursing	Helping a needy individual or family locate food, clothing, or shelter.
NAAJK	Swallowing therapy, General, Interventions, Nursing	Facilitating swallowing and preventing complications of impaired swallowing.
NAAJL	Monitoring device management, General, Interventions, Nursing	Continuous monitoring the output of an apparatus which observes and records particular conditions or phenomena.
NAAJM	Temperature regulation, General, Interventions, Nursing	Attaining and/or monitoring body temperature within a normal range.
NAAJN	Temperature regulation, intraoperative, General, Interventions, Nursing	Attaining and/or monitoring desired intra-operative body temperature.
NAAJQ	Transport, General, Interventions, Nursing	Moving a patient from one location to another.
NAAJR	Triage, General, Interventions, Nursing	Establishing priorities of patient care for urgent treatment while allocating scarce resources.
NAAJS	Truth telling, General, Interventions, Nursing	Use of the whole or partial truth or decision delay to promote the self-determination and well-being of the patient.
NAAJT	Unilateral neglect management, General, Interventions, Nursing	Protecting and safely reintegrating the affected part of the body while helping the patient adapt to disturbed perceptual abilities.
NAAJU	Bladder training, General, Interventions, Nursing	Improving bladder function for those with urge incontinence by increasing the ability of the bladder to hold urine and the ability of the patient to suppress urination.
NAAJX	Urinary elimination management, General, Interventions, Nursing	Maintenance of an optimum urinary elimination pattern. Also see codes NAAOC, NAAKA, NAAKB and NAAAO.
NAAJY	Urinary habit training, General, Interventions, Nursing	Establishing a bladder emptying pattern to prevent incontinence for persons with limited cognitive ability who have urge, stress, or functional incontinence.
NAAJZ	Assistive device therapy, individual, General, Interventions, Nursing	Actions to manage products to aid in caring for oneself.

Interventions

General

ABC Code	Procedure Description	Expanded Definition
NAAKA	Urinary incontinence care, General, Interventions, Nursing	Assistance promoting continence and maintaining perineal skin integrity. Also see codes NAAJX, NAAOC, NAAKB and NAAAO.
NAAKB	Urinary retention care, General, Interventions, Nursing	Assistance relieving bladder distention. Also see codes NAAJX, NAAOC, NAAKA and NAAAO.
NAAKC	Ventilation assistance, non mechanical, General, Interventions, Nursing	Promoting an optimal spontaneous breathing pattern that maximizes oxygen and carbon dioxide exchange.
NAAKD	Environmental management, violence prevention, General, Interventions, Nursing	Monitoring and manipulating the physical environment to decrease the potential for violent behavior directed toward self, others, or environment.
NAAKE	Vital signs monitoring, General, Interventions, Nursing	Collection and analysis of cardiovascular, respiratory, and body temperature to determine and prevent complications.
NAAKF	Wheelchair positioning, General, Interventions, Nursing	Placement of a patient in a properly selected wheelchair to enhance comfort, promote skin integrity and foster independence.
NAAKG	Wound care, general, General, Interventions, Nursing	Preventing wound complications and promoting wound healing.
NAAKH	Wound care, closed drainage, General, Interventions, Nursing	Maintaining a pressure drainage system at the wound site.
NAAKI	Wound irrigation, General, Interventions, Nursing	Flushing an open wound to cleanse and remove debris and excessive drainage.
NAAKJ	Infant care, each hour, after first 48 hours, General, Interventions, Nursing	Additional hour providing developmentally appropriate family-centered care to a child under one year of age. For initial time, see codes CEEAO and CEEAP.
NAAKK	Area restriction, General, Interventions, Nursing	Limiting patient mobility to a specified area for safety or behavior management.
NAAKL	Aspiration precautions, General, Interventions, Nursing	Preventing or minimizing risk factors in the patient at risk for aspirations.
NAAKN	Breast examination, General, Interventions, Nursing	Inspection and palpation of the breasts and related areas.
NAAKR	Coping enhancement, General, Interventions, Nursing	Assisting the patient to adapt to perceived stressors, changes or threats which interfere with meeting life demands and roles.

General

ABC Code	Procedure Description	Expanded Definition
NAAKS	Prosthesis care, General, Interventions, Nursing	Care of a removable appliance worn by a patient and the prevention of complications associated with its use.
NAAKU	Ostomy care, General, Interventions, Nursing	Maintaining elimination through a stoma and care of surrounding tissue.
NAAKV	Venous access device maintenance, General, Interventions, Nursing	Managing the patient with prolonged venous access via tunneled, non-tunneled catheters and implanted ports.
NAAKW	Splinting, General, Interventions, Nursing	Stabilizing, immobilizing, and/or protecting an injured body part with a supportive appliance.
NAAKX	Shock management, General, Interventions, Nursing	Promoting adequate tissue perfusion for a patient with severely compromised intravascular volume.
NAAKY	Lavage, 1 ear, General, Interventions, Nursing	Irrigation or washing out of the cavity of one ear.
NAAKZ	Cataract care, individual, General, Interventions, Nursing	Actions performed to control cataract conditions.
NAALA	Lavage, 2 ears, General, Interventions, Nursing	Bilateral irrigation or washing out of the cavity of both ears.
NAALB	Colonic irrigation, General, Interventions, Nursing	Introduction of various liquids into the colon through the rectum.
NAALC	Enema, General, Interventions, Nursing	Introduction of a solution into the lower gastro intestinal tract for cleansing or therapeutic purposes.
NAALE	Emotional support, each additional 15 minutes, General, Interventions, Nursing	Additional fifteen minute period of direct provision on reassurance, acceptance and encouragement during time of stress. For initial time, see code NAADR.
NAALF	Eating disorders management, General, Interventions, Nursing	Educating on prevention and treatment of severe diet restriction and over-exercising or bingeing and purging of food and fluids.
NAALG	Energy management, General, Interventions, Nursing	Regulating energy use to treat or prevent fatigue and optimize functional activity.
NAALH	Active listening by provider, General, Interventions, Nursing	Attending closely to and significance of verbal and nonverbal messages of a patient.

General

ABC Code	Procedure Description	Expanded Definition
NAALJ	Anesthesia administration, presurgical, General, Interventions, Nursing	Presurgical preparation for and administration of anesthetic agents and monitoring of patient responsiveness during administration.
NAALK	Caregiver support, General, Interventions, Nursing	Providing information, advocacy and support to facilitate primary patient care by someone other than a healthcare professional.
NAALM	Surgical preparation, General, Interventions, Nursing	Providing care immediately prior to surgery and verification of required procedures and/or tests and documentation in the clinical record.
NAALN	Pre-surgical assistance, General, Interventions, Nursing	Assisting the surgeon or dentist with pre-operative procedures and care of the patient.
NAALO	Shock management, sepsis, each additional 15 minutes, General, Interventions, Nursing	Additional fifteen minute period facilitating the delivery of oxygen and nutrients to systemic tissue with removal of cellular waste products in a patient with severe infection. For initial time, see code NAAIB.
NAALP	Surgical assistance, General, Interventions, Nursing	Assisting the surgeon or dentist with operative procedures and care of the patient.
NAALQ	Hemorrhage control, each additional 15 minutes, General, Interventions, Nursing	Additional fifteen minute period reducing or eliminating rapid and excessive blood loss. For initial time, see code NAAEP.
NAALR	Substance use treatment, drug withdrawal, each additional 15 minutes, General, Interventions, Nursing	Additional fifteen minute period of supportive care of patient with physical and psychosocial problems associated alcohol or drug use. For initial time, see code NAAJC.
NAALS	Substance use treatment, overdose, each additional 15 minutes, General, Interventions, Nursing	Additional fifteen minute period monitoring, treating and emotional support of a patient who has ingested prescription or over-the-counter drugs beyond the therapeutic range. For initial time, see code NAAJE.
NAALT	Exercise therapy, ambulating, General, Interventions, Nursing	Assisting a patient to walk and to maintain or restore autonomic and voluntary body functions during treatment and recovery from illness or injury. Also see code NAANG.
NAALU	Chemotherapy care, General, Interventions, Nursing	Actions performed to administer and monitor anti-neoplastic agents.
NAALW	Decubitus care stage 1, General, Interventions, Nursing	Actions performed to prevent skin breakdown.

General

ABC Code	Procedure Description	Expanded Definition
NAALX	Decubitus care stage 2, General, Interventions, Nursing	Actions performed to manage tissue breakdown.
NAALY	Decubitus care stage 3, General, Interventions, Nursing	Actions performed to manage skin destruction.
NAALZ	Decubitus care stage 4, General, Interventions, Nursing	Actions performed to manage open wounds.
NAAMA	Diabetic care, individual, General, Interventions, Nursing	Actions performed to control diabetic conditions.
NAAMB	Edema control, individual, General, Interventions, Nursing	Actions to manage excess fluid in tissue.
NAAMC	Electrolyte management hypercalcemia, each additional 15 minutes, General, Interventions, Nursing	Fifteen minute period promoting calcium balance and preventing complications resulting from serum calcium levels higher than desired. For initial time, see code NAAER.
NAAMD	Electrolyte management hyperkalemia, initial contact, first hour, General, Interventions, Nursing	Initial hour promoting potassium balance and preventing complications resulting from serum potassium levels higher than desired. For additional time, see code NAAME.
NAAME	Electrolyte management hyperkalemia, each additional 15 minutes, General, Interventions, Nursing	Additional fifteen minute period promoting potassium balance and preventing complications resulting from serum potassium levels higher than desired. For initial time, see code NAAMD.
NAAMF	Electrolyte management hypermagnesemia, initial contact, first hour, General, Interventions, Nursing	Initial hour of promoting magnesium balance and preventing complications resulting from serum magnesium levels higher than desired. For additional time, see code NAAMG.
NAAMG	Electrolyte management hypermagnesemia, each additional 15 minutes, General, Interventions, Nursing	Additional fifteen minute period promoting magnesium balance and preventing complications resulting from serum magnesium levels higher than desired. For initial time, see code NAAMF.
NAAMH	Electrolyte management hypernatremia, initial contact, first hour, General, Interventions, Nursing	Initial hour promoting sodium balance and preventing complications resulting from serum sodium levels higher than desired. For additional time, see code NAAMI.
NAAMI	Electrolyte management hypernatremia, each additional 15 minutes, General, Interventions, Nursing	Additional fifteen minute period promoting sodium balance and preventing complications resulting from serum sodium levels higher than desired. For initial time, see code NAAMH.

General

ABC Code	Procedure Description	Expanded Definition
NAAMJ	Electrolyte management hyperphosphatemia, initial hour, General, Interventions, Nursing	Initial hour promoting phosphate balance and preventing complications resulting from serum phosphate levels higher than desired. For additional time, see code NAAMK.
NAAMK	Electrolyte management hyperphosphatemia, each additional 15 minutes, General, Interventions, Nursing	Additional fifteen minutes promoting phosphate balance and preventing complications resulting from serum phosphate levels higher than desired. For initial time, see code NAAMJ.
NAAML	Electrolyte management hypocalcemia, initial hour, General, Interventions, Nursing	Initial hour promoting calcium balance and preventing complications resulting from serum calcium levels lower than desired. For additional time, see code NAAMM.
NAAMM	Electrolyte management hypocalcemia, each additional 15 minutes, General, Interventions, Nursing	Additional fifteen minutes promoting calcium balance and preventing complications resulting from serum calcium levels lower than desired. For initial time, see code NAAML.
NAAMO	Electrolyte management hypokalemia, initial contact, first hour, General, Interventions, Nursing	Initial hour promoting potassium balance and preventing complications resulting from serum potassium levels lower than desired. For additional time, see code NAAMP.
NAAMP	Electrolyte management hypokalemia, each additional 15 minutes, General, Interventions, Nursing	Additional fifteen minute period promoting potassium balance and preventing complications resulting from serum potassium levels lower than desired. For intial time, see code NAAMO.
NAAMQ	Electrolyte management hypomagnesemia, initial contact, first hour, General, Interventions, Nursing	Initial hour promoting magnesium balance and preventing complications resulting from serum magnesium levels lower than desired. For additional time, see code NAAMR.
NAAMR	Electrolyte management hypomagnesemia, each additional 15 minutes, General, Interventions, Nursing	Additional fifteen minutes promoting magnesium balance and preventing complications resulting from serum magnesium levels lower than desired. For initial time, see code NAAMQ.
NAAMS	Electrolyte management hyponatremia, initial contact, first hour, General, Interventions, Nursing	Initial hour promoting sodium balance and preventing complications resulting from serum sodium levels lower than desired. For additional time, see code NAAMT.
NAAMT	Electrolyte management hyponatremia, each additional 15 minutes, General, Interventions, Nursing	Additional fifteen minutes promoting sodium balance and preventing complications resulting from serum sodium levels lower than desired. For initial time, see code NAAMS.

General

ABC Code	Procedure Description	Expanded Definition
NAAMU	Electrolyte management hypophosphatemia, initial hour, General, Interventions, Nursing	Initial hour promoting phosphate balance and preventing complications resulting from serum phosphate levels lower than desired. For additional time, see code NAAMV.
NAAMV	Electrolyte management hypophosphatemia, each additional 15 minutes, General, Interventions, Nursing	Additional fifteen minutes promoting phosphate balance and preventing complications resulting from serum phosphate levels lower than desired. For initial time, see code NAAMU.
NAAMW	Emergency center triage, General, Interventions, Nursing	Establishing priorities and initiating treatment in an emergency center.
NAAMX	Genetic risk identification, individual, General, Interventions, Nursing	Identification and analysis of potential genetic risk factors in an individual.
NAAMY	Genetic risk identification, group, General, Interventions, Nursing	Identification and analysis in a group setting of potential genetic risk factors.
NAAMZ	Genetic risk identification, family, General, Interventions, Nursing	Identification and analysis in a family setting of potential genetic risk factors.
NAANA	Hearing aid care, individual, General, Interventions, Nursing	Actions performed to manage a hearing aid. Also see codes DDADF or BACAK.
NAANB	Hemofiltration therapy, first hour, General, Interventions, Nursing	First hour cleansing the blood via a hemofilter controlled by the hydrostatic pressure of the patient. For additional time, see code NAANC.
NAANC	Hemofiltration therapy, each additional hour, General, Interventions, Nursing	Additional hour of cleansing the blood via a hemofilter controlled by the hydrostatic pressure of the patient. Must be used with code NAANB.
NAAND	Inhalation therapy, individual, General, Interventions, Nursing	Managing breathing treatments.
NAANE	Intake, output, General, Interventions, Nursing	Actions performed to measure the amount of fluid/food and excrement of waste. Also see code NAAEF for fluid only.
NAANF	Medication side effects, individual, General, Interventions, Nursing	Controlling untoward reactions or conditions to prescription drugs. Also see codes NAAGA and NBAAC.
NAANG	Mobility therapy, individual, General, Interventions, Nursing	Advising and instructing on mobility deficits. Also see code NAALT.

Interventions

General

ABC Code	Procedure Description	Expanded Definition
NAANH	Nausea management, General, Interventions, Nursing	Prevention and alleviation of nausea.
NAANI	Pacemaker care, individual, General, Interventions, Nursing	Managing an electronic device that provides a normal heartbeat.
NAANJ	Prompted voiding, General, Interventions, Nursing	Promotion of urinary continence through timed verbal toileting reminders and positive social feedback for successful toileting.
NAANK	Pruritis management, General, Interventions, Nursing	Preventing and treating itching.
NAANL	Radiation therapy care, individual, General, Interventions, Nursing	Administering and monitoring radiation therapy.
NAANM	Remote electronic surveillance, General, Interventions, Nursing	Purposeful and ongoing acquisition of patient data via electronic modalities (telephone, video conferencing, e-mail) from distant locations, as well as interpretation and synthesis of patient data for clinical decision-making.
NAANN	Respiratory care, individual, General, Interventions, Nursing	Managing pulmonary hygiene.
NAANO	Sexual assault crisis intervention, initial contact, first hour, General, Interventions, Nursing	Initial hour of crisis intervention and support following a sexual assault. For additional time, see code NAANP.
NAANP	Sexual assault crisis intervention, each additional 15 minutes, General, Interventions, Nursing	Additional fifteen minutes providing crisis intervention and support immediately following a sexual assault. For initial time, see code NAANO.
NAANQ	Sexual assault documentation of history, initial contact, 45 minutes, General, Interventions, Nursing	Initial forty-five minutes completing sexual assault history. For additional time, see code NAANR.
NAANR	Sexual assault documentation of history, each additional 15 minutes, General, Interventions, Nursing	Additional fifteen minutes completing sexual assault history. For initial time, see code NAANQ.
NAANS	Sexual assault forensic evidence collection, initial contact, first hour, General, Interventions, Nursing	Initial hour collecting and documentating forensic evidence. For additional time, see code NAANT.
NAANT	Sexual Assault Forensic Evidence Collection, each additional 15 minutes, General, Interventions, Nursing	Additional fifteen minutes collecting and documentating forensic evidence. For initial time, see code NAANS.

General

ABC Code	Procedure Description	Expanded Definition
NAANU	Sexual assault physical injury assessment, initial contact, first hour, General, Interventions, Nursing	Initial hour of head-to-toe assessment and documentation of injuries. For additional time, see code NAANV.
NAANV	Sexual assault physical injury assessment, each additional 15 minutes, General, Interventions, Nursing	Additional fifteen minutes of head-to-toe assessment and documentation of injuries. For initial time, see code NAANU.
NAANW	Sexual assault pregnancy risk education, initial contact, 30 minutes, General, Interventions, Nursing	Initial thirty minutes evaluating pregnancy risk and educating patient about preventive treatment options or future testing. For additional time, see code NAANX.
NAANX	Sexual assault pregnancy risk education, each additional 15 minutes, General, Interventions, Nursing	Additional fifteen minutes evaluating pregnancy risk and educating patient about preventive treatment options or future testing. For initial time, see code NAANW.
NAANY	Sexual assault securing forensic evidence, General, Interventions, Nursing	Securing forensic evidence from an outside source.
NAANZ	Sexual assault, sexually transmitted infection assessment and evaluation, initial contact, 30 minutes, General, Interventions, Nursing	Initial thirty minutes of risk evaluation of contracting a sexually transmitted infection, education about risk factors and implications and preventive treatment options, as well as future testing recommendations. For additional time, see code NAAOA.
NAAOA	Sexual assault, sexually transmitted infection assessment and evaluation, each additional 15 minutes, General, Interventions, Nursing	Additional fifteen mintes of risk evaluation of contracting a sexually transmitted infection, education about risk factors and implications and preventive treatment options, as well as future testing recommendations. For initial time, see code NAANZ.
NAAOB	Telephone triage, General, Interventions, Nursing	Telephone encounter to determine the nature and urgency of a problem and to provide directions for the level of care required.
NAAOC	Urinary catheter irrigation, individual, General, Interventions, Nursing	Actions to flush out a urinary catheter. Also see codes NAAJX, NAAKA, NAAKB and NAAAO.
NAAOD	Circulatory care, venous insufficiency, General, Interventions, Nursing	Promotion of venous circulation.
NAAOE	Vomiting management, General, Interventions, Nursing	Prevention and alleviation of vomiting.
NAAOF	Developmental enhancement, individual adolescent, General, Interventions, Nursing	Facilitating optimal physical, cognitive, social and emotional growth during the transition from childhood to adulthood.

General

ABC Code	Procedure Description	Expanded Definition
NAAOG	Developmental enhancement, group of adolescents, General, Interventions, Nursing	Facilitating optimal physical, cognitive, social and emotional growth in a group setting during the transition from childhood to adulthood.
NAAOH	Simple massage, General, Interventions, Nursing	Stimulation of the skin and underlying tissues with degrees of hand pressure to decrease pain, produce relaxation and/or improve circulation.
NAAOI	Acid base management, metabolic alkalosis, initial stabilization, General, Interventions, Nursing	Initial promotion of acid-base balance and prevention of complications resulting from serum HCO3 levels higher than desired. For additional time, see code NAAOJ.
NAAOJ	Acid base management, metabolic alkalosis, each additional 15 minutes, General, Interventions, Nursing	Additional fifteen minute period of promoting acid-base balance and preventing complications resulting from serum HCO3 levels higher than desired. For initial time, see code NAAOI.
NAAOL	Ear care, General, Interventions, Nursing	Treatment, prevention or minimization of threats to ear or hearing.
NAAOM	Acid base management, respiratory alkalosis, initial stabilization, General, Interventions, Nursing	Initial promoting acid-base balance and preventing complications resulting from serum pCO2 levels lower than desired. For additional time, see code NAAON.
NAAON	Acid base management, respiratory alkalosis, each additional 15 minutes, General, Interventions, Nursing	Additional fifteen minute period promoting acid-base balance and preventing complications resulting from serum pCO2 levels lower than desired. For initial time, see code NAAOM.
NAAOO	Exercise promotion, General, Interventions, Nursing	Facilitation of regular physical exercise to maintain or advance to a higher level of fitness and health.
NAAOP	Substance use treatment, alcohol withdrawal, initial hour, General, Interventions, Nursing	Initial hour of patient care experiencing sudden cessation of alcohol consumption. For additional time, see code NAAOQ.
NAAOQ	Substance use treatment, alcohol withdrawal, each additional 15 minutes, General, Interventions, Nursing	Additional fifteen minute period of patient care experiencing sudden cessation of alcohol consumption. For initial time, see code NAAOP.
NAAOR	Blood sugar management, initial hour, General, Interventions, Nursing	Initial hour of managing or preventing and treating hyperglycemia or hypoglycemia. For additional time, see code NAAOS.
NAAOS	Blood sugar management, each additional 15 minutes, General, Interventions, Nursing	Additional fifteen minute period managing or preventing and treating hyperglycemia or hypoglycemia. For initial time, see code NAAOR.

General

ABC Code	Procedure Description	Expanded Definition
NAAOT	Airway management, General, Interventions, Nursing	Facilitation of potency of air passages.
NAAOV	Hypovolemia management, General, Interventions, Nursing	Intravascular fluid volume in a patient who is volume depleted.
NAAOW	Surgical precautions, General, Interventions, Nursing	Minimizing the potential for iatrogenic injury to the patient caused by a surgical procedure.
NAAOX	Touch, General, Interventions, Nursing	Providing comfort and communication through purposeful tactile contact.
NAAOY	Umbilical line tube care, General, Interventions, Nursing	Managing a newborn with an umbilical catheter.
NAAOZ	Recreation therapy, General, Interventions, Nursing	Recreation to promote relaxation and enhancement of social skills.
NAAPA	Infection control techniques, General, Interventions, Nursing	Use of universal precautions for minimizing the acquisition and transmission of infectious agents.
NAAPB	Laser precautions, General, Interventions, Nursing	Limiting injury to the patient related to laser use.
NAAPC	Family planning, unplanned pregnancy, General, Interventions, Nursing	Facilitation of decision making regarding pregnancy outcome.
NAAPD	Resuscitation, fetus, General, Interventions, Nursing	Emergency measures to improve placental perfusion or correct fetal acid-base status.
NAAPE	Cesarean section care, General, Interventions, Nursing	Preparation and support of patient delivering a baby by Cesarean section.
NAAPF	Health screening, General, Interventions, Nursing	Evaluating health risks or problems through history, examination and other procedures.
NAAPG	Infection prevention, General, Interventions, Nursing	Preventing and early detecting infection.
NAAPH	Infection control, intraoperative, General, Interventions, Nursing	Preventing nosocomial infection in the operating room.
NAAPI	Environmental management, home preparation, General, Interventions, Nursing	Home preparation for a safe and effective delivery.
NAAPJ	Immunization or vaccination management, General, Interventions, Nursing	Monitoring immunization status, facilitating access to and providing immunizations to prevent communicable disease.

Interventions

General

ABC Code	Procedure Description	Expanded Definition
NAAPK	Code management, General, Interventions, Nursing	Emergency measures to sustain life.
NAAPL	Delirium management, General, Interventions, Nursing	Providing a safe and therapeutic environment for a patient experiencing an acute confusional state.
NAAZZ	Undefined, narrative required, General, Interventions, Nursing	Anywhere else undefined general nursing interventions. Narrative required.

Nursing Education

Patient education and counseling

ABC Code	Procedure Description	Expanded Definition
NBAAC	Medication monitoring training, Patient education and counseling, Nursing Education, Nursing	Teaching the techniques for consistent observation of relevant measurements or findings to facilitate safe and effective use of prescription and over-the-counter drugs. Teaching non-medical personnel how to monitor the taking of the medications at appropriate time intervals and the recognition of side effects. Also see codes NAAGA and NAANF.
NBAAD	Patient prescribed activity or exercise, Patient education and counseling, Nursing Education, Nursing	Preparing a patient to achieve and/or maintain a prescribed level of activity.
NBAAE	Progressive muscle relaxation, Patient education and counseling, Nursing Education, Nursing	Tensing and releasing of successive muscle groups while attending to the resulting differences in sensation.
NBAAF	Risk identification training, Patient education and counseling, Nursing Education, Nursing	Counseling a patient who has health risk factors.
NBAAG	Teaching prescribed medication, Patient education and counseling, Nursing Education, Nursing	Advising a patient to safely take prescribed medications and monitor for effects.
NBAAH	Preoperative education, individual, Patient education and counseling, Nursing Education, Nursing	Facilitating pre-admission diagnostic testing, preparing and educating the patient.
NBAAI	Disease process education, individual, Patient education and counseling, Nursing Education, Nursing	Assisting a patient understand information related to a specific disease.
NBAAJ	Treatment procedure education, individual, Patient education and counseling, Nursing Education, Nursing	Achieving for patient to understand and mentally prepare for a prescribed procedure or treatment.

Patient education and counseling

ABC Code	Procedure Description	Expanded Definition
NBAAK	Preoperative education, group, Patient education and counseling, Nursing Education, Nursing	Facilitating pre-admission diagnostic testing, preparing and educating in a group setting.
NBAAL	Disease process education, group, Patient education and counseling, Nursing Education, Nursing	Assisting a patient in a group setting understand information related to a specific disease.
NBAAM	Treatment procedure education, group, Patient education and counseling, Nursing Education, Nursing	Achieving for patient in a group setting to understand and mentally prepare for a prescribed procedure or treatment.
NBAAO	Developmental enhancement, Patient education and counseling, Nursing Education, Nursing	Teaching parents or caregivers to facilitate the optimal gross motor, fine motor, language, cognitive, social and emotional growth of preschool or school-aged children.
NBAAP	Culture brokerage, Patient education and counseling, Nursing Education, Nursing	Bridging, negotiating, or linking the orthodox healthcare system with a patient and family of a different culture. Additional training and certification are needed to perform this service. See referral codes ADYAF through ADYAK if referring to a person or entity who is trained to provide this service to the public.
NBAAQ	Allergy proofing, Patient education and counseling, Nursing Education, Nursing	Teaching a patient or nonmedical caretaker techniques for eliminating or reducing allergens in the environment.
NBAAR	Cognition, teaching stimulation and nurturance, individual, Patient education and counseling, Nursing Education, Nursing	Teaching a parent or caregiver techniques for giving care and excitation to increase the kowledge of the patient.
NBAAS	Cognition, teaching stimulation and nurturance, group, Patient education and counseling, Nursing Education, Nursing	Teaching a parent or caregiver in a group setting techniques for giving care and excitation to increase the knowledge of the patient.
NBAAT	Coping skills, permanent disability, individual, Patient education and counseling, Nursing Education, Nursing	Teaching a patient with a permanent disability alternative means or methods for support ability of nerves, muscles and bones to perform or coordinate specific activities.
NBAAU	Coping skills, permanent disability, group, Patient education and counseling, Nursing Education, Nursing	Teaching patients with a permanent disability in a group setting alternative means or methods for support ability of nerves, muscles and bones to perform or coordinate specific activities.
NBAAV	Cost containment, Patient education and counseling, Nursing Education, Nursing	Management and facilitation of efficient and effective use of resources.

Patient education and counseling

ABC Code	Procedure Description	Expanded Definition
NBAAX	Grief coping skills, Patient education and counseling, Nursing Education, Nursing	Helping deal effectively with keen mental suffering or distress over a recent affliction or loss.
NBAAY	Patient education on universal precautions, Patient education and counseling, Nursing Education, Nursing	Teaching a patient or nonmedical caretaker techniques of universal precautions.
NBAAZ	Religious ritual enhancement, individual, Patient education and counseling, Nursing Education, Nursing	Facilitating participation in religious practice.
NBABA	Religious ritual enhancement, group, Patient education and counseling, Nursing Education, Nursing	Facilitating participation in religious practice in a group setting.
NBABB	Self catheterization teaching, individual, Patient education and counseling, Nursing Education, Nursing	Instruction of patient in sterile technique and insertion of a flexible tube into their urethra.
NBABP	Blood sugar management training, individual, Patient education and counseling, Nursing Education, Nursing	Teaching about prevention and treatment of hyperglycemia or hypoglycemia.
NBABQ	Blood sugar management training, group, Patient education and counseling, Nursing Education, Nursing	Teaching a group about prevention and treatment of hyperglycemia or hypoglycemia.
NBABR	Blood sugar management training, family, Patient education and counseling, Nursing Education, Nursing	Teaching family members to assist an individual to prevent and treat hyperglycemia or hypoglycemia.
NBABS	Humor therapy, Patient education and counseling, Nursing Education, Nursing	Teaching a patient to perceive, appreciate and express what is funny amusing or ludicrous to establish relationships, relieve tension, release anger, facilitate learning or cope with painful feelings.
NBABT	Specific lifestyle risk factor education, individual, Patient education and counseling, Nursing Education, Nursing	Training for lifestyle risk factors, determining health risks and prioritizing risk reduction strategies.
NBABU	Specific lifestyle risk factor education, group, Patient education and counseling, Nursing Education, Nursing	Training for lifestyle risk factors, determining health risks and prioritizing risk reduction strategies in a group setting.
NBABV	Learning readiness enhancement, individual, Patient education and counseling, Nursing Education, Nursing	Improving the ability and willingness of an individual to receive information.

Patient education and counseling

ABC Code	Procedure Description	Expanded Definition
NBABW	Learning readiness enhancement, group, Patient education and counseling, Nursing Education, Nursing	Improving the ability and willingness in a group to receive information.
NBABX	Home maintenance assistance, Patient education and counseling, Nursing Education, Nursing	Helping a patient and family to maintain the home as a clean, safe and pleasant place.
NBAZZ	Undefined, narrative required, Patient education and counseling, Nursing Education, Nursing	Anywhere else undefined patient education and counseling. Narrative required.

Public health

ABC Code	Procedure Description	Expanded Definition
NBBAA	Case management, Public health, Nursing Education, Nursing	Coordinating care and advocating for specified individuals and patient populations across settings to reduce cost and resource use, improve quality of health care and achieve desired outcomes.
NBBAD	Communicable disease management, Public health, Nursing Education, Nursing	Working with a community to decrease and manage the incidence and prevalence of contagious diseases in a specific population.
NBBAE	Community disaster preparedness, Public health, Nursing Education, Nursing	Preparing a community for an effective response to a large scale disaster.
NBBAF	Community health development, Public health, Nursing Education, Nursing	Working with a community to identify health concerns, mobilize resources and implement solutions.
NBBAG	Community surveillance, Public health, Nursing Education, Nursing	Purposeful and on-going acquisition, interpretation and synthesis of data for decision-making in the community.
NBBAH	Conflict mediation, Public health, Nursing Education, Nursing	Facilitating constructive dialogue between opposing parties to resolve disputes in a mutually acceptable manner.
NBBAI	Consciousness, recognition teaching, individual, Public health, Nursing Education, Nursing	Instructing when aprofessional help is needed for a dependent child or adult by monitoring the physical signs and consciousness level.
NBBAJ	Consultation, individual, Public health, Nursing Education, Nursing	Working with an individual to enable individuals, families, groups or agencies to achieve identified goals.

Nursing Education

Public health

ABC Code	Procedure Description	Expanded Definition
NBBAK	Consultation, group, Public health, Nursing Education, Nursing	Use of expert knowledge to work with those in a group setting who seek help in problem-solving to enable individuals, families, groups or agencies to achieve identified goals.
NBBAL	Consultation, family, Public health, Nursing Education, Nursing	Working with a family to enable individuals, families, groups or agencies to achieve identified goals.
NBBAM	Contamination disposal, Public health, Nursing Education, Nursing	Teaching a patient or nonmedical caretaker proper techniques for handling and disposing of contaminated materials.
NBBAN	Environmental risk protection, Public health, Nursing Education, Nursing	Preventing and detecting disease and injury in populations at risk from environmental hazards.
NBBAO	Fiscal resource management, Public health, Nursing Education, Nursing	Procuring and directing financial resources to assure development and continuation of programs and services.
NBBAP	Long range parenting planning and decision making, individual, Public health, Nursing Education, Nursing	Teaching an individual effective ways of providing support, nurturing, stimulation and physical care for dependent adult or child on a long term basis.
NBBAQ	Long range parenting planning and decision making, group, Public health, Nursing Education, Nursing	Teaching in a group setting effective ways of providing support, nurturing, stimulation and physical care for dependent adult or child on a long term basis.
NBBAR	Long range parenting planning and decision making, family, Public health, Nursing Education, Nursing	Teaching a family effective ways of providing support, nurturing, stimulation and physical care for dependent adult or child on a long term basis.
NBBAS	Parenting safety, individual, Public health, Nursing Education, Nursing	Teaching an individual safety measures for development stages of a dependent child or adult.
NBBAT	Financial resource assistance, Public health, Nursing Education, Nursing	Assisting an individual and family to secure and manage health care finances.
NBBAU	Parenting safety, group, Public health, Nursing Education, Nursing	Teaching safety measures in a group setting for developmental stages of a dependent child or adult.
NBBAV	Parenting safety, family, Public health, Nursing Education, Nursing	Teaching a family about safety measures for developmental stages of a dependent child or adult.
NBBAW	Parenting, age appropriate discipline training, individual, Public health, Nursing Education, Nursing	Teaching age appropriate discipline to provide support, nurturance, stimulation and physical care for a dependent adult or child.

Public health

ABC Code	Procedure Description	Expanded Definition
NBBAX	Parenting, age appropriate discipline training, group, Public health, Nursing Education, Nursing	Teaching age appropriate discipline in a group setting to provide support, nurturance, stimulation and physical care for a dependent adult or child.
NBBAY	Parenting, age appropriate discipline training, family, Public health, Nursing Education, Nursing	Teaching age appropriate discipline to a family to provide support, nurturance, stimulation and physical care for a dependent adult or child.
NBBAZ	Parenting, nutritional requirements, individual, Public health, Nursing Education, Nursing	Teaching realistic expectations regarding growth and development for the maturation of a child or adult.
NBBBA	Parenting, nutritional requirements, group, Public health, Nursing Education, Nursing	Teaching in a group setting realistic expectations regarding growth and developmentfor the maturation of a child or adult.
NBBBB	Parenting, nutritional requirements, family, Public health, Nursing Education, Nursing	Teaching a family realistic expectations regarding growth and development for the maturation of a child or adult.
NBBBC	Parenting, stimulation and nurturance, individual, Public health, Nursing Education, Nursing	Teaching an individual verbal, facial, tactile and other age appropriate stimulation and nurturing for a dependent child or adult.
NBBBD	Parenting, stimulation and nurturance, group, Public health, Nursing Education, Nursing	Teaching in a group setting verbal, facial, tactile and other age appropriate stimulation and nurturing for a dependent child or adult.
NBBBE	Parenting, stimulation and nurturance, family, Public health, Nursing Education, Nursing	Teaching a family verbal, facial, tactile and other age appropriate stimulation and nurturing for a dependent child or adult.
NBBBF	Program development, Public health, Nursing Education, Nursing	Planning, implementing and evaluating coordinated activities to enhance wellness or to prevent, reduce, or eliminate health problems in a group or community.
NBBBG	Promotora, community, Public health, Nursing Education, Nursing	Educating a community to improve health, welfare or environmental conditions.
NBBBH	Promotora, community outreach, each hour, Public health, Nursing Education, Nursing	One hour period of community canvassing to locate individuals in need of information and helping locate community resources to improve their health, education, welfare or environmental conditions.
NBBBI	Promotora, individual, Public health, Nursing Education, Nursing	Sducating an individual to improve health, welfare or environmental conditions.
NBBBJ	Promotora, group, Public health, Nursing Education, Nursing	Educating in a group setting to improve health, welfare or environmental conditions.

Public health

ABC Code	Procedure Description	Expanded Definition
NBBBK	Promotora, family, Public health, Nursing Education, Nursing	Educating a family setting to improve health, welfare or environmental conditions.
NBBBL	Residential safety, individual, Public health, Nursing Education, Nursing	Teaching a patient or nonmedical caretaker techniques for creating a safe environment to protect the entire household.
NBBBM	Residential safety, group, Public health, Nursing Education, Nursing	Teaching a group of patients or nonmedical caretakers techniques for creating a safe environment to protect the entire household.
NBBBN	Residential safety, family, Public health, Nursing Education, Nursing	Teaching a family techniques for creating a safe environment to protect the entire household.
NBBBO	Resiliency promotion, individual, Public health, Nursing Education, Nursing	Assisting individuals in development, use and strengthening of protective factors in coping with environmental and societal stressors.
NBBBP	Resiliency promotion, group, Public health, Nursing Education, Nursing	Assisting a group in development, use and strengthening of protective factors in coping with environmental and societal stressors.
NBBBQ	Resiliency promotion, family, Public health, Nursing Education, Nursing	Assisting a family in development, use and strengthening of protective factors in coping with environmental and societal stressors.
NBBBR	Resiliency promotion, community, Public health, Nursing Education, Nursing	Assisting community groups in development, use and strengthening of protective factors in coping with environmental and societal stressors.
NBBBS	Role change, coping skills, individual, Public health, Nursing Education, Nursing	Teaching an individual beneficial movement from one set of expected behavioral characteristics to another.
NBBBT	Role change, coping skills, group, Public health, Nursing Education, Nursing	Teaching in a group setting beneficial movement from one set of expected behavioral characteristics to another.
NBBBU	Role change, coping skills, family, Public health, Nursing Education, Nursing	Teaching a family beneficial movement from one set of expected behavioral characteristics to another.
NBBBV	Staff development, Public health, Nursing Education, Nursing	Developing, maintaining and monitoring staff competence.
NBBBW	Toddler nutrition teaching, individual, Public health, Nursing Education, Nursing	Individual instruction on nutrition and feeding during the second and third years of life.

Public health

ABC Code	Procedure Description	Expanded Definition
NBBBX	Toddler nutrition teaching, group, Public health, Nursing Education, Nursing	Instruction in a group setting on nutrition and feeding during the second and third years of life.
NBBBY	Toddler safety teaching, individual, Public health, Nursing Education, Nursing	Individual instruction on safety during the second and third years of life.
NBBBZ	Toddler safety teaching, group, Public health, Nursing Education, Nursing	Instruction in a group setting on safety during the second and third years of life.
NBBCA	Vehicle safety promotion, individual, Public health, Nursing Education, Nursing	Assisting to reduce unintentional injuries in motorized and non-motorized vehicles.
NBBCB	Vehicle safety promotion, group, Public health, Nursing Education, Nursing	Assisting in a group setting to reduce unintentional injuries in motorized and non-motorized vehicles.
NBBCC	Vehicle safety promotion, community, Public health, Nursing Education, Nursing	Assisting a community to reduce unintentional injuries in motorized and non-motorized vehicles.
NBBCD	Sports injury prevention, youth, individual, Public health, Nursing Education, Nursing	Reducing sports-related injury in a young athlete.
NBBCE	Sports injury prevention, youth, group, Public health, Nursing Education, Nursing	Reducing sports-related injury in young athletes in a group setting.
NBBCF	Health education, individual, Public health, Nursing Education, Nursing	Developing and providing patient instruction and learning to facilitate voluntary adaptation of positive behavior conducive to health.
NBBCG	Health education, family, Public health, Nursing Education, Nursing	Developing and providing patient instruction in a family setting and learning to facilitate voluntary adaptation of positive behavior conducive to health.
NBBCH	Health education, group, Public health, Nursing Education, Nursing	Developing and providing client instruction in a group setting and learning experiences to facilitate voluntary adaptation of behavior conducive to health in individuals.
NBBCI	Health education, community, Public health, Nursing Education, Nursing	Developing and providing instruction in a community setting and learning to facilitate voluntary adaptation of positive behavior conducive to health.
NBBZZ	Undefined, narrative required, Public health, Nursing Education, Nursing	Anywhere else undefined general public health procedure. Narrative required.

Communication disorders

ABC Code	Procedure Description	Expanded Definition

Communication disorders

ABC Code	Procedure Description	Expanded Definition
NBCAD	Speech and language communication therapy, individual, Communication disorders, Nursing Education, Nursing	Teaching an individual compensatory communication strategies, eliciting verbal and non-verbal responses, visualmotor, writing and numeric processes and addressing deficiencies in vocal sounds, symbols, signs or gestures.
NBCAE	Speech and language exercise therapy, base of tongue and pharyngeal, individual, Communication disorders, Nursing Education, Nursing	Teaching, drilling and observing activity to increase tone and improve coordinated mobility and reflexes of the tongue and throat muscles to aid swallowing and communication in patients.
NBCAF	Speech and language exercise therapy, bolus control, individual, Communication disorders, Nursing Education, Nursing	Teaching, drilling and observing chewing techniques, including tongue and orofacial muscle coordination in swallowing softened, small ball-sized pieces of food in patients.
NBCAG	Speech and language exercise therapy, control of drooling, individual, Communication disorders, Nursing Education, Nursing	Teaching, drilling and observing techniques to prevent or reduce saliva dribble from in patients.
NBCAH	Speech and language exercise therapy, elicit phonation, individual, Communication disorders, Nursing Education, Nursing	Teaching, drilling and observing techniques towartds speech through vibration of the vocal chords in patients.
NBCAI	Speech and language exercise therapy, individual, Communication disorders, Nursing Education, Nursing	Teaching, drilling and observing physical activity to increase tone, power, range of motion and mobility of the tongue to improve communication.
NBCAJ	Speech and language exercise therapy, orofacial, individual, Communication disorders, Nursing Education, Nursing	Teaching, drilling and observing physical activity to maintain or improve the muscles of the mouth, tongue, lips and face to improve communication.
NBCAK	Speech and language exercise therapy, swallowing and positioning, individual, Communication disorders, Nursing Education, Nursing	Teaching, drilling and observing swallowing and positioning techniques to improve communication.
NBCAL	Speech and language exercise therapy, thermal stimulation, individual, Communication disorders, Nursing Education, Nursing	Teaching, drilling and observing use of heat and/or cold to normalize or improve communication.
NBCAM	Speech and language feeding procedure teaching, individual, Communication disorders, Nursing Education, Nursing	Teaching, drilling and observing techniques to prevent or reduce problems in eating, swallowing, and dribble of solids and liquids.
NBCAN	Speech and language rehabilitation, anomia, individual, Communication disorders, Nursing Education, Nursing	Teaching, drilling and practicing the naming of objects.

Communication disorders

ABC Code	Procedure Description	Expanded Definition
NBCAO	Speech and language rehabilitation, apraxia, individual, Communication disorders, Nursing Education, Nursing	Educating and practicing individually to perform purposeful movements without paralysis and the true nature, use and meaning of things so that proper vocalization or action may follow.
NBCAP	Speech and language rehabilitation, dysarthia, individual, Communication disorders, Nursing Education, Nursing	Educating and practicing individually to alleviate difficulties due to disturbances of muscular control so that others may properly perceive and understand the meaning when listening to the patient.
NBCAQ	Speech and language rehabilitation, dysphagia, individual, Communication disorders, Nursing Education, Nursing	Educating and practicing individually to alleviate difficulty in swallowing, stemming from any cause.
NBCAR	Speech and language rehabilitation, expressive language, individual, Communication disorders, Nursing Education, Nursing	Educating and practicing individually to alleviate difficulties in speaking a native language, so that others may properly perceive and understand the meaning when listening to the patient.
NBCAS	Speech and language rehabilitation, intelligibility, individual, Communication disorders, Nursing Education, Nursing	Educating and practicing individually to make speech capable of being understood by the listener.
NBCAT	Speech and language rehabilitation, intelligibility, group, Communication disorders, Nursing Education, Nursing	Educating and practicing in a group setting to make speech capable of being understood by the listener.
NBCAU	Speech and language rehabilitation, receptive language, individual, Communication disorders, Nursing Education, Nursing	Educating and practicing individually to alleviate difficulty in perceiving and understanding when listening to native or acquired spoken language.
NBCAV	Speech and language rehabilitation, voice phonation disorders, individual, Communication disorders, Nursing Education, Nursing	Educating and practicing for proper production of speech sounds through vocal folds of the larynx.
NBCZZ	Undefined, narrative required, Communication disorders, Nursing Education, Nursing	Anywhere else undefined general communication disorders. Narrative required.

Procedure Index

A.A.T., see Animal assisted therapy

A.D.D., see Hyperactivity

Abdominal exercise   **BBAAA**

Abortion counseling, see Unplanned pregnancy, Pregnancy termination

Abuse protection

  Adult

    Individual   **CDAAK**

    Group   **CDAAL**

  Child

    Individual   **CDAAR**

    Group   **CDAAS**

  Domestic partner

    Individual   **CDAAZ**

    Group   **CDAHW**

  Elder

    Individual   **CDABC**

    Group   **CDABD**

  Institution and organizational

    Individual   **CDAEZ**

    Group   **CDAIP**

Acid base management

  Initial   **NAAAQ**

  Additional   **NAAAR**

  Metabolic acidosis

    Initial   **NAAAS**

    Additional   **NAAAT**

  Metabolic alkalosis

    Initial   **NAAOI**

    Additional   **NAAOJ**

  Respiratory acidosis

    Initial   **NAAAU**

    Additional   **NAAAV**

  Respiratory alkalosis

    Initial   **NAAOM**

    Additional   **NAAON**

Acid base monitoring   **NAAAW**

Active listening by provider, see also, Counseling   **NAALH**

Active listening training

  Individual   **CDABL**

  Group   **CDABM**

  Family   **CDABN**

Activities of daily living, see Daily living activities

Activity or Exercise codes   **BBAAA-BBAZZ**

  see also, Therapeutic Exercise

Activity therapy, see also, Exercise

  Individual   **CDAAJ**

  Group   **CDAHU**

Acupressure, see also, Oriental Massage   **CBGAA**

Acupuncture, see also, Oriental Medicine

  Initial   **CABAE**

  Additional   **CABAF**

  Aquapuncture   **CADAA**

  Auricular acupuncture   **CABAB**

  Cauterizing laser   **CACAA**

  Electrical   **CACAD**

  Non-cauterizing laser   **CACAG**

  Trigger point needling   **CABAG**

Acupuncture anesthesia

  Initial 2 hours   **CAAAB**

  Cesarean section   **CAAAD**

  Cesarean section delivery   **CAAAD**

  Dental acupuncture   **CAAAA**

  Each additional hour   **CAAAE**

  Induction of labor   **CAAAC**

  Surgical, initial   **CAAAB**

Acupuncture general codes   **CABAB-CABZZ**

Acupuncture needles, see Supply and Product Index

Acuscope, see also, Microelectronic current   **BDAAD**

Adjustments, see Closed joint adjustment, Osteopathic manipulation, Chiropractic manipulations, Naturopathic manipulations

Advocate, see Culture brokerage

Aerobics, see also, Exercise

  Low impact   **BBAAW**

  Step   **BBAAX**

Agreement contracting, see also, Counseling   **NAAGP**

Ahara counseling, see also, Ayurvedic medicine   **CHAAA**

AIDS, see HIV, HTLV

AIDS prevention, see Infection control

Airway insertion, stabilization   **DDCAC**

Airway management

  Artificial airway management   **NAABB**

  General   **NAAOT**

  Suctioning   **NAAAY**

Alexander Technique, see also, Bodywork and Massage   **CBBAA**

Allergen solutions, see Supply and Product Index   **ECAAA-ECAZZ**

Allergic reaction care   **NAAGZ**

Allergy injection

  With provision of extracts

    Initial injection   **DDBCQ**

    Additional injection   **DDBDB**

  Without provision of extracts

    Initial injection   **DDBCR**

    Additional injection   **DDBDC**

Allergy management   **DEPAK**

Allergy profile

  1 to 8 items   **DEPAA**

  1 to 16 items   **DEPAR**

  1 to 24 items   **DEPAS**

Allergy proofing   **NBAAQ**

Allergy testing, see also, Autoimmune panel, Spice profile

  Food allergy profile, 1 to 8 Items   **DEPAB**

  Food allergy profile, 1 to 16 items   **DEPBR**

  Food allergy profile, 1 to 24 items   **DEPBS**

  Inhalants profile   **DEPAG**

  Intracutaneous

    General   **DEPAL**

    Sequential and incremental   **DEPAN**

    With allergenic extracts, immediate type reaction   **DEPAM**

  Percutaneous

    Sequential and incremental   **DEPAP**

    With allergenic extracts, immediate type reaction   **DEPAO**

  Skin End Point Titration   **DEPAQ**

Allergy testing codes   **DEPAA-DEPZZ**

Allergy testing/ treatment codes, see also, NAET   **BEAAO-BEAZY**

Alternative Birth Center, see Free standing birth facility, Hospital based birth center facility

Amino acid analysis

  44 metabolites, plasma   **DECAG**

  Qualitative, 44 metabolites, urine   **DECAE**

  Quantitative, 44 metabolites, urine   **DECAF**

Amino acid supplement   **FAAZZ**

Amma therapy   **CBGAB**

Amnioinfusion   **CECAN**

Amputation care   **NAABA**

Analgesic, see also, Pain management, Patient controlled analgesia

  Intramuscular administration   **DDBDH**

  Intravenous administration   **DDBDG**

Analysis and interpretation

  Computer data   **ADDAA**

  Laboratory findings   **ADDAB**

Procedure Index

Procedure Index

-C-

Procedure Index

-E-

-F-

-G-

Procedure Index

Homeopathic preparations	
Recommending	ADXAB
Homeopathic training	
Individual	AEAAO
Group	AEAAS
Hope instillation	NAAEQ
Hormone Profile	
Female	DEOAA
Female, comprehensive	DEOAB
Male	DEMAC
Male, comprehensive	DEMAB
Post menopause	DEOAC
Post menopause, comprehensive	DEOAD
Hospice care, see Dying care	
Hospital based birth center facility	
Charge D	CECBG
Charge D2	CECBH
House call	
Existing client	
5 minutes, diagnostician	AADAA
10 minutes, diagnostician	AADAB
15 minutes, diagnostician	AADAC
25 minutes, diagnostician	AADAD
40 minutes, diagnostician	AADAE
60 minutes, diagnostician	AADAF
90 minutes, diagnostician	AADAG
120 minutes, diagnostician	AADAH
150 minutes, diagnostician	AADAI
New client	
10 minutes, diagnostician	AACAA
20 minutes, diagnostician	AACAB
30 minutes, diagnostician	AACAC
45 minutes, diagnostician	AACAD
60 minutes, diagnostician	AACAE
90 minutes, diagnostician	AACAF
120 minutes, diagnostician	AACAG
150 minutes, diagnostician	AACAH
Existing client	
15 minutes, limited diagnostician	ACDAA
30 minutes limited diagnostician	ACDAB
60 minutes limited diagnostician	ACDAC
New client	
45 minutes limited diagnostician	ACCAB
60 minutes limited diagnostician	ACCAC
HTLV, see also, HIV	
HTLV and HIV antibody, Western blot	DEJAO
HTLV1 with analysis and antibody detection	DEJAN
Hubbard Tank	BADAD
Human sexuality education	
Individual	CDAGJ
Group	CDAGK
Humor therapy, see also, Counseling	NBABS
Hydrotherapy, see also, Colonic irrigation	
Constitutional hydrotherapy	BADAJ
Constitutional hydrotherapy with sine	BADAI
Percussion	BADAQ
Hygiene, see also, Self care assistance	
Bathing	NAABC
Ear care	NAAOL
Foot care	NAAEG
Hair care	NAAEI
Nail care	NAAGB
Hyperactivity, see also, Inattention	CDAAN
Hypercalcemia, see Electrolyte management	
Hyperglycemia, see Blood sugar management	

Hyperkalemia, see Electrolyte management	
Hypermagnesemia, see Electrolyte management	
Hypernatremia, see Electrolyte management	
Hyperphosphatemia, see Electrolyte management	
Hyperpyrexia treatment, see Fever treatment	
Hyperthermia, see Malignant hyperthermia precautions	
Hypervolemia management	NAAFA
Hypnotherapy, Clinical	CDAAD
Hypnotherapy, see also, Autogenic training	CDAAG
Hypocalcemia, see Electrolyte management	
Hypoglycemia, see Blood sugar management	
Hypokalemia, see Electrolyte management	
Hypomagnesemia, see Electrolyte management	
Hyponatremia, see Electrolyte management	
Hypophosphatemia, see Electrolyte management	
Hypothermia treatment	
One area	BAAAC
Entire body	BAAAD
Hypovolemia management, see also, Fluid management	NAAOV

-I-

Ice massage, see also, Cold therapy	BAAAE
Ice pack	BAAAA
Immunization, see Vaccination	
Impaction management	NAACT
Impedance measuring device, see also, Ed. Kinesiology	BDBAB
Impulse control, see also, Counseling	NAAFK
Impulse control training	
Individual	CDADA
Group	CDADB
Family	CDADC
Inattention, see also, Hyperactivity	CDAIA
Incision site care	NAAFL
Indigenous medicine codes	CHAAA-CHCZZ
Induction of labor, see Labor induction	
Infant care, each hour after first 24 hours	NAAKJ
Infant care codes, see Newborn care codes	
Infant care teaching	
Individual	CEEAK
Group	CEEAS
Infant massage	CBEAG
Infant nutrition teaching, see also, Bottle feeding, Breastfeeding	
Individual	CEEAT
Group	CEEAU
Infant safety teaching	
Individual	CEEAV
Group	CEEAW
Infection control education	NBAAY
Infection control techniques	NAAPA
Infection control, intraoperative	NAAPH
Infection prevention	NAAPG
Infertility, see Family planning, Fertility preservation	
Infrared hemorrhoid cauterization	BAEAF
Infrared light therapy, see Light therapy	
Inhalation therapy	NAAND
Injections	
Intra arterial	
One substance	DDBBQ
Two or more substances	DDBBR
Intracutaneous	
One substance	DDBBS
Two or more substances	DDBBT
Intramuscular	
Autogenous solution	DDBBJ

Procedure Index

Postural drainage, see Cough enhancement

Postural Integration, see also, Bodywork — CBBAQ

Posture, see Body mechanics

PPV, see Newborn Resuscitation

Pradhamana Nasya, see also, Ayurvedic medicine — CHABC

Prati Marshya, see also, Ayurvedic medicine — CHABD

Preconceptional counseling, see also, Family planning — CEFAK

Pregnancy, see also, Childbirth — CEBAP

Pregnancy termination care

Initial — CEAAW

Additional — CEAAX

Pregnancy termination counseling — CEABL

Prenatal care

4 to 6 visits — CEBAA

7 or more visits — CEBAB

Complete — CEBAC

Prenatal Care codes, see also, Childbirth — CEBAA-CEBZZ

Prenatal massage — CBEAT

Prenatal monitoring of uterus — CEBAE

Preoperative education

Individual — NBAAH

Group — NBAAK

Preparation, see Compounding

Preparatory sensory information — NAAHG

Prescribe

Homeopathic remedy — ADZAD

Nutritional supplements — ADZAA

Oral chelation agents — ADZAF

Oriental herb or botanical — ADZAB

Pharmaceutical — ADZAG

Western herb or botanical — ADZAC

Prescribed diet teaching, see also, Nutritional education

Individual — AEBAM

Group — AEBAN

Pressure management — NAAHI

Pressure ulcer

Care — NAAHJ

Prevention — NAAHK

Pre-surgical assistance — NAALN

Products, see Supply and Product Index

Program development — NBBBF

Progressive muscle relaxation — NBAAE

Prolapse, see Pessary management

Promotora

Individual — NBBBI

Group — NBBBJ

Family — NBBBK

Community — NBBBG

Community outreach — NBBBH

Prompted voiding — NAANJ

Proprioceptive Neuromuscular Facilit., see also, Massage — CBEAQ

Prostate specific antigen — DEMAL

Prostatic acid phosphate panel — DEMAI

Prostatic massage, see also, Naturopathic — CFBAD

Prosthesis, see also, Rehabilitation

Prosthesis care — NAAKS

Prosthetic movement education — BCAAB

Pruritis management — NAANK

Psychiatric evaluation services — CDBAU

Psychological test interpretation, see also, Testing, Evalua! — CDBAR

Psychological testing

Brief assessment — CDBAP

Comprehensive — CDBAQ

See also, Testing, Evaluation and Interpretation of mental health

Psychomotor skills teaching

Individual — CBDAR

Group — CBDAQ

Psychotherapy, see also, Counseling

Inpatient

Initial — CDAGZ

Additional — CDAHA

Group — CDAHG

Family — CDAHE

Couples — CDAHD

Multi Family — CDAHF

Initial — CDAHB

Additional — CDAHC

Public health, see also, Health education

Public health codes — NBBAA-NBBZZ

Pulmonary embolus care — NAAHL

Pulmonary or vital capacity breathing study, see Ordering pulmonary or vital capacity breathing study

Pulmonary services, see Ordering pulmonary or vital capacity breathing study

Putrefied skin, see Maggot therapy

-Q-

Qigong, see also, Movement modalities

Individual — BBABM

Group — BBABN

-R-

Radiation therapy care — NAANL

Radiation therapy management — NAAHM

Radiological films, see Analysis and interpretation

Radiology procedure codes, see Ordering x-rays

Raktamoksha, see also, Ayurvedic medicine — CHAAD

Range of motion codes — BDFAA-BDFZZ

Rape, see Sexual assault

Rape trauma treatment

Initial — NAAHN

Additional — NAAHO

Rapid intravenous fluid resuscitation, see Resuscitation

Reading therapy, see Bibliotherapy

Reality orientation, see also, Counseling

Individual — CDAFV

Group — CDAFW

Rebirthing, see also, Counseling — CDAAI

Recommend

Homeopathic preparation — ADXAB

Nutritional supplements — ADXAA

Oral Chelation agent — ADXAC

Oriental herb or botanical — ADXAD

Western herb or botanical — ADXAE

RECOVERING

10 day program — BCAAE

Each 2 hours — BCAAF

Recreation therapy, see also, Counseling — NAAOZ

Rectal medication administration, see Medication administration

Rectal prolapse management — NAAHQ

Referral

Hypnotherapy — ADYAF

Meditation service or class — ADYAK

Rebirthing services — ADYAG

Specialist — ADYAL

Tai Chi class — ADYAI

Yoga class — ADYAJ

-R-

Reflexology	CBEAU
Rehabilitative, see Self care, Therapeutic exercise	
Rehabilitative cardiac care	NAABU
Rehabilitative codes	BCAAA-BCAZZ
Relaxation massage	CBEAV
Relaxation therapy, see also, Autogenic training	
Individual	CDAEL
Group	CDAEM
Religious, see Compulsive behavior treatment	
Religious abuse, see Abuse protection	
Religious ritual enhancement	
Individual	NBAAZ
Group	NBABA
Reminiscence therapy, see also, Counseling	CDAFX
Remote electronic surveillance	NAANM
Reports, see Analysis and Interpretation	
Reservoir medication dispensing	ADZAJ
Residential safety	
Individual	NBBBL
Group	NBBBM
Family	NBBBN
Resiliency promotion	
Individual	NBBBO
Group	NBBBP
Family	NBBBQ
Community	NBBBR
Respiratory acidosis, see Acid base management	
Respiratory alkalosis, see Acid base management	
Respiratory care	NAANN
Respiratory monitoring	NAAHS
Respite care	NAAHT
Restraint, see Physical restraint	
Resuscitation	
Fetus	NAAPD
Neonate	NAAHU
Rapid intravenous fluid resuscitation	DDBDD
Risk identification	NAAAA
Risk identification training	NBAAF
Role change, coping skills	
Individual	NBBBS
Group	NBBBT
Family	NBBBU
Role enhancement training, see also, Counseling	
Individual	CDADQ
Group	CDADR
Family	CDADS
Rolfing, see also, Ergonomics	CBBAR
Rosen Method, see also, Bodywork	CBBAS
Russian conditioning, see also, Massage	CBEAW
Ryodoraku, see also, Tests and Measurements	BDAAC

-S-

Safe sex education, see also, Counseling	
Individual	CDADT
Group	CDADU
Safety, see Parenting, Residential safety	
Safety surveillance	NAAHW
Saliva analysis	
Adrenocortex stress profile	DEFAA
Antigliadin or gluten antibodies	DEFAB
Saliva analysis codes	DEFAA-DEFZZ
Sanitation, see Sanitation	
Sauna, see also, Heat, Water Therapies	BACAH

-S-

Scar therapy, see also, Oriental medicine	
Manual	CFCAC
Moxa	CADAD
Scotch Douche, see Percussion hydrotherapy	
Seclusion	
Initial hour	NAAIQ
Each re-evaluation	NAAIS
Second midwife assist with delivery	
Initial hour	CECBN
Additional hour	CECBO
Security enhancement	NAAIU
Sedation, see Anesthesia, Conscious sedation	
Seizure management	NAAIW
Seizure precautions	NAAIY
Self awareness enhancement, see also, Counseling	
Individual	CDADV
Group	CDADW
Self care assistance, see also, Hygiene	
Bathing, hygiene	NAAJD
Dressing	NAAHX
Feeding	NAAHY
Other	NAAJB
Toileting	NAAIA
Self care training, see also, Rehabilitative	
Individual	BCAAG
Group	BCAAH
Family	BCAAC
Self catheterization teaching	NBABB
Self esteem enhancement, see also, Counseling	
Individual	CDADX
Group	CDADY
Self harm, see Behavior management	
Self hypnosis, see Autogenic training	
Self massage training, see also, Activity or Exercise	
Individual	BBABH
Group	BBABG
Self modification assistance training, see also, Counseling	
Individual	CDAEA
Group	CDAEB
Self responsibility facilitation, see also, Counseling	
Individual	CDAEC
Group	CDAED
Family	CDAEE
Sensory Integration, see also, Bodywork	CBBAT
Sex education, see Human sexuality education	
Sexual, see Compulsive behavior treatment	
Sexual abuse, see Abuse protection	
Sexual assault, see also, Rape trauma treatment	
Crisis intervention	
Initial contact, first hour	NAANO
Additional	NAANP
Documentation of history	
Initial contact, first 45 minutes	NAANQ
Additional	NAANR
Forensic evidence collection	
Initial contact, first hour	NAANS
Additional	NAANT
Physical injury assessment	
Initial contact, first hour	NAANU
Additional	NAANV
Pregnancy risk education	
Initial contact, first 30 minutes	NAANW
Additional	NAANX
Securing forensic evidence	NAANY

Procedure Index

Procedure Index

I-19

Weight reduction assistance

Individual	AEBAK
Group	AEBAL

Wellness visit

15 minutes	ABAAA
30 minutes	ABAAB
45 minute s	ABAAC
60 minutes	ABAAD
90 minutes	ABAAE
120 minutes	ABAAF

Western blot, see HTLV, HIV antibody

Western botanical training

Individual	AEAAM
Group	AEABC

Western herb or botanical

Compounding	ADZAL
Prescribing	ADZAC
Recommending	ADXAE
Dispensing	ADZAP

Western herb or botanical codes GBAAA-GBZZZ

Wet mount, see also, Laboratory DEJAD

Wheelchair positioning NAAKF

Whirlpool, see also, Water BADAG

Woman, see Midwifery, Female testing

Work conditioning, see also, Ergonomics

Initial	BCBAA
Additional	BCBAB

Work conditioning codes BCBAA-BCBZZ

Worker safety management

Individual	BCBAC
Group	BCBAD

World healing, see Indigenous medicine

Wound bleeding reduction NAABK

Wound care

Closed drainage	NAAKH
General	NAAKG

Wound irrigation NAAKI

-X-

X-rays, see Ordering x-rays

-Y-

Yoga, see also, Activity or Exercise

Individual	BBABK
Group	BBABF

Yoga Basti, see also, Ayurvedic medicine CHAAY

-Z-

Zero Balancing, see also, Bodywork CBBBC
Zone therapy, see also, Massage CBEBJ

Supply and Product Index

Part A: Physical Supplies and Solutions

-A-

A-Acetylcysteine	ECBAA
Abdominal binders and support	EAAAA
Acupuncture needles, disposable	EAAAB
Additives or preservatives hypersensitivity	
Up to 15 items	ECAAC
16 to 30 items	ECAAD
Adrenal cortical extract	ECBAB
Allergy solution	
Danders, hair, feathers, up to 15 items	ECAAI
Environmental chemicals, up to 15 items	ECAAJ
Environmental chemicals, 16 to 30 items	ECAAK
Environmental chemicals, 31 to 60 items	ECAAL
Food dyes and colors, up to 12 items	ECAAQ
Haptens, toxic mineral hypersensitivity	ECAAT
IgE for 100 vegetarian foods	ECAAU
IgE for 96 general foods	ECAAV
IgG4 for 100 vegetarian foods	ECAAW
IgG4 for 96 general foods	ECAAX
Inhalants profile, with IgE for 47 inhalants	ECABB
Lecithin hypersensitivity	ECABC
Medications hypersensitivity, up to 15 items	ECABG
Medications hypersensitivity, 16 to 30 items	ECABH
Mold hypersensitivity, up to 15 items	ECABI
Mold hypersensitivity, 16 to 30 items	ECABJ
Pokeweed mitogen hypersensitivity	ECABK
Spice profile, with separate IgE profiles	ECAAA
Spice profile, with separate IgG4 profiles	ECAAB
Stinging insect venom, 1 item	ECABL
Stinging insect venoms, 2 items	ECABM
Stinging insect venoms, 3 items	ECABN
Stinging insect venoms, 4 items	ECAAR
Stinging insect venoms, 5 items	ECAAO
Sulfite hypersensitivity	ECABQ
Tricophyton hypersensitivity	ECABP
Alpha-1 Antitrypsin	ECAAE
Ankle canvass splint	EAAAC
Antibiotic	ECBAC
Aredia	ECBAD
Arm and shoulder immobilizer	EAAAD
Autoimmune panel	ECAAF

-B-

Back frame support	EAAAE
Bandages and wraps	EAAAF
Benzoate hypersensitivity	ECAAG
Braces, hinged	EAACF

-C-

Calcium	ECBAF
Calcium bersonate and additives	ECBAE
Candida antigen	ECAAH
Casting materials	EAAAG
Cervical cap	EAACP
Cervical collar, fitted	EAAAH
Cervical exerciser, home use	EAAAI
Cervical pillow, therapeutic	EAAAJ
Cervical roll	EAAAK
Chromium	ECBAG

-C-

CMBZM	ECBAH
Colema board	EAAAL
Compresses	EAAAM
Copper	ECBAI
Cryotherapy, cervical contour	EAAAN
Cryotherapy, home use, eye	
Home use, eye	EAAAO
Home use, large	EAAAP
Home use, medium	EAAAQ
Home use, small	EAAAR
Cupping supplies	EAACJ

-D-

Deferoximine mesylate	ECBAJ
Diaphragm	EAACP
Dimeracaprol, 1% procaine	ECBAK

-E-

EDTA	ECBAL
Elastic bandages	EAAAS
Electro needles	EAACK
Epstein Barr	
Early antigen	ECAAM
Nuclear antigen	ECAAN

-F-

Folic acid	ECBAM
Fomentel	EAAAT
Food and inhalants	ECAAP

-G-

Germanium	ECBAN
Glutathione	ECBAO
Gut mucosal immunity	ECAAS

-H-

Hand grip exerciser, home use	EAAAU
Hemoglobinometer	EAACO
Heparin	ECBAP
Hepatitis A vaccine	ECBAQ
Hepatitis B vaccine	ECBAR
Holster arm sling	EAAAV
Hot pack	
Large	EAAAW
Small	EAAAX
Hydrochloric acid	ECBAS
Hydrocortisone with additives	ECBAT
Hydrogen peroxide	ECBAU
Hydrogen peroxide with additives	ECBAV

-I-

Ice pack	
Large	EAAAY
Small	EAABA

Supply and Product Index

Supply and Product Index

Part B: Herbs, Botanicals, Homeopathic Preparations and Flower Essences

Western and Oriental herbs and botanicals are listed by Latin, common and Oriental name.
Homeopathic preparations and flower essences are listed by Latin name.

-A-

Angustura spuria	HABBT
Abelmoschus moschatus	HAAAA
Abies canadensis	HAAAB
Abies nigra	HAAAC
Abrus precatorius	HAAAE
Acalypha indica	HAAAG
Acer negundo	HAADZ
Acetanilidum	HAAAH
Aceticum acidum	HAAAI
Achillea filipendulina	GCAAA
Achillea millefolium	
Flower essence	GCAAB
Homeopathic	HAACZ
Pink, Flower essence	GCAAC
Yarrow formula	GCAAD
Achyranthes aspera	HAAAJ
Aconite napellus	HAAAK
Aconitinum	HAAAL
Aconitum cammarum	HAAAM
Aconitum ferox	HAAAN
Aconitum lycotonum	HAAAO
Actea spicata	HAAAP
Adder's tongue	GBEAG
Adelheidsquelle aqua	HAAAQ
Adonis vernalis	HAAAR
Adoxa moschatellina	HAAAS
Adrenalinum	HAAAT
Aesculus carnea	GCAAE
Aesculus glabra	HAAAV
Aesculus hippocastanum	
Bud, Flower essence	GCAAG
Herb	HAAAW
White, Flower essence	GCAAF
Aethiops antimonialis	HAAAX
Aethiops mercurialis	HAAAU
Aethusa cynapium	HAAAY
Agaricus emeticus	HAABA
Agaricus muscarius	HAABB
Agaricus pantherinus	HAABC
Agaricus phalloides	HAABD
Agave americana	HAABE
Agave tequilana	HAABF
Agkistrodon contortrix	HAAGJ
Agnus castus	HAABG
Agraphis nutans	HAABH
Agrimonia eupatoria	GCAAH
Agrimony herb	GBAAE
Agrostemma githago	HAABI
ah jao	GAABJ
ai ye	GAABH
Ailanthus altissima	HAABJ
Alchemilla arvensis	HAABK
Alchemilla vulgaris	HAABL
Alcohol, ethyl alcohol	HAABM
Aletris farinosa	HAABN
Alfalfa leaf	GBMAE
alga	GALAA
Allium cepa	HAABO

-A-

Allium sativum	
Flower essence	GCAAI
Homeopathic	HAABP
Alloxanum	HAABQ
Alnus rubra	HAABR
Aloe socotrina	HAABS
Aloe vera	
Flower essence	GCAAJ
Homeopathic	HAABT
Alstonia constricta	HAABU
Alumen	HAABV
Alumina	HAABX
Alumina silicata	HAABW
Aluminum acetate	HAABY
Alumroot	GBHAF
Amanita bulbosa	HAABD
Amaranthus caudatus	GCAAK
Ambra grisea	HAACA
Ambrosia artemisiifolia	HAACB
American angelica	GBAAK
American aspen	GBPAQ
American black alder	GBPAT
American blackberry	GBRAE
American foxglove	GBGAE
American larch	GBLAA
American pennyroyal	GBHAB
American spikenard	GBAAP
American water smartweed	GBPAL
American wormseed	GBCAI
Ammonium	
Aceticum	HAACD
Benzoicum	HAACE
Bromatum	HAACF
Carbonicum	HAACG
Causticum	HAACH
Iodatum	HAACI
Muriaticum	HAACJ
Phosphoricum	HAACK
Picricum	HAACL
Valerianicum	HAACM
Amorphophallus rivieri	HAACN
Ampelopsis quinquefolia	HAACO
Amygdalus amara aqua	HAACQ
Amygdalus persica	HAACR
Amylenum nitrosum	HAACS
Anacardium occidentale	HAACT
Anacardium orientale	HAACU
Anagallis arvensis	HAACV
Andira araroba	HAAGK
Anemone pulsatilla	HAAFZ
Anemopsis californica	HAACX
Anethum graveolens	GCAAL
Angelica archangelica	GCAAM
Angelica atropurpurea	HAACY
Angelica sinensis	HAADA
Angophora lanceolata	HAADB
Angustura vera	HAADC
Anhalonium lewinii	HAADD
Anilinum	HAADE

I-23

Supply and Product Index

Supply and Product Index

I-25

Supply and Product Index

Calluna vulgaris	GCAAY
Calochortus albus	GCABU
Calochortus leichtlinii	GCABA
Calochortus monophyllus	GCABB
Calochortus tolmiei	GCABC
Calotropis gigantea	HACBD
Caltha palustris	HACBE
Camphora bromata	HACBF
Campsis tagliabuana	GCABD
Canada goldenrod	GBSAM
Canadian hemp	GBAAN
Cancer root	GBOAC
cang erci	GAXAA
cang zhu	GAABO
Canker root	GBCAQ
Cannabis indica	HACBI
Cannabis sativa	HACBJ
Cantharis vesicatoria	HACBK
cao guo	GAAAQ
Capsella bursa pastoris	HACGX
Capsicum minimum	HACBL
Capsium annuum	GCABE
Carbo animalis	HACBM
Carbo vegetabilis	HACBN
Carbolicum acidum	HACBO
Carbon tetrachloride	HACBP
Carboneum	HACBT
Carboneum hydrogen	HACBQ
Carboneum oxygen	HACBR
Carboneum sulphuratum	HACBS
Carcinosin	HACBU
Carduus benedictus	HACBV
Carduus marianus	HACBW
Carlsbad aqua	HACBX
Carolina pink	GBSAN
Carpinus betulus	GCABF
Carya alba	HACBY
Cascara sagrada	
Herb	GBRAB
Homeopathic	HACCA
Cassia acutifolia	HACGV
Castanea sativa	GCABG
Castanea vesca	HACCC
Castilleja miniata	GCABH
Castor equi	HACCD
Castor oil	GBOAB
Castoreum	HACCE
Cataria nepeta	HACCF
Catnip	GBNAC
Caulophyllum thalictroides	HACCG
Causticum	HACCH
Ceanothus americanus	HACCI
Ceanothus integerrimus	GCABI
Celandine herb	GBCAG
Cement	HACCK
Cenchris contortrix	HAAGJ
Centaurea solstitialis	GCABJ
Centaurea tagana	HACCM
Centaurium erythraea	GCABK
Centella asiatica	HACDZ
Cephaelis ipecacuanha	HACEE
Cephalanthus	HACCN
Ceratostigma willmottiana	GCABL
Cereus giganteus	GCABM

Cereus serpentinus	HACCP
Cerium oxalicum	HACCQ
Cervus campestris	HACCR
Cetraria islandica	HACCS
Chaenomeles speciosa	GCABN
chai hu	GABAL
Chamomilla matricaria	HACCT
chan tui	GACAO
chang shan	GADAE
Chaparral	GBLAB
Chaparro amargoso	HACCU
Chaulmoogra	HACCV
che qian	GAPAT
che qian zi	GAPAT
Cheiranthus cheiri	HACCW
Chelidonium majus	HACCX
Chelone glabra	HACCY
chen xiang	GAAAW
Chenopodium olidum	HACDB
Chenopodium vulvaria	HACDA
chi fu ling	GAPBB
chi shao yao	GAPAA
chi shi zhi	GAHAB
chi xiao dou	GAPAJ
Chickweed	GBSAO
Chicory root	GBCAJ
Chimaphila maculata	HACDC
Chimaphila umbellata	HACDD
China arsenicosum	HACDE
China salicylicum	HACDH
China sulphuricum	HACDI
Chininum muriaticum	HACDJ
Chiococca racemosa	HACAI
Chionanthus virginica	HACDK
Chloralum hydratum	HACDL
Chloramphenicol palmitate	HACDM
Chloroformum	HACDN
Chlorpromazine	HACDO
Chlorum aqua	HACDP
Choke cherry	GBPAU
Cholesterinum	HACDR
Christmas tree	GBTAB
Chromicum acidum	HACDS
Chromium kali sulphuratum	HACDT
Chrysanthemum leucanthemum	HACDU
Chrysanthemum maximum	GCABO
Chrysanthemum morifolium	GCABP
Chrysophanicum acidum	HACDW
Chrysothamnus nauseosus	GCABQ
chuan bei mu	GAFAE
chuan jiao zi	GAZAA
chuan lian zi	GAMAH
chuan niu xi	GACBN
chuan shan jia	GAMAD
chuan xiong	GALAH
Cichorium intybus	
Flower essence	GCABR
Homeopathic	HACDX
Cicuta maculata	HACDY
Cicuta virosa	HACEA
Cimarron	GBLAI
Cimex lectularius	HACEB

Supply and Product Index

Supply and Product Index

-D-

Dew plant	GBDAE
di fu zi	GAKAB
di gu pi	GALAW
di long	GALAV
di yu	GASAC
Dicentra chrysantha	GCACG
Dicentra formosa	GCACH
Dichapetalum cymosum	HADAG
Dictamnus albus	HADAH
Digitalis purpurea	HADAI
Digitoxinum	HADAK
ding jin cao	GAMAG
ding xiang	GACAG
Dioscorea villosa	HADAL
Diosma lincaris	HADAM
Diphtheria	HADAN
Diphtherinum	HADAO
Dipteryx odorata	HADBB
Dirca palustris	HADAP
DNA	HADAQ
Dodecatheon hendersonii	GCACI
don gua ren	GABAD
dong chong xiao cao	GACBE
Dorema ammoniacum	HADBC
Doryphora decemlineata	HADAS
dou chi jiang	GALAO
Dracunculus vulgarus	HAAFB
Dragon's root	GBAAW
Dropberry	GBPAJ
Drosera rotundifolia	HADAT
du huo	GAAAU
du zhong	GAEAI
Duboisia myoporoides	HADAU
Duboisinum	HADAX
Dudleya cymosa	GCACJ
Dysentery bacillus	HADAW

-E-

e zhu	GACBL
Eastern arbor vitae	GBTAC
Echallium elaterium	HAEAE
Echinacea angustifolia	HAEAA
Echinacea purpurea	
Flower essence	GCACK
Homeopathic	HAEAB
Elaeis guineensis	HAEAC
Elaps corallinus	HAEAD
Elderberry	GBSAD
Elecampane root	GBIAB
Electricitas	HAEAF
Emetic root	GBAAY
Emetine	HAEAG
English oak	GBQAA
Eosinum	HAEAH
Ephedra vulgaris	HAEAI
Epigea repens	HAEAJ
Epilobium palustre	HAEAK
Epiphegus virginiana	HAEAL
Epiphysterinum	HAEAM
Equisetum hyemale	HAEAN
Erechthites hieracifolia	HAEAO
Ergotinum	HAEAP
Erigeron canadense	HAEAQ

-E-

Eriodictyon californicum	
Flower essence	GCACL
Homeopathic	HAEAR
Erodium cicutarium	
Flower essence	GCACM
Homeopathic	HAEAS
Eryngium aquaticum	HAEAT
Eryngium maritimum	HAEAU
Erythraea chilensis	HAEAZ
Erythrinus erythrinus	HAEAV
Erythronium purpurea	GCACN
Erythroxylon coca	HAEBW
Eschscholzia californica	
Flower essence	GCACO
Homeopathic	HAEAW
Eserinum	HAEAX
Etherum	HAEAY
Eucalyptus globulus	HAEBA
Eucalyptus leaf	GBEAH
Eugenia jambos	HAEBB
Euonymus americanus	HAEBD
Euonymus atropurpurea	HAEBE
Euonymus europaea	HAEBF
Eupatorium aromaticum	HAEBG
Eupatorium perfoliatum	HAEBH
Eupatorium purpureum	HAEBI
Euphorbia	
Amygdaloides	HAEBJ
Corollata	HAEBK
Cyparissias	HAEBL
Heterodoxa	HAEBM
Hypericifolia	HAEBN
Ipecacuanhae	HAEBO
Lathyris	HAEBP
Officinarum	HAEBQ
Peplus	HAEBC
Pilulifera	HAEBR
Polycarpa	HAEBS
Euphrasia officinalis	HAEBT
Eupionum	HAEBU
European beech	GBFAA
Evening primrose	GBOAA
Everlasting onion	GBAAH
Eysenhardtia polystachia	HAEBV

-F-

Fabiana imbricata	HAFAA
Fagopyrum	HAFAB
Fagus sylvatica	
Flower essence	GCACP
Homeopathic	HAFAC
False jasmine	GBGAC
False wintergreen	GBPAY
fan feng	GASAQ
fan xie yeh	GASAN
fang feng	GALAD
Feather few	GBPAX
fei zi	GATAF
Fel tauri	HAFAD
feng wei cao	GAPBK
Ferrum	
Aceticum	HAFAE
Arsenicosum	HAFAF

Supply and Product Index

Supply and Product Index

Hedeoma pulegioides	HAHAF
Hedra helix	HAHAG
Hedysarum desmodium	HAHAH
hei di yu	GASAC
hei pu huang	GATAO
Helianthemum nummularium	GCACT
Helianthus annuus	
Flower essence	GCACU
Homeopathic	HAHAJ
Heliotropinum	HAHAK
Helix tosta	HAHAL
Hellebore	GBVAC
Helleborus fetidus	HAHAM
Helleborus niger	HAHAN
Helleborus orientalis	HAHAO
Helleborus viridis	HAHAI
Heloderma suspectum	HAHAP
Helonias dioica	HAHAQ
Henbane	GBHAK
Hepar sulphuris	HAHAR
Hepatica triloba	HAHAS
Heracleum sphondylium	HAHAT
Hibiscus rosa sinensis	GCACV
Himalaya ProSelect	
Abana 60, 720 mg tablets	FDAAQ
Cystone 100, 620 mg tablets	FDAAR
Gasex 120, 450 mg tablets	FDAAA
Geriforte 60, 920 mg tablets	FDAAS
Geriforte liquid, 200 ml	FDAAT
Glucosim 120, 500 mg tablets	FDAAB
Kilose 60, 500 mg capsules	FDAAC
Koflet 200 ml liquid	FDAAD
Koflet 24 lozenges	FDAAE
Koflet sugar free 200 ml liquid	FDAAF
Liv 52, 120 tablets 515 mg	FDAAU
Liv 52, 200 ml liquid	FDAAV
Menstrim 200 ml liquid	FDAAG
Mentat 200 ml liquid	FDAAW
Mentat 60, 490 mg tablets	FDAAX
Mentat JR 120, 490 mg tablets	FDAAY
Pilexim 100, 570 mg tablets	FDAAH
Prostane 100, 630 mg tablets	FDAAI
Rumalaya 80, 820 mg tablets	FDAAJ
Septilin 200 ml liquid	FDAAK
Septilin 80, 820 mg	FDAAL
Septilin JR 120, 425 mg tablets	FDAAM
Speman 100, 630 mg tablets	FDAAN
Styplon 80, 670 mg tablets	FDAAO
Tentex Forte 90, 500 mg tablets	FDAAP
Vegelax 50, 800 mg capsules	FDAAZ
Hippomane mancinella	HAHBS
Hippomanes	HAHAU
Hippozaeninum	HAHAV
Hippuricum acidum	HAHAW
Hirudo medicinalis	HAHAX
Histamine	HAHAY
Hoitzia coccinea	HAHBA
Homarus americanus	HAHBB
Homeria collina	HAHBC
hong hua	GACAF
hong zao	GAZAE
Hop tree	GBPAV
Horehound herb	GBMAC
Horse balm	GBCAO

Horse chestnut	GBCAD
Horseradish	GBCAN
Horsetail	GBEAC
Hot pepper	GBCAB
Hottonia palustris	GCACW
hou po	GAMAB
hou zao	GAMAA
Hound's tongue	GBCAV
hu huang	GAPAN
hu jiao	GAPAR
hu lu ba	GATAK
hu ma ren	GASAO
hu po	GASBD
hu shi cao	GAOAE
hu tao ren	GAJAA
huai hua	GASAU
huai jiao	GASAU
huai niu xi	GAAAB
huang bai	GAPAK
huang jing	GAPAW
huang lian	GACBD
huang qi	GAAABN
huang qin	GASAK
huang yao zi	GADAG
Humulus lupulus	HAHAZ
huo xiang	GAAAF
Hura brasiliensis	HAHBD
Hura crepitans	HAHBE
Hydrangea aborescens	HAHBF
Hydrastinum muriaticum	HAHBG
Hydrastis canadensis	HAHBH
Hydrobromicum acidum	HAHBI
Hydrocyanicum acidum	HAHBK
Hydrogen	HAHBL
Hydrophis cyanocinctus	HAHBM
Hydrophyllum virginianum	HAHBN
Hyoscyamine	HAHBO
Hyoscyamus niger	HAHBP
Hypericum perforatum	
Flower essence	GCACX
Homeopathic	HAHBQ
Hypothalamus	HAHBR
Hyssop leaf	GBHAM

-I-

Iberis amara	HAIAA
Ichthyolum	HAIAB
Ictodes foetidus	HAIAC
Ignatia amara	HAIAD
Ilex aquifolium	
Flower essence	GCACY
Homeopathic	HAIAE
Ilex paraguayensis	HAIAF
Ilex vomitoria	HAIAG
Illecebrum paronychia	HAIAZ
Impatiens gladulifera	GCADA
Imperatoria ostruthium	HAIAH
Indian corn	GBSAQ
Indian cup plant	GBSAJ
Indigofera tinctoria	HAIAI
Indium	HAIAJ
Indolum	HAIAK
Influenza	HAIAL

Supply and Product Index

-I-

Insulinum	HAIAM
Inula helenium	HAIAN
Iodium	HAIAO
Iodoformum	HAIAP
Ipomoea purpurea	
Flower essence	GCADB
Homeopathic	HAIAR
Iridium	HAIAS
Iridium chloride	HAIAT
Iris douglasiana	GCADC
Iris foetidissima	HAIAU
Iris germanica	HAIAW
Iris germanica var florentina	HAIAV
Iris tenax	HAIAX
Iris versicolor	HAIAY
Iron weed	GBVAF

-J-

Jacaranda caroba	HAJAB
Jacaranda gualandai	HAJAC
Jalap	GBCAP
Jasminum officinale	HAJAE
Jatropha curcas	HAJAF
Jatropha urens	HAJAG
ji li	GATAI
ji xue teng	GAMAJ
ji xue teng	GAMAQ
jiang can	GABAG
jiang huan	GACBL
jiang xiang	GADAA
jie geng	GAPAU
jin bu huan	GALBB
jin jie	GASAI
jin qian cao	GALBD
jin sha teng	GALBC
jin yin hua	GALAS
jin ying zi	GARAH
jiu bai	GAAAM
jiu zi	GAAAL
ju hua	GACAM
juan bai	GASAL
jue ming zi	GACAH
Juglans cinerea	HAJAI
Juglans regia	
Flower essence	GCADD
Homeopathic	HAJAJ
Juncus effusus	HAJAK
Juniper berries	GBJAC
Juniperus communis	HAJAL
Juniperus sabina	HAJAO
Juniperus virginianus	HAJAM
Justicia adhatoda	HAJAN

-K-

Kali	
Aceticum	HAKAA
Arsenicosum	HAKAB
Bichromicum	HAKAC
Bromatum	HAKAZ
Carbonicum	HAKAD
Chloricum	HAKAE

-K-

Kali	
Chlorosum	HAKAF
Citricum	HAKAG
Cyanatum	HAKAH
Ferrocyanatum	HAKAI
Hypophosphoricum	HAKAJ
Iodatum	HAKAK
Muriaticum	HAKAL
Nitricum	HAKAM
Oxalicum	HAKAN
Permanganicum	HAKAO
Phosphoricum	HAKAP
Silicicum	HAKAQ
Sulphuricum	HAKAR
Tartaricum	HAKAS
Telluricum	HAKAT
Kalmia latifolia	HAKAU
Karwinskia humboldtiana	HAKAX
ke zi rou	GACAL
ke zi rou	GATAB
Kerosolenum	HAKAY
Kreosotum	HAKBC
ku shen	GASAV
kuan dong hua	GATAN
kuan jin teng	GATAE
kun bu	GALAA

-L-

Labrador tea	GBLAD
Laburnum anagyroides	HALBZ
Lac caninum	HALAA
Lac defloratum	HALAB
Lac felinum	HALAC
Lac humanum	HALAD
Lac vaccinum	HALAE
Lac vaccinum coagulatum	HALAF
Lacerta agilis	HALAG
Lachesus mutus	HALAH
Lachnanthes tinctoria	HALAI
Lacticum acidum	HALAJ
Lactis vaccini floc	HALAK
Lactuca virosa	HALAM
lai fu zi	GARAA
Lamium album	HALAN
Lapathum sylvestris	HALAO
Lapis albus	HALAP
Lappa arctium	HALAQ
Lapsana communis	HALAR
Larix decidua	GCADE
Larkspur	GBDAC
Larrea tridentata	
Flower essence	GCADF
Homeopathic	HALCL
Lathyrus latifolius	GCADG
Lathyrus sativus	HALAS
Latrodectus hasselti	HALAT
Latrodectus kalipo	HALAU
Latrodectus mactans	HALAL
Lavandula officinalis	GCADH
Lecithinum	HALAX
Ledum palustre	HALAY
lei wan	GAPAX

Supply and Product Index

Supply and Product Index

-M-

Mercurius	
Praecipitatus albus	HAMBQ
Precipitatus ruber	HAMBX
Sulphocyanatus	HAMAU
Sulphuricus	HAMBY
Vivus	HAMCA
Methylene blue	HAMCB
mi meng hua	GABAK
Micromeria douglasii	HAMCD
Mikania cordifolia	HAMDC
Milk weed	GBAAM
Mimosa humilis	HAMCF
Mimosa pudica	HAMCG
Mimulus aurantiacus	GCADQ
Mimulus cardinalis	GCADR
Mimulus guttatus	GCADS
Mimulus kelloggii	GCADT
Mimulus lewisii	GCADU
Mirabilis jalapa	HAMBZ
Mitchella repens	HAMCH
mo yao	GAMAS
Momordica balsamica	HAMCI
Momordica charantia	HAMAZ
Monardella odoratissima	GCADV
Monterey cypress	GBCAU
Moon seed	GBMAF
Morbillinum	HAMCJ
Morgan bacillus	HAMCK
Morphine	HAMCL
Moschus	HAMCM
Motherwort herb	GBLAF
mu bie zi	GAMAM
mu dan pi	GAMAP
mu dan pi	GAPAA
mu gua	GACAK
mu tong	GAAAH
mu xiang	GASAG
mu zei	GAEAE
Mucuna pruriens	HAMDB
Mucuna urens	HAMCN
Mugwort herb	GBAAV
Murex trunculus	HAMCO
Muriaticum acidum	HAMCP
Musa sapientum	HAMCQ
Muscarine	HAMCR
Mygale lasiodora	HAMCT
Myosotis arvensis	HAMCU
Myosotis sylvatica	GCADW
Myrica cerifera	HAMCV
Myristica sebifera	HAMCW
Myrtus chekan	HAMCY
Myrtus communis	HAMDA

-N-

Nabalus serpentaria	HANAA
Naja atra	HANAB
nan gua zi	GACBJ
Naphthaline	HANAC
Narcissus pseudonarcissus	HANAD
Narcotinum	HANAE
Natrium	
Arsenicosum	HANAG
Cacodylicum	HANAH

-N-

Natrium	
Carbonicum	HANAI
Fluoratum	HANAJ
Hypochlorosum	HANAK
Iodatum	HANAL
Lacticum	HANAM
Muriaticum	HANAN
Nitricum	HANAO
Nitrosum	HANAP
Phosphoricum	HANAQ
Salicylicum	HANAR
Selenicum	HANAS
Silicofluoricum	HANAT
Sulphuricum	HANAU
Sulphurosum	HANAV
Nectrianinum	HANAW
Nelumbo nucifera	GCADX
Nemophila menziesii	GCADY
Nepenthes distillatoria	HANAY
Nerium oleander	HANAZ
Nettle	GBUAB
New Jersey tea	GBCAF
Niccolum metallicum	HANBA
Niccolum sulphuricum	HANBB
Nicotiana alata	GCAEA
Nicotiana tabacum	HANBN
Nicotinum	HANBC
Nigella sativa	HANBD
Nitri spiritus dulcis	HANBE
Nitro muriatic acid	HANBG
Nitrogenium oxygenatum	HANBH
niu bang zi	GAAAY
North American ginseng	GBPAA
nu zhen zi	GALAJ
nuo dao gen	GAOAG
Nuphar luteum	HANBI
Nux moschata	HANBJ
Nux vomica	HANBK
Nyctanthes arbortristis	HANBL
Nymphea odorata	HANBM

-O-

Oatstraw	GBABB
Ocimum basilicum	GCAEB
Ocimum canum	HAOAA
Oenanthe aquatica	HAOAB
Oenothera biennis	HAOAC
Oenothera wolfii	GCAED
Olea europaea	GCAEC
Oleum animale	HAOAE
Oleum jecoris aselli	HAOAF
Oleum wittnebianum	HAOAZ
Oniscus asellus	HAOAG
Ononis spinosa	HAOAH
Onosmodium molle	HAOAI
Oophorinum	HAOAU
Operculina turpenthium	HAOAJ
Opuntia vulgaris	HAOAL
Orchitinum	HAOAM
Oreodaphne californica	HAOAN
Origanum majorana	HAOAO

Supply and Product Index

-P-

Pituitaria glandula	HAPBY
Pix liquida	HAPCA
Plantago major	HAPCB
Plantain	GBPAG
Platanus racemosa	HAPCC
Platinum metallicum	HAPCD
Platinum muriaticum	HAPCE
Platinum muriaticum natronatum	HAPCF
Plectranthus fruticosus	HAPCG
Pleurisy root	GBABA
Plumbago litteralis	HAPCH
Plumbum aceticum	HAPCI
Plumbum chromicum	HAPCJ
Plumbum iodatum	HAPCK
Plumbum metallicum	HAPCL
Pneumococcinum	HAPCM
Podophyllum peltatum	HAPCN
Pokeroot	GBPAE
Polygala senega	HAPCZ
Polygonum aviculare	HAPCO
Polygonum punctatum	HAPCP
Polygonum sagitatum	HAPCQ
Polypody	GBPAN
Polyporus pinicola	HAPCR
Populus candicans	HAPCS
Populus tremula	GCAEI
Populus tremuloides	HAPCT
Prickly ash	GBXAA
Primula obconica	HAPCV
Primula veris	HAPCW
Primula vulgaris	HAPCX
Princes feather	GBAAJ
Prinos verticillatus	HAPCY
Propylaminum	HAPDA
Proteus bacillus	HAPDB
Prunella vulgaris	GCAEJ
Prunus cerasifera	GCAEK
Prunus laurocerasus	HAPAZ
Prunus padus	HAPDC
Prunus spinosa	HAPDD
Prunus virginiana	HAPDE
Psorinum	HAPDF
Ptelea trifoliata	HAPDG
pu gong ying	GATAA
pu huang	GATAO
Pulex irritans	HAPDH
Pulmo vulpis	HAPDI
Pulsatilla nuttaliana	HAPDJ
Punica granatum	
Flower essence	GCAEL
Homeopathic	HAPDR
Purple coneflower	GBEAA
Pyrethrum parthenium	HAPDL
Pyrogen	HAPDM
Pyrus americanus	HAPDN

-Q-

qian cao	GARAJ
qian dan	GAMAK
qian hu	GAPAG
qian nian jian	GAHAC
qian niu zi	GAPAH
qian shi	GAEAN

-Q-

qiao mai	GAFAA
qin jiao	GAGAD
qin pi	GAFAD
qing hao	GAABF
qing mu xiang	GAABC
qing pi	GACAV
qu mai	GADAD
Quassia amara	HAQAA
Queen Ann's lace	GBDAB
Quercus glandium spiritus	HAQAC
Quercus robur	GCAEM
Quillaya saponaria	HAQAD

-R-

Radium bromatum	HARAA
Ranunculus acris	
Flower essence	GCAEN
Homeopathic	HARAC
Ranunculus bulbosus	HARAD
Ranunculus ficaria	HARAE
Ranunculus glacialis	HARAF
Ranunculus repens	HARAG
Ranunculus sceleratus	HARAH
Raphanus sativus niger	HARAI
Ratanhia peruviana	HARAJ
Rattlesnakeroot	GBPAI
Rauwolfia serpentina	HARAK
Red clover blossom	GBTAF
Red elm	GBUAA
Red maple	GBAAA
Red puccoon	GBSAE
Red raspberry leaf	GBRAD
ren dong teng	GALAQ
ren shen	GAGAG
Reserpine	HARAL
Resina itu	HARBK
Rhamnus californica	HARAM
Rhamnus catharticus	HARAN
Rhamnus frangula	HARAO
Rheum palmatum	HARAP
Rhodium metallicum	HARAR
Rhodium oxydatum nitricum	HARAQ
Rhododendron chrysanthum	HARAS
Rhus aromatica	HARAT
Rhus diversiloba	
Flower essence	GCAEO
Homeopathic	HARAU
Rhus glabra	HARAV
Rhus toxicodendron	HARAW
Rhus venenata	HARAX
Ribonucleinicum acidum	HARAY
Ricinus communis	HARBA
Robinia pseudoacacia	HARBB
Roman camomile	GBMAD
Rorippa nasturtium aquaticum	HARAZ
Rosa californica	GCAEP
Rosa canina	
Flower essence	GCAEQ
Homeopathic	HARBC
Rosa damascena	HARBD
Rosmarinus officinalis	
Flower essence	GCAER
Homeopathic	HARBE

Supply and Product Index

Supply and Product Index

Supply and Product Index

-T-

Tropaeolum majus	
Flower essence	GCAFI
Homeopathic	HATBU
tu fu ling	GASAS
tu si zi	GACBM
Tuberculinum	HATBV
Tuberculinum aviare	HATBW
Turnera aphrodisiaca	HATAZ
Tussilago farfara	HATCA
Tussilago fragrans	HATBX
Tussilago petasites	HATBY

-U-

Ulex europaeus	GCAFJ
Ulmus campestris	HAUAA
Ulmus procera	GCAFK
Uncaria tomentosa	HAUAB
Upas tiente	HAUAD
Uranium nitricum	HAUAE
Urea pura	HAUAF
Uricum acidum	HAUAG
Urinum humanum	HAUAH
Urtica urens	HAUAI
Usnea barbata	HAUAJ
Ustilago maydis	HAUAK
Uva ursi	HAUAL
Uva ursi leaf	GBAAR

-V-

Vaccininum	HAVAB
Vaccinium myrtillus	HAVAA
Valeriana officinalis	HAVAC
Vanadium metallicum	HAVAD
Vanilla aromatica	HAVAE
Variolinum	HAVAF
Venus mercenaria	HAVAG
Veratrinum	HAVAH
Veratrum album	HAVAI
Veratrum nigrum	HAVAJ
Veratrum sabadilla	HAVAZ
Veratrum viride	HAVAK
Verbascum flower	GBVAD
Verbascum thapsus	
Flower essence	GCAFL
Homeopathic	HAVAL
Verbena hastata	HAVAM
Verbena officinalis	GCAFM
Veronal	HAVAN
Vesicaria communis	HAVAO
Vespa crabro	HAVAP
Vetiveria zizanioides	HAVBC
Viburnum opulus	HAVAQ
Viburnum prunifolium	HAVAR
Viburnum tinus	HAVAS
Vichy aqua	HAVAT
Vinca minor	HAVAU
Viola odorata	
Flower essence	GCAFN
Homeopathic	HAVAV
Viola tricolor	HAVAW
Vipera berus	HAVAX

-V-

Virginia creeper	GBVAJ
Virginia skullcap	GBSAG
Virginia snakeroot	GBAAS
Viscum album	HAVAY
Vitex trifolia	HAVBA
Vitis vinifera	GCAFO
Voeslau aqua	HAVBB

-W-

wa leng zi	GAAAX
wang buliuxing	GAVAA
Water cabbage	GBNAD
Watercress	GBNAB
wei ling xiang	GACBA
White lettuce	GBNAA
White mullein leaf	GBVAK
White Pine	GBPAF
Wiesbaden aqua	HAWAA
Wild ginger	GBAAX
Wild indigo	GBBAA
Wild sarsaparilla	GBAAO
Wild senna	GBCAC
Wild yam	GBDAD
Wildbad aqua	HAWAB
Winter green	GBGAB
Wood strawberry leaf	GBFAD
Wormwood herb	GBAAU
wu bei zi	GARAE
wu jia pi	GAAAA
wu ling zhi	GATAM
wu mei	GAPBF
wu wei zi	GASAH
wu yao	GALAL
wu yi	GAUAA
wu zhu yu	GAEAO
Wyethia helenoides	HAWAC

-X-

Xanthorrhea arborea	HAXAB
Xanthorrhiza apifolia	HAXAC
Xanthoxylum fraxineum	HAXAD
Xerophyllum tenax	HAXAE
xhiang fu	GACBQ
xi gua	GACAX
xi qian cao	GASAP
xi xin	GAABI
xi yan she	GAGAG
xi yang shen	GAPAB
xia ku cao	GAPBD
xian he cao	GAAAG
xian mao	GACBK
xiang ru	GAEAB
xiao hui xiang	GAFAB
xiao ji	GACAJ
xiao jin ying	GARAG
xin yi	GAMAB
xing ren	GAPBE
X-rays	HAXAA
xu duan	GADAK
xuan fu hua	GAIAB

Supply and Product Index

NIC Code Index

The NIC index maps the Nursing Interventions Classification (NIC) system to the ABC Codes. The NIC Codes and titles are referenced for each appropriate ABC Code. NIC Codes are primarily referenced in the Nursing and Mental Health sections of the ABC Coding System.

0000

0140	Body mechanics promotion	CBDAN
0180	Energy Management	NAALG
0200	Exercise Promotion	NAAOO
0201	Exercise Promotion: Strength Training	
	Individual	BBAAZ
	Group	BBABL
0202	Exercise Promotion: Stretching	
	Individual	BBABA
	Group	BBAAY
0221	Exercise Therapy: Ambulating	NAALT
0222	Exercise Therapy: Balance therapy	BBABO
0224	Exercise Therapy: Joint Mobility	
	Individual exercise	BBBAF
	Group exercise	BBBAE
0226	Exercise Therapy: Muscle Control	BBABP
0410	Bowel Incontinence Care	NAABM
0412	Bowel Incontinence Care: Encopresis	NAABL
0420	Bowel Irrigation, Enema	NAALC
0430	Bowel Management	NAABN
0440	Bowel Training	NAABO
0450	Constipation/ Impaction Management	NAACT
0460	Diarrhea Management	NAADD
0470	Flatulence Reduction	NAAEE
0480	Ostomy Care	NAAKU
0490	Rectal Prolapse Management	NAAHQ
0550	Bladder Irrigation	NAABE
0560	Pelvic floor exercise	BBABR
0570	Urinary Bladder Training	NAAJU
0580	Urinary Catheterization	
	Urinary catheter placement	DDCBN
	Urinary catheter irrigation	NAAOC
0582	Urinary catheter placement, intermittent	DDCBN
0590	Urinary Elimination Management	NAAJX
0600	Urinary Habit Training	NAAJY
0610	Urinary Incontinence Care	NAAKA
0612	Urinary Incontinence Care: Enuresis	NAADS
0620	Urinary Retention Care	NAAKB
0630	Pessary Management	CEABJ
0640	Prompted Voiding	NAANJ
0740	Bed rest care	NAABD
0762	Cast Care: Maintenance	NAABX

0764	Cast Care: Wet	NAABY
0840	Patient positioning	NAAHB
0842	Intraoperative positioning	NAAFN
0844	Neurologic positioning	NAAGD
0846	Wheelchair positioning	NAAKF
0910	Splinting	NAAKW
0940	Traction/ Immobilization Care	
	Manual Traction, gravity guidance	CBDAM
	Manual Traction	BBCAA
	Mechanical Traction	BBCAB
0960	Transport	NAAJQ

1000

1020	Diet Staging	NAADE
1030	Eating Disorders Management	NAALF
	Eating disorders therapy, individual	CDAHH
	Eating disorders therapy, group	CDAHI
	Eating disorders therapy, family	CDAHJ
1050	Feeding	NAADY
1052	Bottle Feeding	CEEAF
1054	Breastfeeding Assistance	CEEAH
	Breastfeeding education	CEEAI
	Lactation counseling	CEDAI
1056	Enteral tube infusion	
	Enteral tube feeding	DDBBM
	Enteral tube injection	DDBBN
	Enteral tube placement	DDCAL
1080	Gastrointestinal Intubation	
	G. I. tube care	NAACZ
	G. I. tube placement, intubation	DDCAP
	G. I. tube removal, extubation	DDCAQ
1100	Nutrition Management	AEBAE
1120	Nutrition Therapy	ADBAF
1160	Nutritional Monitoring	AEBAO
1200	Total Parental Nutrition Administration	DDADQ
1240	Weight Gain Assistance	
	Individual	AEBAG
	Group	AEBAH
1260	Weight Management	
	Individual	AEBAI
	Group	AEBAJ
1280	Weight Reduction Assistance	
	Individual	AEBAK
	Group	AEBAL
1320	Acupressure	CBGAA
1340	Cutaneous stimulation	NAACX

1380	Heat/Cold Application	
	Heat	BACAC - BACZZ
	Cold	BAAAA - BAAZZ
1400	Pain Management	
	Patient pain management, initial	NAAGN
	Patient pain management, additional	NAAGO
	Training, individual	CDAFS
	Training, group	CDAIH
1450	Nausea management	NAANH
1460	Progressive Muscle Relaxation	NBAAE
1480	Simple Massage	NAAOH
1540	Transcutaneous Electrical Nerve Stimulation	BABAD
	TENS unit purchase for home use	EAABV
	TENS unit replacement pads	EAABW
1570	Vomiting management	NAAOE
1610	Bathing	NAABC
1620	Contact lens care	NAACU
1630	Dressing	NAADG
1640	Ear Care	NAAOL
1650	Eye Care	NAADW
1660	Foot Care	NAAEG
1670	Hair Care	NAAEI
1680	Nail Care	NAAGB
1710	Oral Health Maintenance	NAAGI
1720	Oral Health Promotion	NAAGJ
1730	Oral Health Restoration	NAAGK
1750	Perineal Care	CEDAF
1770	Postmortem Care	
	Initial contact	NAAHE
	Additional	NAAHF
1780	Prosthesis Care	NAAKS
1800	Self-Care Assistance	NAAJB
	Self care training, individual	BCAAG
	Self care training, group	BCAAH
	Self care training, family	BCAAC
1801	Self-Care Assistance: Bathing/Hygiene	NAAJD
1802	Self-Care Assistance: Dressing/Grooming	NAAHX
1803	Self-Care Assistance: Feeding	NAAHY
1804	Self-Care Assistance: Toileting	NAAIA
1850	Sleep Enhancement	NAAIM
1860	Swallowing Therapy	NAAJK
1870	Drainage tube care	NAAAD
1872	Tube Care: Chest	
	Chest tube care	NAAAC
	Chest tube placement for drainage	DDCAG
1874	Tube Care: Gastrointestinal	
	Gastrointestinal tube care	NAACZ
	G.I. tube removal, extubation	DDCAQ

3620	Suturing	
	Referral for suturing	ADWAF
	Undefined skin suturing	DGEZZ
3620	Suturing	
	Vaginal suturing	CEDAJ
	Episiotomy	CEDAG
3660	Wound Care	NAAKG
3662	Wound Care: Closed Drainage	NAAKH
3680	Wound Irrigation	NAAKI
3740	Fever Treatment	NAAEA
3780	Heat Exposure Treatment	NAAEL
3800	Hypothermia Treatment	
	one area	BAAAC
	entire body	BAAAD
3840	Malignant Hyperthermia Precautions	NAAEZ
3900	Temperature Regulation	NAAJM
3902	Temperature Regulation: Intraoperative	NAAJN

4000

4010	Bleeding precautions	NAABF
4020	Bleeding reduction	NAABI
4021	Bleeding Reduction: Antepartum uterus	
	Initial stabilization	CEBAG
	Additional Time	CEBAH
4022	Bleeding Reduction: Gastrointestinal	
	Initial stabilization	NAABG
	Additional Care	NAABH
4024	Bleeding Reduction: Nasal	NAABJ
4026	Bleeding Reduction: Postpartum uterus	
	Initial stabilization	CEDAD
	Additional Care	CEDAE
4028	Bleeding Reduction: Wound	NAABK
4030	Blood Products Administration: Intravenous	DDADI
4040	Cardiac Care	DDBDK
4044	Cardiac Care: Acute	
	Initial care	NAABQ
	Additional Care	NAABR
4046	Cardiac Care: Rehabilitative	NAABU
4050	Cardiac precautions	NAABV
4062	Circulatory Care: Arterial Insufficiency	NAAIZ
4064	Circulatory Care: Mechanical Assist Device	
	Initial hour	NAACG
	Additional 4 hours	NAACH
4066	Circulatory Care: Venous insufficiency	NAAOD
4070	Circulatory precautions	NAACI

4974	Communication enhancement: Hearing deficit	NAACN
4976	Communication enhancement: Speech deficit	NAACO
4978	Communication enhancement: Visual deficit	NAACP

5000

5000	Complex relationship building	
	Individual	CDAAX
	Group	CDAHV
5020	Conflict Mediation	NBBAH
5100	Socialization Enhancement	
	Individual	CDAGC
	Group	CDAHX
5210	Anticipatory Guidance	CDAAM
5220	Body image enhancement	
	Individual	CDACK
	Group	CDACL
5230	Coping Enhancement	
	Patient coping enhancement	NAAKR
	Coping Enhancement Training	
	Individual	CDACM
	Group	CDACN
	Family	CDACO
5240	Counseling	CDABJ
	Individual	CDAGV
	Couples	CDAGW
	Group	CDAGX
	Family	CDAGY
5242	Genetic Counseling	CEFAI
5244	Lactation Counseling	CEDAI
5246	Nutritional Counseling	
	Individual	AEBAA
	Group	AEBAB
5247	Preconception Counseling	CEFAK
5248	Sexual Counseling	
	Individual	CDAEH
	Group	CDAEI
5250	Decision Making Support	
	Individual	CDACP
	Group	CDACQ
	Family	CDACR
5260	Dying Care	
	Initial Care	ADEAP
	Additional Care	ADEAQ
5270	Emotional Support	
	Initial Care	NAADR
	Additional Care	NAALE

5430	Support Group	CDAGF
5440	Support System Enhancement	
	Individual	CDAFC
	Group	CDAFD
	Family	CDAFE
5450	Therapy Group	
	Psychotherapy, group	CDAHG
	Counseling, group	CDAGX
5460	Touch	NAAOX
5465	Therapeutic Touch	CBCAB
5470	Truth Telling	NAAJS
5480	Values Clarification	
	Individual	CDAFL
	Group	CDAFM
5510	Health Education	
	Individual	NBBCF
	Group	NBBCH
	Family	NBBCG
	Community	NBBCI
5520	Learning Facilitation	
	Individual	CDAFN
	Group	CDAGU
5540	Learning Readiness Enhancement	
	Individual	NBABV
	Group	NBABW
5562	Parent education: Adolescent	
	Teen parent education, individual	CDABO
	Teen parent education, group	CDAIO
5566	Parent education: Childrearing family	CDAAT
	Child development education	
5568	Infant care teaching	
	Individual	CEEAK
	Group	CEEAS
5580	Preparatory Sensory Information	NAAHG
5602	Teaching: Disease Process	
	Individual	NBAAI
	Group	NBAAL
5604	Teaching: Group	See other codes
5606	Teaching: Individual	See other codes
5610	Teaching: Preoperative	
	Individual	NBAAH
	Group	NBAAK
5612	Teaching: Prescribed Activity/Exercise	
	Patient prescribed activity or exercise	NBAAD
5614	Teaching: Prescribed Diet	
	Individual	AEBAM
	Group	AEBAN

5960	Meditation Facilitation	
	Individual	CDADD
	Group	CDADE

6000

6000	Simple Guided Imagery	CDAAF
6040	Simple Relaxation Therapy	
	Individual	CDAEL
	Group	CDAEM
6140	Code Management	NAAPK
6160	Crisis Intervention Counseling	
	Individual	CDAAY
	Family	CDAIF
	Crisis intervention peer training, group	CDAIG
6200	Emergency Care	NAADQ
6240	First Aid	
	Initial care	NAAEC
	Additional Care	NAAED
6260	Organ Procurement	NAAGL
6300	Rape-Trauma Treatment	
	Initial	NAAHN
	Additional	NAAHO
	See also SANE Codes	NAANO - NAAOA
6320	Resuscitation	NAAHU
6340	Suicide Prevention	
	Initial	NAAJH
	Additional	NAAJI
	Counseling	CDAGE
6360	Triage: Disaster	NAAJR
6364	Triage: Emergency Center	NAAMW
6366	Triage: Telephone	NAAOB
6400	Abuse Protection Support	
	Individual	CDAAK
	Group	CDAAL
6402	Abuse Protection Support: Child	
	Individual	CDAAR
	Group	CDAAS
6403	Abuse Protection Support: Domestic Partner	
	Individual	CDAAZ
	Group	CEAHW
6404	Abuse Protection: Institutional and organizational	
	Individual	CDABC
	Group	CDABD
6408	Abuse Protection, Religious	
	Individual	CDAEZ
	Group	CDAIP

Code Tree

A - Clinical practice charges
    A - Diagnostician
        A - New client in office
        B - Existing client in office
        C - New client house call
        D - Existing client house call
        E - New client nursing facility
        F - Existing client nursing facility

    B - Periodic
        A - Wellness visit, new or existing client

    C - Limited diagnostician
        A - New client in office
        B - Existing client in office
        C - New client house call
        D - Existing client house call
        E - New client nursing facility
        F - Existing client nursing facility
        Z - General

    D - Generalservice and reference codes
        A - Consultation between providers
        B - Expanded services
        C - Phone conversations
        D- Interpretive services
        E - Hospice care
        W - Performing
        X - Recommending
        Y - Ordering and referring
        Z - Prescription, preparation and dispensing

    E - Education
        A - General
        B - Nutritional counseling

B - Multi specialty treatments
    A - Physical modalities
        A - Cold
        B - Electrical or magnetic
        C - Heat
        D - Water
        E - Light therapy
        F - Mechanical
        G - Sound
        H - General

    B - Movement modalities
        A - Activity or exercise
        B - Joint mobilization
        C - Traction
        D - General
        E - Aquatic

B - Multi specialty treatments
- *C - Rehabilitative*
  - A - General
  - B - Work conditioning

- *D - Tests and measurements*
  - A - General
  - B - Body composition
  - C - Electronic muscle testing
  - D - Manual muscle testing
  - E - Physical performance
  - F - Range of motion

- *E - General*
  - A - Allergy

C - Practice specialties
- *A - Oriental Medicine*
  - A - Anesthesia
  - B - General
  - C - Modalities
  - D - Therapies

- *B - Somatic education and massage*
  - A - Body Mind
  - B - Bodywork
  - C - Energy work
  - D - Ergonomics
  - E - Massage
  - F - General
  - G - Oriental massage

- *C - Chiropractic services*
  - A - Chiropractic manipulation
  - B - Closed joint adjustment
  - C - Strapping

- *D - Mental Health*
  - A - Counseling
  - B - Testing, evaluation and interpretation

- *E - Midwifery services*
  - A - General
  - B - Antepartum
  - C - Delivery
  - D - Postpartum
  - E - Newborn care
  - F - Family planning

- *F - Naturopathic manipulation*
  - A - Osseous
  - B - Visceral
  - C - General

- *G - Osteopathic manipulation*
  - A - Manipulation
  - B - General

C - Practice specialties

    H - Indigenous healing
        A - Ayurvedic medicine
        B - Native American
        C - Curandera

D - Laboratory and office procedures

    A - Heart and vascular studies
        A - Electrocardiogram
        B - Extracranial arteries and veins
        C - Extremity veins and arteries
        D - Plethysmography
        E - Quantitative vascular studies
        F - General heart or vascular

    B - Neurological
        A - Electromyogram
        B - Nerve conduction procedures
        C - Somatosensory services
        D - General neurological procedures

    C - Pulmonary
        A - Pulmonary evaluation services
        B - Spirometry
        C - Vital capacity
        D - General pulmonary services

    D - Substance administration
        A - General
        B - Injections
        C - Insertion and removal management

    E - Laboratory
        A - General blood analysis
        B - Mineral analysis
        C - Nutritional analysis
        D - Metabolic analysis
        E - Blood vitamin analysis
        F - Saliva analysis
        G - Stool analysis
        H - Tissue and bone
        I - Urinalysis
        J - General laboratory services
        K - Organ and disease panels
        L - Chemical screening
        M - Male testing
        O - Female testing
        P - Allergy
        Z - Sample collection

    F - Radiology
        A - General
        B - Cervical spine
        D - Lumbosacral spine
        E - General spine
        F - Thoracic spine
        G - Computer enhanced radiology services

D - Laboratory and office procedures

    G - Minor surgical
        A - Nail
        B - General procedures of the skin
        C - Skin excision
        D - Shaving skin lesions
        E - Skin suturing
        F - General

    H - General procedures and services
        A - Spectroscopy
        B - Irradiation
        C - Thermography

E - Supplies

    A - Physical devices
        A - General

    B - Topical applicants
        A - General

    C - Solution
        A - Allergen
        B - General

F - Nutritional supplements

    A - Amino acids
        A - General

    B - Enzymes
        A - General

    C - Minerals
        A - General

    D - Other
        A - General

    E - Oral chelation with natural agents
        A - General

    F - Oxidative
        A - General

    G - Vitamins
        A - General

G - Herbs and botanicals

    A - Oriental
        A-Z Scientific name A - Z

    B - Western
        A-Z Scientific name A - Z

G - Herbs and botanicals
    C - General
        A - Flower essences

H - Homeopathic preparations
    A - General
        A-Z Scientific name A - Z

N - Nursing
    A - Interventions
        A - General

    B - Nursing Education
        A - Patient education and counseling
        B - Public health
        C - Communication disorders